Unix Shell Programming Tools

McGraw-Hill Unix Series Titles:

Maxwell	*Unix Network Management Tools*	0-07-913782-2
Medinets	*Unix Shell Programming Tools*	0-07-913790-3
Ross	*Unix System Security Tools*	0-07-913788-1

To order or receive additional information on these or any other McGraw-Hill titles, in the United States please call 1-800-722-4726, or visit us at www.computing.mcgraw-hill.com. In other countries, contact your McGraw-Hill representative

Unix Shell Programming Tools

David Medinets

McGraw-Hill

New York • SanFrancisco • Washington, D.C. • Auckland • Bogotá • Caracas
Lisbon • London • Madrid • Mexico City • Milan • Montreal • New Delhi
San Juan • Singapore • Sydney • Tokyo • Toronto

McGraw-Hill

*A Division of The **McGraw·Hill** Companies*

Printed in the United States of America

2 3 4 5 6 7 8 9   AGM/AGM   9 0 4 3 2 1 0 9

P/N 0-07-039733-3

Part of

ISBN 0-07-913790-3

*The sponsoring editor for this book was Simon Yates and the production supervisor was Clare Stanley. It was set in Sabon by **TIPS** Technical Publishing*

Printed and bound by Quebecor/Martinsburg.

McGraw-Hill books are available at special quantity discounts to use as premiums and sales promotions, or for use in corporate training programs. For more information, please write to the Director of Special Sales, McGraw-Hill, 11 West 19th Street, New York, NY 10011. Or contact you local bookstore.

This book is printed on recycled, acid-free paper containing a minimum of 50% recycled, de-inked fiber.

Contents

Code Listings

Introduction

Welcome to *Unix Shell Programming Tools*. What makes this book different from other Unix books? Quite simply, it is focused on programming. You won't find discourses on the best text editor or why one Unix version is better than another in this book. Nor will you find information about Unix system administration. Here, you'll only find simple advice on how to create programs that perform the tasks you need them to do.

This book is different in other ways, as well. One of the biggest is how Bash, Perl and Tcl are all used to illustrate programming concepts. Bash, of course, is what is commonly considered as the *shell*, while both Perl and Tcl are called *programming languages*. All three can be used to create programs; each has its own strengths. Being able to pick a particular language for a specific task will make you a stronger programmer.

I've packed this book with as many code examples as possible because that's how *I* like to learn. Additionally, I have liberally added comments to the examples. When you return to this book, in a month or a year, you won't need to read the text to remember what an example does. Simply read the comments and your memory should be jogged well enough to remember the details.

Who Should Use This Book?

Unix Shell Programming Tools should be read by anyone seeking to learn how to program in the Unix environment. Basic skills, such as how to list a directory and edit a file, are *not* covered.

If you are already familiar with Perl or Tcl, reading this book lets you transfer many of your skills to creating Bash programs.

What Do I Need?

In order to effectively use this book you need access to two things: a computer running Bash, and a text editor such as *vi* or *emacs*. That's it! You don't even need to have a local computer running Bash. If you have a way to telnet into an ISP's computer, and that computer uses Bash, then you can use this book.

How to Use This Book

There are several ways to use this book. If you're not too familiar with programming, start at the beginning and work your way to the end. Each chapter builds on the last, giving you an understanding of basic concepts before the more complex concepts.

More experienced programmers might want to skip to Chapter 5, "Controlling the Shell," read Chapter 8, "Pattern Matching," and then move on the Chapter 12, "Customizing the Tools."

Code Listings

Many readers prefer to type in most of the example code by hand. This helps them focus on the code one line at a time. If you do this, remember that you don't need to copy the comments! Not copying the comments makes most listings much shorter.

All of the code examples are on the Web at *http://www.codebits.com/spt*.

After each example, try experimenting a little to see what happens. Change a few lines, or add a couple. Don't be afraid to purposely introduce syntax errors so that you can see the errors that arise.

One of the most important attributes of a learning experience is that it should be fun. If you are getting frustrated over a topic, take a break. Talk with a colleague. Then go back to the program.

Conventions

The following conventions are used in this book:

- Codelines, functions, and any text you see onscreen appear in a special `monospace` typeface.

- Filenames and variable names are set in *italic*.

- New terms are also in *italic*.

- Case is important in Perl and Tcl programming. Always pay attention to uppercase and lowercase in variable and function names.

- Commands and keywords are set in **boldface**.

•If you are required to type text, the text you must type appears in boldface. For example, "type **cd examples**."

- ```
  // this style is used for author's comments in the code. They should
  // not be entered into your scripts.
  ```

Overview

Part I, " Fundamentals," consists of the first eight chapters of this book. These chapters discuss the fundamentals of Shell, Perl, and Tcl Programming. Chapter 1, "Playing With Shells," introduces you to shells and processes. It provides the foundation for the rest of the book. Then Chapter 2, "Variables and Operators," discusses how to store and manipulate data using Bash. Going one step further, Chapter 3, "Procedures," shows how to create nuggets of functionality that can be used again and again. With procedures under your belt, Chapter 4, "Script Execution Commands," provides information at the script level. After controlling scripts, it's good to also know how to control the shell itself— which is the environment in which the script runs. Chapter 5, "Controlling the Shell," fulfills this need.

After you read the first five chapters, you'll have a good understanding of the general nature of shell programming. Chapters 6 and 7 cover the basics of Perl and Tcl respectively. And then comes one of the more difficult chapters: Chapter 8, "Pattern Matching," delves into some details of how to match patterns of text.

Part II, "Using the Toolkit," explores the utilities that come with the Bash shell. Just like no man is an island, the shell is not isolated, either. It comes loaded with hundreds of utilities just waiting for your use. Chapter 9, "Examining the Tools," looks at many of the more important utilities and provides some short examples of how they can be used. Chapter 10, "Portability Issues," looks at how Bash, Perl, and Tcl differ from each other and how they are similar. Chapter 11, "Debugging Concepts," shows you some debugging techniques that are useful when your scripts don't work correctly. And finally, Chapter 12, "Customizing the Tools," shows longer examples in all three languages—Bash, Perl, and Tcl.

Appendix A, "Internet Resources," talks about some of the ways to get information about Shell Programming from the World Wide Web. Appendix B, "The ASCII Table," is a list of the ASCII codes for your convenience, should you need to reference them.
  ```

Playing with Shells

This chapter introduces you to shells and processes. You see the different types of shells available and read about Bash in particular. Bash, Perl,
and Tcl scripts are also introduced, and their differences are briefly mentioned. Last, features common
to most shells are mentioned.

Let's get some really basic information out of the way first. Unix is an operating system. It mediates between the CPU, disk drives, memory, monitors, keyboards, and other pieces of hardware. When you look at a Unix screen, you're not really seeing "Unix," you're seeing a program run by the operating system that monitors and responds to the keyboard. That program is called the *login shell*. The login shell is a user interface to the Unix operating system. Figure 1.1 shows a diagram that depicts this situation.

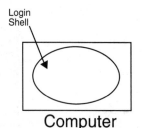

Figure 1.1 *The login shell monitors the command line.*

I'm not certain of the origin of the term *shell*. If I had to guess, I would say it relates to how everything you do at the keyboard is enveloped by that monitoring program—the login shell. This is an important concept to understand. When you enter commands on the keyboard, the shell program interprets them.

Shell programs are also called command interpreters.

For example, let's say that you run a program that displays process statistics—the *ps* program. The *ps* program runs inside the shell program. You might want to picture the shell as a big balloon. When the calculator program is run, the balloon swells up to accommodate it (because the calculator program essentially runs inside the shell). When the calculator program is finished, the balloon shrinks.

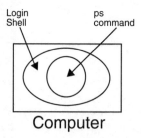

Figure 1.2 *Shell programs can run other programs.*

The *ps* program is executed as a process inside the computer. *Processes* are simply individual commands being run by the computer. Each process has its own memory and access permissions.

You can even run a shell program inside another shell program. The shell program inside the balloon is called a *child shell*. The following series of commands shows you a child process in action:

```
$ echo $SHLVL
1
$ bash
$ echo $SHLVL
2
$ exit
$ echo $SHLVL
1
```

Notice how the number displayed by the **echo** command (corresponding to the level of shell *nesting*) increases? This shows that the child shell is displaying the value. The **exit** command returns back to the parent shell.

Exploring Access Permissions

If this is the first time you're looking into programming—as opposed to simply running programs—you might be unfamiliar with access permissions. *Access permissions* are used to control access to files. Restrictions can be based on the file's owner, the file's group, and all other users. There are three types of access for each of these groups: read, write, and execute.

Access permissions are changed by the **chmod** command.

Because access permissions are part of the file system structure on all Unix systems and are so integral to shell programming, let's look at a couple examples of them.

```
$ echo "A Test" > test.dat
$ mkdir test_dir
$ ls -l test.dat test_dir
total 2
-rw-rw-r--  1 medined medined     7  [date] test.dat
drwxrwxr x  2 medined medined  1024  [date] test_dir2
$ rm -r test_dir
$ rm test.dat
```

For some special files, the first character can be something besides a dash or a "d." Those files are more likely than not used by system administrators and aren't covered in this book.

The first column of the **ls –l** command contains the access permissions for each file listed. As shown in Figure 1.3, you interpret the first column by breaking it into four sections: d, rwx, rwx, and r x.

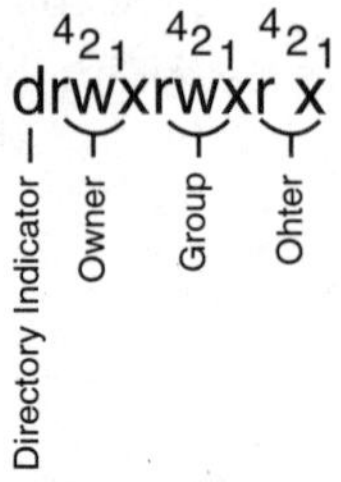

$$4\,2\,{}_1 \quad 4\,2\,{}_1 \quad 4\,2\,{}_1$$

drwxrwxr x

Directory Indicator ─┘ Owner ─┘ Group ─┘ Ohter ─┘

Figure 1.3 *You can grant read, write, and execute permissions to the file owner, the file owner's group, or to all other users.*

Although it might be counter-intuitive, directory information is stored inside files. And the first section indicates whether or not the file contains directory information. If it does, the first section displays a d; it is blank for normal files.

The next three sections use a simple same notation to indicate if the user, group, or other categories have read, write, or execute access to the file.

The next section of this chapter lets you create and run a shell script. It also briefly shows how to use the **chmod** command to control the access permissions. The "421" numbers in Figure 1.3 are explained there.

Running a Shell Script

The first shell script in this book shows how to display a line of text. The first step is to create the script using any text editor. Then change the file permissions so that it's executable. Last, you'll see how to run the brand-new script.

A *script* file consists of an ordinary text file containing a series of shell commands. Shell commands are free form with just a few syntax rules. The more complex rules are mentioned as the need arises later in the book. For now, here are the basics:

- Leading spaces are ignored. Therefore, always indent your script lines to aid in your future understanding of the code. My preferences about script indenting are clearly shown in the examples, so I won't belabor the point.

- Commands are sometimes terminated with a semi-colon but always with a newline. If you'd like to continue a command across lines, place a backslash (\) character at the end of the line. The \ character forces the shell to ignore the newline.

- Spaces, tabs, and blank lines are irrelevant outside of strings— one space after a command or option is as valid as ten.

- Anything after a hash (#) character is ignored unless the # character is inside a string. This lets you easily add comments to your scripts.

TIP

A string is a series of characters enclosed in quotes. Characters are things like the letter "A" and the number "3." Appendix B, "The ASCII Table," lists all the available characters.

Use any text editor to create the file in Listing 1.1.

NOTE

If you are unfamiliar with Unix editors, follow these steps to create the *hello* file using the *vi* editor.

1. Use the command **vi hello** to start the editor.

2. Use the letter **i** to enter insert mode.

3. Enter the first line of the script. If you make a mistake, use the backspace key to erase the mistake and then retype it.

4. Use the **Enter** key to start the second line.

5. Enter the second line of the script. If you make a mistake, use the **backspace** key to erase the mistake and then retype it.

6. Use the **Escape** key to exit insert mode.

7. Use the **:wq** command to write the file and quit the editor.

Use the **man vi** command to become familiar with **vi**'s commands. There are also numerous Internet sites devoted to the **vi** editor.

Listing 1.1 *hello—Your First Shell Script*

```
#!/bin/bash
# The first line of "Congo" by Michael Crichton
echo "Dawn came to the Congo rain forest."
```

You can run this script using the following commands:

```
% chmod +x hello
% ./hello
Dawn came to the Congo rain forest.
```

The first line of the *hello* script tells the shell which program should be used when running this script. In this case, it is the file */bin/bash* (which on my system is the Bash program).

CAUTION   This interpretation of the # character is an anomaly. Normally, the # character is used to begin comments—the shell usually ignores any characters after the # character. Only if the # character is on the first line of a script does it have the special ability to determine which program executes the script.

The **chmod** command changes the file permissions of the *hello* file so that the shell can execute it simply by using the file name on the command line.

The **echo** command sends its arguments to the monitor. Actually, its actions are a bit more complicated than that because the arguments are sent to something called *STDOUT*, which is usually the display. Chapter 5, "Controlling the Shell," discusses *STD-OUT*.

Exploring Shell Programming

Shell programming is nearly always used to automate a task—as compared to creating an accounting or spreadsheet application. The shell has very few tools for interacting with users. At most, you can ask the user a question and receive a text response.

Because I believe more full-featured languages should be used when user interaction is needed, this book doesn't cover how to read and parse input.

Shell scripts are also used to customize "normal" shell commands or programs. For example, one of my most used scripts is very simple. All it does is run the **mount** command on my floppy disk drive.

Shell scripts are also useful for:

- checking disk usage

- maintaining a system log

- monitoring user activity

- and hundreds of other tasks.

Counting Shells

As with calculator programs (of which there are hundreds), there is more than one type of shell. In fact, shells actually have a family history! However, there are plenty of web sites that detail the different shells, so I won't go into the history here.

http://www.mit.edu/afs/athena/user/w/c/wchuang/www/unix/ Unix/Shell_history.txt is one of the pages with this type of information. I found this page through Altavista by searching for the phrase "Unix Shell History."

The *Bourne* shell and the *C* shell are the ancestors of the shell family. The Bourne-related shells vary in several respects from the C-related shells.

In order for you to avoid getting lost in details about how a particular shell works, my advice is to download a free copy of Bash (if you're not already using it) from *http://www.gnu.org* and use it. This ensures that you're using a modern, stable shell.

The main advantage of using Bash, in my opinion, is that it is offered under the "copyleft" license. You can install Bash on all of your computers regardless of manufacturer. This lets you have a consistent programming environment to work in.

If you'd like to read some comments about why the csh shell isn't good for programming, try this URL:　　**CAUTION**

http://www.perl.org/CPAN/doc/FMTEYEWTK/versus/csh.whynot

Exploring Shell Features

Shells have many features in common. The following sections briefly discuss some of these features.

Aliases

Aliases are used to create shortcut commands that stand in for full command lines. For example, many people use an alias of **ll** to mean *ls –l* or *la* to mean *ls –a*. Aliases are only peripherally related to shell programming. Mainly, they are used to reduce the amount of typing needed at the command line.

TIP   When I start working with a new web server, I frequently create an alias to display the last 10 lines of the server log file.

The **alias** command is fully documented in the Bash **man** page.

When creating shell script, sometimes you want to ensure that you're using a "basic" shell command instead of an alias (somebody might have aliased **ls** to **ls –a**). You can avoid the alias by using the full pathname of the command. In the case of **ls**, the full pathname is **/bin/ls**.

Command Substitution

One of the shell's nicer features is the ability to do command substitution. You can combine the output of one command inside another using backtick notation. This might sound like a wacky idea at first, but as you gain proficiency you'll find that it's a powerful technique.

Some of the examples in Chapter 12, "Customizing the Tools," use command substitution, so I'll only give a simple example here. Let's say you created a file called *ls_info* that contained a single line:

```
*.c
```

You could incorporate the contents of the *ls_info* file into an **ls** command line like this:

```
% ls `cat ls_info`
one.c two.c
```

The command Bash executes is really **ls *.c**. The output of the **cat ls_info** command replaces the **cat ls_info** part of the original command line.

You might ask why I call this a powerful technique. The answer is that command substitution lets you set parameters around commands. Imagine that the **ls `cat ls_info`** command was inside a script and further imagine that a user changed the contents of the *ls_info* file. What would happen when the script is run? The **ls** command automatically executes using the changed contents of the *ls_info* file.

Background Processing

Another useful feature of shells is the ability to run multiple programs or scripts at the same time. When this happens, the program in control of the keyboard is said to be in the foreground. Any other programs run in the background.

This feature comes in handy when you know a program will take a long time to finish and doesn't need your input—it'll just percolate quietly to itself while running. The **find** command frequently takes a long time to run and is a good candidate for background processing. Let's take a look at an example:

```
% find / -name "hello" -print > find.log &
% date
Wed Apr 15 22:43:59 EDT 1998
% date
Wed Apr 15 22:46:23 EDT 1998
[1]+ Exit 1     find / -name "hello" -print >find.log
% cat find.log
/data/tk8.0/library/demos/hello
/home/medined/hello
/usr/lib/tk8.0/demo/hello
```

The two **date** commands show that time has passed while the **find** command was running. They also show that the login shell retains keyboard control. The **find** command can display error messages; however, it can't access the keyboard. When the background process is done, the shell displays a message indicating the exit code of the process. Because the **find** command sent its output to the *find.log* file (you'll learn about the > operator in Chapter 5,

"Controlling the Shell"), it is easy to read the list of found files using the **cat** command.

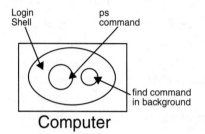

Computer

Figure 1.4 *The login shell can run one command in the fore-ground (controlling the keyboard) as well as one or more background commands—like the* **find** *command.*

Variables

All shells have the ability to store information in variables. *Variables* are named pieces of information. They are fully discussed in Chapter 2, "Variables."

Pipes

Unix is perhaps most famous for its philosophy of building complex commands out of simple commands. The building process is possible because of pipes. *Pipes* let you connect the output of one command to the input of another in a nearly seamless manner. Figure 1.5 shows how the **ls** command's output can be piped to the **sort** command.

Figure 1.5 *Pipes connect the output of one command to the input of the next.*

Try the following command:

```
% ls | sort -r
```

Your output should display one file per line in reverse sorted order, like this:

```
unmount_floppy
mount_floppy
hello
find.log
```

Redirection

The previous section briefly described the concept of pipes. Redirection is a related concept. *Redirection* lets you change where a program looks for input and where a program sends output.

Let's use the **sort** command to examine redirection. When you run the **sort** command from the command line, it might look like this:

```
% sort
10
9
^D        <- press control and D to end input.
9
10
```

The **sort** command looked to the keyboard for input and sent its output to the monitor. If you have a few hundred numbers to sort, this behavior isn't very useful. However, you can use redirection to tell the **sort** command to look at a data file for its input.

```
% sort < unsorted.dat
9
10
```

Notice how the < character represented redirection *into* the **sort** command. By the way, the *unsorted.dat* file contains the following lines:

```
10
9
```

The > character represents redirection *out of* the **sort** command.

```
% sort < unsorted.dat > sorted.dat
% cat sorted.dat
9
10
```

The "location" where input is gotten from is called *STDIN*, while the output "location" is called *STDOUT*. More details about *STDIN* and *STDOUT* are given in Chapter 5, "Controlling the Shell."

Figure 1.6 shows the situation before redirection, and Figure 1.7 shows the situation after redirection.

Figure 1.6 *The "normal" situation of input and output.*

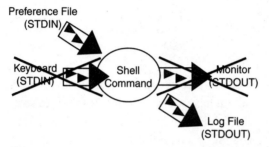

Figure 1.7 *Input and output after redirection has taken place.*

Pattern Matching

All shells have the ability to display files that have a txt extension or to display files that begin with the letter a. This ability is called *pattern matching*. Because this book has an entire chapter, Chapter 8, devoted to pattern matching, no examples are given here.

Special Characters

You might have already noticed there are many characters that have special meanings to the shell. Table 1.1 lists them and gives a short description of each. Unfortunately, you need to master most of them in order to become truly fluent in shell programming. There are no shortcuts.

Table 1.1 *Characters with Special Meanings to the Shell*

Character	Description
"	Double quotes are used to hide spaces, tabs, and most other special characters from the shell. This lets `"David Medinets"` be seen as one value instead of two. In the same vein, `"David < Medinets"` also indicates one value and the redirection interpretation of the < character is ignored.
'	Single quotes hide *all* special characters from the shell, except the ending single quote.
`	Backticks are used for command substitution. The output from the command inside the back quotes replaces the backticked string in the original command. You can see examples of backticked strings in the "Command Substitution" section earlier in this chapter and in Chapter 12, "Customizing the Tools."
\	A backslash character hides only the following character from the shell. In other words, the character following the backslash loses any special meaning. As a trivial example, you could use `David\ Medinets` to represent one value instead of two.
;	The semi-colon lets you put more than one command on a line. However, one command per line is considered more readable.
&	The ampersand, when placed at the end of a command, puts that command into the background. You can see an example of this in the "Background Processing" section earlier in this chapter.
( )	Parens are used to create command grouping. Examples of command groups are in the "Sequencing Your Commands" section of Chapter 5.

Table 1.1 *Characters with Special Meanings to the Shell (Cont'd)*

Character	Description
{ }	Curly braces are used to create command blocks for shell procedures. Examples of procedures are shown in Chapter 3, "Procedures."
|	Pipes are used to connect the output of one command to the input of another. An example using a pipe is given in the "Pipes" section earlier in this chapter.
> < &	These three characters are used to indicate that redirection needs to take place. Redirection is mentioned in the "Redirection" section earlier in this chapter and in Chapter 5.
* ? [ ] ~ !	These six characters are used for filename pattern matching. Pattern matching is extensively discussed in Chapter 8, "Pattern Matching."
$	The $ character indicates the beginning of a variable name. Many examples of variables are given in Chapter 2, "Variables."
#	The # character begins comments in script files. Simply start any line with a pound sign and the shell ignores it.
\<space\> \<tab\> \<newline\>	These characters, collectively, are called *whitespace* for the obvious reason. Whitespace is used to separate words in shell commands.

The Shell/Perl/Tcl Bridge

As the Unix community matures, it has become obvious that as a programming environment the shell is too limiting. Languages like Perl and Tcl have become very popular as replacements for shell scripting.

This book attempts to form a bridge between the three languages. While the focus of the book is using the shell for programming, brief introductions to Perl and Tcl are also provided. After finishing this book, you'll have a solid grounding in Perl and Tcl.

At the very least, you'll be able to look at someone else's code and figure out what it does.

Summary

This chapter serves as a backdrop for the rest of the book. All of the concepts presented here are explored further in various parts of the book.

The chapter began with a description of Unix and shells. When you log into a Unix system, the keyboard and monitor are "attached" to a login shell. This shell interacts with you and does your bidding.

As you run commands, they are executed as child processes. If you desire, you can place child processes in the background so you can continue working while they continue processing.

Unix uses access permissions to control who can read, write and execute files. These permissions are associated with each file and directory. The **chmod** command changes permissions when needed. The **ls** command displays the current permissions for each file when the **-l** option is used.

In order to execute a script file, the **chmod +x scriptfile** command is used. From then on, simply using the name of the script file executes it.

Mention was made of the many different types of shells that are available. However, only the Bash shell is covered in this book because it seems to be the most modern, the cheapest (it's free), and the most stable.

The Bash shell has many features that make a programmer's life easier. Some of them—like word completion—only affect you at the command line and not while programming. Therefore, those features were not covered. Aliases, command substitution, background processing, variables, pipes, redirection, pattern matching, and the shell's special characters were mentioned. Each of these topics is discussed in more detail later in the book.

Chapter 2, "Variables," introduces you to variables and how they are used to store information.

Variables and Operators

This chapter discusses variable use in the shell—specifically Bash. You learn how to manipulate variables and what kinds of variables exist. A brief discussion of how variable substitution is done and the internal shell commands that interact with variables round out the chapter.

When shell scripts need to hold a piece of information for later use—(perhaps a filename) they store it in a variable. Variables are chunks of computer memory that hold changeable values. You (or the shell) give each variable a name so that it's easy to refer to.

Listing 2.1 displays a short script that simply assigns a value of *monday.dat* to a variable called *logfile*.

Listing 2.1 *assign_logfile—A Simple Variable Assignment*

```
#!/bin/bash

# The following line is the assignment command.
logfile="monday.dat"

echo "The value of logfile is:"

# The dollar sign is used to access a variable's value.
echo "$logfile."
```

Here is an example of this script in action:

```
% chmod +x assign_logfile
% ./assign_logfile              <- execute the file.
The value of logfile is:
monday.dat                      <- the correct value is
                                <- displayed.
% echo $logfile
                                <- yikes! how come no value
                                <- is displayed?
```

Listing 2.1 shows that variables are, by default, only accessible in the shell that creates them. Before exploring this issue further, let's look at the $ character and how it's used in the script to access the value of a variable.

When assigning a value to a variable, you use only the variable's name (on the left side of the assignment). For example:

```
logfile="monday.dat"
```

However, when accessing the variable's value, some character is needed to let the shell know that a variable substitution is to be done. Variable substitution replaces the variable's name with its value, and Bash uses the $ character to signal that the substitution needs to be made. For example:

```
echo "The log file name is $logfile."
```

Variable Substitution

Replacing a variable's name with its value.

For more information about how to use variables inside of quoted strings, see the "Bash Quoting Rules" section later in this chapter. **FRI**

Now let's return to the issue of why the **echo $logfile** command doesn't display anything when run from the command line, but displays the log file's name when run inside the script.

You might recall from Chapter 1 that each script runs inside its own shell—scripts are nearly totally enclosed and cut off from other programs except for the files that they open. Well, that description is not totally accurate. Each shell, irrespective of scripts that might be running, has memory that is devoted to holding information about its variables.

The variable information that the shell maintains is called the shell's "environment." The *assign_logfile* script changes its own environment when the assignment statement is made. The first **echo $logfile** command works because it is run from within the *same environment* as the assignment command. The second **echo** command doesn't work because it is run from the *parent shell* of the *assign_logfile* script.

The parent shell of the *assign_logfile* script is your login shell, which is also called the current shell (i.e., the shell you're currently interacting with via the keyboard).

You can force a script to affect the environment of the current shell by using the **source** command (which executes all the commands in the script regardless of the script file's permissions). For example:

```
% source assign_logfile      <- execute the file.
The value of logfile is:
monday.dat                   <- the correct value is
                             <- displayed.

% echo $logfile
monday.dat                   <- the correct value is
                             <- displayed.
```

source

> *A command that lets scripts affect the environment of their parent shells.*

TIP

> Some programmers use the period as a shorthand representation of the **source** command. I feel using a period is prone to misinterpretation and is too easy to miss when reading a script.

You've now seen how to affect the parent shell of a script. What if you need to affect a child shell? That's when the **export** command comes in handy.

export

> *A command that lets scripts affect the environment of their children shells.*

Listing 2.2 holds a short script that displays the value of the *logfile* variable. Let's use it to demonstrate the **export** command using the script in Listing 2.3.

Listing 2.2 *display_logfile—Display the Value of the logfile Variable*

```
#!/bin/bash

echo "logfile is $logfile."
```

Listing 2.3 *export_logfile—A Simple Variable Assignment*

```
#!/bin/bash

# The following line is the assignment command.
logfile="monday.dat"

# call the display script before using export
echo "Before Export:"
./display_logfile

export logfile

# call the display script after export
echo "After Export:"
./display_logfile
```

Here is an example of this script in action:

```
% unset logfile
% chmod +x export_logfile
% ./export_logfile
Before Export:
logfile is
After Export:
logfile is monday.dat
% ./display_logfile
logfile is
```

Because the second running of the *display_logfile* script displays the value of the *logfile* variable, you can see the effect of the **export** command. It gives the child script—the second running of **display_logfile**—access to the *logfile* variable. You can see that the parent script—the login shell—still doesn't see the *logfile* variable because the *display_logfile* script, when run from the command line, doesn't display a value for *logfile*.

> The *logfile* variable needs to be unset or undefined for this test to work as shown, just in case you ran the **source** command earlier in the chapter. If the **unset** command isn't issued, the *logfile* variable might be displayed by the **display_logfile** run from the command line.

NOTE

You might be wondering why the **source** and **export** commands are needed. Couldn't the various shells be granted free access to change their parent and children shells?

While you think about the answer to this question, remember that Unix is multi-threaded and runs multiple processes. Can you imagine what would happen if one process created 50 children and each of these children tried to update a variable in its parent's environment? Which child's **assignment** command would have precedence and why? These would not be easy questions to answer.

Let's take a look at another example using the **export** command. This time you create a variable in the login shell and then try to access it inside a child shell.

*The **unset** command removes a variable from the environment. It's a handy command to know about when testing scripts that use environment variables.*

Try the following series of commands:

```
% count=19          <- assign a value to count.
% echo $count       <- display count's value.
19
% bash              <- start a child shell.
% echo $count       <- display count's value.
                    <- No Value!
% exit              <- leave the child shell.
% echo $count       <- display count's value.
19                  <- The value is back!
```

This series of commands shows that the *count* variable defined in the current or login shell is not accessible in the child shell.

CAUTION Make sure that you don't leave any spaces around the equal sign in your **assignment** commands or use the **let** command as described in the "The let Command" section later in this chapter.

Now use the **export** command to make the *count* variable available to the child shell:

```
% export count=19   <- assign a value to count
                    <- and export it.
% bash              <- start a child shell.
% echo $count       <- display count's value.
19                  <- The value is displayed.
% exit              <- leave the child shell.
```

Notice that the **export** command can be used as part of the **assignment** command. This feature helps to shrink your scripts and reduce cross-referencing. If the **export** command were run later in the script and you were trying to understand what the script was doing, you'd need to check the **assignment** command to see what its value was.

The bottom line is that you need to be a little careful when modifying variables to ensure that you're letting the correct shell access them.

Variable names are case-sensitive.

Listing 2.4 contains a script that shows how variable names are case-sensitive in Bash. Each of the three variables used in this script is different from the others, as proven by the values displayed by the *echo* statement.

Listing 2.4 *case_sensitive—Bash Variable Names Are Case-Sensitive*

```
#!/bin/bash

logfile=one.txt
LogFile=two.txt
LoGfile=three.txt

echo $logfile $LogFile $LoGfile
```

Here is an example of this script in action:

```
one.txt two.txt three.txt
```

Variable Substitution

Earlier in this chapter, you saw how the $ character is used to indicate that variable substitution is needed. When you need to actually display the $ character, use the \ character to tell the shell to ignore the $ character's special meaning. For example:

```
% logfile="test.dat"
% echo "The value of \$logfile is $logfile."
The value of $logfile is test.dat.
```

Notice that the variable name ended with a period in the last example. If you run into a situation where you need to add a suffix to a variable's value, then you need to use curly braces to delimit the variable name. For example:

The \ character, used in front of the $ character, tells the shell to ignore the $ character's special meaning.

```
% word="large"
% echo "He was a ${word}r man."
He was a larger man.
```

The curly braces around the variable name tell the shell where the name starts and ends.

The shell has some notations that can be used with the curly braces. Table 2.1 shows all of the curly brace notations.

Table 2.1 *Using Curly Braces for Variable Substitution*

Notation	Description
${VARIABLE}	Basic variable substitution. The curly braces delimit the start and end of the variable name.
${VARIABLE:-DEFAULT}	This notation returns the *DEFAULT* value if *VARIABLE* has no value.
${VARIABLE:=DEFAULT}	This notation returns the *DEFAULT* value if *VARIABLE* has no value. In addition, *VARIABLE* is assigned the *DEFAULT* value if it's not set.
${VARIABLE:+VALUE}	This notation returns *VALUE* if *VARIABLE* is set. Otherwise, a blank string is returned.
${#VARIABLE}	This notation returns the length of the value of *VARIABLE* unless *VARIABLE* is * or @. In the special case of * or @, the number of elements in *$@* is returned. Remember that *$@* holds the list of parameters to the script.
${VARIABLE:?MESSAGE}	This notation returns the *MESSAGE* value if *VARIABLE* has no value. The shell also displays the name of *VARIABLE,* so this notation might be useful for error trapping.

FRI   For information about more advanced variable substitution using regular expressions, see the section "Metacharacters for Variables" in Chapter 8, "Pattern Matching" on page 237.

Listing 2.5 *varsub—Using the Variable Substitution Notation*

```
#!/bin/bash

logfile="web.log"
echo "\${logfile} Example:"
echo " logfile is ${logfile}."
echo
unset logfile

echo "\${logfile:-www.log} Example:"
```

```
echo " logfile is ${logfile:-www.log}."
echo " logfile is $logfile."
echo
unset logfile

echo "\${logfile:=inet.log}."
echo " logfile is ${logfile:=inet.log}."
echo " logfile is $logfile."
echo
unset logfile

logfile="web.log"
echo "\${logfile:+The logfile variable is set.} Example:"
echo "${logfile:+The logfile variable is set.}"
unset logfile
echo "The next line is blank because logfile has been
unset."
echo "${logfile:+The logfile variable is set.}"
echo
unset logfile

logfile="web.log"
echo "\${#logfile} Example:"
echo "There are ${#logfile} characters in '$logfile'."
echo
unset logfile

echo "\${logfile:?Please specify a logfile name!} Example:"
echo "logfile is ${logfile:?Please specify a logfile
name!}"
echo "logfile is $logfile."
```

> Notice how the *logfile* variable is unset after each example? The
> variable was reset to ensure that the environment returns to its
> original condition after each example. This type of programming
> (keeping changes local to a section of code) helps to reduce coding
> errors.

TIP

Here is an example of this script in action:

```
% chmod +x varsub
% ./varsub
${logfile} Example:
  logfile is web.log

${logfile:-www.log} Example:
```

```
    logfile is www.log
    logfile is .

${logfile:=inet.log} Example:
    logfile is inet.log
    logfile is inet.log

${logfile:+The logfile variable is set.} Example:
The logfile variable is set.
The next line is blank because logfile has been unset.

${#logfile} Example:"
There are 7 characters in 'web.log'.

${logfile:?Please specify a logfile name!} Example:
varsub: logfile: Please specify a logfile name!
```

The script in Listing 2.5 uses all five types of `${}` notation. Notice that the `${logfile:-www.log}` example leaves the *logfile* variable in an unset state; the **echo** command displays no value for *logfile*. On the other hand, the `${logfile:=inet.log}` example does assign a value to *logfile*, as evidenced by the next **echo** command, which shows a value for *logfile*.

The `${:+}` notation could be handy if you need to set one variable based on another's being set. For example:

```
bSendEmail=${emailAddr:+true}
```

In your scripts, you can use the value of *bSendEmail* to determine if email should be sent. The following bit of code:

```
if [ bSendEmail = "true" ]
then
    # send email
fi
```

is easier to understand than this:

```
if [ -n emailAddr ]
then
    # send email
fi
```

Whenever possible, use variable names wisely to create self-documenting scripts.

For more information about the **if** command, see "The if Com- **FRI**
mand" in Chapter 4, "Script Execution Commands" on page 74.

> I like to start variable names that will only be valued true or false **TIP**
> with a lowercase b to indicate their boolean nature.

Position Variables

The shell uses *position* variables to access script parameters. If you
create a script to process two files, you might need to find out the
names of the files to be processed. The filenames passed to the
script are stored in the variables, *$1* and *$2*. You can access any
number of parameters simply by placing a dollar sign in front of its
associated number. When accessing any parameters past the tenth,
you need to use curly braces around the number. For example,
${14} and ${19}.

Listing 2.6 shows a script that displays its parameters using
position variables.

Listing 2.6 *display_parameters—Using Position Variables to
Display Script Parameters*

```
#!/bin/bash

echo "\$0 = *$0*"
echo "\$1 = *$1*"
echo "\$2 = *$2*"
echo "\$3 = *$3*"
```

Here is an example of this script in action:

```
% chmod +x process
% ./process one.dat two.dat
$0 = *process*
$1 = *one.dat*
$2 = *two.dat*
$3 = **
```

This scripts illustrates two main points. First, sometimes it's useful to surround values with asterisks so that you can more easily
tell when a variable is empty. Notice that $3 is empty. This makes
good sense, because only two parameters are passed to the script.

Second, the *$0* variable holds the name of the script itself. This variable might be used to create log files that are easily associated with the script.

There are three other variables that are related to the positional variables:

$*   This variable contains a list of the parameters.

$@   This variable contains a list of the parameters.

$#   This variable contains the number of parameters.

Bash maintains both the *$** and the *$@* variables to make porting scripts from other shell programs easier.

Listing 2.7 contains the *listparam* script, which demonstrates use of the *$**, *$@*, and *$#* variables.

Listing 2.7 *listparam—Using the $*, $@, and $# Variables*

```
#!/bin/bash

echo "There are $# parameters."
echo "The parameters are *${*}*"
echo "The parameters are *$@*"
```

Here is an example of this script in action:

```
% chmod +x listparam
% ./listparam one two three
There are 3 parameters.
The parameters are *one two three*
The parameters are *one two three*
```

Notice how the curly braces were used in the second **echo** command so that the variable's value could be surrounded by asterisks. The curly braces come in handy in more than one situation.

The *$@* variable will become very useful to you after you read about the **for** command in Chapter 4, "Script Execution Commands." Listing 2.8 gives you a preview by using the **for** command to display file information about files specified as parameters to a script.

Listing 2.8 *listfiles—Using the for Command with the $@ Variable*

```
#!/bin/bash

for file in $@
do
   ls -l $file
done
```

Here is an example of this script in action:

```
% chmod +x listfiles
% ./listfiles listfiles listparam
-rwxr-xr-x 1 medined user   60 Apr 1 19:04 listfiles
-rwxr-xr-x 1 medined user   77 Apr 1 19:04 listparam
```

Let's examine the *$@* variable on the third line. It holds a list of the command-line parameters. The **for** statement examines the *$@* variable and places the parameters, one at a time, into the file variable. The file variable is then used by the **ls** command to determine which file to examine.

Process Variables

Bash uses several variables to find out information about processes. For example, you can use the *$?* variable to determine if a command succeeded or failed.

There are four process variables:

$?   This variable contains zero if the last command succeeded. Any other value indicates failure.

$$ This variable holds the current process id.

$-   This variable contains a list of the shell options that are turned on.

$!   This variable holds the process id of the last executed background process.

Let's take a look at the *$?* and *$$* variables. The *$-* variable is discussed in the "The set Command" section of Chapter 9, "Examining the Tools."

The following example shows the *$?* variable in action:

```
% ls listfiles
listfiles
% echo $?
0
% ls ltfiles
ls: ltfiles: No such file or directory
% echo $?
1
```

In the Unix shell, a value of zero means that a command has
succeeded. By examining the value of *$?*, you can determine that
the second **ls** command failed. Obviously, *$?* is more useful for
non-interactive commands, like inside scripts, which are run in the
background (i.e., when no one is sitting there reading whatever
error messages might appear). You can also use the **exit** command
in your scripts to indicate success or failure. For example, you
might have a set of scripts performing some compression and
backup chores. A controlling script might be used to start the
chores and to send email when the *$?* variable indicates one of the
scripts failed.

FRI   For more information about sending email, see Chapter 9,
"Examining the Tools."

The *$$* variable holds the id of the current process. It can be
handy in a number of ways. Among other things, you can use *$$* to:

• create a unique filename

```
% echo `date` > /tmp/$$.out
% cat /tmp/$$.out
Sat Apr 4 11:54:02 EST 1998
% ls /tmp/$$.out
29287.out
```

• determine which user is running the current process

```
% ps u | grep $$ | awk '{print $1}'
medinets
```

• access the */proc* directory structure for information about the
  current process.

```
% cat /proc/$$/status
Name:    bash
State:   S (sleeping)
...
```

> The */proc* directory is a pseudo-filesystem that is used as an inter-   **NOTE**
> face to kernel data structures (including those that are used to track
> running processes). Normally, only system administrators need to
> know the details about the */proc* directory, so I will avoid describing
> it in this book. You can find more information about */proc* by using
> the **man proc** command. If you don't have the man pages loaded
> on your system, this URL should help *http://hegel.ittc.ukans.edu/top-
> ics/linux/man-pages/man5/proc.5.html.*

Bash Quoting Rules

You've seen quite a few examples so far of using the **echo** command to display the value of variables. Now let's look at the rules
behind the usage. There are three kinds of quotes you can use in
shell scripts:

- double quotes—Double quotes around text stop the shell from
  interpreting most special characters. For example, the # character doesn't begin comments inside double quotes, it simply indicates a pound sign. However, the $, `, and " characters keep
  their special meanings.

- single quotes—Single quotes around text stop all character
  interpretation except for the single quote character.

- backticks—Backticks around text indicate command substitution. The shell command inside the backticks is executed, and
  the resulting output is substituted for the backticked text. All
  special characters are interpreted normally.

The following series of commands shows how the rules for double quotes work:

```
% echo "\"Well said,\" said she."
"Well said," said she.
% echo "The value of \$logfile is $logfile."
The value of $logfile is foo.dat.
% echo "Yesterday was `date '+%B %d' --date '1 day ago'`."
Yesterday was April 03.
```

The second and third commands show that the dollar sign and
backtick characters retain their special meanings.

Using the backslash character forces the shell to ignore the following character's special meaning.

The following series of commands show how the rules for single quotes work:

```
% echo '\"Well said,\" said she.'
\"Well said,\" said she.
% echo '"Well said," said she.'
"Well said," said she.
% echo 'The value of \$logfile is $logfile.'
The value of \$logfile is $logfile.
% echo 'Yesterday was `date '+%B %d' --date '1 day ago'`.'
Yesterday was `date '+%B %d' --date '1 day ago'`.
```

These examples show that even the dollar sign and backtick characters lose their special meaning inside single quotes.

Because backticks were used in the double quote and single quote examples, no further backtick examples are needed.

Operators

Operators tell the computer what actions to perform. The shell, like most languages, has many operators. The examples earlier in the chapter used the *assignment* operator. As you read about the other operators, you'll undoubtedly realize that you are familiar with some of them. Trust your intuition. The definitions you already know will probably still be true.

Operators are instructions you give to the computer so that it can perform some task. All operators cause actions to be performed on operands. An *operand* can be a literal value (like 3 or 23.3), a variable (like $count), or an expression (like $count + 1). A good working definition of an expression is some combination of operators and operands that are evaluated as a unit.

Operands are recursive in nature. The expression 1 + 9 (two operands and a plus operator) can be considered as one operand with a value of 10. For example, (1 + 9) - 2 is an expression that consists of two operands subtracted from each other. The first operand is (1 + 9) and the second operand is 2.

Understanding precedence is key to being able to decipher expressions. The order of precedence indicates which operand should be evaluated first in each expression or subexpression. I like to think about operators in the same way I would give instructions to the driver of a car. I might say "turn left" or "turn right."

These commands could be considered directional operators in the same way that + and mathematical operators say "add this" or "subtract this." If I yell "stop" while the car is moving, on the other hand, it should supersede the other commands. This means that "stop" has precedence over "turn left" and "turn right."

Table 2.2 lists all of the operators used by the shell in order of decreasing precedence. Operators with a higher level of precedence are evaluated before operators of a lower level of precedence.

Table 2.2 *Shell Operators and Their Order of Precedence*

Level	Operator	Description
13	-, +	Unary minus, Unary positive
12	!, ~	Logical negation, Bitwise inversion or one's complement
11	*, /, %	Multiplication, Division, Modulus
10	+, -	Addition, Subtraction
9	<<, >>	Bitwise left shift, Bitwise right shift
8	<=, >=, <, >	Less than or equal to, Greater than or equal to, Less than, Greater than
7	==, !=	Equality, Inequality
6	&	Bitwise AND
5	^	Bitwise XOR
4	|	Bitwise OR
3	&&	Logical AND
2	||	Logical OR
1	=, +=, -=, *=. /=, %=, &=, ^=, |=, <<=, >>=	Assignment, Evaluate the operator then assign

NOTE You might think that Table 2.2 lists a lot of operators. You're wrong; this list is actually fairly modest. For example, the shell does not support the *exponentiation* operator. For this and more advanced operators, you need to use Perl or Tcl.

Before discussing some of the more esoteric operators, let's take a look at how order of precedence affects expression evaluation:

```
% echo $[ 1 + 2 * 4 ]
9
% echo $[ (1 + 2) * 4 ]
12
```

NOTE   The $[] notation tells the shell to evaluate the expression inside the square brackets. The "Expression Substitution" section later in this chapter discusses the $[] notation.

The first command evaluates the multiplication operator first because its precedence level is 11 versus the precedence level of 10 for addition. Therefore, the first command becomes echo $[1 + 8] or 9.

The second command uses parentheses to force evaluation of the addition operator first. Expressions in parentheses are always evaluated first.

The Modulus Operator

The *modulus* operator is used to find the remainder of the division between two operands. For example, 9 % 7 equals 2 because 9 / 7 equals 1 with 2 left over.

The modulus operator is useful when scripts need to iterate over a list and do something every so many elements. Listing 2.9 shows how to determine every third element in a list.

Listing 2.9 *modulus—Using the Modulus Operator to Process Every Third Element*

```
#!/bin/bash

count=1
for element in $@
do
  if test $[ $count % 3 ] = 0
  then
    echo $element
  fi
  let count=$count+1
done
```

Here is an example of this script in action:

```
% chmod +x modulus
% ./modulus one two three four five six
three
six
```

The only tricky part of the modulus script is the **test** command. The **test** command is fully discussed in Chapter 9, "Examining the Tools," so it is only briefly described here. The expression that needs evaluation, $count % 3, is within the $[] notation. And the value that the expression should be compared to is on the right side of the equals sign. Thus, when $count reaches three, the expression inside the square brackets evaluates to zero and the *echo* statement is executed.

Notice that every third item is printed. By changing the value on the right side of the modulus operator, you can affect which items are processed. Changing the value to five means that a message will be printed every five items.

The Bitwise Operators

Bitwise operators work at the single bit level on two operands. Each bit in the first operand is compared to its corresponding bit in the second operand (except for the inversion operator that only acts on one operand).

Table 2.3 provides details about each of the bitwise operators used by the shell.

Table 2.3 *The Bitwise Operators*

Operator	Description
~op1	The INVERSION operator converts all 1 bits to 0 and all 0 bits to 1 in op1.
op1 << op2	The SHIFT LEFT operator moves the bits in op1 to the left op2 bits, discards the far left bits, and assigns the rightmost bits a value of 0. Each bitwise move to the left effectively multiplies op1 by 2.

Table 2.3 *The Bitwise Operators (Cont'd)*

Operator	Description
op1 >> op2	The SHIFT RIGHT operator moves the bits in op1 to the right op2 bits, discards the far right bits, and assigns the far left bits a value of 0. Each move to the right effectively divides op1 in half.
op1 & op2	The AND operator compares the corresponding bits in op1 and op2 and generates, for each bit, a result of 1 if both bits are 1; otherwise it returns 0.
op1 ^ op2	The EXCLUSIVE-OR operator compares the corresponding bits in op1 and op2 and generates, for each bit, a result of 1 if the bits are complementary (i.e., not the same); otherwise it returns 0.
*op1	op2*	The OR operator compares the corresponding bits in op1 and op2 and generates, for each bit, a result of 1 if either or both bits are 1; otherwise it returns 0.

The Logical Operators

Logical operators allow programs to make decisions based on multiple conditions. Each operand is evaluated to a true or false value. Then the true or false values of the operands are used to determine the overall value of the expression.

Table 2.4 lists the four different ways that two operands can be combined using the *&&* *(AND)* operator. You can see that only if both operands are true is the result true.

Table 2.4 *The && Result Table*

Operand1	Operand2	Operand1 && Operand2
0	0	0
1	0	0
0	1	0
1	1	1

Table 2.5 lists the four different ways that two operands can be combined using the || *(OR)* operator. You can see that if either operand is true, the result is true.

Table 2.5 *The || Result Table*

Operand1	Operand2	Operand1 || Operand2
0	0	0
1	0	1
0	1	1
1	1	1

The Assignment Operators

The basic assignment has already been used in many previous examples in this chapter. It simply places the value of the expression on the right side of the equal sign into the variable on the left side of the equal sign.

The shell also has shortcut assignment operators that combine the basic assignment operator with another operator. For example, instead of saying `let $count = $count + $change` you could say `let $count += $change`. The advantage of using shortcut operators—besides having less characters to type—is that your intentions regarding assignment are more clear.

Expression Substitution

In the last section, you saw the `$[]` notation used to evaluate expressions. You can also use `$(())` to evaluate expressions. But I prefer to use `$[]` because it has fewer characters and seems less confusing.

All shell expression evaluation is done using integers. The divide by zero error is the only math error that is trapped. A divide by zero error message looks like this:

```
% echo $[ 12 / 0 ]
bash: 12 / 0 : division by 0 (remainder of expression is
"")
```

The $[] notation is very flexible because it can accept numbers using different bases, not only decimal and hexadecimal. For example:

```
% echo $[ 2#10 + 1]
3
% echo $[ 7#10 + 1]
8
% echo $[10#8 + 1]
9
```

You can use this [base#]n notation for any base from 2 to 36. If the [base#] is omitted, then base 10 is used.

The shell also supports the standard 0x and 0X prefixes to indicate hexadecimal numbers. For example:

```
% echo $[ 0x10 + 1]
17
```

Standard Shell Variables

The shell uses many variables. Some systems have non-standard variables in addition to the standard set.

Table 2.6 lists the standard variables used by Bash and a brief description of each. Variables that seem important for script programming are described in more detail after the table.

Table 2.6 *Variables Used by the Shell*

Name	Description
allow_null_glob_expansion	Determines if the shell lets pathname patterns expand to a null string or to the pattern itself. Set this variable to "true" to force this behavior.
auto_resume	Controls how the shell interacts with the user and job control. Run the **man bash** command for more information.
BASH	Holds the full pathname used to invoke the instance of Bash running the current shell.

Table 2.6 *Variables Used by the Shell (Cont'd)*

Name	Description
BASH_VERSION	Holds the version number of the current Bash instance. This book was developed using Bash version 1.14.7(1).
cdable_vars	Determines if the argument to the **cd** command is a variable whose value is the directory to switch to. Set this variable to "true" to force this behavior.
CDPATH	Holds the search path for the **cd** command.
command_oriented_history	Determines if the shell attempts to save all lines of a multiple-line command in the same history entry. Set this variable to "true" to force this behavior.
ENV	Holds the filename, if any, used to initialize new shells.
EUID	Holds the effective user id of the current user.
FCEDIT	Holds the name of the default editor for the **fc** command.
FIGNORE	Holds a colon-delimited list of suffixes to ignore when performing filename completion.
glob_dot_filenames	Determines if the shell includes filenames beginning with a dot when doing filename expansion. Set this variable to "true" to force this behavior.
histchars	Controls history expansion and tokenization. Run the **man bash** command for more information.
HISTCMD	Holds the history number of the current command.

Table 2.6 *Variables Used by the Shell (Cont'd)*

Name	Description
HISTCONTROL	Determines whether commands go into the history and if duplicate commands are ignored. Valid values are `ignorespace`, `ignoredups`, and `ignoreboth`.
HISTFILE	Holds the filename where the command history is stored. The default is `~/.bash_history`.
HISTFILESIZE	Holds the maximum number of lines contained in the history file. The default number is 500.
HISTSIZE	Holds the number of commands to remember.
HOME	Holds the home directory of the current user.
HOSTFILE	Holds the filename that is read when the shell does hostname completion.
HOSTTYPE	Uniquely describes the type of machine on which the shell is running.
IFS	Holds a list of characters used as field separators by Bash's expansion and word-splitting internal routines. The default separators are spaces, tabs, and newlines.
IGNOREEOF	Controls how the shell reacts to the `EOF` (`Ctrl-D`) character. When a shell encounters a `Ctrl-D` or `0x04` character in its input, it usually exits. However, if the *IGNOREEOF* variable is set to a number, the shell ignores that number of `EOF` characters before exiting. If set to a non-number, the default value is 10. This variable only affects interactive shells.

Table 2.6 *Variables Used by the Shell (Cont'd)*

Name	Description
INPUTRC	Holds the filename of the *readline* initialization file.
LINENO	Holds the current sequential line number of the current script or function. Its value is not meaningful outside the context of a script or function.
MAIL	Holds the filename where the shell should look for new mail. *MAIL* is mutually exclusive with the *MAILPATH* variable.
MAILCHECK	Holds the number of seconds between mailbox checks.
MAILPATH	Holds a colon-separated list of pathnames to be checked for mail.
MAIL_WARNING	Determines if the shell prints a "mailfile has been read" message.
noclobber	Determines if the shell overwrites existing files when doing I/O redirection. Set this variable to "true" to force this behavior.
no_exit_on_failed_exec	Determines if a non-interactive shell exits when a command fails. Set this variable to "true" to force this behavior.
nolinks	Determines if the shell follows symbolic links when executing commands that change the current working directory. Set this variable to "true" to force this behavior.
notify	Determines if the shell reports terminated background jobs immediately or if it waits until the next primary prompt is displayed.
OLDPWD	Holds the previous working directory as set by the **cd** command.

Table 2.6 *Variables Used by the Shell (Cont'd)*

Name	Description
OPTARG	Holds the value of the last option argument process by the **getopts** command.
OPTERR	Controls whether the shell displays error messages from the **getopts** command. A value of 1 means that messages are displayed.
OPTIND	Holds the index of the next argument to be processed by the **getopts** command.
OSTYPE	Uniquely describes the operating system on which the shell is running.
PATH	Holds the search path for commands. This colon-separated list of directories is system-dependent. When a command needs to be executed, the shell looks for a related script or program files in each directory in the list until the command is found or the list is exhausted—at which point an error is displayed.
PPID	Holds the process id of the parent shell.
PROMPT_COMMAND	Holds the command line, if any, to be executed before each primary prompt.
PS1	Holds the primary prompt for the shell. Many format specifier characters can be used with this variable. See the Bash man page for more information.
PS2	Holds the secondary prompt for the shell. Many format specifier characters can be used with this variable. See the Bash man page for more information.
PS3	Holds the prompt for the **select** command.

Table 2.6 *Variables Used by the Shell (Cont'd)*

Name	Description
PS4	Holds the prompt used during execution tracing. Many format specifier characters can be used with this variable. See the Bash man page for more information.
PWD	Holds the current working directory as set by the **cd** command.
RANDOM	Holds a different random number each time it is used.
REPLY	Holds the default variable used by the **read** command when no argument is supplied.
SECONDS	Holds the number of seconds since the current shell instance was started. If you assign a value to *SECONDS*, the next time *SECONDS* is used it returns the number of seconds since the assignment plus the assigned value.
SHLVL	Incremented each time a new instance of the shell is started to create a child shell.
TMOUT	Holds the number of seconds to wait for input after displaying the primary prompt. If no input has been received in the allotted time, the shell exits.
UID	Holds the user id of the current user.

You can list all of the variables used in your shell using the **set** and **env** commands. Here is the output from running the **env** command in a newly started login session on my computer:

```
USERNAME=
ENV=/home/medined/.bashrc
HISTSIZE=1000
HOSTNAME=localhost.localdomain
LOGNAME=medined
HISTFILESIZE=1000
```

```
MAIL=/var/spool/mail/medined
TERM=linux
HOSTTYPE=i386
PATH=/usr/local/bin:/bin:/usr/bin:/usr/X11R6/bin:/usr/bin/
mh:/home/medined/bin
HOME=/home/medined
SHELL=/bin/bash
PS1=(\#) \T [\w] \u>
USER=medined
OSTYPE=Linux
MM_CHARSET=ISO-8859-1
SHLLVL=1
LS_COLORS=mi=34
_=/usr/bin/env
```

From the above list, you can see that my path is `/usr/local/`
`bin:/bin:/usr/bin:/usr/X11R6/bin:/`. When I need to work with
scripts in my current directory—say for testing purposes—I use
this command:

```
PATH=".:$PATH"
```

That simple command adds the current directory, symbolized by
the dot, to the beginning of the path. Thus, scripts in my current
directory are found before scripts found in directories later in the
path.

Some of the variables shown above are not standard shell variables. The various Red Hat Linux logon scripts created them.

Variable Affecting Commands

The shell has several commands that work with variables. And several of them seem to duplicate each other's features. For example,
you can create global (or exported) variables using the **declare**,
export, and **typeset** commands. In fact, **typeset** is a synonym for
the **declare** command.

The declare Command

Syntax:

```
declare [options] [name[=value]]
```

Synopsis:
    Used to display or set variables.

The **declare** command understands four options:

-*f* displays only function names.

-*r* creates read-only variables. Read-only variables can't be assigned new values or unset unless the **declare** or **typeset** command is used.

-*x* creates exported variables.

-*i* creates integer variables. If you attempt to assign text to an integer variable, a zero is actually assigned instead.

By using a **+** instead of a **-**, you can reverse the meaning of an option.

If no parameters are used, **declare** displays a list of currently defined variables and functions.

Let's take a closer look at the -*r* option:

```
% declare -r title="Paradise Lost"
% title="Xenogenesis"
bash: title: read-only variable
% declare title="Xenogenesis"
% echo $title
Xenogenesis
% typeset title="The Longing Ring"
% echo $title
The Longing Ring
```

This example shows that only the **declare** or the **typeset** command can change the value of a read-only variable.

The export Command

Syntax:

```
export [options] [name[=value]]
```

Synopsis:

Used to create variables that are passed to child shells.

The **export** command understands four options:

-- signifies the end of options. All subsequent parameters are arguments.

-*f* signifies that the names (in the name-value pairs) are functions.

-*n* converts a global variable into a local variable. In other words, the named variables are no longer passed to child shells.

-*p* displays a list of global variables.

If no parameters are used, the -*p* parameter is assumed and a list of global variables is displayed:

```
% export
declare -x ENV="/home/medined/.bashrc"
declare -x HISTFILESIZE="1000"
...
declare -xi numPages="314"
declare -xr title="The Longing Ring"
declare -xri numChapters="32"
```

One interesting feature of this display is that it tells you which variables are integer-only, read-only, or both.

The let Command

Syntax:

```
let expression
```

Synopsis:

Used to evaluate integer expressions.

The **let** command evaluates integer expressions. It is commonly used to increment a counter variable, as shown in Listing 2.10

Listing 2.10 *let—Using the let Command*

```
#!/bin/bash

count=1
for element in $@
do
  echo "$element is element $count"
  let count+=1
done
```

Here is an example of this script in action:

```
% chmod +x let
% ./let one two three
one is element 1
two is element 2
three is element 3
```

If you prefer to use spaces in your expressions, enclose the expression in double quotes:

```
let "count += 1"
```

The local Command

Syntax:
```
local [name[=value]]
```

Synopsis:

Used to create variables that are *not* passed to child shells. This command is only valid inside of procedures.

Simply put, the **local** command creates a variable that is not accessible by child shells. However, you can only use the **local** command from within functions. From the command line or in scripts, you can use the `VARIABLE=VALUE` **assignment** command.

If `local` is used without arguments, a list of currently defined local variables is sent to standard output.

Chapter 3, "Procedures," has information about how to create and use procedures.

The readonly Command

Syntax:
```
readonly [options] [name[=value]]
```

Synopsis:

Used to display or set read-only variables.

The **readonly** command understands two options:

-- signifies the end of options. All subsequent parameters are
   arguments.

-f creates read-only functions.

If no parameters are used, **readonly** displays a list of currently defined read-only variables and functions.

The set Command

Syntax:
```
set [--abefhkmnptuvxldCHP] [-o option] [name[=value]]
```

Synopsis:

Used to set or reset various shell options.

The **set** command performs many different functions—not all of which are related to variables. Because the other commands in this section duplicate those variable options available through the **set** command, the **set** command is not described here. Instead, see the "The set Command" section in Chapter 9, "Examining the Tools."

The shift Command

Syntax:

```
shift [n]
```

Synopsis:

Used to shift position variables.

The **shift** command adjusts the positional variables so that the value of $3 is assigned to $2 and the value of $2 is assigned to $1. This ripple effect affects any positional variables that are defined when the **shift** command executes. The **shift** command is often used to check parameters of procedures for specific values—such as when setting flag variables for options.

The section "The shift Command" in chapter 3, "Procedures," has more detailed information.

The typeset Command

Syntax:

```
typeset [options] [name[=value]]
```

Synopsis:

Used to display or set variables.

The **typeset** command is a synonym for the **declare** command. Please see the section "The declare Command" earlier in this chapter for more information.

The unset Command

Syntax:

```
unset [options] name [name...]
```

Synopsis:

Used to undefine variables.

The **unset** command understands two options:

-- signifies the end of options. All subsequent parameters are arguments.

-*f* creates read-only functions.

The **unset** command removes the specified variables and functions from the shell's environment. Note that *PATH, IFS, PPID, PS1, PS2, UID,* and *EUID* cannot be unset. If you unset the *RANDOM, SECONDS, LINENO,* or *HISTCMD* variables, they lose their special properties.

Summary

Variables are used quite a bit in the shell. Quite often they are used to control shell behavior, as evidenced by the *IGNOREEOF* variable. At other times they are simply used to hold important values like the *HISTSIZE* variable.

The shell understands the difference between integer variables and text variables. When integer variables are assigned text values, the shell quietly replaces the text with a zero value.

The shell also incorporates the concept of variable scope—although it's not quite as advanced as "full-blown" computer languages. In the shell, local variables are only accessible by the current shell. Global variables are accessible by child shells.

The shell recognizes the $ character as an indicator that variable substitution needs to take place. When the shell sees a $ and a variable name, both are replaced with the variable's value. *${VARI-ABLE}, ${VARIABLE:-DEFAULT}, ${VARIABLE:=DEFAULT}, ${VARIABLE:+VALUE}, ${#VARIABLE},* and *${VARI-ABLE:?MESSAGE}* are all notations that provide additional flexibility when using variable substitution.

Variable names that consist only of numbers are reserved by the shell to indicate parameters passed to scripts and procedures. They are called position variables. When using positions higher than 9, use curly braces around the variable name. For example, ${13} and ${15}.

The *$?, $$, $-,* and *$!* variables hold information about processes. *$?* indicates the success or failure of the last command. *$$* is the current process id. *$-* is a list of shell options that are turned on (see the **set** command entry in Chapter 9, "Examining the Tools"). And *$!* is the process id of the last executed background process.

There are three types of quotes used by the shell: double quotes, single quotes, and backticks. In general, quoting is a means of turning off the special meaning of characters. For example, the ; character typically indicates that a new command is starting. However, inside quotes the ; character has no special meaning. Backticks tell the shell to execute the command inside the backticks and substitute the command output for the backticked text.

The shell does understand a limited number of operators, as shown in Table 2.2. However, when using them, you need to surround expressions with the $[] or $(()) notation and the expression should be assigned to some variable, otherwise the shell executes the resulting value as a command.

Table 2.6 lists the standard shell variables, of which there are quite a few. Not too many of them are directly related to shell programming, however, so you don't need to learn the entire list right away.

The **declare, export, let, local, readonly, set, shift, typeset**, and **unset** commands work with variables. Although the **declare** command can create both global and read-only variables, it might help script readability if you use the more specific **export** and **readonly** commands.

The next chapter, "Procedures," shows you how to create your own commands.

Procedures

This chapter discusses how to create packages of commands called *procedures*. These packages can be called whenever needed and are used to store sets of commands that are called often within a script. They help to keep your script small and tidy because the same sequence of commands doesn't need to be repeated many times throughout the script.

Shell procedures are rarely used because, by their nature, shell scripts tend to be small and straightforward. However, occasionally you'll need the extra kick provided by procedures.

One of their biggest benefits is that they allow you to create advanced aliases. Instead of simply aliasing **ls -l** to **ll**, you can get more creative by using and manipulating parameters in your procedures. This chapter only goes into the basics of procedure syntax and how to use parameters. Chapter 10, "Customizing the Tools," shows more advanced examples of procedures in action.

Procedure

A block of commands that has been given a name for later use.

Procedures are blocks of shell commands that are given names so you can use them wherever they are needed. Procedures organize your code into easy-to-understand and easy-to-use pieces. They let you build your scripts slowly, testing them along the way.

As you prepare to implement a complex script, you should break the script into several tasks and create a procedure for each task. As you develop a small army of procedures, you'll find that writing scripts becomes easy—sometimes as easy as stringing your procedures together in a new way. This is called *code reuse*.

When procedures are *sourced*, they are defined just as if you were typing the shell commands they comprise. Procedures are sourced using the **source** command (using a . instead of source also works). The command lines following Listing 3.1 show the **source** command in action. Basically speaking, the **source** command means that the script is not run inside a subshell. Instead, it's run in the current shell.

You can simply call procedures (after sourcing) from the shell command line. Many procedures, in fact, are created to enhance existing shell commands. Other procedures are created to combine commands or to process the output of one command before displaying it.

What does a procedure look like? Listing 3.1 shows a procedure that tracks *tar* file extractions. The *untar* procedure creates an audit trail that lists the name of the *tar* file used and the files inside it, and then moves the *tar* file to a storage partition. A full explanation of the script follows the listing.

Listing 3.1 *untar—Creating an Audit Trail for the tar Command*

```
#!/bin/bash

untar () {
    cp $1 /store                            #1
    echo "----------" >> ~/tar.log          #2
    echo $1 >> ~/tar.log                    #3
    date >> ~/tar.log                       #4
    tar tf $1 >> ~/tar.log                  #5
    tar xvf $1                              #6
    rm $1                                   #7
    ln -s /store/$1 $1                      #8
}
```

This script, while straightforward, does quite a few things:

1. Copies the *tar* file to the */store* directory. On my system, the */store* directory is a separate partition that I use solely to store *tar* files so I will have them in case an emergency arises in the future.

2. Appends a separator line to a log file in the user's home directory. This log file records tar activities for future audits.

3. Appends the name of the *tar* file to the log file.

4. Appends a timestamp to the log file.

5. Appends a list of the files inside the *tar* file to the log file.

6. Extracts the files inside the *tar* file.

7. Removes the *tar* file to save space in the current partition.

8. Creates a symbolic link to the new location of the *tar* file (in the */data* partition) in the current directory. This symbolic link is frequently not needed, but it's cheap in terms of disk space.

Running the *untar* script, as is, requires that the */store* directory already exist and for you to be able to write to it. If this is not the case, either comment out lines 1, 7, and 8 or simply create a store directory in your home directory and change lines 1 and 7 to use ~/ *store* instead of plain */store*.   **NOTE**

Some of this syntax should already be familiar to you. The *$1* positional variable was discussed in Chapter 2, "Variables and Operators," where it was used to access the command-line parameters. In Listing 3.1, it's used to access parameters passed to the procedure. In this case, it's the name of the *tar* file that is being untarred.

Here is an example of the script in action:

```
% chmod +x untar
% source untar
% untar medined.tar
```

FRI

"The for Command" section in Chapter 4 shows you how to change the *untar* function to handle multiple *tar* files.

Notice that you don't need any special mechanisms to run the procedure. You simply use it like any other shell command—after the script has been sourced, of course. Interestingly enough, you can run the *untar* procedure from either the command line or from another script file. Once you source the procedure, it becomes a part of the shell, usable anywhere a "normal" Bash command can be used.

The **untar** command does not display any output. Instead, the information is sent to a log file called *~/tar.log*. If you try this procedure, check out the log file created in your home directory. My log file, after the above sequence of commands, looks like this:

```
- - - - - - - - - -
medinets.tar
Sat Mar 14 15:42:31 EST 1998
name.pl
desk.pl
pen.pl
```

This output shows that on March 14, 1998 at 3:42 in the afternoon I extracted three files from the *medinets.tar* file. If you work with *tar* files a lot, this information might come in handy if you need to remember which *tar* file a specific file came from.

As mentioned earlier, you can use the *untar* procedure (or any other procedure you create) inside scripts. Calling a procedure means the shell stops executing the current series of commands. Execution flow jumps to the commands inside the procedure.

When the procedure is finished, the shell jumps back to the point at which the procedure was called. Program execution continues from that point onward. The basic syntax for procedure definition is:

```
procedure_name () {
}
```

That's it—nothing complicated at all. Simply use your own procedure name in place of *procedure_name* and place the procedure's commands between the curly braces.

Using Variables Inside Procedures

Chapter 2, "Variables," introduced you to the positional variables—$1, $2, and so forth. When using these variables along with procedures, the shell saves the variables' values before entering the procedure and restores them after the procedure exits.

Let's look at this behavior more closely. Listing 3.2 shows a procedure that simply displays how many parameters are passed to it.

Listing 3.2 *03lst02.sh—A Simple Procedure that Prints the Amount of Parameters It Gets*

```
test () {
    echo $#
}
```

Try the following series of commands using Listing 3.2:

```
medined> source 03lst02.sh
medined> test one two three
3
medined> test one
1
medined> test
0
```

The $# special variable always contains the number of parameters passed to your script. What happens to the value of $# inside a procedure? Listing 3.3 shows you.

Listing 3.3 *03lst03.sh—Exploring the Value of $# Inside Procedures*

```
#!/bin/bash

test_two () {
    echo "Test Two: $#"
}

test () {
    echo "Test One: $#"
    test_two one two three
    test_two
    echo "Test One: $#"
}
```

Try the following series of commands using Listing 3.3:

```
medined> source 03lst03.sh
medined> test one
Test One: 1
Test Two: 3
Test Two: 0
Test One: 1
```

From the output, you can tell that the $# variable was saved before *test_two* was called, and then restored to its original value after *test_two* exited.

The same behavior can be seen with the positional variables. Let's replace the $# in Listing 3.3 with positional variables, in Listing 3.4.

Listing 3.4 *03lst03.sh—Exploring Positional Variables Inside Procedures*

```
#!/bin/bash

test_two () {
    echo "Test Two: $1 $2 $3 $4 $5"
}

test () {
    echo "Test One: $1 $2 $3 $4 $5"
    test_two one two three
    test_two
    echo "Test One: $1 $2 $3 $4 $5"
}
```

Here is an example of this script in action:

```
medined> source 031st04.sh
medined> test one two
Test One: one two
Test Two: one two three
Test Two:
Test One: one two
```

> The *$0* special variable is always unchanged.   **NOTE**

The shift Command

The **shift** command adjusts the positional variables so that the value of $3 is assigned to $2 and the value of $2 is assigned to $1. This ripple effect affects any positional variables that are defined when the **shift** command executes. The **shift** command is often used to check parameters to procedures for specific values—such as when setting *flag* variables for options as shown in the next example.

Listing 3.5 checks all of its parameters for a *--x* option and then takes the next parameter as the name of a logfile.

Listing 3.5 *test_shift—Using the shift Command to Set Flag Variables*

```
#!/bin/bash

for element in $@
do
    # ignore all elements except "--x"
    if test "$1" = "--x"
    then
        logfile=$2
    fi
    shift
done

echo "logfile=$logfile"
```

Here is an example of this script in action:

```
% chmod +x test_shift
% test_shift one two three
logfile=
% test_shift one --x shift.log three
logfile=shift.log
```

FRI   For more information about the **test** command, see Chapter 9,
"Examining the Tools."

When the loop encounters a --*x* string as one of the parameters,
the *logfile* variable is assigned to the value of the next parameter
(which is *$2)*. The **shift** command ensures that each parameter, in
turn, is examined.

CAUTION   When testing the script in Listing 3.5, I tried to use a -x string
with the **test** command and ran into some strange behavior.
That's why the two dashes are used in the script. I didn't investigate this behavior further because the --x works for this example.

You might notice that the script tests the parameter holding the
logfile name for the --*x* string. Obviously, this test is not needed.
However, the performance penalty is small.

Creating Local Procedure Variables

You can see, from Listings 3.3 and 3.4, that the shell saves and
restores the value of positional variables. In effect, the positional
and *$#* variable are given local values when a procedure is entered.
Regular variables, however, don't get this special treatment. Normally, they have global values. Listing 3.6 illustrates the global
nature of most variables.

Listing 3.6 *03lst06.sh—Variables are Global by Default*

```
#!/bin/bash

test_two () {
    test_var=5
    echo "Test Two: $test_var"
}
```

```
test () {
    test_var=1
    echo "Test One: $test_var"
    test_two
    echo "Test One: $test_var"
}
```

Try the following series of commands using Listing 3.6:

```
medined> source 03lst06.sh
medined> test
Test One: 1
Test Two: 5
Test One: 5
```

These results show that the *test_two* procedure was able to "permanently" change the value of *$test_var* (the initial value wasn't restored when the procedure was exited). This means *$test_var* is global to both procedures.

You can use the **local** command to change this behavior. With the **local** command, changes made to variables inside procedures don't affect other procedures. Listing 3.7 demonstrates this.

Listing 3.7 *03lst07.sh—The local Command in Action*

```
#!/bin/bash

test_two () {
    local test_var=5
    echo "Test Two: $test_var"
}

test () {
    test_var=1
    echo "Test One: $test_var"
    test_two
    echo "Test One: $test_var"
}
```

Try the following series of commands using Listing 3.7:

```
medined> source 03lst07.sh
medined> test
Test One: 1
Test Two: 5
Test One: 1
```

Notice how the original value of *$test_var* is preserved.

The **local** command comes in handy if you create large scripts that contain many procedures. Keeping variable values local to a procedure makes them easier to understand because changes in one procedure won't affect other procedures.

Returning Values From Procedures

The return value of a procedure is always the return value of its last executed command.

NOTE   If you prefer, you don't need to use the *return()* function to return a value, because Bash will automatically return the value of the last expression evaluated. I prefer to use the *return()* function and be explicit so that there is no mistaking my intention.

You might have used programming languages that distinguish between functions and subroutines. The difference is that a function returns a value and a subroutine does not. Bash makes no such distinctions. All procedures, commands, programs, and scripts have a return value—even it's only the default value of success (i.e., zero).

Summary

Procedures are important for every programmer to become familiar with. When a new Bash procedure is defined, it seems to become a part of the shell and is invoked just like any command. The syntax to define a procedure is quite simple:

```
procName () {
}
```

Parameters to procedures are stored in the positional parameter variables described in Chapter 2, "Variables and Operators." When a procedure is called, the values of the current positional variables are processed, so that the parameters used by the procedure don't overwrite their values. Then, when the procedure is finished, the original values of the positional variables are restored.

The *$#* variable holds the number of parameters passed to your procedure or script. It is handy for iterating over the parameter list.

The **shift** command shifts the values of the positional variables down one position. So, for example, the value of $3 is assigned to $2 and the value of $2 is assigned to $1. **shift** is another handy tool to use when you need to iterate over the parameter list.

Most shell variables are global in scope, which means that every procedure and script can access them. However, you can create local variables (variables only accessible inside one procedure) using the **local** command.

The last section of the chapter mentions that every command in Bash has a return value. You can store return values in variables and test them using the **test** command as discussed in Chapter 9, "Examining the Tools."

The next chapter, "Script Execution Commands," shows how to control what happens inside your scripts. Your scripts can be a little more intelligent after you see how to handle loops and make decisions.

Script Execution Commands

This chapter discusses commands that let you control the execution of your script. So far in this book you've mostly seen shell scripts that execute sequentially, top to bottom. While you'll have occasion to use sequential scripts, most of the time you'll need more flexibility. The commands in this chapter provide the ability to test return values of procedures and commands and to execute statement blocks more than once. You'll also see how to trap signals and leave scripts at will instead of only at the end of the script file.

Script flexibility, or control, is provided by the commands listed in Table 4.1. These commands let you make decisions, repeatedly execute a block of commands (also called looping), and control your scripts in other ways.

Table 4.1 *Commands for Controlling Script Execution*

Command	Description
break	The **break** command leaves the current command block.
case	The **case** command is an alternative to the *if* statement. It is normally used when you need to make a decision based on a variable that has many possible values.
continue	The **continue** command skips the remaining commands in a command block. It's used in conjunction with the **for**, **while**, and **until** commands.
exit	The **exit** command forces a script to end. It is very useful when error conditions are detected.
for	The **for** command iterates over a set (or list) of values, executing a specific block of statements once for each value in the list.
if	The **if** command lets you decide on one or more courses of action.
trap	The **trap** command lets your script intercept signals and act on them. If your script does something particularly critical, you might want to trap certain signals to avoid interruptions. The **trap** command is also used for running "cleanup" commands just before the script exits.
until	The **until** command repeatedly executes a command block until a test succeeds (returns a zero).
while	The **while** command, like the **until** command, repeats a command block. However, instead of stopping when the test succeeds, it stops when the test fails (i.e., returns non-zero).

CAUTION   In order to avoid confusing readers of your shell scripts (or yourself!), try to pick variable and procedure names that aren't similar to shell commands.

The rest of this chapter discusses these commands in more detail. First, the **exit** and **trap** commands are discussed. Then, decision-making commands are discussed. Next, looping commands are explained. Finally, the chapter closes with the jump commands—**break** and **continue**.

The exit Command

Syntax:

```
exit [n]
```

Synopsis:

Forces a script to end, returning the value of *n* to the calling process.

The **exit** command lets you communicate—in a limited way—between two scripts. It is used to assign an exit value for one script that can be evaluated in the other. Let's look at how this can be accomplished with the following three small scripts.

Listing 4.1 shows the *success* script. When run, it simply exits with a zero value, which is the standard success indicator.

Listing 4.1 *success—A Command that Always Returns the Value for Success*

```
#!/bin/bash

exit 0
```

Listing 4.2 shows the *failure* script. When run, it simply exits with a value of one, which is the standard failure indicator. Actually, any non-zero value signifies failure. Some programs assign specific meanings to different non-zero values.

Listing 4.2 *failure—A Command that Always Returns the Value for Failure*

```
#!/bin/bash

exit 1
```

Listing 4.3 *test_return—A Command that Tests Its First Parameter or Argument*

```
#!/bin/bash

if `$1`
then
  echo "The Test Worked."
else
  echo "The Test Failed."
fi
```

FRI

For more information about the **if** command, see the section "The if Command" later in this chapter.

Here is an example of these scripts in action:

```
% chmod +x success failure test_return
% ./test_return success
The Test Worked.
% ./test_return failure
The Test Failed.
```

The *test_return* script runs its argument and tests its exit value. If the exit value is zero, then success is assumed and the first **echo** command is run. Otherwise, failure is assumed and the second **echo** command is run.

The *success* and *failure* scripts explicitly told the **exit** command what value to use; you can also substitute a shell command for the literal value. For example, the line of code below is perfectly okay:

```
exit `failure`
```

Assuming that you've already created the *failure* script, this might be a nice way to make your script files more readable—at the expense of some extra CPU cycles. However, when moving your scripts from one machine to another you'd need to also move the *success* and *failure* scripts. So perhaps this isn't the greatest idea after all.

The trap Command

Syntax:
```
trap [-l] [[commands] signals]
```

Synopsis:

Lets your script intercept signals and, optionally, acts on them.

What's a signal? Good question. A signal is sent to your script by the shell when specific things happen. For example, if your script dials into another machine, a signal would be generated if the phone line goes dead—the *SIGHUP* or *hangup* signal.

The simplest use of the **trap** command is to use it to ignore signals. If you wanted your script to ignore the CTRL-C key combination, you would use the following line of code earlier in your script:

```
trap "" 2
```

or

```
trap "" SIGINT
```

Listing 4.4 contains a program that reads lines of input from the keyboard (actually standard input, but let's not be too technical). The user can press CRTL-C without causing the program to break. As long as the user only enters "a" and then presses <ENTER>, the script loops. If any other input is read, the script ends.

Listing 4.4 *test_sigint—A Script to Use for Experimenting with SIGINT*

```
#!/bin/bash
trap "" SIGINT

input="a"

while [ $input = "a" ]
do
    echo "Type 'a' to continue, anything else to quit:"
    read input
done

echo "The script is done."
```

First run the script with the **trap** command commented out (use the # character at the beginning of the second line). This results in the following output:

```
% chmod +x test_sigint
% test_sigint
Type 'a' to continue, anything else to quit:
a                <- while "a" is entered, the script loops.
Type 'a' to continue, anything else to quit:
 ^C              <- CRTL-C is pressed. And the script exits.
```

Notice that when CRTL-C is pressed the script immediately exits. The final **echo** command is not executed.

Now let's try Listing 4.4 with the **trap** command active. Remove the # character that you used to comment out the trap line. Here is the script in action:

```
% test_sigint
Type 'a' to continue, anything else to quit:
a                    <- while "a' is entered, the script loops.
Type 'a' to continue, anything else to quit:
^C                   <- CRTL-C is pressed. And nothing happens.
Type 'a' to continue, anything else to quit:
w
the end
The script is done.
```

At this point, you might be wondering what other kinds of signals the shell might use. You can find out the signal numbers and mnemonic names by using the **-l** option of the **trap** command:

```
% trap -l
 0) EXIT          1) SIGHUP       2) SIGINT       3) SIGQUIT
 4) SIGILL        5) SIGTRAP      6) SIGIOT       7) SIGBUS
 8) SIGFPE        9) SIGKILL     10) SIGUSR1     11) SIGSEGV
12) SIGUSR2      13) SIGPIPE     14) SIGALRM     15) SIGTERM
16) SIGJUNK(16)  17) SIGCHLD     18) SIGCONT     19) SIGSTOP
20) SIGTSTP      21) SIGTTIN     22) SIGTTOU     23) SIGURG
24) SIGXCPU      25) SIGXFSZ     26) SIGVTALRM   27) SIGPROF
28) SIGWINCH     29) SIGIO       30) SIGPWR      31) SIG-
JUNK(31)
```

Table 4.2 briefly describes each of these signals:

Table 4.2 *Signal List*

Signal Number	Mnemonic Name	Type	Description
0	EXIT	Termination	This signal is received when the script exits.
1	SIGHUP	Termination	This signal reports that a user's terminal is disconnected.

Table 4.2 *Signal List (Cont'd)*

Signal Number	Mnemonic Name	Type	Description
2	SIGINT	Termination	This signal is received when the user types the INTR or interrupt character, which is normally Control-C.
3	SIGQUIT	Termination	This signal is received when the user types the QUIT character, which is normally Control-\. A core dump is produced by this signal.
4	SIGILL	Program Error	This signal is usually received when an executable has been corrupted. It means that the CPU is being asked to execute bad or privileged instructions.
5	SIGTRAP	Program Error	This signal is produced by the CPU's breakpoint instruction. It is typically used by debuggers.
6	SIGIOT (SIGABRT)	Program Error	
7	SIGBUS	Program Error	This signal indicates an invalid memory address was referenced.
8	SIGFPE	Program Error	This signal indicates a fatal arithmetic error.
9	SIGKILL	Termination	This signal is always fatal. It can't be handled or ignored.

Table 4.2 *Signal List (Cont'd)*

Signal Number	Mnemonic Name	Type	Description
10	SIGUSR1	Miscellaneous	This signal is reserved for your use. The system won't generate it. *SIGUSR1* and *SIGUSR2* are sometimes used for interprocess communication.
11	SIGSEGV	Program Error	This signal indicates an invalid access to a valid memory address.
12	SIGUSR2	Miscellaneous	This signal is reserved for your use. The system won't generate it. *SIGUSR1* and *SIGUSR2* are sometimes used for interprocess communication.
13	SIGPIPE	Operation Error	This signal indicates a problem with a broken pipe—the connection between two processes has failed in some way.
14	SIGALRM	Alarm	This signal indicates that a timer has expired.
15	SIGTERM	Termination	This signal is a request to terminate a program or script. Because it can be handled, it is a "polite" way to ask.
16	SIGJUNK(16)	Miscellaneous	
17	SIGCHLD	Job Control	This signal indicates a child process has terminated.

Table 4.2 *Signal List (Cont'd)*

Signal Number	Mnemonic Name	Type	Description
18	SIGCONT	Job Control	This signal can't be handled or ignored. It simply starts a stopped process.
19	SIGSTOP	Job Control	This signal can't be handled or ignored. It simply stops a process.
20	SIGTSTP	Job Control	This signal "politely" requests your program or script to stop. It's used when files and memory need to be placed into a specific state—perhaps for security—before a process stops.
21	SIGTTIN	Job Control	This signal indicates that a background process is trying to read input from the terminal.
22	SIGTTOU	Job Control	This signal indicates that a background process is trying to write output to the terminal.
23	SIGURG	Async I/O	This signal indicates that urgent or out-of-band data has arrived on a socket.
24	SIGXCPU	Operation Error	This signal indicates that a CPU time limit has been reached. Some systems place limits on the amount of CPU time each process can use.

Table 4.2 *Signal List (Cont'd)*

Signal Number	Mnemonic Name	Type	Description
25	SIGXFSZ	Operation Error	This signal indicates that a file size limit has been reached. Some systems place a limit on how much disk space a user can use.
26	SIGVTALRM	Alarm	This signal indicates the expiration of a timer that measures CPU time used by the current process. Some systems place limits on the amount of CPU time each process can use.
27	SIGPROF	Alarm	This signal is used by code profiling programs.
28	SIGWINCH	Miscellaneous	This signal indicates that a window (in X Windows) has changed size.
29	SIGIO	Async I/O	This signal indicates that a terminal or socket is ready for I/O. Rarely, you might find that *SIGIO* indicates a file is ready for I/O.
30	SIGPWR	Miscellaneous	This signal indicates a change in status for your Uninterruptible Power Supply. It might also have other power-related interpretations.
31	SIGJUNK(31)	Miscellaneous	Undocumented

If you want to do something when a signal is received, you need to create a signal handler. For example, let's say that you want to display a parting message ("Bye Bye") when a script ends. To accomplish this task, you need to take these steps:

1. Develop the script to display the parting message.

2. Trap the EXIT signal.

The first step is easy enough. It's simply an **echo** command like this:

```
echo "Bye Bye"
```

This command is given to the **trap** command as a parameter enclosed in single quotes. Listing 4.5 shows how to combine the **echo** and **trap** commands.

Listing 4.5 *PARTING_MSG—Using the **trap** Command to Display a Parting Message*

```
#!/bin/bash
trap 'echo "Bye Bye"; exit' EXIT

echo "Line One"
```

Here is an example of this script in action:

```
% chmod +x parting_msg
% ./parting_msg
Line One
Bye Bye
```

Notice how `echo "Line One"` is printed before the `"Bye Bye"` message? This shows the signal handler is created, but doesn't get triggered until the script ends (generating the *EXIT* signal).

Signal handlers are also called event or interrupt handlers.

The if Command

Syntax 1:

```
if test-commands
then
  .. commands ..
fi
```

Syntax 2:

```
if test-commands
then
  .. commands ..
else
  .. commands ..
fi
```

Syntax 3:

```
if test-commands
then
  .. commands ..
elif test
  .. then
commands ..
      else
  ..       commands ..
fi
```

Synopsis:

Lets you decide on one or more courses of action.

Many times, scripts decide which set of command blocks to execute based on some criteria. For instance, if a configuration file for a certain application doesn't exist, you might need to create one.

```
if test ! -e config.dat
then
  echo "Create the file."
fi
```

FRI   For more information about the **test** command, see "The test Command" on page 390 in Chapter 9, "Examining the Tools."

The **test** command can check for a variety of conditions. In the above example, it checks to see if a file called *config.dat* exists in the current directory. Then the ! (or bang) character negates the sense of the test, so the **test** command returns true if the file doesn't exist and false if the file exists.

Recently, I worked on an application where the development computer had a different directory structure from the production computer. Therefore, I created a variable indicating which directory should be used by the script. I used an **if** command similar to this:

```
if test "$HOSTNAME" = 'waswaldo'
then
  working_dir="/usr/waswaldo/project_one"
else
  working_dir="/usr/local/project_one"
fi
```

When the script is run on the *waswaldo* computer, the first assignment statement is executed and *working_dir* is set to */usr/waswaldo/project_one*. On any other computer (including the production computer) the *working_dir* variable is set to */usr/local/project_one*.

If you need to decide between more than two options, you can either use the **case** command (discussed in the next section) or use an **elif** clause in your **if** command. For example:

```
if test "$HOSTNAME" = 'waswaldo'
then
  working_dir="/usr/waswaldo/project_one"
elif test "$HOSTNAME" = 'thor'
  working_dir="/usr/thor/project_on"
else
  working_dir="/usr/local/project_one"
fi
```

This script sequence sets the *working_dir* variable to one of three values.

The next section on *case* statements shows what many programmers feel is a better technique for dealing with situations where a single variable needs to be tested for different values.

The case Command

Syntax:

```
case string
in
  regular_expression_1)
    .. commands ..
    ;;
  regular_expression_2)
    .. commands ..
    ;;
  *)
    .. commands ..
    ;;
esac
```

Synopsis:

   Makes a decision based on many values of a single variable.

   The **case** command is great when you need to test one variable
for many different values—like checking a variable called
GIVEN_NAME for specific first names in order to initialize some
variables. Your *case* statement, in this instance, might look like
this:

The
*GIVEN_*
NAME
variable was
defined ear-
lier in the
chapter in
the section
"The trap
Command."

```
case $GIVEN_NAME
in
 David*)
  echo "David, Welcome. You have ALL privileges."
  ;;
 Kathy*)
  echo "Kathy, Welcome. You have READ privileges."
  ;;
 *)
   echo "Sorry, I don't know you. Please go away."
   exit 1
   ;;
esac
```

   The example shows the flexibility of the **case** command. The
GIVEN_NAME variable is tested again in the two regular expressions, *David** and *Kathy**. If the value of the *GIVEN_NAME*
variable starts with either "David" or "Kathy," the associated
echo command is executed. The last regular expression, *,

matches all strings. Therefore, if no other match is found, the last set of commands is run.

For more information about regular expressions, see Chapter 8, "Pattern Matching." **FRI**

The for Statement

Syntax:

```
for variable [in list]
do
   .. command block ..
done
```

Synopsis:

Iterates over a list of values executing a specific block of statements once for each value in the list.

There are two keys to understanding the **for** statement. One is the concept of command blocks and the other is the concept of iteration.

A command block is a set of commands that you want to execute together. In the syntax entry above, the command block is surrounded by the **do** and **done** keywords.

An iteration—for the purposes of this discussion—is a single execution of the command block.

Command Block

A set of commands executed together.

Iteration

A single execution of a command block.

Putting these definitions together results in the **for** command, which iterates over a list of values, executing a command block once for each value in the list.

One of the simplest uses of the **for** command is to find the largest number in a list:

Listing 4.6 *04LST06—Using the for Command to Find the Largest Number*

```
#!/bin/bash

max_n=0
for n in 9 8 7 6 5 4 3 2 1
do
  if test $max_n -lt $n
  then
    max_n=$n
  fi
done
echo "The maximum value is $max_n."
```

Here is the script in action:

```
% chmod +x 04lst06
% ./04lst06
The maximum value is 9.
```

I'll admit this example is a bit simplistic, but we can use it to show how the variable *n* takes on each successive value in the list. Let's examine the value of the *max_n* and *n* variables for the first two iterations of the **for** command:

Table 4.3 *Examining the Value of Variables from Listing 4.6*

Iteration Number	Value of max_n	Value of n
1	0	9
2	9	8

Can you see how the **if** command assigns a value of 9 to *max_n* on the first iteration of the loop? Good. On the second iteration, *n* has a value of 8, which is less than *max_n*, and therefore no **assignment** command is performed.

You can also use the **for** command to iterate over all of the files in a directory. Listing 4.7 displays the number of files in the current directory.

Listing 4.7 *file_count—Using the for Command to Count the Number of Files in a Directory, Version 1*

```
#!/bin/bash

file_count=0

for file in *
do
  if test ! -d file
  then
    file_count=$file_count+1
  fi
done

echo "There are $file_count files."
```

For more information about using the asterisk character, see Chapter 8, "Pattern Matching." **FRI**

Here is the script in action:

```
% chmod +x file_count
% ./file_count
There are 0+1+1+1+1+1+1+1+1+1 files
```

Why did this happen?

When you simply use `file_count=$file_count+1`, Bash assumes you want to concatenate strings. In order to actually increment the *file_count* variable by one, you need to use the **let** command. Listing 4.8 shows the corrected *file_count* script.

Listing 4.8 *file_count—Using the for Command to Count the Number of Files in a Directory, Version 2*

```
#!/bin/bash

file_count=0

for file in *
do
  if test ! -d $file
  then
    let file_count=$file_count+1
  fi
done

echo "There are $file_count files."
```

Here is the script in action:

```
% chmod +x file_count
% ./file_count
There are 11 files.
```

Now the script displays the correct number of files.

Another method of generating the list is to use backticks. Let's say you need to perform some task on the second column of information in a file. Listing 4.9 contains a script that uses the **for** and **cut** commands to iterate over the second column of a data file.

Listing 4.9 *display_second—Using the* **for** *and* **cut** *Commands to Display the Second Column from a Data File*

```
#!/bin/bash

for line in `cut -f2 display_second.dat`
do
  # commands to perform task
  echo "Processing on '$line' completed."
done
```

Listing 4.10 contains a data file that can be used with the *display_second* script.

Listing 4.10 *display_second.dat—A Two-Column Data File for Use with the display_second Script*

The {tab} notation is used to symbolize an actual tab character.

```
one_01{tab}two_01
one_02{tab}two_02
```

Here is the script in action:

```
% chmod +x display_second
% ./display_second
Processing on two_01 completed.
Processing on two_02 completed.
```

The technique of using backticks is very powerful and has many uses. You'll see additional uses of backticks throughout this book.

There is one more way to generate a list for use by the **for** command. You can simply not supply a list, in which case the shell uses the $* variable.

FRI   For more information about the $* variable, see "Position Variables" on page 27 in Chapter 2, "Variables and Operators."

Listing 4.11 shows the *listless_ for* loop in action.

Listing 4.11 *listless_for—Using the for Command and the Implicit $ * Variable*

```
#!/bin/bash

for item
do
  echo $item
done
echo "Program Ended."
```

Here is the script in action:

```
% chmod +x listless_for
% listless_for one two three
one
two
three
Program Ended.
```

The last example of this section expands on Listing 3.1 in Chapter 3, "Procedures," which defines an **untar** command. You might recall that the **untar** command only let you work with one *tar* file at a time. Listing 4.12 shows you how to change the *untar* procedure to handle multiple *tar* files.

Listing 4.12 *untar_multi—Creating an Audit Trail for the* **tar** *Command*

```
untar () {
  for file in $@
  do
    echo "Processing $file."
    cp $file /store
    echo "----------" >> ~/tar.log
    echo $file >> ~/tar.log
    date >> ~/tar.log
    tar tf $file >> ~/tar.log
    tar xvf $file
    rm $file
    ln -s /store/$file $file
  done
}
```

The differences between Listing 4.12 and Listing 3.1 are displayed in bold text.

Here is the script in action:

```
% chmod +x untar_multi
% source untar_multi
% untar one.tar two.tar three.tar
Processing one.tar.
Processing two.tar.
Processing three.tar.
```

The changes between Listing 4.12 and Listing 3.1 are minor. The *$@* special variable was used to get a list of parameters to the function. And the *$1* variable was replaced by the *$file* loop variable.

FRI

For more information about the *$@* special variable, see Chapter 2, "Variables and Operators."

The next section talks about another command used for looping, the **while** command.

The while Command

Syntax:

```
while test-commands
do
   .. commands ..
done
```

Synopsis:

Repeatedly executes a command block until the **test** command fails and returns a non-zero value.

In the last section, you learned about the **for** command, which uses a list to control how many times a statement block is executed. In this section, you read about the **while** command, which doesn't use a list to control looping. Rather, a **test** command is executed and its return value is evaluated. When the return value is zero, the **while** command ends.

Let's see how you can use the **while** command to perform a command block a specific number of times. Listing 4.12 uses a **while** command to count backwards from five to one.

Listing 4.13 *count_backwards_while—Using the **while**
Command to Count Backwards From One to Five*

```
#!/bin/bash

count=5
while test $count -gt 0
do
  echo $count
  let count=$count-1
done
echo "The end count is $count."
```

Here is the script in action:

```
% chmod +x count_backwards_while
% ./count_backwards_while
5
4
3
2
1
The end count is 0.
```

This script executes the command block five times, as shown by
its output. It's important to note that the value of *count* ends up as
0 and not 1 as you might expect upon casually looking at the code.
When *count* is still 1, the **test** command is true, so the command
block is executed again, thereby decrementing *count* to 0. Then,
the next time the **test** command is executed, it fails and the loop
ends with *count* equal to 0.

It's useful to note that if the **test** command fails the first time,
the command block is never executed. You can see this behavior by
reversing the **test** command of the previous example:

```
while test $count -lt 0
```

Here is the new script in action:

```
% ./count_backwards
The end count is 5.
```

This example shows that the command block is never evaluated
if the **test** command fails when the loop starts.

A more advanced example of the **while** command might be to create a procedure that totals or sums a series of numbers. Listing 4.14 shows one way this might be done.

Listing 4.14 *add_numbers—Using the* **while** *Command to Total or Sum a Series of Numbers*

```
#!/bin/bash

total=0
while read
do
    if [ ! -z $REPLY ]
    then
        let total=$total+$REPLY
    fi
done
echo "The total is $total"
```

Here is the script in action:

```
% chmod +x add_numbers
% ./add_numbers
12
24
                        <- Type CTRL-D to end input.
The total is 36
```

This example uses the **read** command to get a line of input from the user and, if the input is not zero length, adds the input string to the total variable. The [ ] characters are shorthand for the **test** command used in earlier examples. The other new point in this example is the use of the CTRL-D character to end user input. Unix uses the CTRL-D character to indicate the end of a file. Because **read** really gets input from the *STDIN* file handle (in this case, standard input is the keyboard), the CTRL-D character ends the input stream, making **read** return *failure* and ending the *while* loop.

NOTE   Many of the examples in this chapter use a command called **test** to control looping. However, you can use any command to control a loop, even another script. Use your imagination and be creative.

The until Command

Syntax:

```
until test-commands
do
   .. statements ..
done
```

Synopsis:

Repeatedly executes a command block until a **test** command succeeds or returns zero.

The **until** command is identical to the **while** command except that instead of testing for failure, it tests for success. In order to demonstrate the **until** command, we can use the same script we used for the **while** command (Listing 4.12) and simply change the test from **-gt** to **-lt** as shown in Listing 4.15:

Listing 4.15 *count_backwards_until—Using the* **until** *Command to Count Backwards From One to Five.*

```
count=5
until test $count -lt 0
do
  echo $count
  let count=$count-1
done
echo "The end count is $count."
```

Here is the script in action:

```
% chmod +x count_backwards_until
% ./count_backwards_until
5
4
3
2
1
0
The end count is -1.
```

The big difference between this example and the one in Listing 4.12 is that the value of *count* winds up as -1 instead of 0. This happens because 0 is not less than 0; therefore, the command block is executed one additional time.

The break Command

Syntax:

```
break [n]
```

Synopsis:

Leaves the current command block.

The **break** command leaves a command block immediately. For example, you might want to execute a command five times, unless an error condition is detected (at which point you want to exit), as shown in Listing 4.16.

Listing 4.16 *test_break—Using the* **break** *Command to Leave a Loop's Command Block*

```
count=5
while $count -gt 0
then
   .. commands ..
   if test -e error_file_flag
     break;
   fi
done
```

If one of the commands inside the statement block creates an *error_file_flag* file, then the **while** command is exited and no further iterations are done.

You can use the **break** command to break out of a nested loop command by supplying the number of loops to leave. First, let's look at an example of a nested loop using the **break** command, as shown in Listing 4.17.

Listing 4.17 *nested_loop—How to Break out of a Nested Loop*

```
#!/bin/bash

x=3
while test $x -gt 0
do
  y=3
  while test $y -gt 0
  do
    echo "[$x, $y]"
    if test $y -eq 2
    then
```

```
      echo "breaking."
      break 1;
    fi
    let y=$y-1
  done
  let x=$x-1
done
```

Here is the script in action:

```
% chmod +x nested_loop
% ./nested_loop
[3, 3]
[3, 2]
breaking.
[2, 3]
[2, 2]
breaking.
[1, 3]
[1, 2]
breaking.
```

You can see that every time the inner loop variable of *y* is equal to 2, the inside loop is broken, and the outer loop goes through another iteration. *y* is called a loop variable because it controls the iterations of the inner loop.

Now let's see what happens if you tell **break** to exit from two loops:

Listing 4.18 *double_loops—Breaking out of Two Nested Loops*

```
#!/bin/bash

x=3
while test $x -gt 0
do
  y=3
  while test $y -gt 0
  do
    echo "[$x, $y]"
    if test $y -eq 2
    then
      echo "breaking."
      break 2;
    fi
    let y=$y-1
  done
  let x=$x-1
done
```

Here is the script in action:

```
% chmod +x double_loops
% ./double_loops
[3, 3]
[3, 2]
breaking.
```

This time, as soon as the **break** command is reached, both loops are terminated.

The continue Command

Syntax:

```
continue [n]
```

Synopsis:

Skips the remaining commands in a command block.

The **continue** command starts the next iteration of a loop command immediately. Can you figure out what would happen if you replaced the **break** command in Listing 4.18 with a continue statement? Listing 4.19 does exactly that.

Listing 4.19 *using_continue—Using the* **continue** *Command*

```
#!/bin/bash
x=3
while test $x -gt 0
do
  y=3
  while test $y -gt 0
  do
    echo "[$x, $y]"
    if test $y -eq 2
    then
      echo "continuing"
      continue;
    fi
    let y=$y-1
  done
  let x=$x-1
done
```

Here is the script in action:

```
% chmod +x double_loops
% ./double_loops
[3, 3]
[3, 2]              <- these two lines
continuing         <- indefinitely repeat
[3, 2]
continuing
[3, 2]
continuing
```

Why was an infinite loop created by using the **continue** command instead of the **break** command? It was because the script never got to execute the code lines that decrement x and y, therefore the **test** commands never result in failure.

The situation only changes a little if you use a **continue 2** command. As with the **break** command, you can use the **continue** command with an argument that specifies the number of loops that are to be affected. When **continue 2** is used, the script displays:

```
% ./double_loops
[3, 3]             < - - these
[3, 2]             < - - three lines
continuing         < - - infinitely repeat.
[3, 3]
[3, 2]
continuing
```

Summary

The nine shell commands covered in this chapter let you control the execution of your scripts. They can be broken into the following four categories:

- miscellaneous—**exit** and **trap**.

- decision commands—**if** and **case**.

- looping commands—**for, while**, and **until**.

- jump commands—**break** and **continue**.

Together these commands give you enormous flexibility in how your scripts execute. The **exit** command lets you stop a script anywhere. The **trap** command lets you either ignore signals or kick off some commands whenever a signal is detected. The **if** command is great for making decisions among a small number of options. When greater flexibility is needed, the **case** statement can be used. It can test a variable for any number of values, and execute different commands or a group of commands for each value specified. The **for**, **while**, and **until** commands are used to control looping. The **for** command iterates over the values in a list. The **while** and **until** commands loop until a **test** command fails or succeeds. Finally, the **break** and **continue** commands give you fine control over exactly how and when loop iterations begin and end.

The next chapter, "Controlling the Shell," discusses many different aspects of how commands interact with the shell. It goes into detail about how commands can be made to execute in the background, how to sequence commands so that the execution of a command is made dependent on the execution of another, and many other topics.

Controlling the Shell

This chapter covers some odds and ends of shell programming. You learn to create a command list to execute more than one command at a time, and why this technique is useful. Additionally, you learn how to provide input to a program using a file instead of the keyboard, and many other interesting techniques.

Creating Command Lists

Chapter 1 points out that each shell command is a process. For simplicity's sake, not too much detail is given about processes. However, you need to know more details about processes before you can fully understand command lists.

> For the purposes of this chapter, the terms command and process are nearly interchangeable. A command list is more than one command combined to form a single command.

Every command produces an exit value when it stops. A typical successful command has an exit value of zero. Any other exit value indicates a failure of some sort. You might find it useful to assign exit values to indicate specific problems. For example, your scripts could use an exit value of 5 to indicate that an initialization file was not found. As an alternative, you could use the values between 200 and 250 to indicate different types of input errors.

A command list can use the exit value of one command to control whether or not another command is executed. For example, you might not want to begin a backup process if an initialization file doesn't exist.

Table 5.1 shows the notation used when creating command lists.

Table 5.1 *The Three Types of Command Lists*

Notation	Description
a && b	The *and* list type executes *b* if and only if *a* succeeds. This is shorthand for: *if a then b*.
a || b	The *or* list type executes *b* if and only if *a* fails. This is shorthand for: *if not a then b*.
a ; b	The *sequential* list type simply executes *a*, then *b*. The exit value of *b* becomes the exit value for the list.

Let's look at examples of each type. The *and* type prevents b from executing if a succeeds. When might you need this ability? You could use it to make sure an initialization file exists before running a program:

```
test -e init.dat && count_users
```

This line uses the **test** command to see if a file called *init.dat* exists. If it does, the shell executes the *count_users* program.

The *or* list type can be used to create the initialization file if needed:

```
test -e init.dat || create_init
count_users
```

This line uses the **test** command to check for *init.dat*. If it doesn't exist, the *create_init* program is run. Finally, the **count_users** command is run.

For more information about the **test** command, see Chapter 9, **FRI** "Examining the Tools."

Using a combination of these two list types lets you make intelligent scripts that check the system's status before running critical applications.

Creating Compound Commands

A *compound command* executes a command list as if it were a single command. The exit value of the last command in the list becomes the exit value of the entire compound. Table 5.2 shows the two types of compound commands.

Table 5.2 *The Two Types of Compound Commands*

Notation	Description
(list)	A parenthesized list executes all of its commands inside the same child shell. Variable assignment and commands like **cd,** which change the environment of the shell, *do not remain in effect* after the list is finished executing.

Table 5.2 *The Two Types of Compound Commands (Cont'd)*

Notation	Description
{ list }	An expression inside curly braces executes all of its commands inside the current shell. Variable assignment and environment changes *remain in effect* after the list is finished executing. Note that a space is required after the initial curly brace.

CAUTION   Don't confuse parentheses used for compound commands with parentheses used to affect operator precedence in expressions. Expressions are only used in assignment or decision statements. If a parenthesis is at the beginning of whatever you're looking at, there's a good chance that it's a compound command.

The *(list)* notation lets you combine several commands together in the same child shell. This ability is especially useful if you need to temporarily change the environment variables.

A classic example of this type of compound command is:

```
parentDir=`(cd ..; pwd)`
```

This line sets the *parentDir* variable to the name of the parent directory. If the current directory is */var/local*, then *parentDir* is set to */var*. Let's see what happens by running the following commands interactively:

```
% PS1="[\w] % "                     # 1
[/var/local] % cd ..; pwd           # 2
/var
[/var] % cd local
[/var/local] % (cd ..; pwd)         # 3
/var
[/var/local] %
```

The line numbered 1 changes the shell's prompt so the current directory is displayed—making it easier to see the results of the commands.

The line numbered 2 executes two commands, the **cd** command and the **pwd** command. The **cd** command changes to a new directory; the **pwd** command displays the current working directory. Notice that the **cd** command changes the current directory, which isn't the behavior we need. The goal is to retrieve the name of the parent directory without changing the current shell.

The parenthesized expression in the line numbered 3 runs the same commands as line 2, except that they are run in a child shell, thereby insulating the login shell from them. The **cd** command affects the child shell normally, so **pwd** displays the name of the login shell's parent directory.

Now let's return to our original compound command example:

```
parentDir=`(cd ..; pwd)`
```

Backticked strings are executed, and the resulting output replaces the backticked string in the original command. Therefore, this example reduces to:

```
parentDir=/var
```

> By the way, even in the "more powerful" Perl and Tcl languages, escaping to the shell using `(cd ..; pwd)` might be the easiest way to determine the parent directory name. Learning the fundamentals (i.e., the shell language) is always a good idea.
>
> **TIP**

The next example displays an error message if the *init.dat* file doesn't exist. Before running this example, I made sure that no *init.dat* file existed, so the error was sure to happen.

> When running tests or examples (e.g., from this book!), it's very important to determine what your initial environment should be for the tests to produce the expected results. The only thing that should change when you run tests or examples should be the code.
>
> **NOTE**

```
% test -e init.dat || echo "Bad File."
Bad File
% echo $?  # display the exit value of last command.
0
```

You can see the command list in this example has an exit value of 0 (indicating success). However, we know that the *init.dat* file doesn't exist. So why is the command considered a success? Because the last command executed is **echo,** and **echo** returns success if it successfully displays its message.

At times, it will make more sense to have a non-zero exit value. This can be done using a compound command:

```
% test -e init.dat || (echo "Bad File."; exit 1)
Bad File.
% echo $?
1
```

The **exit** command ends a compound command's subshell—not the login shell or any script in which you might use this technique.

Could you also use the following compound command?

```
% (test -e init.dat || echo "Bad File."; exit 1)
Bad File.
% echo $?
1
```

The exit value still remains 1. However, there is a flaw in this compound command. Can you spot it? If the *init.dat* file exists, this compound command still returns 1. You need for it to return 0.

Let's go back to the working version of the compound command. By adding another **test** command, you can exit the parent shell:

```
test -e init.dat || (echo "Bad File."; exit 1)
test $? = 1 && exit
...
# more commands
...
```

As you work with shell scripting, you'll find many uses for the *()* notation. I once needed to add an end-of-file delimiter between two files before sending them to a processing program. Using a compound command worked very well:

```
% $FILE1="monday.dat"
% $FILE2="tuesday.dat"
% (cat $FILE1; echo "~~~~"; cat $FILE2) | audit
```

If you only need to combine the two files, you can use *cat* *$FILE1 $FILE2*. Using the subshell lets you insert any type of information you need between the two files.

Redirecting Input/Output

The topic of redirection is briefly mentioned in Chapter 1, where redirection is shown to change where a program looks for input and where a program sends output. Figure 5.1 should serve as a reminder of the mechanism.

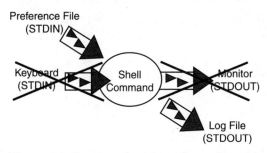

Figure 5.1 *Input and output after redirection has taken place.*

You already know (from Chapter 1) that every program has an associated standard input (*STDIN*) and standard output (*STDOUT*). All programs also have a standard error (*STDERR*). Beneath the covers, *STDIN*, *STDOUT*, and *STDERR* are file handles—they point to the locations where the actual input and output happen. *STDIN* usually points to your keyboard. *STDOUT* and *STDERR* usually point to your monitor.

> *STDIN, STDOUT,* and *STDERR* point to the locations where input and output take place. Under the covers, they are file handles and are associated with the file descriptor numbers 0, 1, and 2, respectively. You can also use file descriptor numbers 3 through 9. **NOTE**

Every file accessed by Unix has its own file descriptor number. *STDIN* is always 0. *STDOUT* is always 1. And *STDERR* is always 2. The file descriptors from 3 to 9 can be used for any purpose you dream up. The "Using Advanced Redirection" section shows examples of using the higher numbered file descriptors.

Unix views any file as a simple series of bytes—no one byte is more important than any other. One series of bytes is as good as the next when it comes to getting input. Therefore, from a program's point of view, getting input from a file is just as good as getting input from the keyboard. Likewise, sending data to a file instead of to the monitor is okay, too.

NOTE   By convention, some bytes have special meanings (see Appendix B—The ASCII Table). For example, a byte that has a value of 9 is considered a tab character. Nearly all programs understand these conventions. Thus, displaying or printing a byte that has a value of 9 performs a tab action.

Our goal in the following sections is to learn the notation used by the shell to indicate input and output redirection.

Controlling Input

Programs can get input from three places: the keyboard, a file, or in-line. Getting input from the keyboard is a no-brainer—it's the default, after all—so we'll skip it. First, let's look at getting input directly from a file.

Getting input from a file uses this syntax:

```
command < input_file
```

It's up to you to ensure that the data in *input_file* is correct and has the right format. If the command is looking for input that has two columns and *input_file* has three columns, the result of the redirection won't be what you expected.

Getting input in-line uses this syntax:

```
command << END
line one
line two
END
```

NOTE   Many books and programmers refer to in-line input as being a "here document." I've never liked that term because it sounds awkward and is not descriptive.

Many people find this type of input to be counterintuitive. However, the effort to become familiar with in-line input pays off handsomely when you combine it with variable substitution. Your scripts suddenly become easier to understand. For example, let's see how in-place input can be used to send email:

```
$TO_MAIL_ADDR="medined@planet.net"
$SUBJECT="This is a test."
$NAME="David"
mail $TO_EMAIL_ADDR -s $SUBJECT << END

$NAME, sorry about the delay.
Please be patient, I'll be back from
vacation in June.
.
END
```

This short script shows how to use in-line input to send parameterized email messages. By changing the value of the three variables, you can change the contents of the email message and to whom it is sent.

> You can parameterize your scripts by extracting changeable information into variables. Then you only need to make changes in the variable initialization section of your script in order to change the script's actions. **NOTE**

You can use input redirection in some non-obvious ways. For example, you can use it to provide input to a **while** command. Listing 5.1 contains a data file used by the *send_status* script of Listing 5.2. The *send_status* script uses the email addresses in the data file to send mail about the system status.

Listing 5.1 *input.dat—A List of Email Addresses for the send_status Script*

```
medined
jake@affy.com
barbie
```

Listing 5.2 *send_status—Using Redirection with the while Command*

```
#!/bin/bash

while read ADDRESS
do
  echo "Sending mail to $ADDRESS"
  mail $ADDRESS -s "Status Report" << END
The status is just fine.
END
done < input.dat
```

Here is an example of this script in action:

```
% chmod +x send_status
% ./send_status
```

By itself, this script might not seem too exciting. But when you combine it with an auditing program and run it every night, it becomes the solution to an administrative task.

Controlling Output

Directing a program's output to go to a file is a little more difficult than input redirection. But that's only because you might have to worry about whether the target file already exists. Fortunately, Bash provides a *noclobber* option to help you. But we're getting ahead of ourselves. Let's start with the most basic output redirection:

```
% echo "Testing" > test.dat
% cat test.dat
Testing
```

Redirection of the **echo** command's output actually creates the specified file or, if the file already exists, overwrites it. For example:

```
% echo "one" > test.dat
% cat test.dat
one
% echo "two" > test.dat
% cat test.dat
two
```

If your situation requires you to prevent overwriting, use Bash's built-in **set** command to turn on the *noclobber* option:

Use the set – o noclobber command to prevent overwriting existing files.

```
% set -o noclobber
% echo "one" > test.dat
% cat test.dat
one
% echo "two" > test.dat
bash: test.dat: Cannot clobber existing file
% echo $?
1
```

When the *noclobber* option is turned on, the shell won't let output redirection overwrite files. You can use the *$?* variable to test the exit value of the **echo** command.

In addition to using redirection to create files, you can append output to existing files like this:

```
% echo "two" >> test.dat
% cat test.dat
one
two
```

Most programs send their error messages to *STDERR* instead of *STDOUT*. This separation of normal output from error output can be very handy at times. Remember the unsightly error message that appeared when *noclobber* was set and you tried to overwrite the *test.dat* file? Let's use *STDERR* redirection to stop it from displaying on the monitor.

```
% set -o noclobber
% echo "one" > test.dat
% cat test.dat
one
% echo "two" 2> error.dat > test.dat
% echo $?
1
% echo "two" 2> error.dat > test.dat
bash: error.dat: Cannot clobber existing file
```

The 2> notation tells the shell to redirect *STDERR*. In this case, we're directing *STDERR* to a file called *error.dat*. Notice the error message does not display the first time the 2> redirection is used. On the other hand, the second time that *STDERR* redirection is attempted, the error message is displayed. Why? Because the *error.dat* file exists and the *noclobber* option is turned on, the shell has no choice but to ignore the redirection and display the error message on your monitor. The second message can be avoided by using the *2>>* notation—thereby appending to the *error.dat* file instead of trying to create it.

The *>|* notation provides an alternative to appending when *noclobber* has been turned on. When the *>|* notation is used, it overrides the *noclobber* option, letting you overwrite files on an as-needed basis:

```
% set -o noclobber
% echo "one" > test.dat
% cat test.dat
one
% echo "two" > test.dat
bash: test.dat: Cannot clobber existing file
% echo "two" >| test.dat
% cat test.dat
two
```

If you want to simply ignore a program's output, redirect the output to the */dev/null* file. When the program ends, the */dev/null* file is closed and automatically deleted.

CAUTION   When redirecting output to */dev/null* you might run out of disk space if a program generates a lot of output or runs continuously without stopping. The program must end in order for the shell to close the */dev/null* file and delete it.

The Pipe

As you've seen, redirection can be quite handy. The next step beyond redirecting from or to a file is to make the output of one program the input of another. More technically, this means making the *STDOUT* of program A the *STDIN* of program B. This technique is called a *pipe*.

Unix pipes connect the output of one program to the input of another.

Unix programmers use this feature frequently. One advantage of this technique is that no temporary files are created, so no cleanup is needed.

The vertical bar character is used to indicate a pipe. For example,

```
% ls *.dat | sort -r
c.dat
b.dat
a.dat
```

The above command line connects the output of the **ls** command to the input of the **sort** command. The *–r* option of the **sort** command causes the **sort**'s lines of input to be sorted in reverse order.

There is no practical limit to the number of pipes used on a command line. If you need the list of files in reverse order to be processed again, just tack the next command to the end of the line:

```
% ls *.dat | sort -r | processing_program
```

Each command is executed inside its own child shell. So, if the first program changes the environment, those changes don't affect the second program.

All of the sub-commands are executed before the exit value of the command is determined. Therefore, don't ever place commands in the middle of a pipe sequence into the background.

You can place a ! character in the front of piped sequence in order to negate the exit value. The following example shows what this syntax looks like:

```
% sorted_files=`ls *.dat | sort -r`
% echo $?
0
% echo $sorted_files
c.dat b.dat a.dat
% sorted_files=`! ls *.dat | sort -r`
% echo $?
1
% echo $sorted_files
c.dat b.dat a.dat
```

Notice that using the ! character does not change the value of the *sorted_files* variable. This might seem strange, until you realize that the value of *sorted_files* comes from the *output* of the **sort** and not its exit value. The ! character negates the exit value, but doesn't affect the output of the command.

One of the more interesting uses of a pipe is to send output to the **for** command. Most programmers only use pipes to form connections between "normal" commands and frequently forget that in Unix, **for** loops are also considered commands.

The example script in Listing 5.3 is quite contrived. It counts the number of files belonging to the medined group in the current directory. The purpose of the script is to show how the pipe command works in this situation. There are better ways to perform this specific task.

The following example also uses the **awk** command, which is not covered in this book. **awk** is a powerful program that is used mainly for text processing. In my opinion, Perl is almost always a better choice for text processing. However, Unix programmers need to be flexible at all times—so, for this example, **awk** is used.

Listing 5.3 *findpipe—Using a Pipe Between the find and for Commands*

```
#!/bin/bash

# initialize the variables.
group_to_find="medined"

# run the find command looking for dat files
# then send the output to the for command.

find . -name "*.dat" | for file in *
do

   # use the awk command to grab the group name.

   group=`ls -l $file | awk '{print $4}'`

   # test to see if we're interested in this
   # file by comparing the file's group to the
   # one we're looking for.

   if [ "$group" = "$group_to_find" ]
   then
      let file_count=$file_count+1

      # Since the for command is operating inside
      # a child shell, we need to use a temporary
      # file in order to communicate back to the
      # parent shell. This echo command overwrites
      # a temporary file in the /tmp directory.
```

```
    echo $file_count >| /tmp/$$_count
  fi
done
```

```
# Now that the count is done we can use the cat
# command to display the number of files on the
# standard output. Then the temporary file is
# removed - all good programs should clean up
# after themselves.
```

```
cat /tmp/$$_count
rm /tmp/$$_count
```

Here is an example of this script in action:

```
% chmod +x findpipe
% ./findpipe
33
```

This script is the most complex so far in this book. The important point to understand about it is why the temporary file is needed. Because the **for** command is executed in a child shell, the value of the *file_count* variable is not available to the parent shell. The **echo** command is used to "store" the value of *file_count* into a temporary file. Each time the variable is incremented, the contents of the temporary file are updated. When the **for** command is finished, the **cat** command displays the contents of the temporary file.

If needed, you can use the *findpipe* script as a component of a larger command. For example, let's use the output of *findpipe* to initialize a *num_files* variable:

```
% num_files=`./findpipe`
% echo num_files
33
```

After examining Listing 5.3, you might also have guessed that the **pipe** command can also be used at the end of the **for** command. Listing 5.4 shows an alternative version of the **findpipe** command called **findpip1**. Many of the comments from Listing 5.3 apply to Listing 5.4 and are not repeated.

Listing 5.4 *findpip1—Using a Pipe Between the* **find** *and* **for**
Commands

```
#!/bin/bash

# Instead of piping the output of the find
# command to for, in this example backticks
# are used to create a list.

for file in `find . -name "*.dat"`
do
  group=`ls -l $file | awk '{print $4}'`
  if [ "$group" = "medined" ]
  then
    let file_count=$file_count+1
    echo $file_count
  fi
done | tail -n 1
```

Here is an example of this script in action:

```
% chmod +x findpip1
% ./findpip1
33
```

This script is quite a bit simpler than the earlier version. All of
the code dealing with the temporary file is gone. Can you see why?

Because the output of the **for** command is sent to the **tail** command, the issues with child and parent shells are avoided. The **tail**
command only displays the last line of the **for** command's output,
which displays the last value of *file_count* that was displayed.

By the way, you can also use the following command to find out
the number of dat files owned by the medined group:

```
find . -name "*.dat" -group "medined" | wc -l
```

This command is somewhat simpler and faster than the earlier
examples. The solution you use depends on your particular needs.

TIP

> Remember that Unix frequently has many ways to accomplish the
> same objective. Try experimenting with different commands. Only
> through research and experimentation can you become a Unix
> wizard.

Using Advanced Redirection

The advanced redirection techniques shown here are probably the most complex topics in this book. Only the topic of pattern matching comes close. However, by building from simple examples to more complex examples, I've made the techniques as easy to understand as possible.

Our first example shows how to combine two output streams into one—*STDERR* is combined with *STDOUT*.

An output stream is simply the lines or bytes of output generated by a program or script.

```
% (date '+%B %d'; ls -l *.foo) >ls.log 2>&1
% cat ls.log
May 10
ls: *.foo: No such file or directory
```

The **date** command sends its output to *STDOUT*, while the **ls** command (because there aren't any files with an extension of *foo*) generates errors that are sent to *STDERR*. When the *ls.log* file is displayed, you can see that both *STDOUT* and *STDERR* have been merged. You could merge the streams in the opposite direction and have *STDOUT* merge into *STDERR*, but that would go against convention.

You can merge any two output streams using *m>&n* notation. The output going to the *m* file descriptor is merged with the output going to the *n* file descriptor.

That example wasn't too hard, was it? Let's take the next step by looking at the file descriptors 3 through 9. Unix only reserves file descriptors 0, 1, and 2—the rest are yours to use as you see fit.

The next example looks at using file descriptor 4 to temporarily hold an exit value for a first command in a pipe sequence. Normally, the exit value of a pipe sequence of commands is the exit value of the last command executed. Because each command is executed in its own child shell, the exit values of the earlier commands are lost.

You can use redirection to save the exit value of one of the earlier commands. The only caveat is that the normal *STDOUT* needs to be redirected to a file.

```
% status=`(a; echo $? >&4 | b > so.dat 2>se.dat) 4>&1`
```

This is quite a complex command. As with all complicated commands, the best way to understand this one is to break it down into components. The innermost command is:

```
(a; echo $? >&4 | b > so.dat 2>se.dat)
```

This compound command, in turn, is really two commands `a;` `echo $? >&4` and `b > so.dat 2>se.dat`. A pipe is used to connect the output of a with the input of `b`.

Let's look at `a;` `echo $? >&4` more closely. What exactly is happening? You know that the > character causes output redirection and that `m>&n` merges two output streams. It turns out that if no value is specified for *m*, the default is *STDOUT*, or 1. So `>&4` means that the output originally destined for file descriptor 1 is sent to file descriptor 4. So, the result of `a;` `echo $? >&4` is that the exit value of the a program is sent, as output, to file descriptor 4.

Now let's look at `b > so.dat 2>se.dat`. This command is pretty straightforward. Both *STDOUT* and *STDERR* are being redirected to files. Because the first command sends its output to file descriptor 4, that's where the output from b would go if not redirected.

In simplified form, the original command was:

```
% status=`(...) 4>&1`
```

By now, you probably recognize the *4>&1* notation; it means that the output stream going to file descriptor 4 is being redirected to file descriptor 1. But wait, you might be thinking, isn't file descriptor 1 the same as *STDOUT*? Yes, it is. The only output coming from the backticked string is that of the `echo $?` command—the exit value of program a. The assignment statement assigns the exit value to the *status* variable, which can be used as needed.

Learning to use file descriptors in this manner involves a lot of trial and error. But, on those rare occasions where this technique is needed, there is no other path to success.

Reading Input

Although shell programs do not generally require a lot of interaction with users, you can use the **read** command to request a line of input from *STDIN*.

The general syntax for the **read** command is:

```
read [variable_name, ...]
```

If you don't provide a variable name, the line of input is assigned to *REPLY*.

If you provide a single variable name, the whole line of input is assigned to it. If you provide more than one variable name, the line of input is broken up into words and assigned to the variables one by one. The last variable on the command line gets whatever words are left over.

Here are some examples of the **read** command:

```
% read                    <- use the default variable
This is a great day!      <- which is named REPLY.
% echo $REPLY
This is a great day!
```

This is a simple example. The default variable is used to hold the entire line of input.

```
% read one two            <- use your own variables
This!is a great day!
% echo "*$one* *$two*"
*This!is* *a great day!*  <- spaces end words,
                          <- not exclamation characters
```

This example is slightly more difficult. The first variable is assigned the value of the first word from the line of input. But how are words delimited? It turns out that Bash has a variable called *IFS* (short for Internal Field Separator) that holds the word-delimiting characters. Normally, the space, tab, and newline characters delimit words. This is why, in the last example, the first word was "This!is". Any English-speaking person can tell that "This!is" should be two words, but Bash only knows about the space, tab, and newline characters.

You can make Bash a little more intelligent by adding the exclamation character to the end of the *IFS* variable. For example:

```
% IFS="$IFS\!"
% read one two
This!is a great day!
% echo "*$one* *$two*"
*This *is a great day!
```

Now the shell recognizes that "This" and "is" are separate words. Notice that the delimiting character, the exclamation, disappears. The shell tosses the delimiting characters away.

NOTE Pay close attention to the way that the exclamation character was appended to the *IFS* variable. If the exclamation character is not "escaped" by the slash, the shell interprets it as a special character related to the shell's command history. This book doesn't cover the topic of command history. If you're interested, the best place to start learning about command history is in the Bash man page (use the **man bash** command).

If you decide that you don't want to make a long-lasting change to your shell environment by changing the *IFS* variable, you can use a compound command like this:

```
% (IFS="$IFS\!"; read one two; echo "*$one* *$two*")
This!is!a!great!day.
*This* *is!a!great!day.*
```

Listing 5.6 shows how to use the *IFS* variable in conjunction with the **read** command to read a list of email addresses from a data file and send email to them. Listing 5.5 shows a sample data file that can be used with the *postmsg* script in Listing 5.6.

Listing 5.5 *mail.dat —The Input File for the sndmail Script*

```
david:medinets:medined@planet.net
jane:conner:jconner@affy.com
```

Listing 5.6 *postmsg—Using the IFS Variable and the* **read** *Command to Report Status Via Email*

```
#!/bin/bash

# Hold the old value of IFS for later.
storage="$IFS"
```

```
# Append the current date to the subject
# line using a backticked string.
subject="System Status - `date '+%B %d'`"

# The colon character is used as the delimiter
# in the data file.
IFS=":"

# The read command returns non-zero when the
# end-of-file is reached, so it can be used as
# the condition clause of the while command.
#
while read fname lname email
do

# display a message so the user knows something is
# happening.
echo "Sending email to $fname $lname."

# Using in-script input to supply the email
# message to the mail command.
mail $email -s $subject << MAIL_END
   $fname, the status is good.
   .
MAIL_END
done

# Replace the original value of the IFS variable.
IFS=$storage
```

Here is an example of this script in action:

```
% chmod +x postmsg
% ./postmsg
Sending email to david medinets.
Sending email to jane conner.
```

In order to actually run *postmsg* yourself, you need to change the email addresses in the *mail.dat* file to some that your own system recognizes.

Frequently, the **read** command is used to pause the display in order to let the user view some messages, as shown in Listing 5.7.

Listing 5.7 *pause—Using the read Command to Display a "Press Enter to Continue" Message*

```
#!/bin/bash

for n in 0 1 2 3 4 5 6
do
  if test $n -eq 3
  then
    echo "Press <ENTER> to continue."
    read
  fi
  echo "$n: This is a test."
done
```

Here is an example of this script in action:

```
% chmod +x pause
% ./pause
0: This is a test.
1: This is a test.
2: This is a test.
Press <ENTER> to continue.
                          <- here is where the read command
                          <- waited for me to hit enter.
3: This is a test.
4: This is a test.
5: This is a test.
6: This is a test.
```

In some situations, you might need to request some information from the user, but provide a default value if only the Enter key is pressed. Let's look at what happens if you provide a default value for the **read** command.

```
% NAME="Angelo"
% echo -n "What is your name?"
% read NAME
                    <- Just hit the ENTER key.
% echo "*$NAME*"
**                  <- An empty string.
```

The **read** command sets the *NAME* variable to an empty string if only the Enter key is pressed. Therefore initializing *NAME* before the **read** command is not the solution.

You can use the test command to see if the *NAME* variable is empty using the –z option. Then you can use a command list to assign the default value if needed.

```
% echo -n "What is your name?"
% read NAME
                    <- Just hit the ENTER key.
% test -z $name && name="Angelo"
% echo "*$NAME*"
*Angelo*            <- The default value.
% read NAME
Tex                 <- Type a real name.
% test -z $name && name="Angelo"
% echo "*$NAME*"
*Tex*               <- The real name.
```

Using the "–" File

The – file asks a program to read from the standard input instead of from a file. At first glance, this might seem unnecessary. After all, it's standard input—so programs should automatically read from it, right?

It turns out that there are many programs that want you to specify the files they should use on the command line. One of the commonly used programs is the **diff** command. **Diff** is used to compare two files and display differences between them.

Nicolas Riley (on the #unix IRC channel) once told me how he used the – file so that users wouldn't get copies of articles they submitted to his mailing list. He used the following code:

```
% FROM="john@affy.com"

$ LIST=`echo $FROM | cat - input.dat | \
> sort | uniq -u | xargs echo`
```

The *input.dat* file looks like this:

```
mike@affy.com
john@affy.com
bob@affy.com
```

The complicated command in this example deserves a closer look. The echo $FROM | cat - input.dat produces the following output:

```
john@affy.com
mike@affy.com
john@affy.com
bob@affy.com
```

You can see the *$FROM* variable is prepended to the contents of the *input.dat* file. Then this output is sorted and only unique lines are kept:

```
mike@affy.com
bob@affy.com
```

Finally, the **xargs** command reads those two lines and sends them to the **echo** command for the final result:

```
mike@affy.com bob@affy.com
```

Quite a lot of Unix programming is done by combining small commands until the desired results are achieved. Because of this, it is vital to become familiar with all of the different commands available to you on the command line. Chapter 9, "Examining the Tools," provides a good start in this direction by listing many of the commands and explaining how to use their options.

Using Device Files

In Unix, all of the hardware devices connected to your computers are represented by device files in the */dev* directory. *Device files* are merely a convenient way for the operating system (or you) to communicate with the hardware. They provide a consistent way to send and receive information.

Most of the aspects of device files fall into the realm of system administration instead of programming and won't be covered here. However, you should know some basics. Table 5.3 shows some of the different types of device files.

Table 5.3 *All Devices Files Are Located in /dev*

File Name	Description
/dev/fd0	Associated with floppy drive A.
/dev/hda	Associated with the first physical (as opposed to logical) drive in your system.
/dev/mouse	Associated with your mouse.
/dev/sda	Associated with the first SCSI drive in your system.
/dev/lp0	Associated with your parallel port—normally your printer.
/dev/null	This device accepts bytes and then ignores them. It is frequently used when the output from a program is not needed.
/dev/tty	Associated with your terminal.
/dev/ttyS0	Associated with the first serial port.
/dev/zero	This device is a byte emitter. You can read an infinite number of zero bytes from */dev/zero*.

If you have more than one of any type of device, they are represented by changing the suffix of the device file. For example, serial port two is represented by */dev/ttyS1*.

If you take a look at the */dev* directory in your system, you'll see files that don't correspond to existing devices. On my system, for example, there is a */dev/sda* file and I don't have a SCSI disk.

Device files are, in some ways, used just like regular files. However, some devices have special requirements. Most of the disk-based device files need to be made known to Unix before being used. The **mount** command is used for this purpose. It tells Unix what kind of disk is being used and where its files and directories will attach to the rest of the Unix file system. I use the following command to make my floppy disk accessible:

```
mount -t msdos /dev/fd0 /mnt/floppy
```

This command line tells Unix that I will be using an MS-DOS-formatted diskette and that its files will be accessible through /*mnt*. After running the **mount** command, I can use the following command to see all of the files on the diskette:

```
ls /mnt/floppy
```

The /*mnt* directory is considered the mounting point for the diskette. You can unmount the diskette with this command:

```
unmount /mnt/floppy
```

CAUTION The mount point directory must already exist before you issue the **mount** command or an error message will be displayed.

Don't ever use /*tmp* or a subdirectory of /*tmp* as a mounting point! Many systems automatically delete files in the /*tmp* directory when space is needed or after a certain amount of time has elapsed.

Using Exec

The **exec** command can do a number of interesting things because it runs commands in place of the current shell. Most of the time this ability is used to change your current shell. For example, the command exec /bin/csh causes you to start using the C shell instead of Bash.

The **exec** command can also be used to semi-permanently redirect output to a file descriptor. This technique lets you use a file descriptor other than *STDOUT* or *STDERR*, as shown in Listing 5.8.

Listing 5.8 *to_log—Using the* **exec** *Command and Redirection to Create a Log File*

```
#!/bin/bash

exec 3> /tmp/log

for file in *
do
   echo "`date +%B %d %H:%I:%S`" - Processing $file" >&3
```

```
# do some file processing
done
```

Here is an example of this script in action:

```
% chmod +x to_log
% ./to_log
% cat /tmp/log
May 17 19:07:48 - Processing init.dat
May 17 19:07:48 - Processing to_log
```

By using this technique you can use several log files simultaneously. Perhaps one log file holds messages about directories and another holds messages about files. As an alternative, you could use a different log file for each user. The possibilities and permutations are numerous.

Another way to use **exec** is to redirect *STDOUT* and then restore *STDOUT* to normal. Listing 5.9 redirects *STDOUT* for most of the script, but restores *STDOUT* back to the terminal before the last command.

Listing 5.9 *Listing 5.9[em]stdout1—Using the exec Command to Redirect STDOUT and then Restoring It*

```
#!/bin/bash

exec > /tmp/standard_output

echo "This line is going to the file."
echo "This line too."

exec > /dev/tty
echo "This line is going to the display."
```

Here is an example of this script in action:

```
% chmod +x stdout1
% ./stdout1
This line is going to the display.
% cat /tmp/standard_output
This line is going to the file.
This line too.
```

The */dev/tty* device file represents the display connected to your login shell. So if you redirect *STDOUT* to */dev/tty,* you essentially restore it to normal.

Using Eval

Chapter 9, "Examining the Tools," has a section called "The eval Command."

The **eval** command concatenates its parameters and then executes the newly created command. This effectively results in a second round of variable substitution. This functionality has some fascinating uses. First, look at a very basic use of **eval**:

```
$ function="ls *.dat"
$ eval $function
cat.dat    cut.dat    mail.dat
$ function="ls -l *.dat"
$ eval $function
-rw-rw-r—   1 medined medined   45   May 9 15:42 cat.dat
-rw-rw-r—   1 medined medined   45   May 9 15:42 cut.dat
-rw-rw-r—   1 medined medined   45   May 9 15:42 mail.dat
```

In this example, the same command eval $function produces two different results because the value of $function changes. Using this technique, you indirectly run commands. At times, this can be handy. For example, perhaps you need to let users run different commands but you always want the results to be logged:

```
% eval "$function >> $USER.log"
% ls $USER.log
medined.log
```

Using the *$USER* variable lets each user have his own log file.

It's time to move on to something more complicated—arrays. An array is a list of items, like this fruit array: apples, pears, and oranges. Manipulating lists of information is usually easier than using separate variables for each one. In some languages, you can reference the first element of the fruit array with this type of notation: fruit[1], which is equal to apples.

Bash doesn't have any support for arrays. But you can create fake arrays using the **eval** command. I think it's easier to see a working example of this technique before reading an explanation. Listing 5.10 contains a list of appointments. Listing 5.11 holds a script that reads the list and displays the appointment for either the current date or a date specified on the command line.

Listing 5.10 *eval.dat—A Data File Holding Appointments Used for the **eval** Command Example*

```
mm=01 dd=12 yy=1998 msg='Appt with Dr. Katz'
mm=03 dd=09 yy=1998 msg='Golf w/Jackie, Lunch w/John'
mm=04 dd=20 yy=1998 msg='Anniversary Dinner'
```

Listing 5.11 *eval.sh—Using the **eval** Command to Find Appointments*

```bash
#!/bin/bash

# Show the user what parameters are needed
# if the wrong number of parameters was
# supplied on the command line.
if [ $# -ne 3 -a $# -ne 0 ]
then
  echo "Usage: eval.sh OR eval.sh {mm} {dd} {yyy}"
  exit 0
fi

# Read the data file. Each line of the
# data file results in a separate environment
# variable holding a single day's appointments.
while read DATA
do
  # Execute each line that is read. This creates four
  # variables called mm, dd, yy, and msg.
  eval $DATA

  # Create a variable called DATEBOOK_{date} where
  # the date part is created by combining the mm, dd,
  # and yy variables read from the input file. The msg
  # variable is assigned to the newly created DATEBOOK
  # variable.

  # The ${mm} notation is used because the underscore
  # is a valid character for use in a variable's name.
  # The curly braces serve to delimit the variable name.
  # If they weren't used, Bash would see a variable called
  # $mm_.

  eval "DATEBOOK_${mm}_${dd}_$yy='$msg'"
done < eval.dat

# This next section of code builds the {date} portion
# of the DATEBOOK variable. This date is the one for
# which the appointments are displayed.
```

```
if [ $# -eq 3 ]
then
  curdate="$1_$2_$3"
else
  curdate="`date '+%m_%d_%Y'`"
fi

# Display the datebook entry.
echo "Datebook Entry For $curdate:"
eval "echo \$DATEBOOK_$curdate"
```

The *while* loop in the above example generates and executes the following three command lines:

```
DATEBOOK_01_12_1998='Appt with Dr. Katz'
DATEBOOK_03_09_1998='Anniversary Dinner'
DATEBOOK_04_20_1998='Golf w/Jackie, Lunch w/John'
```

In many ways, these three variables can be looked at as a three-dimensional array, because the three components (month, day, and year) can all vary independently. The *DATEBOOK_01_12_1998* variable is equivalent to *DATEBOOK[01][12][1998]* in other computer languages. I call this technique, where each dimension is converted into part of the variable name, *flattening the array.*

TIP

Here is an advanced tip: You can flatten any array by incorporating the array indexes directly into a variable's name. However, this technique is only available in a language that lets you generate and execute commands on-the-fly (in other words, in languages that have the **eval** command or its equivalent).

As you create your own scripts, you'll find that the **eval** command is critical to your success. Often, its ability to create and execute commands on-the-fly is invaluable.

Using Background Processes

The shell that you communicate with through the keyboard, your login shell, normally runs one program at a time. You enter a command, the associated program is executed, and the results are displayed. You enter another command, the next program is executed, and the results are displayed again. This allows for a nice, orderly progression of command, execution and view of the results.

A problem arises, however, when one of the programs that you run takes a long time to finish. For example, suppose you're using the **find** command to search for all backup files more than two weeks old. Such a command might take five minutes or more to complete. In the meantime, your terminal is unusable because the **find** command has control of it.

The solution to this problem is to make the **find** command run in the background. When programs are run in the background, they no longer control your keyboard. In fact, it's hard for them to get input at all, unless you pipe it into them from a file.

Background processes can be quite convenient. They let you run more than one program at once. In fact, you can run lots of programs at once.

Every time a program is executed, it is assigned a Process ID number, or PID. The PID can be used to find information about a running program. Once the program is finished, the PID goes away.

Programs are placed into the background by adding an ampersand (&) to the end of a command line. For example:

```
% find / -name "temp.dat" -print &
[1] 301
% find: /etc/uucp: permission denied
find: /var/spool/at: Permission denied
date
Mon Jun 22 14:13:01 EDT 1998
[1]+ Exit 1     find / -name "temp.dat" -print
%
```

The number in square brackets tells you how many background processes you've started. In this case, the **find** command is the first background process. The second number, the 301, is the Process ID. Every time you start a new background process, you'll see a new PID. This PID is also displayed by the **ps** command:

```
% ps
PID TTY STAT TIME COMMAND
263   1 S    0:00 /bin/login -- medined
301   1 R    0:00 find / -name temp.dat -print
323   1 R    0:00 ps
```

I've italicized the relevant line in the output from the **ps** command. The important information consists of the PID, the TTY, and the command line that is being executed.

Just as important as knowing how to start background processes is knowing how to stop them. Let's create a background process that never ends, so you can learn how to stop runaway or misbehaving processes. The script in Listing 5.12 never ends, because background processes are disconnected from the keyboard. Therefore, without any input, the **read** command just waits forever.

Listing 5.12 *background.sh—A Never-ending Script*
```
read
```

Let's start a few never-ending background processes:

```
% background.sh &
[1] 341
% background.sh &
[2] 342

[1] Stopped (tty input)    background.sh
% background.sh &
[3] 343

[2] Stopped (tty input)    background.sh
% ps
PID TTY STAT TIME COMMAND
327   1 S    0:00 /bin/login — medined
328   1 T    0:00 -bash
341   1 T    0:00 -bash
342   1 T    0:00 -bash
343   1 T    0:00 -bash
344   1 R    0:00 ps

[3] Stopped (tty input)    background.sh
```

The **ps** command shows all three background process (the italicized lines). Each process is stopped because it is waiting for input from the TTY—because of the unsatisfied **read** command.

There are two ways to get rid of the background jobs. You can log out or use the **kill** command, as shown here:

```
% kill -SIGKILL 341 342 343
[1]- Killed   background.sh
```

```
[2]+ Killed    background.sh
[3]+ Killed    background.sh
% ps
PID TTY STAT TIME COMMAND
327  1 S   0:00 /bin/login — medined
328  1 T   0:00 -bash
348  1 R   0:00 ps
```

It's important to note that only one command is placed into the background at a time. If you enter the command find / -name "sam.dat" -print; find / -name "jon.dat" -print &, then only the last **find** command is executed in the background. The first **find** command is executed in the foreground, and the terminal is locked until the command finishes.

You can use a compound command to avoid this problem like this:

```
(find / -name "sam.dat" -print; \
 find / -name "jon.dat" -print ) &
```

> Compound commands are discussed in the "Creating Compound Commands" section earlier in this chapter.   **NOTE**

Summary

This chapter looks at the many different ways that you can interact with and control Bash. It starts by explaining that a command list lets you run two or more commands on a single command line. Command lists use the *&&*, ‖ *and* ; notation to connect one command with another. The *&&* notation runs the second command only if the first is successful. The ‖ notation does the opposite, the second command runs only if the first command fails. The ; notation simply sequences the commands—the first command runs, then the second one.

Next, you read about compound commands, of which there are two types. The *(command_list)* notation runs its commands in the same child shell, and any environmental changes do not remain in effect after the commands are finished. The *{ command_list }* notation also runs its command inside the same child shell, but the environment changes remain after the commands finish.

You can redirect input into a program or redirect output from a program. Input redirection uses the < *file* or the << *label* notation. The < *file* notation lets you substitute the contents of a file for input from the keyboard. The << *label* notation lets you place the required input directly on the command line (and therefore directly inside a script).

Output redirection is done using the > *file* notation. If the file doesn't exist it is created unless the *noclobber* variable is set. You can also use the I> notation to avoid overwriting existing files. The >> *file* notation is used to append output to a file. The 2> *file* notation lets you redirect output sent to *STDERR*.

You can merge any two output streams using *m>&n* notation. The output going to the *m* file descriptor is merged with the output going to the *n* file descriptor.

One of the most important concepts in Unix is that of the pipe. Pipes are used to connect the output of one command to the input of another. Because it's so easy to link two programs, programmers are encouraged to write short, focused programs that perform short tasks. Then, using pipes, these programs can be linked together to perform larger tasks.

The **read** command is discussed next. **read** takes a line of input from *STDIN* and stores it either into a variable of your choosing or into *$REPLY*. Optionally, **read** breaks up the input into words and stores the individual words into variables that you specify. If you need to delimit words using any character other than spaces, tabs, or newlines, you'll need to set the *IFS* (short for Internal Field Separator) variable. For example, *IFS="$IFS\!"* adds the exclamation point character to the delimiter list.

Next, the – file name was introduced. Most Unix commands and programs understand that when a dash is used as a file name, it means that *STDIN* should be read instead of a file. This notation is especially useful in pipes when the program on the right side of the pipe (the one accepting input) doesn't normally read from *STDIN*.

Unix uses device files to communicate with hardware. For example, if you need to interact with the system's floppy disk, you might use a file called */dev/fd0*. Some other devices are */dev/mouse* and */dev/lp0*, which allow communication with the mouse and printer, respectively.

The **exec** command is usually used to change your current shell. For example, the command `exec /bin/csh` causes you to start using the C shell instead of Bash. However, it can also be used to semi-permanently redirect a file descriptor (so a descriptor other than *STDOUT* or *STDERR* can be used) inside a script. For example, `exec 3> /tmp/log` redirects file descriptor 3 to a temporary file. After the redirection is set up, you can make use of it like this: `echo "This is a message" >&3`.

After the **exec** command, the **eval** command is discussed. The **eval** command concatenates its parameters and then executes the newly created command, which effectively results in a second round of variable substitution. This technique can be used in a variety of interesting ways — from creating pseudo-arrays to passing the names of commands to scripts for them to execute.

Next, background processes are examined. By running commands in the background, you can run more than one command at the same time. Each command has its own Process ID, or PID. If one of your processes goes awry, you can use the `kill -SIGKILL pid` command to end it.

The next chapter, "Using Perl," introduces the Perl programming language. This versatile language has quickly become the "de facto" system administration language for Unix systems. Additionally, it is used for quite a bit of Internet development. Its scope of features and portability make it a powerful tool in the shell programmer's arsenal.

Using Perl

This chapter takes you on a whirlwind tour of Perl—a very popular programming language. You learn about its basic features, such as its many operators, functions, and file-handling abilities. Perl's pattern matching feature is covered in Chapter 8, "Pattern Matching."

Perl came into widespread usage mainly for its ability to quickly create system utilities and for its use on web servers to create and serve dynamic web pages. However, its use has grown far beyond that limited scope. Today, programmers are using Perl to access databases, create or process XML, and work in many other areas too numerous to mention.

Perl has evolved quite a bit since Larry Wall first created it in 1986. In its first incarnation, Perl was used as a utility to print reports. Larry Wall wrote the first Perl interpreter using a Unix-based C compiler. In some ways, Perl has never outgrown its Unix origins. However, the Perl community has labored mightily in order to port Perl to many computer platforms. You can find Perl running under nearly every flavor of Unix as well as Windows 95 and Windows NT.

Perl seems to have an infinite number of uses. I've used it to automate the creation of tables of contents for my web site. A friend of mine uses Perl to analyze Radius (a user authentication server) scripts. Because of Perl's many built-in functions and its built-in pattern matching, it is ideal for quick, one-shot programs and reports.

On the other hand, Perl's object-oriented features and its ability to limit the scope of variables makes it ideal for robust, long-term programs.

Most of Perl's features work the same on the various Unix and Windows operating systems. The only time you'll have a problem with portability is if you're forking processes or using the timeout feature for sockets under Unix. Perl for Windows doesn't support those two Unix-based features.

After you read this chapter, you'll be able to identify the components of a Perl program. If you're already a programmer or have a little programming experience, you'll be able to create your own Perl programs with no trouble.

If you need to have additional information about Perl after reading this chapter, you can turn to the Perl Usenet newsgroups—*comp.lang.perl* and *comp.lang.perl.misc.*—or read the online version of my Perl introductory book, "Perl 5 by Example," at -*http://www.affy.com/p5be.*

The Features of Perl

Even if you don't create your own Perl scripts from scratch, you might need to modify someone else's. This section will familiarize you with Perl's features, giving you the bird's eye view of the language.

Completeness—Perl has all the elements of a modern computer language. There are variables, decision statements, control statements, loops, and functions. It also allows you to manipulate files and access information about directories.

File I/O—You can use Perl to open files, read and write information, and close files. You can read or write information character by character or record by record.

Pattern Matching—There are very few computer languages that have built-in pattern matching. Pattern matching is used to search for patterns of characters in strings. For example, you might need to find all customers named "John" in a database. The first step to performing the search is creating a pattern or *regular expression* defining the characters you're looking for. In this case, the regular expression is /^*John*/i. The ^ character means that matches start at the beginning of the string and the i means that the case of the string should be ignored. The ^ character is known as a *metacharacter*. The i is a regular expression modifier. Perl has many additional metacharacters and modifiers. They are covered in more detail in Chapter 8, "Pattern Matching."

Reports—Perl has the ability to create simple reports. You define the report format and specify what information should be used. Perl handles the hard work of pagination and information alignment.

Special Variables—Many operations in Perl are controlled by variables. For example, the end of record delimiter is stored in the $/ variable. If all of your data records end with the string "_END_", you can modify $/ and let Perl read your data file record by record.

References—Perl uses references to hold the memory locations of variables. They are mostly used to pass information to subroutines and to create data structures in memory.

Objects—Objects group data and subroutines together. The data describes the objects (size, price, and quantity), and the subroutines act on the data. For example, if you have an inventory item object, you need subroutines to change the quantity on hand and an item's price.

Modules—Modules are used to physically separate subroutines and data into different files. The module files have a file extension of *pm*. Often, modules are object-oriented and each object is defined in a separate module.

Debugger—When you are trying to understand the behavior of Perl code or you are tracking down a bug, Perl's built-in debugger can come in handy. The debugger lets you control the execution of your Perl script.

Command-line Options—When you run the Perl interpreter from the command line, you can specify many different options to change its behavior. For example, the *–c* option tells Perl to only check for syntax errors, not to execute the script.

Perl has many features that are not available in the shell. Perl can do everything the shell can. In some ways, Perl can be thought of as a super-shell.

As much as I'd like to discuss all aspects of Perl, this book covers shell programming and Perl is just one aspect of that topic. Therefore, some topics related to Perl aren't discussed in this chapter. One important topic left out is reports. If you need to know more about Perl, take a look at http://www.perl.org.

Introduction to Perl

The Perl syntax will grow on you, if you let it. Don't assume too quickly that familiar words have entirely different meanings just because you know Perl is a programming language. Trust your instincts. This chapter describes the features of Perl using everyday language wherever possible. Words that are special to Perl or that are computer-related are italicized the first time they are used.

This chapter assumes that Perl is already installed on your system. You can check to see if Perl is installed and find out what version is installed using the **perl –v** command. If Perl is installed, the response should look similar to this:

```
This is Perl, version 5.005_02 built for i686-linux

Copyright 1987-1998, Larry Wall

Perl may be copied only under the terms of either the
Artistic License or the GNU General Public License, which
may be found in the Perl 5.0 source kit.

Complete documentation for Perl, including FAQ lists,
should be found on this system using 'man perl' or 'perldoc
perl'. If you have access to the Internet, point your
browser at http://www.perl.com/, the Perl Home Page.
```

The example code in this book was developed and tested on an older version of Perl. You are probably using Perl 5.003 or later. Some additional features might be available to you, but the examples presented here should work identically on your system.

> **If you're running version 4 or an even older version of Perl, many of the features discussed in this chapter are not available to you. Please try to upgrade to the latest version of Perl.**   **CAUTION**

Now you know Perl is installed. The next step is to create a Perl script and execute it. Type the following Perl script using any text editor and save it to a file called *dummy.pl*.

```
#!/usr/bin/perl
print "Hello, World!\n";
```

The first line of this script (the one with the pound sign) is used to locate the Perl interpreter. Other lines that begin with # are comments, which Perl ignores. You can freely add comments to your scripts using the pound sign.

> **You can find out which directory holds the Perl interpreter using the command which perl. Then change the first line of the script to match whichever directory is displayed. If no directory is displayed or if more than one is displayed, talk to your system administrator to see which Perl executable you should be using.**   **TIP**

The print
subroutine is
similar to the
shell's echo
command.

The second line is a print statement—it calls the built-in *print* subroutine. The *print* subroutine displays the text "Hello, World" on your monitor. Actually, the print statement is a bit more complicated. However, before learning about what really happens when using the *print* subroutine, execute the *dummy.pl* script by making it executable and typing its name or by using this command:

```
perl dummy.pl
```

You should see the words "Hello, World" displayed on your monitor.

Now let's look at the **print** function a bit closer. It actually sends the "Hello, World" text to *STDOUT*. In the above example, the monitor is viewed as a write-only file by the Perl program.

FRI

For more information about *STDOUT*, see Chapter 5, "Controlling the Shell."

Subroutines,
functions,
and com-
mands are
similar to
each other.
For most
purposes, we
use these
terms inter-
changeably.

The \n at the end of the print statement is a newline character. Some terminals require an entire line of output (or a minimum number of characters) to be sent before characters are displayed immediately. This is called *buffered I/O*. The newline character, in effect, forces the output line to be displayed. More information about the newline and other special characters is in the "Using Static Information" section, later in this chapter.

Variables in Perl

Variables are vital to every computer program. A *variable* is a named piece of computer memory. A *scalar* variable holds individual items of information. An *array* holds a series or list of information. A *hash* (or associative array) is used when elements of an array need to be accessed by non-numeric means.

Naming Conventions

Shell vari-
ables were
discussed in
Chapter 2,
"Variables."

Perl variable names are case-sensitive, user-defined variables that always start with a type-identifier character and a letter. Scalars start with the $ character, arrays start with the @ character, and hashes start with the % character. Most Perl programmers use a combination of lowercase and uppercase letters for their variable names. Names with all uppercase letters are generally reserved for file handles. Names that begin with an uppercase letter generally indicate a module or package name. See the "Using Modules" section later in this chapter for additional information on modules and packages.

Variable names can be quite long. However, the practical limit is roughly 15 characters. Any longer and you'll get tired of typing the variable name as you enter your code into a text editor.

Scalars

Scalar variable names always start with a dollar sign ($). They can hold one number or one text string at a time. Perl variables always start with a value of zero or the empty string (""). If a number is needed, the value is zero. If a string is needed, the empty string is used. Scalars are assigned values, using the equals sign, like this:

```
$bookNum   = 10;
$bookTitle = "The Scarlet Letter";
$bookNum   = $bookNum + 5;
```

Arrays

Array variable names always start with an at sign (@). They can hold a series of scalar values or elements. Arrays can consist of a mixture of numbers and text in any combination and are assigned values like this:

```
@oddNumbers  = ( 1, 3, 5, 7, 9 );
@weekends    = ( "Saturday", "Sunday" );
@mixed       = ( 1, "Monday", 2, "Tuesday" );
```

The parentheses indicate the beginning and ending of the list of scalars. Individual elements are accessed using a numeric index. You access the first elements of the @*oddNumbers* array using $*oddNumbers[0]*. Notice that the individual element is a scalar and therefore starts with a dollar sign. Also notice that the array index is surrounded by square brackets. Array indexes start at zero. Therefore, while the @*oddNumbers* array has five elements, the last element is referenced by $*oddNumbers[4]*.

You can always access the last element in an array using the –*1* index. The next to last element is –*2* and so on.   **TIP**

Perl combines arrays that are side-by-side into a single array. This means that *((1, 2, 3), (4, 5, 6))* is the same as *(1, 2, 3, 4, 5, 6)*. By combining arrays, Perl ensures that each array element is a scalar value. Some programmers call this behavior *flattening*.

One of Perl's time savers is the *list range* operator. An *operator* indicates you want Perl to perform an action on one or more operands. The list range operator is expressed as two periods together (..) and is used to specify a range of elements in a list. For example, the expression *(0..5)* is shorthand for *(0, 1, 2, 3, 4, 5)*. Likewise, *(A..F)* is shorthand for *(A, B, C, D, E, F)*.

Perl can evaluate arrays in either a list or a scalar context. When evaluating in a list content, all of the elements are used. For example,

```
@array = (0..5);
print "@array\n";
```

This code snippet displays "0 1 2 3 4 5".

TIP

> The $" variable controls which delimiter is displayed between array elements. Its default value is a space. However, you can change it to whatever you like. For example, if you want to print array elements one per line, use $" = "\n"; to assign the newline character as the array element delimiter.

When evaluating an array in a scalar context, the number of elements is returned. For example,

```
@array       = (0..5);
$numElements = @array;
print "$numElements\n";
```

This code snippet displays "6".

Another time saver is the array slice feature. *Array slices* are subsets of existing arrays. For example, suppose you only need the third and fifth elements of an array. Instead of writing:

```
@array = (0..5);
$third = $array[2];
$fifth = $array[4];
```

you could write:

```
($third, $fifth) = @array[2, 4];
```

This line of code assigns the list returned by the array slice on the right of the equals sign to the variables in the list on the left of the equals sign. You can also assign the list from an array slice to an array. You can even use an array slice on the left side of the equals sign to assign values to multiple array elements at once. For example,

```
@array[2, 4] = ($third, $fifth);
```

> Using array slices on both sides of the equals sign efficiently swaps **TIP**
> array elements. For example, *@array[2, 4] = @array[4, 2]* swaps the
> third and fifth elements.

Hashes

Hash variable names always start with a percent sign (%). They can hold a series of scalar index-value pairs. Hashes are assigned values like this:

```
%hash = ( "David", "123 Hardy Rd",
          "Kathy", "45 Darling Lane");
```

The *%hash* variable consists of two index-value pairs. Hash indexes are also known as keys. The first index-value pair is *"David"* and *"123 Hardy Rd"*. The index is *"David"* and the value is *"123 Hardy Rd"*. The index (or key) can be used to directly access the value scalar. For example, *$hash{"Kathy"}* is equal to *"45 Darling Lane"*. Notice that the value is a scalar and therefore starts with a dollar sign. Also notice that curly braces surround the hash index. You can also use => instead of the comma to define the hash. For example:

```
%hash = ( "David" => "123 Hardy Rd",
          "Kathy" => "45 Darling Lane");
```

Associating the value with the index creates individual hash entries. Use curly braces around the index:

```
$hash{"Matt"} = "23 Park Place";
```

Unlike arrays, hashes cannot simply be printed. Instead, you need to iterate over the list of indexes or keys and print each hash entry individually. For example:

```
%hash = ( "David" => "123 Hardy Rd",
          "Kathy" => "45 Darling Lane");

foreach $index (keys(%hash)) {
  print "$index: $hash{$index}\n";
}
```

This code snippets displays:

```
David: 123 Hardy Rd
Kathy: 45 Darling Lane
```

The Perl foreach statement and the shell's for command are similar in nature.

The keys(%hash) section of the code snippet returns a list consisting of the indexes in *%hash*. In this case, the list is ("David", "Kathy"). The *foreach* statement iterates over the list of indexes. Each index value is placed into the *$index* variable, in turn, and the statement inside the curly braces is executed.

Using Static Information

Much of the information used in programs is *static*—it never changes. For example, a graphics program will likely need a specific value for Pi (roughly 3.14). In addition, filenames are sometimes static.

Static numbers are represented in Perl code as themselves. Simply use the number as you were taught in school. In addition to base ten numbers, you can also use base 8 (octal) and base 16 (hexadecimal) numbers. For example, 16_{10} is equivalent to 20_8 and 10_{16} are specified like this:

```
decimal16 = 16;
octal16 = 020;
hex16 = 0x10;
```

NOTE Base conversion is one area where the shell has an advantage over Perl and every other language I know. You can use the *[base#]n* notation in the shell to perform integer arithmetic on numbers in any base from 2 to 36.

Static text is a little more complicated than static numbers. There are two types of static text—single-quoted text and double-quoted text. Single-quoted text is used without any processing. Double-quoted text is subject to variable interpolation before it is used. *Variable interpolation* replaces the variable name with the variable's value. For example,

Variable interpolation is similar to variable substitution in the shell.

```
$age = '14';
print "Charlie is $age years old\n";
```

This code snippet displays "Charlie is 14 years old". Notice that the value of $age has replaced the variable name in the output. The static value of $age is assigned using single-quotes because no variable interpolation is needed. Double-quoted strings take longer to evaluate than single-quoted strings. Therefore, single-quoted strings should be used whenever possible (i.e., whenever there are no variables to interpret).

Double-quoted text also lets you use some special characters, like the newline character, to get different results. The special characters are represented by *escape sequences* in double-quoted strings. Table 6.1 lists Perl escape sequences.

Table 6.1 *Perl's Escape Sequences*

Escape Sequence	Description
\a	Alarm bell
\b	Backspace
\e	Escape
\f	Form feed
\n	Newline
\r	Carriage return
\t	Tab
\v	Vertical tab
\$	Dollar sign
\@	Ampersand

Table 6.1 *Perl's Escape Sequences (Cont'd)*

Escape Sequence	Description
\0nnn	Any octal byte
\xnn	Any hexadecimal byte
\cn	Any control character
\l	Change next character to lowercase
\u	Change next character to uppercase
\L	Change characters following the \L to lowercase until a \E sequence is encountered. Note that you need to use an uppercase L here, lowercase will not work.
\Q	Forces Perl to use the characters following the \Q as literal characters—used when working with regular expressions. The \E sequence ends the literal character mode. Note that you need to use an uppercase Q here; lowercase will not work.
\U	Change characters following the \U to uppercase until a \E sequence is encountered. Note that you need to use an uppercase U here, lowercase will not work.
\E	Terminates \L, \Q, and \U sequences. Note that you need to use an uppercase E here, lowercase will not work.
\\	Backslash

TIP   Perl uses strings and numbers interchangeably. Strings are converted to numbers as needed. If the string doesn't contain a number, a zero value is used. Therefore, never worry about string-to-number or number-to-string conversions.

Using Backticked Strings

Perl sends backticked strings to the operating system for execution. You can use variable interpolation within backticked strings. If you assign a backticked string to an array, the elements of the array will contain the output from the string's execution. For example,

```
$directory = '/usr/bin/';

# Get the output of the ls command.
@output    = `ls $directory`;

# Iterate over the @output array and print
# each element.
foreach (@output) {
  print;
}
```

This code snippet displays the output of the **ls** command. The first line of output is assigned to $output[0]. The last line of output is assigned to $output[-1]. The @output array has as many elements as there are lines of output from the **ls** command.

The **foreach** statement iterates over the list of elements in @output and prints each one. When no temporary variable name is specified in the **foreach** statement, *$_* is used. It just so happens that the **print** function displays the *$_* variable as the default when nothing else is specified.

Each output line is displayed on a separate line of your monitor because the newline character is preserved when the output of the **ls** command is stored in the array elements. Use the **chomp** function to remove the newline character if you don't need it.

Using Statements

Perl interprets script files starting with the first line and executes them sequentially until some decision or condition statement forces the execution path to change. A Perl *statement* is a logical unit of work. Statements can span multiple physical lines in your script file. For exampl:

```
#!/usr/bin/perl
if ($title eq "Perl") { print "The title is Perl.\n"; }
```

executes identically to

```
#!/usr/bin/perl
if ($title eq "Perl") {
  print "The title is Perl.\n";
}
```

The second line in both examples holds the beginning of the *if* statement. The end of the *if* statement is the closing bracket. Notice that the entire statement does not have to be contained on one line.

The *eq* used in the code snippet is an operator. You might have read about operators in Chapter 2, "Variables." Perl has a lot more operators than the shell does. The *eq* operator compares two text strings for equality. In this case, the *$title* variable is being compared to the "Perl" text string.

Statements are built out of variables, operators, and functions. You've already read about variables. The next step is to examine operators. Functions are discussed in the "Functions" section later in this chapter. Finally, all of the statement elements are pulled together in the "Statements" section of the chapter.

Operators

Perl has many operators. An *operator* indicates you want Perl to perform an action on one or more operands. The standard arithmetic operators are addition, subtraction, multiplication, and division. In addition, Perl has operators to assign values, do comparisons, test the status of files, manipulate lists, and do a variety of other things.

You can use more than one operator in a statement. In order to determine which operation is performed first, Perl uses a specific *Order of Precedence*. However, if you use parentheses to explicitly tell Perl how to evaluate your statements, you can effectively ignore the issue of operator precedence. For example, instead of using *5 + 4 * 2*, I use *5 + (4 * 2)*. Operations inside parentheses are evaluated first—they have the highest level of precedence.

Table 6.2 *Perl's Operators*

Operator	Description
()	Parentheses group scalars into lists and change the evaluation order of operations.
[]	Square brackets are used in array slices and provide access to individual array elements.
{}	Curly braces are used to access individual hash entries.
->	The infix dereference operator is used for object-oriented programming.
++	The auto increment operator increments a variable by one.
--	The auto decrement operator decrements a variable by one.
**	The *exponentiation* operator raises a value to a specific power. For example, 2**2 evaluates to four.
!	The logical *not* operator is used in conditional and decision statements—like *if* and *while*.
~	The bitwise *not* operator flips all of the bits in a value. This is also known as taking the complement of a value. If you don't know what the term "bitwise" means, don't worry—you'll probably never need to use this operator.
+	The *plus* operator adds two values together.
-	The *minus* operator subtracts one value from another. The minus sign is also used to create negative numbers.
\	The *reference* operator creates a reference to a value. A *reference* is essentially a pointer to the value. It is used to pass arrays and hashes into functions.
=~ and !~	The *binding* operators force Perl to perform pattern matching operations on a variable other than $_. See Chapter 8, "Pattern Matching," for more information.
*	The *multiplication* operator multiplies one value by another.
/	The *division* operator divides one value by another.

Table 6.2 *Perl's Operators (Cont'd)*

Operator	Description
%	The *modulus* operator returns the remainder of the division of one value by another. For example, *8 % 3* evaluates to *2*.
x	The *repetition* operator repeats a text string for a given number of times. For example, *'a' x 5* evaluates to *'aaaaa'*.
.	The string *concatenation* operator combines one string with another. For example, *'abc' . 'abc'* evaluates to *'abcabc'*.
>>	The bitwise *right shift* operator shifts each bit in a value to the right by a given number of places. For example, *64 >> 2* evaluates to *16*. If you don't know what the term "bitwise" means, don't worry—you'll probably never need to use this operator.
<<	The bitwise *left shift* operator shifts each bit in a value to the left by a given number of places. For example, *64 << 2* evaluates to *256*. If you don't know what the term "bitwise" means, don't worry—you'll probably never need to use this operator.
==, !=	The numeric *equality* and *non-equality* operators are used in conditional expressions.
<, >	The numeric *less-than* and *greater-than* operators are used in conditional expressions.
<=, >=	The numeric *less-than-or-equal-to* and *greater-than-or-equal-to* operators are used in conditional expressions.
<=>	The numeric *spaceship* operator is used in sorting algorithms. For example, *operand1 <=> operand2* returns 1 if operand1 is greater than operand2, 0 if they are equal, and –1 if operand1 is less than operand2.
eq, ne	The text string *equality* and *non-equality* operators are used in conditional expressions.
lt, gt	The text string *less-than* and *greater-than* operators are used in conditional expressions.

Table 6.2 *Perl's Operators (Cont'd)*

Operator	Description
le, ge	The text string *less-than-or-equal-to* and *greater-than-or-equal-to* operators are used in conditional expressions.
cmp	The text string *spaceship* operator is used in sorting algorithms. For example, *operand1* <=> *operand2* returns *1* if *operand1* is greater than *operand2*, *0* if they are equal, and *–1* if *operand1* is less than *operand2*.
&, |, ^	The bitwise *and*, *or*, and *xor* operators are used to perform operations on specific bits in a value. If you don't know what the term "bitwise" means, don''t worry—you'll probably never need to use these operators.
&&, ||	The logical *and* and the logical *or* operators are used in conditional expressions.
..	The array range operator creates sequential series of scalar values. For example, *34..38* evaluates to *34, 35, 36, 37, 38*.
?:	The ternary conditional operator chooses between two values based on the evaluation of a conditional expression. For example, *$numBooks < 5000 ? "Small Library" : "Big Library"* evaluates to *"Small Library"* only if the value of the *$numBooks* variable is less than *5000*. Otherwise, the evaluation results in *"Big Library"*.
,	Commas are used to delimit scalars in lists and to force Perl to evaluate multiple statements where, normally, only one statement is expected.
not	The *not* operator is a low-precedence version of the ! operator.
and, or	The *and* and the *or* operators are low-precedence versions of the && and || operators.
xor	The *xor* operator is a low-precedence version of the ^ operator.

Whew! That's a pretty long list of operators. And I didn't even mention the 27 file test operators listed in the "Using Files" section of this chapter.

Table 6.2 also does not mention the 14 assignment operators. The basic assignment operator is the equal sign. It assigns the value on the right to the variable on the left. For example, `$scalar = 34;` assigns a value of *34* to the *$scalar* variable. The other 13 assignment operators are combinations of some operation with the equal sign—another of Perl's shortcuts. You can use +=, -=, *=, /=, %=, .=, **=, x=, <<=, >>=, &=, |=, ||=, and ^= as assignment operators. For example, `$numBooks += 15;` adds *15* to the value of *$numBooks*.

Functions

Functions are sections of code designed to do a specific task. In order to let you refer to them conveniently, these sections of code are given names. Perl includes both built-in functions and user-defined functions. Use this template to create user-defined functions:

```
Sub functionName {
  # statements
}
```

The *Sub* statement causes Perl to store the subroutine's statements for future use. Function names must start with a letter and can't use $, @, %, or & in their names.

You invoke Perl subroutines like this:

```
...
functionName();
...
```

Some subroutines require information in order to do their work. For example, a subroutine that multiplies two numbers needs to know which numbers to multiply. The specific numbers to use are passed into the subroutine as parameters inside the parentheses at the end of the subroutine name. For example:

```
...
$result = multiply(4, 2);
...
```

Parameters can be accessed using the @_ array inside the sub-routine.

```
Sub multiply {
  my($a, $b) = @_;
  $a * $b;
}
```

Notice the assignment statement used to access the two parameters from the @_ array? The first and second array elements are automatically assigned to the variables inside the parentheses on the left of the assignment operator. Your functions can handle a variable number of parameters using the *foreach* statement (explained later in the chapter) .

The value of the last statement executed becomes the value returned by the subroutine to the main program. In the above example, the last subroutine statement executed is *$a * $b*; the result of this manipulation is assigned to *$result* when the subroutine ends and the *$result = multiply(4, 2)*; assignment statement is finished. Perl provides a **return** function that explicitly indicates the value to return. However, it is not needed (unless, of course, the value you want to return is different from the value of the last statement executed).

The **my** function creates variables local to the **multiply** function. Normally, every section in your Perl script can see all variables. When the **my** function is used, only the current function can access the values of the local variables. Perl also has a **local** function, which creates a different type of local variable. Variables created by **local** can be accessed by the current function and by any functions called from the current function.

Functions by Category

This section lists Perl's functions by category.

- **Array:** chomp, join, keys, map, pop, push, reverse, shift, sort, splice, split, unshift, values

- **Database:** dbmclose, dbmopen

- **Directory:** chdir, closedir, mkdir, opendir, readdir, rewinddir, rmdir, seekdir, telldir

- **File:** binmode, chdir, chmod, chown, chroot, close, eof, fnctl, fileno, flock, getc, glob, ioctl, link, lstat, open, print, printf, read, readdir, readlink, rename, rmdir, seek, select, stat, symlink, sysopen, sysread, syswrite, tell, truncate, umask, unlink, utime, write

- **Group:** endgrent, getgrent, getgrgid, getgrname, getpgrp, setgrent, setpgrp

- **Hash:** delete, each, exists, keys, values

- **Host:** endhostent, gethostbyaddr, gethostbyname, sethostent

- **Input:** getc, read, sysread

- **Inter-process Communication:** msgctl, msgget, msgrcv, msgsnd, pipe, semctl, semget, semop, shmctl, shmget, shmread, shmwrite

- **Math:** abs, atan2, cos, exp, hex, int, log, oct, rand, sin, sqrt, srand

- **Message Queues:** msgctl, msgget, msgrcv, msgsnd

- **Miscellaneous:** bless, defined, do, eval, formline, import, ref, scalar, syscall, tie, tied, undef, untie, wantarray

- **Network:** endnetent, getnetbyaddr, getnetbyname, getnetent, setnetent

- **Output:** die, print, printf, syswrite, warn, write

- **Password:** endpwent, getpwent, getpwname, getpwuid, setpwent

- **Process:** alarm, die, dump, exec, exit, fork, getlogin, getpgrp, getppid, getpriority, kill, setpriority, sleep, system, times, umask, wait, waitpid

- **Protocol:** endprotent, getprotobyname, getprotobynumber, getprotoent, getservbyname, getservbyport, getservent, setprotoent

- **Regular Expression:** grep, pos, quotemeta, reset, split, study

- **Scope:** caller, local, my

- **Service:** endservent, getservbyname, getservbyport, getservent, setservent

- **Socket:** accept, bind, connect, gethostbyaddr, gethostbyname, gethostent, getpeername, getservbyname, getservbyport, getservent, getsockname, getsockopt, listen, recv, select, send, setsockopt, shutdown, socket, socketpair

- **String:** chop, chr, crypt, hex, index, join, lc, lcfirst, length, oct, pack, q, qq, quotemeta, qw, qx, reverse, rindex, split, sprintf, substr, uc, ucfirst, unpack, vec

- **Time:** gmtime, localtime, time

- **UNIX-specific:** chmod, chown, chroot, dump, endgrent, endhostent, endnetent, endprotent, endpwent, endservent, fnctl, fork, getgrent, getgrgid, getgrname, gethostent, getlogin, getnetent, getpgrp, getppid, getpriority, getprotobyname, getprotobynumber, getprotoent, getpwent, getpwname, getpwuid, getservbyname, getservbyport, getservent, ioctl, link, lstat, readlink, select, setgrent, sethostent, setnetent, setpgrp, setpriority, setprotoent, setpwent, setservent, sleep, syscall, times, umask, wait, waitpid

Functions by Name

Table 6.3 lists Perl functions sorted by name.

Table 6.3 *Perl Functions by Name*

Function	Description
abs	Calculates an absolute value.
accept	Accepts a socket connection from clients waiting for a connection.
alarm	Sends a SIGALARM to your script after a specified number of seconds.
atan2	Calculates an arc tangent.

Table 6.3 *Perl Functions by Name (Cont'd)*

Function	Description
bind	Binds a network address to the socket handle.
binmode	On systems that distinguish between text and binary files (like Windows 95 and Windows NT), this function forces binary mode treatment of a file.
bless	Changes the type of the referenced variable to a new type—used for object-oriented programming.
caller	Returns true, in a scalar context, if the current code has been called as a subroutine. Returns details, in an array context, of the calling context comprising the package name, filename, and line of the call.
chdir	Changes the current directory to the directory specified.
chmod	Changes file permissions on Unix operating systems.
chomp	Removes characters at end of a string if they equal the value of the $/ special variable—which is usually the newline character. If the $/ variable contains more than one character, all of those characters are removed.
chop	Removes the last character from a string and returns it.
chown	Changes the ownership of files.
chr	Returns the ASCII character of the specified number.
chroot	Changes the root directory of the current process.
close	Closes a file handle.
closedir	Closes a directory handle.
connect	Attempts to connect to a remote socket.
cos	Calculates a cosine.
crypt	Creates an encrypted string.
dbmclose	Undoes the linking of a hash to a *dbm* file. Use the **untie()** function instead of **dbmclose**.

Table 6.3 *Perl Functions by Name (Cont'd)*

Function	Description
dbmopen	Links a hash to a *dbm* file. Use the **tie**() function instead of **dbmopen**.
defined	Returns true if its parameter has been assigned a value.
delete	Removes an entry from a hash.
die	Terminates execution of the Perl script.
do	Executes the contents of a file as a Perl script—mostly superseded by the **use**() and **require**() functions.
dump	Causes a Unix program to create a binary image or core dump.
each	Allows iteration over the entries in an associative array.
endgrent	Closes the file used by **getgrent**() and other group-related functions.
endhostent	Closes the TCP socket used by **gethostbyname**() and host-related functions.
endnetent	Closes the file used by **getnetent**() and network-related functions.
endprotoent	Closes the file used by **getprotoent**() and protocol-related functions.
endpwent	Closes the file used by **getpwent**() and password-related functions.
endservent	Closes the file used by **getservent**() and server-related functions.
eof	Tests for the end of a file.
eval	Executes its parameters as if they were Perl statements—trapping possible runtime errors before they crash your script.

Table 6.3 *Perl Functions by Name (Cont'd)*

Function	Description
exec	Executes an external system command. *There is no return from this call.* Note that **system** calls external commands and does return.
exists	Returns true if a given key value is an entry in a hash.
exit	Forces the script to end.
exp	Returns the natural log base (e) to the specified power.
fncntl	Superceded by the **fnctl** module.
fileno	Returns the file descriptor for a specified file handle.
flock	Accesses file locks.
fork	Starts a child process.
formline	Allows direct manipulation of the format process by adding values to the format accumulator ($^A)—used mainly as an internal function.
getc	Returns the next character from a file.
getgrent	Returns, in a scalar context, the next group name. Returns, in an array context, information about groups taken from the *group system* file. If called repeatedly, it will iterate through the entries in the *group system* file.
getgrgid	Returns, in a scalar context, the next group name that belongs to a specified group id. Returns, in an array context, information about groups taken from the *group system* file. If called repeatedly, it will iterate through the entries in the *group system* file.
getgrname	Returns, in a scalar context, the next group id that belongs to a specified group name. Returns, in an array context, information about groups taken from the *group system* file. If called repeatedly, it will iterate through the entries in the *group system* file.

Table 6.3 *Perl Functions by Name (Cont'd)*

Function	Description
gethostby-addr	Returns, in a scalar context, the name of the specified host. Returns, in an array context, information about the specified host.
gethostby-name	Returns, in a scalar context, the address of the specified host. Returns, in an array context, information about the specified host.
gethostent	Returns, in a scalar context, the name of the next host in the *system hosts* file. Returns, in an array context, information about the next host in the *system hosts* file.
getlogin	Gets the current login name from the */etc/utmp* system file.
getnetbyaddr	Returns, in a scalar context, the name associated with a specified IP address. Returns, in an array context, information about the IP address.
getnetbyname	Returns, in a scalar context, the IP address associated with a specified host name. Returns, in an array context, information about the host name.
getnetent	Returns, in a scalar context, the name of the next host in the *system networks* file. Returns, in an array context, information about the next host in the *system networks* file. When called repeatedly, it iterates over the information in the *system networks* file.
getpeername	Returns the address of the remote side of a socket.
getpgrp	Returns the current process group for a given pid.
getppid	Returns the pid of the parent process.
getpriority	Returns the current priority of a specified pid, a specified group pid, or a specified uid, or 0 for the current process.
getproto-byname	Returns, in a scalar context, the protocol number assigned to a specified protocol name. Returns, in an array context, information about the protocol.

Table 6.3 *Perl Functions by Name (Cont'd)*

Function	Description
getprotoby-number	Returns, in a scalar context, the protocol name assigned to a specified protocol number. Returns, in an array context, information about the protocol.
getprotoent	Returns information about the next protocol in the *system protocols* file. When called repeatedly, it iterates over the information in the system protocols file.
getpwent	Returns, in a scalar context, the next user name in the *system password* file. Returns, in an array context, information about the next user in the *system password* file. When called repeatedly, it iterates over the information in the *system password* file.
getpwnam	Returns, in a scalar context, the next user id in the *system password* file. Returns, in an array context, information about the next user in the *system password* file.
getpwuid	Returns, in a scalar context, the user name of a specified user id from the *system password* file. Returns, in an array context, information about the specified user id from the *system password* file.
getservby-name	Returns, in a scalar context, the port number of a specific service from the *system services* file. Returns, in an array context, information about the specified service from the *system services* file.
getservbyport	Returns, in a scalar context, the service name associated with a specific port number from the *system services* file. Returns, in an array context, information about the specified port number from the *system services* file.
getservent	Returns, in a scalar context, the next service name from the *system services* file. Returns, in an array context, information about the next service from the *system services* file. When called repeatedly, it iterates over the information in the *system services* file.

Table 6.3 *Perl Functions by Name (Cont'd)*

Function	Description
getsockname	Returns the IP address of a specified socket.
getsockopt	Returns the value of a specified socket option.
glob	Returns a list of files that match a specified expression. For example, **glob("*.txt")** returns a list of all text files in the current directory.
gmtime	Converts an expression into a date and time. Returns, in a scalar context, a string like "Sat Jul 13 07:34:46 1986". Returns, in an array context, a nine-element list of the different date/time components.
grep	Iterates over a list, executing a specified expression for each iteration. Returns, in a scalar context, the number of times the expression evaluated true. Returns, in an array context, a list of the elements that caused the expression to evaluate to true.
hex	Converts a hexadecimal expression into decimal.
import	If a module has an **import** function, the **use** function calls it as the module is being loaded. You can use the **import** function to initialize variables, open files, or do any other setup work.
index	Returns the position of the first occurrence of one string inside another. When called repeatedly, it iterates over all instances of the searched-for string.
int	Returns the integer part of a value.
ioctl	Controls Input/Output operations, mainly used for terminals. It calls the Unix **ioctl** function with the specified parameters.
join	Concatenates all elements of a specified list using a specified delimiter.

Table 6.3 *Perl Functions by Name (Cont'd)*

Function	Description
keys	Returns, in a scalar context, the number of keys (and the number of entries) in a specified hash. Returns, in an array context, a list of the keys in a specified hash.
kill	Sends a signal to a process.
lc	Returns a copy of a specified expression with all letters in lowercase.
lcfirst	Returns a copy of a specified expression with the first letter in lowercase.
length	Returns the number of characters in an expression.
link	Creates a hard link to an existing file.
listen	Listens for connections on a socket.
local	Makes variables local to the current block. However, variables marked using **local** can be seen by functions called from inside the current block.
localtime	Converts an expression into a date and time—possibly localized for your time zone. Returns, in a scalar context, a string like "Sat Jul 13 07:34:46 1986". Returns, in an array context, a nine-element list of the different date/time components.
log	Returns the logarithm of an expression.
lstat	Returns a list that contains information about a symbolic link or file.
map	Iterates over a list, executing a specified expression for each iteration. Returns a list containing the results of the evaluation of each iteration.
mkdir	Creates a directory.
msgctl	Controls message queue operations.
msgget	Returns the message queue id.

Table 6.3 *Perl Functions by Name (Cont'd)*

Function	Description
msgrcv	Retrieves a message from the message queue.
msgsnd	Sends a message to a message queue.
my	Makes variables local to the lexical unit (block or file).
oct	Converts an octal expression into decimal.
open	Opens a file.
opendir	Opens a directory—used for reading file and subdirectory names.
ord	Returns the numeric ASCII code of the first character of a specified expression.
pack	Converts a list into a data structure.
pipe	Opens a pair of connected pipes.
pop	Removes the last element from an array.
pos	Returns the position of the last match produced by the *m//g* regular expression operator.
print	Prints a list to a file. If no file is specified, *STDOUT* is used. The standard output is usually the terminal.
printf	Prints a formatted list to a file.
push	Appends elements to the end of an array.
q	Takes the place of single quotes.
qq	Takes the place of double quotes.
quotemeta	Escapes all metacharacters in an expression.
qw	Returns a list of its parameters evaluated as if they were single-quoted.
qx	Takes the place of backticks or reverse quotes. Backticks are used to execute system commands.
rand	Generates random numbers.

Table 6.3 *Perl Functions by Name (Cont'd)*

Function	Description
read	Reads from a file.
readdir	Returns, in a scalar context, the next file in a directory. Returns, in an array context, a list of all files in a directory—including subdirectory names.
readlink	Returns the value of a symbolic link.
recv	Places information from a socket into a buffer.
ref	Returns the data type of a variable.
rename	Changes the name of a file.
reset	Resets variables in the current package—used with regular expression matching. Using **reset** can reset system variables you might not want to alter—like the *ARGV* and *ENV* variables.
reverse	Reverses, in a scalar context, the characters in a string. Reverses, in an array context, the order of the elements in the array.
rewinddir	Used in conjunction with **opendir**, **readdir**, and **closedir**, lets you start reading directory entries from the beginning of the directory.
rindex	Returns the position of the last occurrence of a substring in a string.
rmdir	Tries to delete a directory. It returns true if the directory is deleted.
scalar	Forces its arguments to be interpreted in a scalar context.
seek	Moves to a specified position in a file.
seekdir	Allows the position in a directory to be reset to a position saved with **telldir**. This is useful when processing directories with **readdir**.

Table 6.3 *Perl Functions by Name (Cont'd)*

Function	Description
select	Changes the default file handle used for the **print** and **write** functions. Also used to manipulate sockets under Unix.
semctl	Controls operations on semaphores.
semget	Finds the semaphore associated with a given key.
semop	Performs semaphore operations like signaling and waiting.
send	Sends the information in a buffer to a socket.
setgrent	Rewinds the */etc/group* file to the start of the file for subsequent accesses using **getgrent**.
sethostent	Determines if name server queries use UDP datagrams or if the socket connection to the name server should stay open.
setnetent	Rewinds the */etc/networks* file used by **getnetent** and other network-related functions.
setpgrp	Sets the current process group for the specified process.
setpriority	Sets the priority of a pid, group pid, or uid for the current process, group, or user.
setprotoent	Rewinds the */etc/protocols* file used by **getprotoent** and other protocol-related functions.
setpwent	Rewinds the */etc/passwd* file used by **getpwent** and other password-related functions.
setservent	Rewinds the */etc/services* file used by **getservent** and other service-related functions.
setsockopt	Sets socket options.
shift	Returns the first element of an array.
shmctl	Controls shared memory.

Table 6.3 *Perl Functions by Name (Cont'd)*

Function	Description
shmget	Finds the id of a shared memory segment.
shmread	Reads information from a shared memory segment.
shmwrite	Writes information from a shared memory segment.
shutdown	Shuts down the connection to a socket.
sin	Calculates the sine of an expression in radians.
sleep	Causes the current process to sleep.
socket	Opens a socket.
socketpair	Creates an unnamed pair of the specified type of sockets in the specified domain.
sort	Sorts a list.
splice	Removes elements from a list.
split	Returns, in a scalar content, the number of fields in an expressions and stores the fields in the @_ array. Returns, in an array context, a list of fields found in an expression.
sprintf	Formats text elements of a list in specific ways.
sqrt	Calculates the square root.
srand	Sets the seed used by the pseudo random number generation algorithm when generating random numbers via **rand**.
stat	Returns a list with information about a specific file.
study	Sets up internal lookup tables based on the string studied so that pattern matching operations can use this information to process the pattern match more quickly.
substr	Returns part of a given string.
symlink	Creates a symbolic link from an existing file to a new file.
syscall	Calls Unix system routines.

Table 6.3 *Perl Functions by Name (Cont'd)*

Function	Description
sysopen	Opens a file using the underlying operating system's **open** function.
sysread	Reads a specified number of bytes into a buffer.
system	Executes an operating system command.
syswrite	Writes a specified number of bytes into a buffer.
tell	Gets the current position in a file.
telldir	Gets the current directory position—used in conjunction with the **seekdir** function.
tie	Binds a variable to a package class.
tied	Returns a reference to an object that is tied to a variable.
time	Returns the current time.
times	Returns a list of four elements representing the amount of time used by the current parent and child processes.
truncate	Truncates a file.
uc	Creates a copy of a string expression with all letters in uppercase.
ucfirst	Creates a copy of a string expression with the first letter in uppercase.
umask	Returns and/or sets the process file mask.
undef	Undefines a variable.
unlink	Deletes the files in a specified list.
unpack	Unpacks data.
unshift	Adds one or more elements to an array.
untie	Breaks the binding between a variable and a package.
utime	Sets the access and modification time of one or more files.

Table 6.3 *Perl Functions by Name (Cont'd)*

Function	Description
values	Returns, in a scalar context, the number of entries in a hash. Returns, in an array context, a list of values in a hash.
vec	Manipulates a bit vector.
wait	Waits for a child process to end.
waitpid	Waits for a specific child process to end.
wantarray	Returns the calling context of the current subroutine.
warn	Prints a list to *STDERR*.
write	Writes a formatted record.

As you can see, Perl has quite a few pre-defined functions. In order to properly harness the power of Perl's many functions, however, you need to know about statements. Statements are discussed in the next section.

Statements

Statements are complete units of instruction to the Perl interpreter. The interpreter evaluates each statement in a script in sequence until a jump or loop command is processed. The simplest statement is 123;—a literal number followed by a semi-colon. The semi-colon is very important. It tells the Perl interpreter that the statement is complete.

Every Perl statement has a value. The last value evaluated becomes the value for the statement. For example, the value of the statement 56 + 3; is 59.

Statement Blocks

Statement blocks group statements into a single unit for execution. The value of the statement block is the value of the last executed statement. In order to create a statement block, simply surround the group of statements within curly braces. For example:

```
{
    $scalar1++;
    $scalar2 += 10;
}
```

If you know that a certain variable is only needed inside a statement block, you can use the **my** function to create a local variable. Changes to a local variable don't affect global variables of the same name. For example:

```
$numRooms =10;
{
  my($numRooms) = 20;
  print "numRooms = $numRooms\n";
}
print "numRooms = $numRooms\n";
```

The above code prints 20 and 10 because the **my** function creates a local version of the $numRooms variable. Variables created with the **my** function can only be used inside the statement blocks in which they are created. If you use **my** outside a statement block, the variables can be used anywhere in the file.

Decision Statements

Decision statements are used to choose between two courses of action. The basic decision statement is the *if* statement. *If* statements look like this:

```
if ($numRooms > 9) {
    print "Very Large House\n";
} elsif ($numRooms > 6) {
    print "Large House");
} else {
    print "House\n";
}
```

When the condition expression in the first line of this example evaluates to true, the first statement block is executed. When the condition evaluates to false, the second statement block is executed. Both the **else** and the **elsif** clauses are optional.

If you need to test for a false value, you can use the *unless* statement. The *unless* statement works exactly opposite to the *if* statement.

```
unless ($color eq "Green") {
    print "Red";
} else {
    print "Green";
}
```

When the condition expression evaluates to false (i.e., `$color` is not "Green"), the first block is evaluated, otherwise the second block is evaluated. Like the *if* statement, the *else* clause is optional.

If and *unless* statements are used so often that Perl has incorporated statement modifiers to create a shorthand decision statement.

```
print "Very Large House\n" if $numRooms > 9;
print "Green" unless $color eq 'Red';
```

Using these modifiers is straightforward. Notice that, by convention, parentheses don't surround the conditional expression.

Loop Statements

Perl has several ways to repeatedly evaluate a statement block. You can use the *while*, *do*, *for* and *foreach* statements.

Table 6.4 *Perl's Loop Statements*

Statement	Description	Example

while	Repeatedly evaluates a statement block as long as the condition is true. The statement block is never evaluated if the condition is false.	`while (condition) {`
		
		`...`
		
		`}`

do	Repeatedly evaluates a statement block. Loop termination is controlled by either a **while** clause or an **until** clause.	`do {`
		
		`...`
		
		`} while (condition);`
		
		`do {`
		
		`...`
		
		`} unless (condition);`

Table 6.4 *Perl's Loop Statements (Cont'd)*

Statement	Description	Example
for	Repeatedly evaluates a statement block. Loop termination is typically controlled by a count variable.	```for (initialization; condition; operation){ ... }```
foreach	Evaluates a statement block for each element in an array.	```foreach (array_var) { ... }```

Many of these loop statements perform similar operations. Choosing which one to use is a matter of deciding which one best matches your program logic.

The *while* statement evaluates the conditional expression before executing the statements inside the block. The *do* statement is guaranteed to execute the statement block at least once. Successive loops are controlled by the condition expression. *do..while* loops continue to loop as long as the condition is true. *do..until* loops continue to loop as long as the condition is false.

For statements are a little more complex than *while* or *do* statements. *For* statements are typically used to execute a statement block for a specified number of times. The initialization clause usually sets the counting variable to zero. The condition clause terminates the loop when it evaluates to true. And the operation clause usually increments or decrements the counting variable.

Foreach statements iterate over the elements of an array. Each time the loop is evaluated, another element is assigned to *$_*. You can specify another variable name instead of *$_* like this:

```
foreach $element (@array) {
  print "$element\n";
}
```

In this example, each array element is assigned to *$element* before each iteration of the loop. The loop is terminated when the last array element is processed.

Quite often, a finer level of control is needed over looping statements. Using the conditional expression only provides one point of
control—at the beginning or end of the loop. What if an error
arises? What if you need to restart the loop?

Perl has a series of jump keywords to help you control loops.
The **last** keyword jumps out of the current statement block. The
next keyword jumps to the next iteration of the loop. The **redo**
keyword restarts the current iteration of the loop. And the **goto**
keyword jumps to a specified label. For example:

```
for (i = 0; i < 10; i++) {
    last if $numRoom = 0;   # jump out of the loop.
    next if $numRoom = 1;   # jump to the i++ clause.
    redo if $numRoom = 2;   # restart the loop.
}
```

Using Files

Files are used to provide long-term storage of information. Information that is only stored in the computer's memory is lost when
the computer is turned off. Writing information to a file on the
computer's hard disk ensures that the information is available
every time the computer is turned on.

Perl controls access to files using file handles. A file handle is
associated with a file using the **open** function. Subsequent use of a
file is done using the file handle in order to specify which file to use.
When all file activity is done, the **close** function is called to disasso-
ciate the file handle with the file.

Three file handles are automatically created when a Perl program is started. These are *STDIN, STDOUT,* and *STDERR* (note
that, by convention, file handles are specified in upper case). The
STDIN file handle is usually associated with the keyboard. The
STDOUT and *STDERR* file handles are usually associated with
the screen. You can use the standard "<" and ">" command-level
redirection characters in order to change the association of the
default file handles.

When reading and writing binary information (as opposed to
text), use the **binmode** function.

After opening a file for input, the <> or diamond operator is
used to read from the file one record at a time—usually one record

is equivalent to one line. Unless you specify a different variable, the input record is placed into *$_*.

> Perl uses the *$_* as a scratchpad variable. Many functions use the *$_* **TIP**
> as the default variable to check for input or to store output.

Reading From Files

Perl seems to be expressly designed for record-based file I/O. The *$/* variable holds the end-of-record delimiter—usually '\n'. The following example shows how to read and display each line of a file.

```
open(INPUT, "<demo.dat")
  or die "Unable to open the demo file.";
print $_ while <INPUT>;
close(INPUT);
```

In this four-line example, the file handle is called *INPUT*. However, it could have been called anything. The < character is used to indicate that you want to read from the file. Because the default action is to open for reading, the < character is optional. The second line is a continuation of the *open* statement. If an error occurs while the file is being opened, the **die** function is executed—the text message is displayed and the script ends. The third line is a *loop* statement. The print clause is repeatedly executed as long as another line (or record) can be read from the input file. After the file has been processed, the *close* statement shuts down the connection between the file handle and the file.

> Notice that the record delimiter (the newline character) is not **TIP**
> stripped from the input records. Use the **chomp** function if you
> need to remove the delimiter.

Writing to Files

When opening files for writing, the > character is used to indicate that you want to write to the file. The **print** function is used to send the information to the file—simply add the file handle to the *print* statement. The following example creates the *new.dat* file by copying the *demo.dat* file.

```
open(INPUT, "<demo.dat")
  or die "Unable to open the demo file.";
open(OUTPUT, ">new.dat")
  or die "Unable to create the new file.";
print OUTPUT $_ while <INPUT>;
close(OUTPUT);
close(INPUT);
```

This example is very similar to the read example you saw in the "Reading From Files" section. Two lines were added and the *print* statement was slightly modified—these changes are shown in bold text.

If a *new.dat* file exists when the above example is executed, it is quietly deleted. Perl has ways to append information to existing files. If you need more information about appending to files, read the documentation available at *http://www.perl.com*.

File Test Operators

Frequently, programmers need to determine the size of a file or if a file exists. Perl uses a *file test* operator in order to get this information. For example, the following code fragment checks for the existence of the *demo.dat* file.

```
print "demo.dat exists!" if -e "demo.dat";
```

You can shorten this conditional expression even further if $_ contains the filename. For example,

```
print "demo.dat exists!" if -e;
```

You can also use a file handle instead of a filename. The special file handle _ (the underscore character) is used when you need to run two or more tests on the same file. Behind the scenes, Perl invokes a system call for each file test. The _ file handle tells Perl to use the file information retrieved from the last system call. For example:

```
print "Readable and Executable\n"
    if -r "test.pl" && -x _;
```

This line of code only displays the message *Readable and Executable* if both conditions are true for the *test.pl* file. By using the underscore file handle, you use the file information that is still in memory. When performing this operation a few hundred times, the time savings start to add up.

Table 6.5 lists all of the available File Test Operators.

Table 6.5 *Perl's File Test Operators*

Operator	Description
-A OP1	Returns the access age of a file OP1 when the program is started.
-b OP1	Returns true if OP1 is a block device.
-B OP1	Returns true if OP1 is a binary file. If OP1 is a file handle, then the current buffer is examined, instead of the file itself.
-c OP1	Returns true if OP1 is a character device.
-C OP1	Returns the inode change age of OP1 when the program is started.
-d OP1	Returns true if OP1 is a directory.
-e OP1	Returns true if OP1 exists.
-f OP1	Returns true if OP1 is a regular file as opposed to a directory, symbolic link, or other type of file.
-g OP1	Returns true if OP1 has the *setgid* bit set.
-k OP1	Returns true if OP1 has the *sticky* bit set.
-l OP1	Returns true if OP1 is a symbolic link. Under DOS, this operator will always return false.
-M OP1	Returns the age of OP1, in days, when the program is started.
-o OP1	Returns true if OP1 is owned by the effective uid. Under DOS, it always returns true.
-O OP1	Returns true if OP1 is owned by the real uid/gid. Under DOS, it always returns true.
-p OP1	Returns true if OP1 is a named pipe.
-r OP1	Returns true if OP1 can be read from.

Table 6.5 *Perl's File Test Operators (Cont'd)*

Operator	Description
-R OP1	Returns true if OP1 can be read from by the real uid/gid. Under DOS, it is identical to -r.
-s OP1	Returns the size of OP1 in bytes. Therefore, it returns true if OP1 is non-zero.
-S OP1	Returns true if OP1 is a socket.
-t OP1	Returns true if OP1 is opened to a *tty*.
-T OP1	Returns true if OP1 is a text file. If OP1 is a file handle, then the current buffer is examined, instead of the file itself.
-u OP1	Returns true if OP1 has the *setuid* bit set.
-w OP1	Returns true if OP1 can be written to.
-W OP1	Returns true if OP1 can be written to by the real uid/gid. Under DOS, it is identical to -w.
-x OP1	Returns true if OP1 can be executed.
-X OP1	Returns true if OP1 can be executed by the real uid/gid. Under DOS, it is identical to -x.
-z OP1	Returns true if OP1's size is zero.

Special Variables

Perl uses many special variables to modify how its functions behave and to store the results of operations. For example, after a pattern match attempt (using the *m//* or *s///* operators), the *$&* variable contains the text, if any, that matched the pattern. Special variables hold the values of environment variables, and can turn on and off debugging options.

The details about how to use many of the special variables, such as the *$^D* variable—which holds the value of Perl's debugging options—are beyond the scope of this book. However, you should be aware that these variables exist, especially because the Perl scripts in Chapter 12, "Customizing the Tools," use several of them.

Table 6.6 groups the special variables into categories and gives a brief one-line description of each. After you've found the variable that you need, you can locate a more complete description in Table 6.7.

Table 6.6 *Perl's Special Variables in Categories*

Category	Variable	Brief Description
Arrays	$"	List element separator, used when printing.
	$[	Base array index.
	$;	Separator for multi-dimensional array emulation.
Files	$.	Record number.
	$/	End-of-record delimiter.
	$|	Controls when buffers are flushed.
	$^F	Maximum system file descriptor.
	$ARGV	Name of file used by <> operator.
	_	File handle which uses the last file's statistics to answer file tests.
	DATA	File handle used to store data inside a script.
	STDERR	Standard error file handle.
	STDIN	Standard input file handle.
	STDOUT	Standard output file handle.
Pattern Matching	$&	Text matched by last successful pattern match.
	$`	Text preceding last successful pattern match.
	$'	Text following last successful pattern match.

Table 6.6 *Perl's Special Variables in Categories (Cont'd)*

Category	Variable	Brief Description
	$+	Text matched by last parentheses in last successful pattern match.
	$*	An alternative to using the /*m* pattern match option.
	$n	Text matching the nth parentheses set in the pattern.
Printing	$,	Output separator for the **print** function.
	$\	Appended as the last parameter to the **print** function.
	$#	Default format for printed numbers.
Processes	$$	Process ID of the current process.
	$?	Status code of the last system operation.
	$0	Name of the Perl script that is being executed.
	$]	Perl's version number.
	$!	Error number or an error message.
	$@	Syntax error, if any, from the last **eval** function executed.
	$<	Real User ID of the current process.
	$>	Effective User ID of the current process.
	$)	Real Group ID of the current process.
	$^T	Time, in seconds, when the script started.
	$^X	Full file path of the Perl interpreter.
	%ENV	Environment variables.
	%SIG	References to the signal handler functions.
Reports	$%	Current page number.

Table 6.6 *Perl's Special Variables in Categories (Cont'd)*

Category	Variable	Brief Description
	$=	Current page length.
	$-	Number of lines left to print.
	$~	Name of the default line format.
	$^	Name of the default heading format.
	$:	End-of-word delimiters for word-wrapping.
	$^L	Page eject and footer text.

Table 6.7 shows a list of Perl's special variables. The order of this list is identical to the list in the file *PERLVAR.HTM*, which comes with your Perl distribution. This table lets you quickly find any special variable you might come across in examples or someone else's scripts.

Table 6.7 *Perl's Special Variables*

Variable Name	Description
$_	The default parameter for a lot of functions. For example, if no other variable is specified, Perl's pattern matching operators search the text stored in $_.
$.	Holds the current record or line number of the file handle that was last read. It is read-only and will be reset to zero when the file handle is closed. This variable is useful when displaying error messages regarding badly formatted input.
$/	Holds the input record separator. The record separator is usually the newline character. However, if $/ is set to an empty string, then two or more newlines in the input file will be treated as one. It is also sometimes useful to assign the formfeed character to $/; this lets you read your input file a page at a time—assuming that you're reading a standard ASCII text file.

Table 6.7 *Perl's Special Variables (Cont'd)*

Variable Name	Description
$,	The output separator for the **print**() function. Normally, this variable is an empty string. However, setting *$,* to a newline might be useful if you need to print each element in the parameter list on a separate line.
$\	Added as an invisible last element to the parameters passed to the **print**() function. Normally an empty string, but if you want to add a newline or some other suffix to everything that is printed, you can assign the suffix to *$*.
$#	The default format for printed numbers. Normally, it's set to *%.20g*, but you can use any of the format specifiers mentioned in the section "The printf Command" of Chapter 9.
$%	Holds the current page number for the default file handle. If you use Perl's **select** function to change the default file handle, *$%* changes to reflect the page number of the newly selected file handle.
$=	Holds the current page length for the default file handle. Changing the default file handle, using Perl's **select** function, changes *$=* to reflect the page length of the new file handle.
$-	Holds the number of lines left to print for the default file handle. Changing the default file handle will change *$-* to reflect the number of lines left to print for the new file handle.
$~	Holds the name of the default line format for the default file handle. Normally, it is equal to the file handle's name.
$^	Holds the name of the default heading format for the default file handle. Normally, it is equal to the file handle's name with *_TOP* appended to it.
$|	If non-zero, flushes the output buffer after every **write**() or **print**() function. Normally, it is set to zero.

Table 6.7 *Perl's Special Variables (Cont'd)*

Variable Name	Description
$$	Holds the process number of the process running the Perl interpreter.
$?	Holds the status of the last pipe close, backtick string, or **system** function.
$&	Holds the string that was matched by the last successful pattern match.
$`	Holds the string that preceded whatever was matched by the last successful pattern match.
$'	Holds the string that followed whatever was matched by the last successful pattern match.
$+	Holds the string that was matched by the last bracket in the last successful pattern match. For example, the statement */Fieldname: (.*)|Fldname: (.*)/ && ($fName = $+);* finds the name of a field even if you don't know which of the two possible spellings is being used.
$*	Changes the interpretation of the ^ and $ pattern anchors. Setting *$** to *1* is the same as using the */m* option with the regular expression matching and substitution operators. Normally, *$** is equal to *0*.
$0	Holds the name of the file containing the Perl script being executed.
$<number>	This group of variables (*$1, $2, $3,* ...) holds the regular expression pattern memory. Each set of parentheses in a pattern stores the string that matches the components surrounded by the parentheses into one of the *$<number>* variables.
$[	Holds the base array index. Normally, it's set to *0*. Most Perl authors recommend against changing it without a very good reason.

Table 6.7 *Perl's Special Variables (Cont'd)*

Variable Name	Description
$]	Holds a string that identifies which version of Perl you are using. When used in a numeric context, it will be equal to the version number plus the patch level divided by 1000.
$"	Holds the separator used between list elements when an array variable is interpolated into a double-quoted string. Normally, its value is a space character. Sometimes setting *$"* to a colon or a newline is useful. Using a colon as the value for *$"* creates a colon-delimited list, while using a newline prints each element on a new line.
$;	Holds the subscript separator for multi-dimensional array emulation.
$!	When used in a numeric context, holds the current value of *errno*. If used in a string context, holds the error string associated with *errno*.
$@	Holds the syntax error message, if any, from the last **eval** function call.
$<	Holds the read uid of the current process.
$>	Holds the effective uid of the current process.
$)	Holds the read gid of the current process. If the process belongs to multiple groups, then *$)* holds a string consisting of the group names separated by spaces.
$:	Holds a string that consists of the characters that can be used to end a word when word-wrapping is done by the ^ report formatting character. Normally, the string consists of the space, newline, and dash characters.
$^D	Holds the current value of the debugging flags.
$^F	Holds the value of the maximum system file description. Normally, it's set to 2.

Table 6.7 *Perl's Special Variables (Cont'd)*

Variable Name	Description
$^I	Holds the file extension used to create a backup file for the in-place editing specified by the *-i* command-line option. For example, it could be equal to ".*bak*."
$^L	Holds the string used to eject a page for report printing.
$^P	Is an internal flag that the debugger clears so that it will not debug itself.
$^T	Holds the time, in seconds, at which the script begins running.
$^W	Holds the current value of the *-w* command-line option.
$^X	Holds the full path name of the Perl interpreter being used to run the current script.
$ARGV	Holds the name of the current file that is being read when using the diamond operator (<>).
@ARGV	This array variable holds a list of the command-line arguments. You can use *$#ARGV* to determine the number of arguments minus one.
@F	This array variable holds the list returned from autosplit mode. Autosplit mode is associated with the *-a* command-line option.
@INC	This array variable holds a list of directories where Perl can look for scripts to execute. The list is mainly used by the *require* statement.
%INC	This hash variable has entries for each filename included by *do* or *require* statements. The keys of the hash entries are the filenames and the values are the paths where the files were found.

Table 6.7 *Perl's Special Variables (Cont'd)*

Variable Name	Description
%ENV	This hash variable contains entries for your current environment variables. Changing or adding an entry only affects the current process or a child process, never the parent process.
%SIG	This hash variable contains entries for signal handlers. For more information about signal handlers, see Chapter 13, "Handling Exceptions."
_	This file handle (the underscore) can be used when testing files. If it is used, the information about the last file tested will be used to evaluate the new test.
DATA	This file handle refers to any data following __END__.
STDERR	This file handle is used to send output to the standard error file. Normally, this is connected to the display, but it can be re-directed if needed.
STDIN	This file handle is used to read input from the standard input file. Normally, this is connected to the keyboard, but it can be changed.
STDOUT	This file handle is used to send output to the standard output file. Normally, this is the display, but it can be changed.

Some of Perl's special variables are hard to understand without examples. Unfortunately, I don't have space in this book to do them justice. The *ENV* hash and the *DATA* file handle are interesting and simple to illustrate with short listings.

As you might know from Chapter 2, "Variables & Operators," environment variables are critical to effective shell programming. Perl lets you read and modify environment variables directly using the *%ENV* hash. While you can change environment variables, those changes will not persist after the process running Perl has ended. The changes will, however, affect the current process and any child processes that are started.

You can print out the environment variables using the script shown in Listing 6.1.

Listing 6.1 *env.pl—Using Perl to Display a List of Environment Variables*

```
#!/usr/bin/perl

foreach $key (keys(%ENV)) {
    printf("%-10.10s: $ENV{$key}\n", $key);
}
```

Here is an example of this script in action:

```
% perl env.pl
ENV        : /home/medined/.bashrc
HISTFILESI: 1000
HISTSIZE   : 1000
HOME       : /home/medined
HOSTNAME   : localhost.localdomain
HOSTTYPE   : i386
LOGNAME    : medined
MAIL       : /var/spool/mail/medined
MM_CHARSET: ISO-8859-1
OSTYPE     : Linux
PATH       : /usr/local/bin:/bin:/usr/bin:/usr/X11...
PS1        : [\u@\h \W]\$
SHELL      : /bin/bash
SHLVL      : 1
TERM       : linux
USER       : medined
USERNAME   :
_          : /usr/bin/perl
```

The *DATA* file handle lets you store data inside your scripts instead of in an external data file. This is a very handy feature if you're sending scripts through the mail to a client for them to execute. Listing 6.2 shows how this feature is used. Everything above the *__END__* line is code, everything below is data.

Listing 6.2 *perl.pl—Using the DATA File Handle With Perl*

```
#!/usr/bin/perl

# The DATA file handle doesn't need to be opened,
# you can just start reading from it.
@list_lines = <DATA>;
```

```
foreach (@list_lines) {
    print("$_");
}

__END__
Line one
Line two
Line three
```

Here is an example of this script in action:

```
% perl data.pl
Line one
Line two
Line three
```

Objects

You've been exposed to a lot of Perl concepts in this chapter. There are only two more that I'll be mentioning—objects and modules. There are no hard-and-fast rules that link objects and modules, but many modules are written to take advantage of Perl's object-oriented features. Because of symbiosis, I need to introduce you to the topic of object-oriented programming. However, I don't have space to go into all of the details. So hang on to your hat, let's look at an overview of objects from Perl's point of view.

NOTE I admit I'm not an object purist. I play fast and loose with the terminology, because I don't think being precise is important. Your getting a general understanding of objects and how to use them is my goal. If you need a rigorous understanding of objects, read a C++ or Java book.

I think of objects as nouns. Desks, chairs, computers are all objects. Every object has properties—color, size, weight, and so forth. And every object has behaviors we associate with it —chairs move, desk drawers open and close. Objects can also contain other objects—a desk can contain a drawer and a drawer, in turn, can contain a pen.

When you walk into a furniture showroom, you might see 50 different pieces of furniture. If they are about 30 inches high and have a flat top, a place for your legs, and perhaps a drawer or two—you realize that all 50 items are desks. This process of generalization is critical to object-oriented programming.

Object-oriented programs move from the general (a definition of a desk) to the specific (an 18th century mahogany rolltop desk) using *classes*. A class defines the characteristics of an object—its properties and behaviors. A generic class can represent many different objects. A more specific class—a subclass—represents fewer objects, but describes each more precisely. Subclasses inherit properties and methods from their parent classes.

The terms *object* and *class* are pretty interchangeable, except that a class might be considered an object described in computer language—whereas an object is just an object.

The design of a class is dependent on the project you're programming. The description of an object, and the class, depend on what needs to be done. If you were attempting to design a school course-scheduling program, your objects would be very different than if you were designing a statistics program.

There are four buzzwords associated with object-oriented programming.

Abstraction: Information about an object (its properties) can be accessed in a manner that isolates how data is stored from how it is accessed and used.

Encapsulation: The information about an object and functions that manipulate the information (its methods) are stored together.

Inheritance: Classes can inherit properties and methods from one or more parent classes.

Polymorphism: A child class can redefine a method already defined in the parent class.

The rest of this section discusses these buzzwords in the context of creating a class that represents pens as an inventory item.

All inventory items have at least a part ID number and a quantity-on-hand number associated with them. Let's use these two properties to create an inventory class:

```
$Inventory = {
   'PART_ID'     => 'PEN1491',
   'QTY_ON_HAND' => 14
};
```

*In my object-
oriented Perl
programs, I
equate a
hash vari-
able with an
object. Each
hash entry—
each key-
value pair—
is a different
property of
the object.*

The { ... } notation returns a reference to an anonymous hash variable. The => notation indicates key-value pairs; each => represents another hash entry. I need to use references to show you object-oriented techniques, but I don't have space to explain them fully. A basic definition of a reference is that it points to a spot in memory. In this case, you'll need to access the anonymous hash later in your code. And because it has no name, you'll need to store the reference value.

The code shown above uses a hash to represent the class. Each property in the class becomes an entry in the hash. This type of representation is fast, easy to program, and easy to extend. If you need to add a new property, perhaps price, all you need to do is add an additional hash entry:

```
$Inventory = {
  'PART_ID'      => 'PEN1491',
  'QTY_ON_HAND' => 14,
  'PRICE'        => 28.50
};
```

You can display the properties like this:

```
print "Part ID:  $Inventory->{'PART_ID'}\n";
print "Quantity: $Inventory->{'QTY_ON_HAND'}\n";
print "Price:    $Inventory->{'PRICE'}\n";
```

You now know how to create an object by hand. Listing 6.3 shows how to create objects programmatically.

Listing 6.3 *inv.pl—Creating Inventory Objects*

```
#!/usr/bin/perl

# Start using a namespace called Inventory.
package Inventory;

  # Define a function that can create a new Inventory
  # object. The new function returns a reference to
  # an anonymous hash containing the two key-value pairs
  # passed to new.
  sub new {
    my($class)  = shift;
    my(%params) = @_
```

```
# Create an anonymous hash and change its type
# to be 'Inventory'. A variable's type can be
# determined with the ref function.
bless {
   "PART_ID"     => $params{'PART_ID'},
   "QTY_ON_HAND" => $params{'QTY_ON_HAND'}
 }, $class;
}

# Switch to using the main, or default, namespace.
package main;

# Create a new Inventory object and store a
# reference to it in the $item variable.
$item = Inventory->new(
   'PART_ID'     => 'PEN1491',
   'QTY_ON_HAND' => 14
);

# Display the object's properties.
print "Part ID:  $item->{'PART_ID'}\n";
print "Quantity: $item->{'QTY_ON_HAND'}\n";
```

Here is an example of this script in action:

```
% perl inv.pl

Part ID:  PEN1491
Quantity: 14
```

The *inv.pl* script introduces two new concepts—the *package* statement and the **bless** function. The *package* statement is essentially used to create new namespaces. Namespaces are used to isolate one set of names from another. In this script we have two namespaces, main and inventory. The **new** function in *inv.pl* can also referred to as **Inventory::new**. The **bless** function changes the type of a variable. In this case, the type of the anonymous hash is changed to $class, which has a value of "inventory."

When the *namespace->function* notation is used, Perl ensures that the first parameter to function is the value of *namespace*. Therefore, to give the script an object-oriented feel, I use the statement my($class) = shift; to retrieve the *namespace*. When I create object-oriented Perl scripts, my class names are also equated to a namespace.

So far you've learned about object-oriented terminology and how to create an inventory object. Let's take the next step and see how to create a pen object. For the purposes of this example, pen objects differ from inventory objects by the addition of one property—*INK_COLOR*.

Listing 6.4 shows one way that pen objects can be defined. The *pen.pl* script builds on the *inv.pl* script. New or changed lines are shown in bold.

Listing 6.4 *pen.pl—Creating Pen Objects*

```perl
#!/usr/bin/perl

package Inventory;

  sub new {
    my($class)  = shift;
    my(%params) = @_


    bless {
      "PART_ID"     => $params{'PART_ID'},
      "QTY_ON_HAND" => $params{'QTY_ON_HAND'}
      }, $class;
  }

# The Pen package defines the Pen object.
package Pen;

  # The ISA array tells Perl who the parents of
  # the current class are.
  @ISA = (Inventory);

  sub new {
    my($class)  = shift;
    my(%params) = @_

    # Create the parent object.
    my($self)   = Inventory->new(@_);

    # Create a key-value entry for the
    # Pen's unique property.
    $self->{'INK_COLOR'} = $params{'INK_COLOR'};

    bless $self, $class;
  }
```

```
package main;

  # Create a new Pen object and store a
  # reference to it in the $item variable.
  $item = Pen->new(
    'PART_ID'      => 'PEN1491',
    'QTY_ON_HAND' => 14,
    'INK_COLOR'    => 'blue'
  );

  # Display the object's properties.
  print "Part ID:   $item->{'PART_ID'}\n";
  print "Quantity:  $item->{'QTY_ON_HAND'}\n";
  print "Ink Color: $item->{'INK_COLOR'}\n";
```

Here is an example of this script in action:

```
% perl pen.pl
Part ID:   PEN1491
Quantity:  14
Ink Color: blue
```

Like the previous listing, *pen.pl* introduces two new concepts—the *@ISA* array and the concept of *$self*. The *@ISA* array lets Perl know which classes (defined by the **package** keyword) are the parents of the current class. In this case, the *Inventory* class is the parent of the *Pen* class. The *$self* variable holds a reference to the object being defined. In essence, it gives the object self-awareness. Through the *$self* variable, you can add new hash entries or modify existing ones.

The topic of object-oriented programming can fill several books. But I've reached the end of the space allotted for the topic in this book—and we still haven't covered such topics as multiple inheritance, calling a parent's methods, and using one class to contain another. If you need more information about Perl's object-oriented features, you can use the **perldoc perlobj** command.

Using Modules

This section introduces you to the concept of modules. Modules are used to group functions and variables together. Grouping functions and variables is important for reusability and documentation purposes. You can define more than one package in a single file.

However, most of the time, programmers place a single package
into a single file and call it a module. Modules have a file extension
of *pm*. A simple module (stored in the *Test.pm* file) might look like
this:

```
package Test;

sub foo {
  print "Inside Test::foo()\n";
}

1;
```

NOTE

As with objects, I only have space to give you an overview of modules. In addition, I can't even touch on Perl libraries. Most Perl libraries have been superseded by modules so their importance has
diminished recently.

Notice that the package name is the same as the filename. Normally, the first letter of the module name is uppercase. The last line
of the module must evaluate to true (or 1) to indicate that the module was loaded correctly.

You may recall the **package** keyword from the earlier section
discussing object-oriented programming. In that section, packages
were used to define objects. In this section, you learn that packages
also define modules. I can't explain why there are so many words
to describe the same action, except to say that words shape your
point-of-view. So when programming with object-oriented
method, you use object-oriented words. At other times, other
words are used.

Module files are typically stored in a directory called */usr/lib/
perl5* (check your system to find the exact location).

Some modules are placed in subdirectories like */usr/lib/Perl5/
Net* or */usr/lib/Perl5/File*.

Some modules are just collections of functions with some "module" stuff added. Modules should follow these guidelines:

• The file name should be the same as the package name.

• The package name should start with a capital letter.

- The file name should have a file extension of *pm*.

- The package should be derived from the *Exporter* class if object-oriented techniques are not being used.

- The module should export functions and variables to the main namespace using the *@EXPORT* and *@EXPORT_OK* arrays if object-oriented techniques are not being used.

Since most modules have their own namespace, you need a way to tell Perl both the namespace and the variable name or function name you're interested in. The :: notation tells Perl which namespace you need:

```
Test::foo();
```

This line of code invokes the **foo** function in the Test package.

Occasionally, you may see a reference to what may look like a nested module. For example, `$Outer::Inner::foo`. This really refers to a module named *Outer::Inner*, so named by the statement: *package Outer::Inner;*. Module designers sometimes use this technique to simulate nested modules.

You can also choose to export function and variable names from the module's namespace to the default namespace (main). Object-oriented modules keep all function and variable names hidden. They are not available directly, you access them through the module name. Remember the *class->function* notation shown in the object-oriented section? However, simple function collections don't have this object-oriented need for secrecy. They want your script to directly access the defined functions. This is done using the *Exporter* class and the *@EXPORT* and *@EXPORT_OK* arrays.

The *Exporter* module supplies basic functionality that gives your script access to the functions and variables inside the module. The **import** function, defined inside the *Exporter* module, is executed at compile-time by the **use** compiler directive. The **import** function takes function and variable names from the module's namespace and places them into the *main* namespace. Thus, your script can access them directly.

The **use** function makes a module's functions available to your script by automatically exporting function and variable names to the *main* namespace by calling a module's **import** function. Most modules don't have their own **import** function; instead they inherit it from the *Exporter* module. You have to keep in mind that the **import** function is not applicable to object-oriented modules. Object-oriented modules should not export any of their functions or variables. For example, if you need to use the Test module, your script might look like this:

```
use Test;

Test::foo();
```

You can use the following lines as a template for creating your own modules:

```
package Module;
  require(Exporter);
  @ISA = qw(Exporter);
  @EXPORT = qw(funcOne $varOne @variable %variable);
  @EXPORT_OK = qw(funcTwo $varTwo);
```

The names in the *@EXPORT* array are always available in the *main* namespace without using the :: notation. Those names in *@EXPORT_OK* are only available if requested in the *use* statement. This small module can be loading into your script using this statement:

```
use Module;
```

Since *use* is a compiler directive, the module is loaded as soon as the compiler sees the directive. This means variables and functions from the module are available to the rest of your script.

NOTE   Some people debate whether Perl compiles scripts or not. To me the issue is irrelevant. Before actually evaluating any lines of code, its syntax is checked—at this point, Perl is acting like a compiler.

If you need to access some of the names in the *@EXPORT_OK* array, use a statement like this:

```
# Make everything except for $varTwo
# available.
```

```
use Module qw(:DEFAULT funcTwo);
```

Once you add optional elements to the *use* directive you need to explicitly list all of the names that you want to use. The *:DEFAULT* is a short way of saying, "give me everything in the *@EXPORT* list."

When more than one module is logically connected to another, they are both placed in a subdirectory of the *lib* directory. For example, most Perl distributions include a *Math* directory which include the files *BigFloat.pm*, *BigInt.pm*, and *Complex.pm*. The subdirectory name is referenced when the files are loaded, using double colons in front of the module name in the *use* statement, like this:

```
use Math::BigFloat;
```

Some modules use constructors and destructors to provide initialization and cleanup services. The module constructor is called the *BEGIN* block, while the module destructor is called the *END* block.

BEGIN blocks are evaluated as soon as they are defined. Therefore, they can include other functions using *do* or *require* statements. Since the blocks are evaluated immediately after definition, multiple *BEGIN* blocks execute in the order they appear in the script. Listing 6.5 shows a script that uses a *BEGIN* block in two different packages, the main package and the *Foo* package.

Listing 6.5 *begin.pl—Using BEGIN blocks*

```perl
#!/usr/bin/perl

# This is the constructor for the main package.
BEGIN {
    print("main\n");
}

# This is the constructor for the Foo package.
package Foo;
    BEGIN {
        print("Foo\n");
    }
```

Here is an example of this script in action:

```
% perl begin.pl
main
Foo
```

END blocks are evaluated just before a script ends. They are even evaluated after **exit** or **die** functions are called. Therefore, they can be used to close files or write messages to log files. Multiple *END* blocks are evaluated in reverse order.

Listing 6.6 *end.pl—Using END blocks*

```
#!/usr/bin/perl

# This is the destructor for the main package.
END {
  print("main\n");
}

# This is the destructor for the Foo package.
package Foo;
  END {
    print("Foo\n");
  }
```

Here is an example of this script in action:

```
% perl end.pl
Foo
main
```

There's only one more topic related to modules that I'd like to cover, using pragmas. A *pragma* is a compiler directive. During the stage where Perl checks the syntax of your script, you can use a pragma to affect Perl's behavior. Some pragmas can also affect the actual running of your script.

Table 6.8 shows a list of the pragmas you can use.

Table 6.8 *Perl's Pragmas*

Pragma	Description
integer	Forces integer math instead of floating point or double precision math.
less	Requests less of something—like memory or cpu time—from the compiler. This pragma has not been implemented yet.
sigtrap	Enables stack backtracing on unexpected signals.
strict	Restricts unsafe constructs. This pragma is highly recommended! Every program should use it.
subs	Lets you predeclare function names.

You can find more information about Perl's modules and pragmas by using the **perldoc perlmod** command.

Summary

This chapter is a brief introduction to Perl. Its purpose is to expose you to a lot of concepts in a short amount of time and space. You now have the knowledge needed to understand other programmers' Perl scripts and, perhaps, to write a few of your own.

In the beginning, Larry Wall dreamt of Perl and life was good. Then, other programmers on the Internet joined forces with Larry and life got even better. Perl is now a full-fledged portable programming language with support for file I/O, pattern matching using regular expressions, reporting features, special variables, references, objects, modules, source-level debugging, and many command-line options.

Perl has three types of variables: scalars, arrays, and hashes. Scalar variables can hold a single unit of information—either text or numeric. Arrays hold a list of scalar values. Hashes hold key-value pairs. Each type of variable uses a different character to begin the variable name: Scalars use $, arrays use @, and hashes use %.

Operators tell Perl which actions to perform at a very low level. Operators are combined with variables and function calls to create statements. Statements are combined to create functions. And functions are combined to create packages or modules.

In this chapter you learn about decision and loop statements. Both types of statements are vital to properly control your program's logic. Decision statements let you choose between two options, while loop statements let you repeatedly execute a group of statements.

Perl, like nearly all other computer languages, can manipulate files. The **open** function is used to form a connection between a file handle and a file. The diamond operator (<>) is used to read a record. And the **close** function is used to shut down the connection between a file handle and a file. The **binmode** function is briefly mentioned as being responsible for ensuring that binary data files are read and written correctly. The file section also mentions Perl's file test operators and how they are used to determine many things—such as size of a file and whether it is read-only.

Next, a short description of objects and object-oriented programming is presented. I hope enough information was presented so you have an understanding of object terminology and can read other people's programs. However, if you need to create more than a few small objects, consider reading a book devoted specifically to object-oriented programming.

Object-oriented programming has its own terminology. This terminology lets you think of objects in a manner independent of computer language. After describing the object or class as a set of properties (information) and methods (functions), the class can be programmed using C++, Perl, or Delphi. The programming language is relegated to the role of an implementation detail.

The four big concepts in object-oriented programming are abstraction, encapsulation, inheritance, and polymorphism. *Abstraction* means to isolate the access of a property from how it's stored. *Encapsulation* means that properties and the methods that act on them are defined together. *Inheritance* means that one class (the child) can be derived from another (the parent), and the child class will have all the properties and methods defined in the parent. *Polymorphism* means that the child class can override properties and methods defined in the parent simply by using the same property or method name.

The chapter shows you how to initialize properties by passing values to an object's **new** function. With this technique, you can use named parameters and therefore create partly initialized objects if needed. Child classes in Perl will not automatically inherit properties from parent classes. However, using anonymous hashes totally avoids this issue because the parent constructor can be explicitly called to create the object. Then, the child can simply add entries to the anonymous hash.

Last, modules are mentioned. Modules are used to group a set of functions and variables together. You read about several guidelines that should be followed when creating modules. For example, package names should have their first letter capitalized and use file extensions of *pm*.

Modules are loaded with the *use* directive. In addition to loading the module, *use* moves variable and function names into the *main* namespace where your script can easily access them. Exporting the names is accomplished using the *@EXPORT* and *@EXPORT_OK* arrays.

You also read about the *BEGIN* and *END* blocks, which are module constructors and destructors. The *BEGIN* block is evaluated as soon as it is defined. *END* blocks are evaluated just before your program ends—in reverse order. The last *END* block defined is the first to be evaluated.

The *use* directive also controls other directives, called pragmas. The most useful pragmas are *integer* and *strict*. Use the *integer* pragma when you need fast integer math. And use *strict* all of the time to enforce good programming habits—like using local variables.

One chapter isn't sufficient to introduce you to Perl in any meaningful way. Still, you've now been exposed to most of Perl's features and syntax. If you need to become proficient in Perl, please continue your research using the Internet. You might start with Chapter 7, the next chapter, which introduces you to Tcl. This relatively new language has been rapidly growing in popularity. Chapter 7, "Using Tcl," covers the basics of functions, file handling, and other important features of the language.

Using Tcl/Tk

This chapter gives you the lowdown on the widely used Tcl language. It teaches you the Tcl basics—substitution, grouping, and creating valid Tcl commands—and takes a look at Tcl's ready-made functions and its support for file handling. Like Perl, Tcl provides some convenient string-handling commands based on regular expressions. You'll find a detailed discussion of regular expressions and related concepts in Chapter 8, "Pattern Matching."

First things first: Tcl is an acronym for Tool Command Language, and Tcl aficionados pronounce the language's name "tickle," trying not to blush as they say it. Tcl was developed by Dr. John Osterhout in the late 1980's. The "tools" in question are software tools, i.e., application programs that do useful things. Tcl was originally developed to script the behavior of the applications that Osterhout and his students created. Much to Osterhout's surprise, Tcl quickly caught on as a general-purpose programming language.

Tcl has been ported to all major platforms, including the major implementations of Unix, the various flavors of Windows, the MacOS, and even to BeOS. Tcl/Tk is often touted as "the cross-platform scripting language," because the Tcl development team has made a conscious effort to make Tcl scripts as portable as possible.

Tcl is a great language for little tasks, such as little five-line utility programs. After all, that's the use it was originally intended to serve. As it turns out, Tcl enthusiasts have also built very large programs in Tcl with excellent results.

One of Tcl's great strengths, and arguably the reason Tcl is so widely used, is that it is readily extensible. Tcl was designed so that developers could easily implement their own additions to the Tcl language—essentially, create their own commands—by writing the extensions in C. Many such extensions have been publicly released, such as *Tcl/Tk* and *Expect*. Furthermore, it's easy for developers to build Tcl into applications as a scripting language for the application, much the same way that Microsoft's Visual Basic for Applications is used as the scripting language for Microsoft's suite of office applications.

The Features of Tcl

Why should you spend time learning Tcl? Look at some of its many features:

Completeness: Tcl is a *bona fide* procedural programming language that supports all of the necessary elements—including variables, decision statements, iteration statements, and recursion—that you need to write any program you like.

Data Structures: Tcl offers a few simple data structures— simple variables, which can hold numbers or strings (transparently converting the format as needed); lists, which contain non-indexed sequences of data; and arrays, which contain indexed lists of data.

File I/O: Tcl scripts can create and destroy files, read from and write to files, and gather basic information about files. It can also process files in any size chunks you like—byte by byte, or line by line.

Pattern Matching: Tcl has built-in support for regular expressions, which makes it a great language for processing text. Pattern matching based on regular expressions adds a whole new dimension of flexibility and power to searching operations, because you can find *patterns* of characters, rather than literal strings. For example, if you're processing an HTML document, you can use regular expressions to find all of the strings that begin with < and end with > —i.e., all of the HTML tags—in the document.

Internet Functionality: The latest implementation of Tcl (version 8.1) includes built-in commands to perform basic network operations. For example, with the single Tcl command **http_get,** you can download the contents of any web page you specify.

Dynamicism: Tcl is a dynamic language—a Tcl script can execute commands *that the script itself has created* as the script runs. In other words, a script can essentially re-write itself as it interacts with the user.

Error Handling: Tcl supports throw-and-catch style error-handling, which makes it easy to create scripts that are both robust (i.e., that handle unexpected results without script failure) and easy to read and modify.

As of this writing, version 8.1 is still in alpha testing, and some implementations of Tcl still don't support http_get.

Debugging: Tcl offers some special commands that make it easy to develop and debug scripts. For example, you can use Tcl's special **trace** command to execute a set of instructions when the value of a particular variable changes, or use the **info** command to gain access to information about the state of the Tcl interpreter.

Extensibility: If the need arises, you can write your own Tcl commands in C. Extending Tcl allows you to add powerful new features to the language without sacrificing Tcl's basic ease of use. There are plenty of freely available extensions to Tcl, including *Tcl/Tk* (which allows you to build a Windows-style graphic interface for your script), *Expect* (which allows your Tcl program to work with interactive programs or processes, such as remote log-ins) and *[incr tcl]* (which adds basic object-oriented programming features to Tcl).

Cross-Platform Compatibility: Tcl (and most Tcl extensions) have been ported to most varieties of Unix, Windows NT/95/98, BeOS, and MacOS. In most cases, Tcl scripts can run *without modification* when moved from platform to platform.

Introduction to Tcl

You'll need a Tcl interpreter on your system to work through the examples in this chapter. You can use tclsh (which behaves in a way that's very similar to Bash), or, if you have X-Windows available, you can use Wish, which is actually a Tcl/Tk interpreter. If you don't have a recent version of tclsh or Wish (which are both at 8.0 in final release and 8.1 in alpha release), point your preferred web browser at *http://www.scriptics.com* for information about downloading the latest binary and source releases.

TIP

Windows and Mac users can also find executable and source versions of tclsh and Wish at http://www.scriptics.com.

If you're not sure if Tcl is installed on your system, try the **which tclsh** command. Or if you're using X Windows, try the **which wish** command at the Bash shell prompt.

Once tclsh (or Wish) is installed on your system, you're ready to roll. Let's start by trying out the tclsh interpreter, which, for practical purposes, behaves like a basic Unix shell, such as Bash or tcsh. Start tclsh by typing its name at your shell's prompt:

```
bash> tclsh
%
```

You'll know that you are talking to Tcl, rather than to the shell, by the % prompt. If you're using X-Windows, you can use the Tcl interpreter built into Wish in exactly the same way that you use tclsh. Just use the Wish command at the shell prompt:

```
bash> wish
%
```

In a departure from my normal shell prompt, I will, in this chapter, use "bash>" for the Bash prompt. This should help to distinguish between executing commands at the Bash command line and executing commands at the Tcl command line. The Tcl command line is indicated by the % prompt.

NOTE

Wish creates a little window for itself that it uses to display any graphic user interface elements that it creates. Because you're only using Wish's Tcl interpreter, you can ignore or minimize the Wish window and concentrate, instead, on the command line.

NOTE

Once you're at Tcl's % prompt, take a look to see which version of Tcl you're working with, using Tcl's **info** command:

```
% info tclversion
8.1
```

As promised, tclsh behaves pretty much like Bash or the C shell and, under Unix, you can use the same commands at the tclsh prompt as you'd use at Bash:

```
% ls -l
myfile.txt
data.txt
hello.tcl
```

Naturally, you can give the Tcl interpreter Tcl commands as well. Here's our old friend *Hello, World* rendered in Tcl:

```
% puts "Hello, World"
Hello, World
```

If tclsh expects you to close an unfinished command (for example, if you have an open left brace with no matching right brace), it uses a pointed prompt (>) until the command is closed as shown here:

```
% puts {
>     Hello, World
> }
Hello, World
```

To bail out of tclsh or Wish and return to the Unix Shell prompt, use the **exit** command:

```
% exit
bash>
```

Of course, you won't want to type Tcl scripts line by line every time you want to execute a Tcl program. As with the Bash and Perl scripts presented earlier in this book, you can store your Tcl script in a text file and execute it whenever you like. To review how this works, use your favorite text editor to enter the script shown in Listing 7.1 and save it in a file called *dummy.tcl*.

Listing 7.1 *dummy.tcl—Using the* **puts** *Command*

```
#!/usr/local/bin/tclsh

puts "Hello, World"
```

Here is an example of this script in action:

```
bash> dummy.tcl
Hello, World
```

By now, the first line of code above probably looks a little familiar. Unix understands the first line as a specification of the program that is to be used to run the script. Tcl regards lines starting with the hash mark (#) as comments, and ignores them.

Your version of tclsh might reside somewhere other than your system's */usr/local/bin* directory. Use the command **which tclsh** at the shell prompt to find out where tclsh lives on your system.

A few moldy old versions of Unix might not understand the *#!* syntax. If you think this is the case on your system, check with your system administrator.

Make sure that the directory that contains *dummy.tcl* is in the system's *PATH*. (See Chapter 2, "Variables and Operators," for information about details about setting the *PATH* environment variable.)

You can execute your Tcl program from within tclsh (or Wish) using Tcl's **source** command. Using **source** is exactly like typing in the script line-by-line at the tclsh prompt. Here's how you'd use **source** to run *dummy.tcl*:

```
bash> tclsh
% source dummy.tcl
Hello, World
```

Understanding Substitution Concepts

Substitution is the heart and soul of Tcl. Once you've mastered substitution and grouping (explained in the next section), you'll be in a position to fully use the power of Tcl. If you don't understand substitution, you'll get frustrated quickly.

There are three basic kinds of substitution in Tcl: variable substitution, which substitutes the value of a variable for the variable's name in a command; command substitution, which replaces a command with the results of the command; and backslash substitution, which replaces a sequence of characters with a special character.

Variable Substitution

Variable substitution is similar to the kind of variable substitution that takes place in Bash . When you add the $ prefix to a variable's name in a Tcl command, the Tcl interpreter substitutes the value of the variable for the variable's name. For example, let's say that we store the value "Mugsy" in the variable named *friend*, like so:

```
% set friend Mugsy
Mugsy
```

Now, if we use *$friend* in a new command, the Tcl interpreter substitutes the value for the name, like so:

```
% puts $friend
Mugsy
```

Without the $ symbol to denote substitution, Tcl treats the variable's name as a literal value, just as it treats any other string of characters:

```
% puts friend
friend
```

Tcl doesn't do anything special with the value of the variable; it doesn't pad it with spaces or add an end-of-line character. The substituted value doesn't need to be part of the command's argument; it can be the command's name, or part of the name, or any slice of the command you like. For example, let's say you set up the following variables:

```
% set comm1 pu
pu
% set comm2 ts
ts
```

Variable substitution doesn't always happen: $ symbols inside a pair of braces are treated as literal $ characters. See the "Grouping with Braces" section later in this chapter for details.

Now, if we like, we can build a new command using substitution to create the whole command, from soup to nuts:

```
% $comm1$comm2 $friend
Mugsy
```

Let's analyze what happened here: Tcl substitutes *pu* for *$comm1* and *ts* for *$comm2*, so it replaces the aggregate *$comm1$comm2* with the aggregate *puts*, which happens to be a Tcl command. Tcl also replaces *$friend* with *Mugsy* so, after substitution, the final command is `puts Mugsy`. Tcl executes this command, just as it would if you had typed it in at the prompt.

Command Substitution

Command substitution behaves in a way that's similar to back-ticked strings in Bash. When a Tcl command is enclosed in square brackets, and the bracketed material is embedded in an "outer" Tcl command, the interpreter evaluates the bracketed material and replaces it with its value.

It's really not as complicated as it might sound. To see how command substitution works, let's use Tcl's **expr** command, which evaluates a mathematical expression, like so:

```
% expr 23 + 45
68
```

Let's say that we want to store the result of this command in a variable, called **result**. First, we wrap up the command that we want to evaluate in square brackets, like so: `[expr 23 + 45]` and embed the bracketed material inside a **set** command:

```
% set result [expr 23 + 45]
68
```

You can get as complicated as you like with command substitution, embedding commands within commands within commands:

```
% puts mirror_result [set result [expr 23 + 45]]
```

As you might suspect, this allows you to write very compact, and very cryptic, code.

Backslash Substitution

"Backslash substitution" is really Tcl's fancy name for "escape sequences." When the Tcl interpreter sees a backslash, it replaces the backslash and one or more subsequent characters with a special character. For example, when the interpreter sees the sequence \n, it replaces \n with the invisible newline character. Similarly, Tcl replaces \$ with $; this is handy when you really want to use a dollar sign inside a string, rather than using it as a marker for variable substitution. For example, variable substitution really screws up a command like this:

```
% set price $2.00
can't read "2": no such variable
```

Backslash substitution solves this problem; essentially, it lets the interpreter know that it shouldn't do variable substitution:

```
% set price \$2.00
$2.00
```

Backslash substitution is also commonly used to break Tcl commands across several lines. Ordinarily, the end-of-line character is used to mark the end of a Tcl command. For example, if we break the command:

```
% expr 1 + 2 + 3 + 4 + 5 + 6
```

onto two lines, the Tcl interpreter returns an error, as below:

```
% expr 1 + 2 + 3 +
syntax error in expression "1 + 2 + 3 +"
```

When we add a backslash to the end of the first line, Tcl replaces the backslash-newline sequence with a plain old space. In other words, as far as Tcl is concerned:

The Tcl interpreter doesn't always perform command substitution on square-bracketed material; square brackets inside a pair of curly braces are treated as literal bracket characters. See the "Grouping with Braces" section later in this chapter for details.

```
% expr 1 + 2 + 3 + \
> 4 + 5 + 6
```

is all on the same line.

Remember that braces override substitution: A backslash inside a pair of braces is just a backslash, not a substitution marker.

Backslash substitution is most helpful for working with Tcl's special grouping and substitution characters. Table 7.1 shows some of the more commonly used escape sequences.

Table 7.1 *Commonly Used Backslash Substitution Sequences*

Escape Sequence	Replacement Character
\$	$
\[	[
\]	]
\{	{
\}	}
\"	"
\\	\
\n	newline
\t	tab
\[newline]	space

Understanding Grouping Concepts

A good understanding of grouping and quoting is essential to the proper use of Tcl. As you learn in the next section of this chapter, Tcl treats all commands as a sequence of words. For example, the **puts** command, which you've already used a few times, looks like this:

```
puts ?channelID? string
```

Tcl assumes that a **puts** command containing two words should put its output to *STDOUT*—i.e., at the command prompt. (Not too surprising, right? After all, this is the same behavior that you see in Perl and shell languages.) If a **puts** command contains three words, the Tcl interpreter assumes that the second word in the

puts command is a channel-ID—a specification of a file, pipeline, socket, or whatever. Thus, trying to print out a string that contains a space creates an error:

```
% puts hello, world
can not find channel named "hello,"
```

In order to persuade Tcl that the phrase *hello world* is a single string, you must group the words together using special characters: braces ({}) or double quotes (" "). (Square brackets, which you will recall are used for command substitution, also serve to group the bracketed command into a single word.) To print out *hello, world* you can use:

```
% puts {hello, world}
hello, world
```

or

```
% puts "hello, world"
hello, world
```

Notice that, in both examples, the Tcl interpreter strips off the character used for grouping, leaving only the grouped material.

Grouping with Braces

Grouping with braces prevents all substitution within the braced material. For example:

```
% puts {these apples are $2\pound [sic]}
these apples are $2\pound [sic]
```

Tcl doesn't try to perform variable substitution on *$2*, it doesn't try to do command substitution on *[sic]*, and it doesn't do back-slash substitution on \\p (or \\pound or any substring thereof.) The interpreter simply outputs the grouped material, exactly as it appears.

If an end-of-line character falls between braces—in other words, if a left brace's matching right brace appears on a subsequent line—the end-of-line characters are treated as part of the grouped material, rather than as a sign that the command is over. A simple example:

```
% puts {hello,
world}
hello, world
```

In this case:

```
{hello,
world}
```

is a single "word," even though it's on two lines, because it is held together by braces. It is common Tcl-coding practice to use braces to break conditional and looping statements across more than one line. To see how this works, take a look at the following snippet of code:

```
if {$ctr = 10} {
    puts "hello, double digits"
}
```

As far as the Tcl interpreter is concerned, the code above consists of three words: the command name, **if**; the condition (the stuff inside the first pair of braces); and the script (the stuff between the second pair of braces). Because there's only one end-of-line character that isn't wrapped up in braces—namely, the end of line after the final brace—the Tcl interpreter treats the block as a single instruction.

Grouping With Quotes

Grouping material with double quotes also causes the Tcl interpreter to treat the grouped material as a single word. However, substitution can take place within quotes. Code like the following will cause the Tcl interpreter to return an error:

```
% puts "These oranges are $1.50 each"
```

Tcl tries to do variable substitution on *$1*. Unless you've set a variable called *1*, this command doesn't work.

You can use double quotes to group material across lines, i.e.:

```
% puts "hello,
world"
hello,
world
```

and you can even use quotes, rather than braces, to build multi-line constructions like the **if** command example that you looked at in the braces example. However, because the interpreter performs substitution on quote-grouped material *before* it evaluates the material, using double quotes to build multi-line structures is not recommended.

Data Structures

Tcl really only has two basic data structures: simple variables and arrays. Simple variables can hold all kinds of data: numbers, strings, and lists. Arrays contain an indexed list of simple variables and, as with Perl's hash tables, the array indices can be either strings or numbers.

One of the things that you'll commonly store in a simple variable is a list—say, a list of filenames or a list of names to be sorted. You don't need to create a special kind of variable in Tcl to store or manipulate a list—you can use a simple variable—but it's handy to think of a list as a special case, because Tcl offers a wide array of built-in tools for managing lists.

Simple Variables

A Tcl variable can hold just about anything that you care to put into it. You don't need to worry about declaring a variable before you use it, or making sure that a variable contains a certain kind of data. Tcl takes care of all of the details for you. For example, let's say that you want to put a number into a variable called x. You create the variable and set its value with a single **set** command:

```
% set x 25
25
```

Then, you can treat the variable as a number, and perform whatever mathematical operations you like on it:

```
% expr $x * 2
50
```

If you prefer to treat the variable as a string of characters, rather than as a number, you can do something like this:

```
% append x " dollars"
50 dollars
```

Tcl takes care of the conversion from number to string automatically; you don't need to explicitly cast or convert the variable before you add the characters to the end of the variable.

Lists

In Tcl, any list of strings separated by spaces can be treated as a list. For example, let's say you initialize a variable called *pets*:

```
% set pets "cats dogs birds"
cats dogs birds
```

Using Tcl's list-handling commands, you can treat the variable *pets* as a list with three elements. For example, you can sort the list with the **lsort** command:

```
% lsort $pets
birds cats dogs
```

or grab a slice, say the first element, of the list with **lrange**:

```
% lrange $pets 0 0
cats
```

Sometimes, of course, you'll want a list element to contain a space. For example, suppose you want to add *anole lizards* to your list. You want *anole* and *lizard* to stay together during sort operations, right? In order to make sure that the two words that make up the name stay together when you add them to the list, you group them with braces, like so:

```
% set pets2 "cats dogs {anole lizards}"
cats dogs {anole lizards}
```

I told you substitution and grouping was the soul of Tcl! As you can see above, Tcl retains the braces when it shows the whole list, to show you that the list item consists of more than one word. However, when you extract the individual item from the list, Tcl strips off the braces for you:

```
% foreach x $pets2 {
>     puts $x
> }
cats
dogs
anole lizards
```

Arrays

Tcl supports array variables. In Tcl, an array is a series of simple variables; each value in the array has its own unique index. Like Perl's hash (associative array) variables, the indices of an array can be a string. To reference a particular value in an array, you use the array's name, followed by the value's index. For example, let's say you have an array called *form_values*, and you'd like to create a value indexed by the string *name:*

```
% set form_values(name) David
David
```

Variable substitution works exactly the same for arrays as it does for simple variables. Thus, to access the *name* slot in *form_values*:

```
% puts $form_values(name)
David
```

Tcl offers a few special commands that you can use to work with array variables. To dump all of the index/value pairs in an array, you can use the **array get** command. For example, to dump the system's *env* variable (which Tcl represents as an array), you'd use:

```
% array get env
HOME c:\\ COMSPEC {C:\WINDOWS\COMMAND.COM} CMDLINE WIN TMP
{C:\WINDOWS\TEMP} WINBOOTDIR {C:\WINDOWS} PROMPT {$p$g}
CLASSPATH {.;C:\VisualCafe\JAVA\LIB;C:\VisualCafe\JAVA\LIB\
SYMCLASS.ZIP;C:\VisualCafe\JAVA\LIB\VECCLASS.ZIP;C:\VisualC
afe\JAVA\LIB\CLASSES.ZIP} PATH {C:\WINDOWS;C:\WINDOWS\
COMMAND;C:\DOS;C:\JDK1.1.3\BIN} WINDIR {C:\WINDOWS} BLASTER
{A220 I5 D1 T4} TEMP {C:\WINDOWS\TEMP}
```

Of course, it's often useful to step through each element of an array and process each value individually. To help with this, Tcl provides the handy **array names** command, which returns a list of all of the indices in an array. You can use **array names** with the **foreach** command to "walk" through each element of the *env* array like this:

The results returned by array get is a list, and you can use Tcl's list-handling tools to work with it.

```
foreach x [array names env] {
    puts "$x"
    # do something interesting with $env($x) here, if you
like
}
```

Using Statements

Now that you've had a basic introduction to the fundamental Tcl concepts of substitution and grouping, and understand Tcl's variables, let's take a look at the construction of basic Tcl statements. Tcl syntax is very simple indeed; every Tcl command is a series of strings, starting with a Tcl command name or procedure name. Period.

This approach is a little different from what you'll find in Perl, shell languages, and languages like C. For example, in a Perl construction like the following, the braces are part of the **if** command's proper syntax, and the Perl compiler will return an error if it can't find the proper punctuation in the expected place (keep in mind that that Perl is not an especially picky language).

```
if $variable {
   `pwd`
}
```

In Tcl, the braces aren't an integral part of the **if** command, and the Tcl interpreter won't return an error if it doesn't see braces. Rather, Tcl expects to see two words after the **if** command, followed by an end-of-line character or semicolon. For example, the following is a perfectly valid (if not especially useful) Tcl command:

```
% if $variable pwd
```

In most real-world situations, the script part of **if** commands is more complex than single-word commands, and so braces are used to group the script into a single Tcl word. However, it is important to understand that the braces are not really part of the command syntax.

Building a Statement

We can divide a Tcl command into four basic components:

Command name: The name of one of Tcl's built-in commands or the name of a procedure that you've written. Every legal command must contain a command name.

Switches: Some Tcl commands support switches, used in much the same way as the switches that you use when you invoke certain

Unix commands like **ls** or **mkdir**. For example, Tcl's **puts** command supports a *–nonewline* switch, which suppresses the new line character that Tcl ordinarily adds when it prints.

Options: Often, a set of related Tcl commands are grouped together under a single command name. *Command options* are used to differentiate between such commands. For example, to get information about the variables defined in the current script, you would use **info vars**; to get information about the version of Tcl that the interpreter supports, you'd use **info tclversion**. In both cases, the command name is **info** but, in the first case, the command option is **vars**, and in the second case, the option is **tclversion**.

Arguments: Many Tcl commands take arguments (i.e., data) for the command to do something with. For example, the **expr** command takes a mathematical expression as an argument and makes itself useful by evaluating the command.

Tcl's Built-in Commands

This section details the commands that are built into Tcl, and, where appropriate, describes important command options. Note that the table does not contain mathematical functions (such as *sin* and *cos*) that are supported by the **expr** command. These functions and Tcl's logical and mathematical operators are documented in Table 7.2.

Table 7.2 *Tcl's Built-in Commands*

Command	Description
append	Concatenates a string to the end of a variable without adding any blank spaces or delimiting characters.
array exists	Determines whether or not an array has been defined.
array get	Returns an array element for a specific array index.
array names	Returns a list of the indices of an array.

Table 7.2 *Tcl's Built-in Commands (Cont'd)*

Command	Description
array set	Creates a new array.
array size	Returns the size of an array, reckoned in the number of index/value pairs.
array startsearch	Iterates through an array.
array nextelement	Returns the next array index in a *startsearch* iteration.
array anymore	Determines if a *startsearch* iteration has returned all of the elements of the array.
array donesearch	Cancels a *startsearch* iteration.
break	Causes the interpreter to jump out of the body of the current command; usually used with looping commands such as **while.**
catch	Executes a block of code (defined within the error command) when the interpreter returns an error.
cd	Changes the current directory (functionally equivalent to the Unix **cd** command).
close	Closes an open channel, such as a file, pipeline, or stream.
concat	Adds a string to the end of a variable.
continue	Skips the rest of the current loop of a looping command (such as **while**), without bailing out of the looping construct completely.
eof	Tests for the end of a file.
error	Causes the Tcl interpreter to return an error.
eval	Evaluates a string as a Tcl command.
exec	Executes a string as a Unix command *in a separate process* from the Tcl interpreter.

Table 7.2 *Tcl's Built-in Commands (Cont'd)*

Command	Description
exit	Terminates execution of the current Tcl script.
expr	Evaluates a string as a mathematical expression.
file atime	Returns the last access time for a file.
file dirname	Returns the name of the directory that contains a file.
file executable	Tests whether or not a file is executable by the current user.
file exists	Tests whether or not a file has been created.
file extension	Returns the extension (if it exists) after the final dot in a file's name.
file isdirectory	Tests whether or not a filename is a directory.
file isfile	Tests whether or not a file is an ordinary file.
file mtime	Returns the time at which the file was last modified.
file owned	Tests whether or not a file is owned by the current user.
file readable	Tests whether or not a file can be read by the current user.
file rootname	Returns the name of the file *stripped of the file's extension, if it exists.*
file size	Returns the size of a file in bytes, or returns an error if the file does not exist.
file stat	Returns an array of system information about a file, including atime, ctime, dev, gid, ino, mode, mtime, nlink, size, type, uid.
file tail	Returns a file's root and extension without the file's directory path.

Table 7.2 *Tcl's Built-in Commands (Cont'd)*

Command	Description
file type	Returns information about the basic type of a file.
file writable	Tests whether a file is writable by the current user.
flush	Flushes any data that has been buffered for output to a file (or channel), but has not been written to the file or channel.
for	Repeats a command or block of commands a certain number of times.
foreach	Repeats a command or block of commands for each element in a list.
format	Prints a string in a particular format.
gets	Reads a line from the command line, a file, pipeline, or other stream.
glob	Returns all filenames in the current (or specified) directory that match a simple variable.
global	Specifies that a variable is a *global* variable to be used by the whole Tcl script, rather than a *local* variable for the use of a procedure.
history	Returns a list of recent commands.
history add	Adds a command's name to the list of commands that history returns.
history	Alters an entry in the list of commands stored in history.
history keep	Alters the number of commands that the history utility stores.
history redo	Re-executes a command stored in the history list.
history substitute	Substitutes a new command for an existing command in the history list.

Table 7.2 *Tcl's Built-in Commands (Cont'd)*

Command	Description
if	Executes commands conditionally (Tcl's basic branching command).
incr	Adds one to a number (similar to Perl and C's ++ operator).
info args	Returns the names of all of the arguments of the current procedure.
info body	Returns the commands in the body of the current procedure.
info commands	Returns a list of all commands, including Tcl's built-in commands, and commands that have been defined with **proc**.
info complete	Tests an expression to make sure that it is a valid Tcl command.
info exists	Tests whether or not a variable or procedure has been defined.
info globals	Returns a list of all of the *global* variables in the current script.
info level	Returns the current level of the stack.
info locals	Returns a list of all of the *local* variables in the current procedure.
info procs	Returns a list of all of the procedures that have been defined with the **proc** command.
info tclversion	Returns information about the version of Tcl that is implemented by the interpreter.
info vars	Returns a list of all of the variables defined in the current Tcl environment, including both user-defined variables and variables that the interpreter automatically creates.

Table 7.2 *Tcl's Built-in Commands (Cont'd)*

Command	Description
join	Makes a string out of a list, optionally adding a delimiter (such as a comma) between elements.
lappend	Adds a new element to the end of a list.
lindex	Returns the list item at a particular position in a list.
linsert	Adds an item at a particular spot in a list.
list	Makes a string into a list.
llength	Returns the number of items in a list.
lrange	Returns a sublist of the items between two positions in a list.
lreplace	Replaces an item or range of items in a list with new item(s).
lsearch	Searches through a list for a particular item.
lsort	Sorts a list.
open	Opens a file (or a pipeline or socket or other kind or stream).
pid	Returns the process ID of a process that has been opened with the **open** command.
proc	Creates a new Tcl procedure.
puts	Writes a string to the display, to a file, or to a pipeline or any other kind of string.
pwd	Prints the working directory (i.e., the same as the basic Unix **pwd** command).
read	Reads data from a file, from the command prompt, or from a socket or any other kind of string.
regexp	Tests a string against a regular expression.
regsub	Substitutes characters within a string, based on regular expression matching.

Table 7.2 *Tcl's Built-in Commands (Cont'd)*

Command	Description
rename	Renames a file or a directory.
return	Returns a value from a Tcl procedure.
scan	Parses a string and puts the results into a variable or variables.
seek	Moves to a particular position within a file or input string.
set	Creates a new variable and sets its value, or sets the value of an existing variable.
source	Runs the Tcl script contained in a file or input stream.
split	Parses a string into a list.
string compare	Tests the lexicographical ordering of two strings.
string first	Returns the index of the first instance of a substring in a string.
string index	Finds the character at a particular position within a string.
string last	Returns the index value of the last instance of a substring within a string.
string length	Returns the length (in characters) of a string.
string match	Determines whether or not two strings match.
string range	Returns the substring between two indices within a string.
string tolower	Returns a lowercase version of a string.
string toupper	Returns an uppercase version of a string.
string trim	Chops off specified leading and trailing characters from a string.
string trimleft	Chops off specified leading characters from a string.

Table 7.2 *Tcl's Built-in Commands (Cont'd)*

Command	Description
string trimright	Chops off specified trailing characters from a string.
subst	Performs substitution on a Tcl command *without evaluating the command.*
switch	Executes one of several blocks of commands.
tell	Returns the current position in a file.
time	Times the execution of a block of commands.
trace	Executes a command when a variable is accessed.
unset	Removes a variable.
uplevel	Executes a script at a different level of the call stack.
upvar	Links to a variable that has been defined at a different level of the call stack; essentially used to pass variables by reference, rather than by value.
while	Creates basic looping control structure.

Expr Commands

In addition to its wide range of built-in commands, Tcl supports many mathematical and logical functions and operators. These functions can't be used as standalone Tcl commands, but they're useful in the context of an **expr** command or a control command, such as **if** or **while**.

For example, suppose that you're interested in calculating square roots. Using Tcl's **sqrt** function at the Tcl prompt returns an error:

```
% sqrt(36)
invalid command name "sqrt(36)"
```

However, using the function makes perfect sense inside an **expr** command:

```
% expr {sqrt(36)}
6.0
```

Tcl also recognizes functions and operators in certain other places, such as the expression part of an **if** command:

```
if {sqrt($x) > 5} {
    puts "$x is more than 25 (or less than [nd]25)"
}
```

Table 7.3 summarizes the mathematical functions built into Tcl.

Table 7.3 *Tcl's Mathematical Functions*

Function	Description
abs(x)	Calculates the absolute value of *x*.
acos(x)	Calculates an *arc cosine*.
asin(x)	Calculates an *arc sine*.
atan(x)	Calculates an *arc tangent*.
ceil(x)	Calculates the *smallest integer* that is *greater than or equal to x*.
cos (x)	Calculates a *cosine*.
cosh(x)	Calculates a *hyperbolic cosine*.
double(x)	Makes *x* into a *floating point number*. This is for display purposes only; Tcl does conversions as necessary for mathematical calculations).
exp(x)	Calculates *e* to the xth power.
floor(x)	Calculates the *largest integer* that is *less than or equal to x*.
fmod(x,y)	Calculates the floating point remainder of *x/y*. For example, *fmod(10,3) = 1*.
hypot(x,y)	Calculates the *square root* of $x^2 + y^2$, i.e., the length of the hypotenuse of the right triangle whose sides are *x* and *y*.
int(x)	Makes *x* into an *integer*. This is for display purposes only; Tcl does conversions as necessary for mathematical calculations).
log(x)	Calculates the *logarithm* of *x*.
pow(x,y)	Calculates *x* to the yth power.

Table 7.3 *Tcl's Mathematical Functions (Cont'd)*

Function	Description
round(x)	Rounds off *x* to the nearest integer.
sin(x)	Calculates the *sine* of *x*.
sinh(x)	Calculates the *hyperbolic sine* of *x*.
sqrt(x)	Calculates the *square root* of *x*.
tan(x)	Calculates the *tangent* of *x*.
tanh(x)	Calculates the *hyperbolic tangent* of x.

Table 7.4 summarizes the operators supported by Tcl.

Table 7.4 *Tcl's Operators*

Operator	Description
~	The bitwise *not* operator flips all of the bits in a value, i.e., calculates the value's complement.
!	The logical *not* operator changes false to true and true to false in expressions that calculate true values.
+	The *plus* operator adds two values together.
[nd]	The *minus* operator subtracts one value from another. The minus sign is also used to create negative numbers.
\	The *reference* operator creates a reference to a value. A reference is essentially a pointer to the value; it is used to pass arrays and hashes into functions. See the "Using References" section for more information.
=~ and !~	The *binding* operators force Perl to perform pattern matching operations on a variable other than $_. See the "Using Regular Expressions" section for more information.
*	The *multiplication* operator multiplies one value by another.
/	The *division* operator divides one value by another.

Table 7.4 *Tcl's Operators (Cont'd)*

Operator	Description
%	The *modulus* operator returns the remainder of the division of one value into another. For example, *8 % 3* evaluates to *2*.
x	The *repetition* operator repeats a text string for a given number of times. For example, *'a' x 5* evaluates to *'aaaaa'*.
.	The string *concatenation* operator combines one string with another. For example, *'abc' . 'abc'* evaluates to *'abcabc'*.
>>	The bitwise *right shift* operator shifts each bit in a value to the right by a given number of places. For example, *64 >> 2* evaluates to *16*. If you don't know what the term "bitwise" means, don't worry—you'll probably never need to use this operator.
<<	The bitwise *left shift* operator shifts each bit in a value to the left by a given number of places. For example, *64 << 2* evaluates to *256*. If you don't know what the term "bitwise" means, don't worry—you'll probably never need to use this operator.
==, !=	The numeric *equality* and *non-equality* operators are used in conditional expressions.
<, >	The numeric *less-than* and *greater-than* operators are used in conditional expressions.
<=, >=	The numeric *less-than-or-equal-to* and *greater-than-or-equal-to* operators are used in conditional expressions.
&, |, ^	The bitwise *and*, *or*, and *xor* operators are used to perform operations on specific bits in a value. If you don't know what the term "bitwise" means, don't worry—you'll probably never need to use these operators.
&&, ||	The logical *and* and logical *or* operators are used in conditional expressions.

Table 7.4 *Tcl's Operators (Cont'd)*

Operator	Description
?:	The ternary *conditional* operator chooses between two values based on the evaluation of a conditional expression. For example, `$numBooks < 5000 ? "Small Library" : "Big Library"` evaluates to *"Small Library"* only if the value of the *$numBooks* variable is less than *5000*. Otherwise, the evaluate results in *"Big Library"*.

Writing Procedures

If Tcl doesn't supply a built-in command to perform a particular function, you can write your own procedure to handle it. Breaking down your script into separate procedures makes it easier to develop your program and makes it easier for you (or someone else) to alter or debug your script later.

For example, let's say you're writing a little script that calculates hex numbers from RGB color values: You want the user to type in the RGB value, such as (51, 102, 102), and have the script return the hex value #336666, so you can plug the hex value into an HTML document in the expected format. It makes sense to break out the actual calculation into a separate procedure. Let's call the new procedure *rgbToHex*. We use the **proc** command to define the new procedure, like so:

```
proc rgbToHex args {
  set hexValue #
  foreach x $args {
    append hexValue [format %02x $x]
  }
  return $hexValue
}
```

Notice that the procedure doesn't read the RGB specification from the command prompt, or do any error checking to make sure that the RGB specification is in the right format; it simply calculates the value and spits it out. That's the way procedures should work in Tcl (and in every language, for that matter). A procedure does one thing, and does it well.

Let's take a closer look at the key lines in the *regToHex* procedure. If you look carefully, you'll see that the whole procedure definition is one big Tcl command; there are no "naked" end-of-line characters that aren't wrapped up in a pair of braces. Thus, as far as the Tcl interpreter is concerned, the procedure consists of four words:

proc   The command name of the command that defines the procedure.

rgbToHex The name of the new procedure that we are defining.

args   The name of the argument(s) that are passed to the procedure. If you use the name *args*, you can pass a list of any length to the procedure, and Tcl will store the list in *args*.

and the body of the command consists of:

```
{
set hexValue #
    foreach x $args {
        append hexValue [format %x $x]
    }
return $hexValue
}
```

Defining a procedure does not cause the procedure to execute immediately. If you type in the *rgbToHex* procedure definition at the prompt, you'll notice that tclsh does not return a hex value; it simply puts up the familiar Tcl prompt to acknowledge that it has accepted the procedure definition. Once you have defined a command with **proc**, you can use the command just like you'd use any of Tcl's built-in commands. For example:

```
% rgbToHex 255 102 204
#ff66cc
```

The Tcl interpreter takes anything after the procedure's name and "feeds" it to the procedure. In the case of *rgbToHex*, it stores the list whose elements are *255*, *102*, and *204* in the simple variable called *args*.

Tcl ordinarily uses local variables in procedures. When you define a variable inside a procedure, the variable doesn't exist outside the procedure—therefore it is called *local*. For example:

```
% proc localVarExample {} {
>    set a 100
> }
% puts $a
can't read "a": no such variable
```

Even if you define a variable with the same name outside a procedure, the procedure's local variable does not affect the global variable defined in the main body of the script. For example:

```
% set a 50
% proc localVarExample {} {
>    set a 100
> }
% localVarExample
100
% puts $a
50
```

Sometimes, however, you do want to change a global variable from within a procedure. Tcl provides a special command, **global**, to handle this situation:

```
% set a 50
% proc localVarExample {} {
>    global a
>    set a 100
> }
% localVarExample
100
% puts $a
100
```

Standard Control Structures

When you use tclsh or Wish to type commands at a Tcl prompt, you don't really need to worry about control structures or the order of program execution. You simply type a command, and Tcl executes the command immediately.

When Tcl executes a script that you have written to a file, it moves in an orderly fashion, executing commands from top to bottom. If there are any procedures defined in the script, Tcl executes the procedure definition, but does not actually execute the procedure until you call the procedure.

However, when you are writing a more complex script, you probably want to use control structures—*conditional statements*, which execute commands or blocks of commands selectively and *looping structures*, which repeat commands or blocks for a certain number of repetitions. Tcl offers a basic set of conditional statements and looping structures.

Conditional Statements

Tcl offers two basic commands that handle conditions: **if** and **switch**.

You had a peek at the **if** command earlier in this chapter. Basically, **if** executes a command or a block of commands if a test expression evaluates to true. Optionally, the **if** command can include an alternate command or command block to execute if the test conditional expression evaluates to false. Thus, **if** is a three- or five-word command:

```
if condition command(s)
```

or

```
if condition command(s) else alternate-commands
```

Here's an example of how **if** (with an *else* clause) might look in real world code:

```
if {$x == black} {
    puts "The color is black"
} else {
    puts "The color is white"
}
```

Remember that the brackets are there for grouping purposes and are not part of the command itself. Before Tcl evaluates the conditional expression, it strips off any braces.

The **switch** command is handy for handling strings that have several different values. You can associate a block of code with any number of strings (or regular expression patterns); if **switch** matches its argument string with any of the strings that are associated with blocks of code, it executes the appropriate code.

For example, consider the following code:

```
% proc trySwitch color {
>     switch $color {
>         red {puts "Apples are red."}
>         blue {puts "The sky is blue."}
>         green {puts "Kermit is green, and it's not easy."}
>         default {puts "Sorry, I don't know that color."}
>     }
> }
% trySwitch red
Apples are red.
% trySwitch yellow
Sorry, I don't know that color.
```

In this example, the **switch** command tests the contents of the variable color against the strings *red, blue,* and *green.* If the value of color matches one of these strings, the **switch** command executes the block that appears immediately after the string. If the **switch** command doesn't match the value of color to one of the strings supplied in the command, it executes the string that appears after the keyword **default**.

Looping Commands

Tcl supports three basic looping commands that you can use to repeatedly execute a command or block of commands. Table 7.5 briefly describes the **while**, **for**, and **foreach** commands.

Table 7.5 *Tcl's Looping Commands*

Command	Description	Format
while	Repeatedly evaluates a statement as long as the test-expression is true. The statement block is never evaluated if the condition is false.	while *test-expression body*
for	Repeatedly evaluates a statement block. Loop termination is typically controlled by a count variable.	for *setup test final body*
foreach	Evaluates a statement block for each element in an array.	foreach *var list body*

The **while** statement is probably the simplest of the looping statements; it simply repeats a block over and over again until the specified test expression evaluates to false. (Be aware that if you're not careful with your test expression, the loop might never end!) For example, the following snippet of code loops through a list of names until it has printed all of the names that start with the letters A through M:

```
% set names "Abe Chuck Ethan Fergie\
Gramps Jim Larry Nathan Pops\
Sam Tim Zach"
% set ctr 0
% while {[string compare N [lindex $names $ctr]] > 0} {
>       puts [lindex $names $ctr]
>       incr ctr
> }
Abe
Chuck
Ethan
Fergie
Gramps
Jim
Larry
```

The key part of this code is the test expression:

```
{[string compare N [lindex $names $ctr]] > 0}
```

If a list element starts with a letter alphabetically preceding the letter *N*, the **string match** returns *1*, so the test expression is true, and the body of the loop is executed. However, if a list element starts with a letter alphabetically following *N*, **string match** returns *-1*, so the test expression evaluates to false, and the loop exits.

The **for** command is typically used to iterate a fixed number of times. For example, to print out the first five elements of the list stored in the variable names, we would use a **for** command that looks like this:

```
% for {set i 0} {$i <= 4} {incr i} {
    puts [lindex $names $i]
}
Abe
Chuck
Ethan
Fergie
Gramps
```

Finally, the **foreach** command is used to repeat a command or block once for each element in a list. It's a snap to print out each of the elements in our list stored in *names*:

```
% foreach x $names {
>       puts $x
> }
Abe
Chuck
Ethan
Fergie
Gramps
Jim
Larry
Nathan
Pops
Sam
Tim
Zach
%
```

Sometimes, you'll just need to bail out of a loop in the middle (it happens to the best of us). Tcl offers two special commands for loop control: **break** and **continue**. The **break** command quits out of the loop command completely, as demonstrated in the following code:

```
% for {set i 0} {$i < 5} {incr i} {
>       if {$i == 3} break
>       puts $i
> }
0
1
2
```

The **continue** command bails out of the current iteration of the loop, but doesn't quit out of the loop completely. Take a close look at the output of the following code—the third loop didn't print, but the fourth generation did.

```
% for {set i 0} {$i < 5} {incr i} {
>       if {$i == 3} continue
>       puts $i
> }
0
1
2
4
```

Using Files

Tcl offers basic support for reading from and writing to files and other kinds of text streams, such as pipelines. Tcl's not quite as slick as Perl in this particular department, but it gets the job done.

Reading From Files

There are three essential steps in reading from a file in Tcl:

1. Open the file with the **open** command.

2. TRead a line from the file with **gets**, or read a fixed number of bytes with **read**. (Repeat this step as necessary to work your way through the file.)

3. Close the file with **close**.

When you use Tcl's **open** command, it returns a unique ID code for the file; you'll need this code for reads from the file and to close the file. It's a standard Tcl idiom to store the ID code in a variable with a name like *myStream* or *myFile*:

```
% set myFile [open thefile.txt]
file2
```

Tcl creates a unique ID for each file that you open, so the Tcl interpreter will not necessarily return file2 as a code for your own open command.

To read a line of code from the current file and put it in a variable called *line,* you use the **gets** command, like so:

```
% gets $myFile line
This is the first line of thefile.txt
```

Typically, you'll want to loop through each line of the file, using the **eof** command to test whether or not you've reached the end of the file. The following code loops through a file and prints it out, line by line:

```
% while {[eof $myFile] == 0} {
>     gets $myFile line
>     puts $line
> }
```

Finally, you'll want to close the file with the close command, like so:

```
close $myFile
```

To read from a pipeline, you use the pipe character and the Unix command's name in the **open** command. For example, to read a list of current users, you'd use a command like this:

```
% set myStream [open |users]
```

Reading from a pipeline and closing the pipeline are handled exactly as if the pipeline were a file.

Writing to Files

If you wish to open a file for writing or appending, you'll need to add an additional argument to the **open** command. This argument is a Tcl-specific code that tells the interpreter what you plan to do with the file. For example, to write to a file, replacing its current contents, you add the **w** code, like so:

```
open thefile.txt w
```

Table 7.6 summarizes the codes used for the **open** command.

Table 7.6 *The Code Used with Tcl's **open** Command*

Code	Description
r	Opens an existing file for reading only. (This is the default.)
r+	Opens an existing file for reading and writing.
w	Opens an existing file for writing only, clobbering any contents that the file contains; if the file does not exist, creates a new file.
w+	Opens an existing file for writing and reading, clobbering any contents that the file contains; if the file does not exist, creates a new file.
a	Opens an existing file for writing only, appending any new content to the end of the current contents.
a+	Opens an existing file for writing and reading, appending any new content to the end of the current contents.

To write to a file, you use the standard **puts** command, adding the file ID between the command name and the string to be written. For example, to create a file that contains the message "Hello, World," you'd use the following:

```
% set myOutfile [open newfile.txt w]
% puts $myOutfile "Hello, World"
% close $myOutfilen
```

Beyond the Shell

The core Tcl language is really only your first taste of the Tcl family of tools. Much of Tcl's popularity stems from Tcl extensions, such as *Tk* and *Expect*, and the ease with which developers can write new, custom extensions to Tcl. Tcl extensions allow you to leverage the Tcl syntax that you have mastered, and to apply your skills with powerful new tools.

Tk is probably the most famous and widely used Tcl extension. In fact, *Tk* is so useful, and so easy to use, that it has been adapted for use with other scripting languages, such as Perl and Scheme. Tcl/Tk (as the extended language is called) allows you to quickly develop a graphical front end for Tcl scripts.

You'll need to use Wish, rather than tclsh, to try the little program below. Tclsh does not support *Tk*. If you've been using Wish throughout the chapter and you minimized the display window, be sure to bring it back!

NOTE

Let's walk through a simple example of Tcl/Tk. Remember the little procedure that performed RGB-to-hex conversions? Let's build a simple interface that make it easy for point-and-click users to perform conversions. First, we'll need the little engine that does all of the work:

```
% proc rgbToHex args {
> set hexValue #
> foreach x $args {
>       append hexValue [format %02x $x]
>    }
> return $hexValue
> }
```

Now, we'll use Tk to build entry boxes where users can type in values for red, green, and blue values, and an entry box to hold the resulting hex value. To build an entry box, we use Tk's **entry** command, like so:

```
% entry .r -textvariable r
```

.*r* is the name of the entry box, and *r* is the name of the Tcl variable in which to store anything that the user enters in the entry box. We'll create a few more entry boxes to hold the green, blue and hex values:

```
% entry .g -textvariable g
% entry .b -textvariable b
% entry .h -textvariable hex
```

We'll use a similar command—called **label**—to create the labels for each entry box.

```
% label .rlabel -text red
% label .glabel -text green
% label .blabel -text blue
% label .hlabel -text hex
```

Next, we'll use Tk's **grid** command to place all of the interface elements in the Wish window:

```
% grid .rlabel -col 1 -row 1
% grid .r -col 2 -row 1
% grid .glabel -col 1 -row 2
% grid .g -col 2 -row 2
% grid .blabel -col 1 -row 3
% grid .b -col 2 -row 3
% grid .hlabel -col 1 -row 4
% grid .h -col 2 -row 4
```

That's our interface. Now, all we need to do is create a button for the user to push, and tie the button to the *rgbToHex* procedure. As you probably guessed, the command that creates the button is simply called **button**.

```
% button .button -text convert -command {
    set hex [rgbToHex $r $g $b]
    . configure -background [rgbToHex $r $g $b]
}
```

The **set** command displays the result in the .h entry box, and the **.configure** command shows the selected color.

Summary

This chapter gives you a good first look at basic Tcl concepts and practices, and a fleeting glimpse of Tcl's most popular extension, *Tk*. Hopefully, you have learned enough to decipher (and even modify) other folks' Tcl programs, and get started on writing your own scripts.

You must understand substitution to understand Tcl. There are three basic kinds of substitution in Tcl: *variable substitution*, marked by the ($) symbol, which substitutes a variable's value for the variables name; *command substitution*, marked by square brackets ([]), which substitute the command's value for the command; and *backslash substitution*, marked by the backslash (\), which is used to implement escape sequences.

Another critical Tcl concept is that of grouping. Tcl uses braces ({}) and double quotes (" ") to group a series of words into a single "word." (Square brackets, used for command substitution, also serve to group the bracketed content.) Braces prevent substitution within the braced material; double quotes allow substitution.

Tcl has two basic data types: *simple variables* and *arrays*. Simple variables can hold just about anything: numbers, strings, or lists. You don't need to initialize simple variables, or specify their type. Tcl converts the contents of the variable between formats as needed. Tcl *arrays*, like Perl hashes, are sequences of simple variables that are indexed by numbers or strings.

You learned about decision and loop statements. Both types of statements are vital to properly control your program's logic. Decision statements let you choose between two options. Loop statements let you repeatedly execute a group of statements.

Tcl offers basic tools for working with files and other text streams, such as pipelines. You open files or streams with the **open** command, and use the resulting file code to read and write to the file or stream with **gets** and **puts**, respectively.

Finally, you saw a little demonstration of Tk and how easy it is to build a graphical, Windows-style application with Tcl/Tk.

This chapter won't make you a Tcl expert, but hopefully it has given you a taste for more. Two good places to continue your research into Tcl are *http://www.tcltk.com*, which contains an extensive set of pointers to Tcl resources, and *http://www.scriptics.com*, the web site of Dr. Osterhout's Tcl-based business and the source of authoritative Tcl documentation and the latest Tcl software.

Pattern Matching

Pattern matching is a wonderful feature of Bash, Perl, Tcl, and other languages. This chapter explains the concept of pattern matching in general and then goes into specifics about each language. One of humanity's best features is our ability to generalize or to pick out common features of disparate objects. At its most basic level, pattern matching takes a description and finds out if an object matches that description. Usually, patterns are matched in text. However, you can also use pattern matching with filenames or the contents of variables.

Pattern Matching

Testing text to see if it matches a description.

Pattern

A series of characters that describe the text you're looking for.

Almost every Unix user knows at least the rudiments of pattern matching. Every time you use the **ls** command with a wildcard character (e.g., to only list PostScript files using a command like **ls *.ps**) or you list all files starting with a certain letter (e.g., using **ls m***), you're using pattern matching.

The rest of this chapter is divided into three main sections. The first section discusses how pattern matching is used by Bash. The second discusses how Perl uses pattern matching. The third shows how Tcl matches patterns.

All three languages rely on *metacharacters* to describe the text to be matched. Metacharacters are characters that have an additional meaning above and beyond their literal meaning. For example, the *?* character has a literal meaning of a question mark. However, in Bash, it can also mean: *match any single character*.

Let's see the *?* character in action:

```
% ls
doo.txt    foo.txt    waswaldo.txt
% ls ?oo.txt
doo.txt    foo.txt
```

This example shows that the *?* metacharacter matches both the *d* in *doo.txt* and the *f* in *foo.txt*.

NOTE   Use the \ (backslash) character to return a character back to its normal meaning. For example, \? actually means a question mark and not "match any character." The backslash is called the escape character, perhaps because it lets characters escape from being treated as metacharacters.

Patterns, the description of the text you're searching for, are also called regular expressions or *regexps*. I don't know the history behind this term, just that it's commonly used.

Regular Expressions

A group of characters and metacharacters used to determine if text matches a description.

Bash

The Bash shell uses pattern matching in several different ways. The most prevalent use of pattern matching is to specify filenames. However, pattern matching is also used with variables, the **case** command, and the **for** command.

Metacharacters for Filenames

Most of the time when using metacharacters in the shell, you'll be looking for filenames. You might need to move all PostScript files or you might need to delete files associated with an old project. These tasks, and more, can be accomplished with pattern matching.

Table 8.1 lists all of the metacharacters used when matching filenames.

Table 8.1 *Metacharacters for Filenames*

Metacharacter(s)	Metameaning
?	The question mark matches any single character.
*	The asterisk matches zero or more of any character.
[ ]	Square brackets create a character list. All characters inside the square brackets are used to match or not match a single character. For example, *[xyz]* matches either *x*, *y*, or *z* but not *xx*, *xy*, or any other combination. Character lists only match a single character regardless of how many characters are in the list. You can use *[a-e]* as shorthand for *[abcde]*. Additionally, using a *!* as the first character of the list negates it. For example, *[!xyz]* matches any character except for *x*, *y*, and *z*.
{ }	Curly brackets are used for pattern expansion. For example, *x{y,z}* matches either *xy* or *xz* and no other text. It is very useful when dealing with directories.

There are two special cases that you need to know about:

1. You can't match a / character. The / character is the name of the root directory and is used as a delimiter for path names.

2. The * character won't match periods at the beginning of files. You must explicitly specify the initial dot in your pattern.

TIP

> Use single or double quotes to control which program expands the pattern. With quotes, the program (e.g., *ls*) expands the pattern. Without quotes, the shell expands the pattern.

When the shell finds filenames that match a pattern, it replaces (or expands) the pattern into a list of filenames that match. For example, *ls f** might become *ls first foo*. This is an important note to remember. Sometimes, you want the command to expand the pattern instead of the shell.

Pattern Expansion
Filename patterns are replaced by a list of matching files.

The two obvious times that shell pattern matching might not be appropriate are when using the **grep** command and when calling Perl or Tcl scripts. Let's look at an example using the **grep** command. The **grep** command searches one or more files looking inside each one for a specified pattern.

FRI

For more information about the **grep** command, see "The grep Command" on page 340 in Chapter 9, "Examining the Tools."

The following example looks in all C files for text lines that contain words beginning with *dav* or *Dav*. Both *foo.c* and *bar.c* contain such patterns, so both should be found by the **grep** command.

```
% ls
foo.c     bar.c     david
% grep [Dd]av* *.c          <- Nothing was found! Why?
% echo grep [Dd]av* *.c
grep david bar.c foo.c      <- Ah, here's the reason.
```

You can use the **echo** command to find out how the shell expands your command lines. In this case, the first argument to **grep**, the *[Dd]av** pattern, matches the *david* file and therefore is replaced. Use single quotes around patterns you don't want the shell to expand:

```
% ls
foo.c      bar.c      david
% grep '[Dd]av*' *.c
bar.c:david-07/97
foo.c:david-09/97
```

In this example, you see that the **grep** command, rather than the shell, expands the pattern by finding matches in the two *.c* files. Notice, however, that the **.c* pattern is expanded by the shell.

There's one more small twist to how the shell expands patterns. If the pattern does not match any filenames, the pattern is left unexpanded. For example:

```
% ls
foo.c      bar.c               <- the david file was removed.
% echo grep [Dd]av* *.c
grep [Dd]av* bar.c foo.c       <- the pattern is unexpanded.
```

In order to gain the maximum benefit from using patterns, you sometimes need to plan ahead and create filename conventions. For example, if you have multiple projects, it might help to assign each project a three-letter prefix code. Then, you can use patterns to manipulate all of the project files at once:

```
% ls
trn_whach.c     trn_qwre.c      trn_sce.c
wed_forc.c      wed_qwsa.c      wed_uyhd.c
% mkdir training
% mv trn_* training
```

This example shows what you might do when the number of files in a project gets to be too many—use the **mv** command to move all of the project files into a subdirectory.

Metacharacters for Variables

When metacharacters are paired with variables, they let you strip off parts of a variable's value and work with the rest. Some examples using project codes should make this concept clear:

```
% project_code='ben_2344'
% echo $project_code
ben_2344
```

```
% echo ${project_code#????}      <- display the project name
2344
% echo ${project_code%?????}     <- display the project
                                 <- number
ben
```

The metacharacters after the # or % are expanded to produce a pattern just like when they are used for filenames.

The first example uses four question marks to strip off the first four characters of the project code, which results in the project name. The second example removes five characters from the end of the variable's value.

Table 8.2 shows the four constructs where you can use metacharacters to work with variables.

Table 8.2 *Metacharacters for Variables*

Syntax	Meaning
${*variable#pattern*}	This construct expands the pattern and then tries to find the *shortest* matching text at the *beginning* of the variable's value. If a match is found, the matching text is deleted and the rest of the text is returned.
${*variable##pattern*}	This construct expands the pattern and then tries to find the *longest* matching text at the *beginning* of the variable's value. If a match is found, the matching text is deleted and the rest of the text is returned.
${*variable%pattern*}	This construct expands the pattern and then tries to find the *shortest* matching text at the *end* of the variable's value. If a match is found, the matching text is deleted and the rest of the text is returned.
${*variable%%pattern*}	This construct expands the pattern and then tries to find the *longest* matching text at the *end* of the variable's value. If a match is found, the matching text is deleted and the rest of the text is returned.

Metacharacters for the case Command

The **case** command is discussed in Chapter 4, "Commands to Control Script Execution." It deserves to be mentioned again because you can use patterns with it. First, let me remind you of the syntax for the **case** command:

```
case string
in
  regular_expression_1)
    .. commands ..
    ;;
  regular_expression_2)
    .. commands ..
    ;;
  *)
    .. commands ..
    ;;
esac
```

Each of the clauses in the **case** command uses a regular expression or pattern for matching the string's value. Any of the metacharacters used for filenames can be used with the **case** command.

Listing 8.1 shows a short script that uses the **case** command to display a project's due date.

Listing 8.1 *duedate—Using Case to Display a Project's Due Date*

```
#/bin/sh

case $1 in
  [Pp][Ee][Nn])
    echo "The pen project is due 11/20/1998."
    ;;
  ben*)
    echo "The ben group of projects are due in January
1999."
    ;;
  *)
    echo "The $1 project is unknown."
    ;;
esac
```

Here is an example of this script in action:

```
% chmod +x duedate
% ./duedate Pen
The pen project is due 11/20/1998.
```

```
% ./duedate foo
The foo project is unknown.
```

Listing 8.1 shows one of the limitations of the pattern matching ability of Bash. It doesn't give you the ability to ignore uppercase and lowercase when making a match. That's why the strange-looking *[Pp][Ee][Nn]* pattern is needed. That pattern matches any uppercase and lowercase text containing the letters *p*, *e*, and *n*—in that order.

TIP

> If you want to avoid the complexity of using *[Pp][Ee][Nn]* as a pattern, check out the **uppercase** and **lowercase** commands in Chapter 10, "Customizing the Tools."

The *ben** pattern was used to recognize all projects that are part of the *ben* group. The group might include *ben_one*, *ben_newyork*, or any other project name that starts with the letters *ben*.

Metacharacters and the for Command

The **for** command lets you use filename metacharacters to create the list that is iterated over. This feature comes in handy when you need to limit which files are processed.

Listing 8.2 shows how to process all of the files in a directory.

Listing 8.2 *process_all—Using the for Command to Process All Files in a Directory*

```
#!/bin/sh

for file in *
do
  echo "$file is being processed."
end
```

Here is an example of this script in action:

```
% chmod +x process_all
% ls
foo.c      bar.c      david
% ./process_all
foo.c is being processed.
bar.c is being processed.
david is being processed.
```

If you only want to process files starting with the letters *b* or *d*, use Listing 8.3 as your template.

Listing 8.3 *process_bd—Processing Files Starting with b or d*

```
#!/bin/sh

for file in [bd]*
do
  echo "$file is being processed."
end
```

Here is an example of this script in action:

```
% chmod +x process_bd
% ls
foo.c      bar.c      david
% ./process_bd
bar.c is being processed.
david is being processed.
```

You can use any of the metacharacters described in "Metacharacters for Filenames" (earlier in this chapter) with the **for** command.

Perl

Perl uses regular expressions for pattern matching, pattern substitution, and character translation. Pattern matching uses the *m//* operator, which returns true if a requested pattern is matched; false otherwise. The substitution operation uses the *s//* operator and replaces one pattern with a replacement pattern. The *tr//* operator translates one set of characters into another. These operators are summarized in Table 8.3.

Table 8.3 *Perl's Regular Expression Operators*

Operator	Description
m/*PATTERN*/	This operator returns true if *PATTERN* is found in $_.
s/*PATTERN*/*REPLACEMENT*/	This operator replaces the sub-string matched by *PATTERN* with *REPLACEMENT*.

Table 8.3 *Perl's Regular Expression Operators (Cont'd)*

Operator	Description
tr/*CHARACTERS*/*REPLACEMENTS*/	This operator replaces characters specified by *CHARACTERS* with the characters in *REPLACEMENTS*.

All three regular expression operators work with a default variable called *$_*, which holds the string that is searched. You might like to think of the *$_* variable as the target of the search. Perl has special binding operators that let you select a different variable as the target of the search (see the section "The Binding Operators" later in this chapter).

Both the matching (*m//*) and the substitution (*s///*) operators perform variable substitution on the *PATTERN* and *REPLACE-MENT* strings. For example, if the value of $book is *Shell Programming Tools*, then m/$book/. is really *m/Shell Programming Tools/*.

Variable Substitution
Replacing the variable name with its value.

If *PATTERN* evaluates to the empty string, the last valid pattern is used. So, if you see a statement like print if //; in a Perl program, look for the previous regular expression operator to see what the pattern is. The substitution operator also uses this interpretation of the empty pattern.

Pattern Delimiters
Every Perl regular expression operator allows the use of alternative *pattern delimiters*. A *delimiter* marks the beginning and end of a given pattern. In the following statement:

```
m//;
```

the slashes (//) are the delimiters. However, you can use any delimiter character. This lets you use the slash character inside patterns. For example, matching a file with the default delimiters looks like this:

```
m/\/medined\/what.dat/
```

The pattern is hard to read because all of the slashes seem to run together (some programmers say they look like upside-down tee-pees). The forward slash is used to escape the backslash so the pattern does not prematurely end. If you use an alternate delimiter, it might look like this:

```
m!/medined/what.dat!
```

or

```
m{/medined/what.dat}
```

These examples are a little clearer. The last example also shows that, if a left bracket is used as the starting delimiter, then the ending delimiter must be the right bracket.

Another method of avoiding the backslash requirement is to use variable substitution. For example:

```
$file = '/medined/what.dat';
m/$file/;
```

Some programmers think this technique yields clearer code than simply changing the delimiters.

If you choose the single quote as your delimiter character, then no variable interpolation is performed on the pattern. However, you still need to use the backslash character to escape any of the metacharacters discussed in the "How to Create Patterns" section later in this chapter.

TIP

I tend to avoid delimiters that might be confused with characters in the pattern. For example, using the plus sign as a delimiter (*m+abc+*) does not help program readability. A casual reader might think that you intend to add two expressions instead of matching them.

The *?* has a special meaning when used as a match pattern delimiter. It works like the */* delimiter, except that it matches only once between calls to the **reset()** function. This feature might be removed in future versions of Perl, so avoid using it.

The Matching Operator (*m//*)

The matching operator (*m//*) finds patterns in strings. One of its more common uses is to look for a specific string inside a data file. For example, you might look for all customers whose first name is *Mark*, or you might look for all names starting with the letter *M*.

The matching operator only uses the *$_* variable as its target. This makes the match statement shorter, because you don't need to specify where to search. Here is a quick example:

```
$_ = "AAA bbb AAA";
print "Found bbb\n" if m/bbb/;
```

The print statement is executed only if the *bbb* character sequence is found in the *$_* variable. In this particular case, *bbb* is found, so the program displays the following:

```
Found bbb
```

The matching operator lets you use variable substitution to create patterns. For example:

```
$needToFind = "bbb";
$_ = "AAA bbb AAA";
print "Found bbb\n" if m/$needToFind/;
```

Using the matching operator is so commonplace that Perl allows you to leave off the *m* from the matching operator as long as slashes are used as delimiters:

```
$_ = "AAA bbb AAA";
print "Found bbb\n" if /bbb/;
```

Using the matching operator to find a string inside a file is very easy because of the *$_* default variable—it's designed to facilitate this type of activity. For example:

```
$target = "M";

open(INPUT, "<findstr.dat");

while (<INPUT>) {
    if (/$target/) {
        print "Found $target on line $.";
    }
}
close(INPUT);
```

> **NOTE** The $. special variable keeps track of the record number. Every time the diamond operators read a line, this variable is incremented.

This example reads every line in the input searching for the letter *M*. When an *M* is found, the print statement is executed. The print statement prints the letter that is found and the line number it was found on.

The matching operator has several options. The *ignore case* option is probably the most useful, followed closely by the option to create an array of all matched text in a targeted string. Table 8.4 shows the options you can use with the matching operator.

Table 8.4 *Options for the Matching Operator*

Option	Description
g	The *g* option causes Perl to find all occurrences of the pattern in the target string. A list of matches is returned, or you can iterate over the matches using a *loop* statement.
i	The *i* option causes Perl to ignore the case of characters in the string.
m	The *m* option causes Perl to treat the string as multiple lines. If you know that your target string contains embedded newline characters, use this option.
o	The *o* option causes Perl to compile the pattern only once. You can achieve some small performance gains with this option. It should be used with variable substitution only when the value of the variable won't change during the lifetime of the program.
s	The *s* option causes Perl to treat the string as a single line.
x	The *x* option lets you use extended regular expressions. Basically, this means that Perl ignores whitespace that's not escaped with a backslash or within a character class. I highly recommend this option so you can use spaces to make your regular expressions more readable. See the section "Example: Extension Syntax" later in this chapter for more information.

All options are specified after the last pattern delimiter. For example, if you want to ignore the case of the characters in the targeted string, you can do this:

```
$_ = "AAA BBB AAA";
print "Found bbb\n" if  m/bbb/i;
```

This program finds a match even though the pattern uses lowercase and the string uses uppercase, because the *i* option was used, telling Perl to ignore the case.

The Substitution Operator (*s///*)

You can replace one pattern with another using the substitution operator (*s///*). It requires two operands, like this:

```
s/a/z/;
```

This statement changes the first *a* in *$_* into a *z*.

You can use variable substitution with *s///* just as you can with the matching operator. For example:

```
$needToReplace    = "bbb";
$replacementText = "1234567890";
$_ = "AAA bbb AAA";
$result = s/$needToReplace/$replacementText/;
```

NOTE   You can use variable substitution in the replacement pattern as shown here, but none of the metacharacters described later in the chapter can be used in the replacement pattern.

This program changes the *$_* variable to hold *AAA 1234567890 AAA* instead of its original value, and the *$result* variable holds *1*—the number of substitutions made.

Frequently, the substitution operator is used to remove substrings. For example, if you want to remove the *bbb* sequence of characters from the *$_* variable, you could do this:

```
s/bbb//;
```

By replacing the matched string with nothing, you have effectively deleted it.

If brackets of any type are used as delimiters for the search pattern, you need to use a second set of brackets to enclose the replacement pattern. For example:

```
$_ = "AAA bbb AAA";
$result = s{bbb}{1234567890};
```

One interesting option of the substitution operator is the capability to evaluate the replacement pattern as an expression instead of a string. You could use this capability to find all numbers in a file and multiply them by a given percentage, for example. You could repeat matched strings by using the string repetition operator. Table 8.5 shows all of the options you can use with the substitution operator.

Table 8.5 *Options for the Substitution Operator*

Option	Description
e	The *e* option causes Perl to evaluate the replacement pattern as an expression. This option changes the interpretation of the pattern delimiters. If used, variable substitution is active even if single quotes are used. In addition, if backticks are used as delimiters, the replacement pattern is executed as a DOS or Unix command. The output of the command is then used as the replacement text.
g	The *g* option causes Perl to find all occurrences of the pattern in the target string. A list of matches is returned, or you can iterate over the matches using a *loop* statement.
i	The *i* option causes Perl to ignore the case of characters in the string.
m	The *m* option causes Perl to treat the string as multiple lines. If you know that your target string contains embedded newline characters, use this option.
o	The *o* option causes Perl to compile the pattern only once. You can achieve some small performance gains with this option. It should be used with variable substitution only when the value of the variable won't change during the lifetime of the program.

Table 8.5 *Options for the Substitution Operator (Cont'd)*

Option	Description
s	The *s* option treats the string as a single line.
x	The *x* option lets you use extended regular expressions. Basically, this means that Perl ignores whitespace that's not escaped with a backslash or within a character class. I highly recommend this option so you can use spaces to make your regular expressions more readable. See the section "Example: Extension Syntax" later in this chapter for more information.

The Translation Operator (tr///)

You can use the translation operator (*tr///*) to change individual characters in the $_ variable. It requires two operands, like this:

```
tr/a/z/;
```

This statement translates all occurrences of *a* into *z*. If you specify more than one character in the pattern character list, you can translate multiple characters at a time. For example:

```
tr/ab/z/;
```

translates all *a* and all *b* characters into the *z* character. If the replacement list of characters is shorter than the target list of characters, the last character in the replacement list is repeated as often as needed. However, if more than one replacement character is given for a matched character, only the first is used. For example:

```
tr/WWW/ABC/;
```

results in all *W* characters being converted to an *A* character. The rest of the replacement list is ignored.

Unlike the matching and substitution operators, the translation operator doesn't perform variable substitution.

The translation operator has options different from the matching and substitution operators. You can delete matched characters, replace repeated characters with a single character, and translate only characters that don't match the character list. Table 8.6 shows the translation options.

Table 8.6 *Options for the Translation Operator*

Option	Description
c	The *c* option complements the match character list. In other words, the translation is done for every character that does not match the character list.
d	The *d* option deletes any character in the match list that does not have a corresponding character in the replacement list.
s	The *s* option reduces repeated instances of matched characters to a single instance of that character.

Normally, if the match list is longer than the replacement list, the last character in the replacement list is used as the replacement for the extra characters. However, when the *d* option is used, the matched characters are simply deleted.

If the replacement list is empty, no translation is done. The operator returns the number of characters that match, though. This is useful when you need to know how often a given letter appears in a string. This feature also can compress repeated characters using the *s* option.

The Binding Operators (=~ and *!~*)

The search, modify, and translation operations work on the $_ variable by default. What if the target string is stored in some other variable? That's where the binding operators come into play. They let you bind the regular expression operators to a variable other than $_. There are two forms of the binding operator: the regular =~ and its complement *!~*.

The following small program shows the syntax of the =~ operator:

```
$scalar       = "The root has many leaves";
$match        = $scalar =~ m/root/;
$substitution = $scalar =~ s/root/tree/;
$translate    = $scalar =~ tr/h/H/;

print("\$match        = $match\n");
print("\$substitution = $substitution\n");
```

```
print("\$translate    = $translate\n");
print("\$scalar       = $scalar\n");
```

This program displays the following:

```
$match        = 1
$substitution = 1
$translate    = 2
$scalar       = THe tree Has many leaves
```

This example uses all three of the regular expression operators with the regular binding operator. Each of the regular expression operators is bound to the *$scalar* variable instead of *$_*. This example also shows the return values of the regular expression operators. If you don't need the return values, you can do this:

```
$scalar = "The root has many leaves";
print("String has root.\n") if $scalar =~ m/root/;
$scalar =~ s/root/tree/;
$scalar =~ tr/h/H/;
print("\$scalar = $scalar\n");
```

This program displays the following:

```
String has root.
$scalar = THe tree Has many leaves
```

The left operand of the binding operator is the string to be searched, modified, or transformed; the right operand is the regular expression operator to be evaluated.

The complementary binding operator is valid only when used with the matching regular expression operator. If you use it with the substitution or translation operator, you get the following message if you're using the *-w* command-line option to run Perl:

```
Useless use of not in void context at test.pl line 4.
```

You can see that the *!~* is the opposite of *=~* by replacing the *=~* in the second line of the previous example:

```
$scalar = "The root has many leaves";
print("String has root.\n") if $scalar !~ m/root/;
$scalar =~ s/root/tree/;
$scalar =~ tr/h/H/;
print("\$scalar = $scalar\n");
```

This program displays the following:

```
$scalar = THe tree Has many leaves
```

The first print line does not get executed because the complementary binding operator returns false.

Metacharacters for Perl Pattern Matching

So far in this chapter, you've read about the different operators used with regular expressions, and you've seen how to match simple sequences of characters. Now we'll look at the wide array of metacharacters that are used to harness the full power of regular expressions. *Metacharacters* are characters that have an additional meaning above and beyond their literal meaning. For example, the period character can have two meanings in a pattern. First, it can be used to match a period character in the searched string—this is its *literal meaning*. Second, it can be used to match *any* character in the searched string except for the newline character—this is its *metameaning*.

When you create patterns, the metameaning is the default. If you really intend to match the literal character, you need to prefix the metacharacter with a backslash. You might recall that the backslash is used to create an escape sequence.

Patterns can have many different components. These components all combine to provide you with the power to match any type of string. The following list of components can give you a good idea of the variety of ways that patterns are created. The section "Pattern Examples" later in this chapter shows many examples of these rules in action.

Variable Interpolation: Any variable is interpolated, and the essentially new pattern is then evaluated as a regular expression. Remember that only one level of interpolation is done. This means that if the value of the variable includes, for example, *$scalar* as a string value, then *$scalar* is not to be interpolated. In addition, backticks do not interpolate within double quotes, and single quotes do not stop interpolation of variables when used within double quotes.

Self-Matching Characters: Any character matches itself unless it is a metacharacter or one of the symbols *$*, *@*, *%*, or *&*. The metacharacters are listed in Table 8.7, and the other characters are used to begin variable names and function calls. You can use the backslash character to force Perl to match the literal meaning of any character. For example, m/a/; returns true if the letter *a* is in the *$_* variable, and m/\$/; returns true if the character *$* is in the *$_* variable.

Table 8.7 *Regular Expression Metacharacters, Metabrackets, and Metasequences*

Metacharacter	Description
|	The *alternation* metacharacter lets you specify two values that can cause the match to succeed. For example, m/a|b/ means that the *$_* variable must contain the *a* or *b* character for the match to succeed.
^	The caret metacharacter matches the beginning of a string or, if the */m* option is used, matches the beginning of a line. It is one of two pattern anchors—the other anchor is the *$*.
.	This metacharacter matches any character except for the newline, unless the */s* option is specified. If the */s* option is specified, the newline is also matched.
$	This metacharacter matches the end of a string or, if the */m* option is used, matches the end of a line. It is one of two pattern anchors—the other anchor is the ^.
*	This metacharacter indicates that the "thing" immediately to the left should be matched zero or more times in order to be evaluated as true.
+	This metacharacter indicates that the "thing" immediately to the left should be matched one or more times in order to be evaluated as true.
?	This metacharacter indicates that the "thing" immediately to the left should be matched zero or one time in order to be evaluated as true. When used in conjunction with the +, _, ?, or {n, m} metacharacters and brackets, it means that the regular expression should be non-greedy and match the smallest possible string.

Table 8.7 *Regular Expression Metacharacters, Metabrackets, and Metasequences (Cont'd)*

Metacharacter	Description
()	The parentheses let you affect the order of pattern evaluation and act as a form of pattern memory. See the section "Pattern Memory" later in this chapter for more information.
(?...)	If a question mark immediately follows the left parenthesis, it indicates that an extended mode component is being specified. See the section "Example: Extension Syntax" later in this chapter for more information.
{n, m}	The curly braces let you specify how many times the "thing" immediately to the left should be matched. *{n}* means that it should be matched exactly *n* times. *{n,}* means it must be matched at least *n* times. *{n, m}* means that it must be matched at least *n* times and not more than *m* times.
[]	The square brackets let you create a character class. For example, m/[abc]/ evaluates to true if *a*, *b*, or *c* is contained in *$_*. The square brackets are a more readable alternative to the alternation metacharacter.
\	This metacharacter "escapes" the following character. This means that any special meaning normally attached to that character is ignored. For example, if you need to include a dollar sign in a pattern, you must use \$ to avoid Perl's variable interpolation. Use \\ to specify the backslash character in your pattern.
\0nnn	Any octal byte.
\a	Alarm.
\A	This metasequence represents the beginning of the string. Its meaning is not affected by the */m* option.

Table 8.7 *Regular Expression Metacharacters, Metabrackets, and Metasequences (Cont'd)*

Metacharacter	Description
\b	This metasequence represents the backspace character inside a character class; otherwise, it represents a *word boundary*. A word boundary is the spot between word (\w) and non-word (\W) characters. Perl thinks that the \W metasequence matches the imaginary characters off the ends of the string.
\B	Match a non-word boundary.
\cn	Any control character.
\d	Match a single digit character.
\D	Match a single non-digit character.
\e	Escape.
\E	Terminate the \L or \U sequence.
\f	Form Feed.
\G	Match only where the previous *m//g* left off.
\l	Change the next character to lowercase.
\L	Change the following characters to lowercase until a \E sequence is encountered.
\n	Newline.
\Q	The \Q metacharacter causes all characters between itself and the \E sequence to be treated literally.
\r	Carriage return.
\s	Match a single whitespace character.
\S	Match a single non-whitespace character.
\t	Tab.
\u	Change the next character to uppercase.

Table 8.7 *Regular Expression Metacharacters, Metabrackets, and Metasequences (Cont'd)*

Metacharacter	Description
\U	Change the following characters to uppercase until a \E sequence is encountered.
\v	Vertical tab.
\w	Match a single word character. Word characters are the alphanumeric and underscore characters.
\W	Match a single non-word character.
\xnn	Any hexadecimal byte.
\Z	This metasequence represents the end of the string. Its meaning is not affected by the /m option.
\$	Dollar sign.
\@	At Sign.

Character Sequences: A sequence of characters matches the identical sequence in the searched string. The characters need to be in the same order in both the pattern and the searched string for the match to be true. For example, `m/abc/;` matches *abc* but not *cab* or *bca*. If any character in the sequence is a metacharacter, you need to use the backslash to match its literal value.

Alternation: The *alternation* metacharacter (|) lets you match more than one possible string. For example, `m/a|b/;` matches if either the *a* character or the *b* character is in the searched string. You can use sequences of more than one character with alternation. For example, `m/dog|cat/;` matches if either of the strings *dog* or *cat* is in the searched string.

TIP	Some programmers like to enclose the alternation sequence inside parentheses to help indicate where the sequence begins and ends.
	`m/(dog|cat)/;`
	However, this affects something called *pattern memory*, which you'll learn about in the section "Pattern Memory" later in the chapter.

Character Classes: Square brackets are used to create character classes. A *character class* is used to match a specific type of character. For example, you can match any decimal digit using m/[0123456789]/;. This matches a single character in the range of zero to nine. You can find more information about character classes in the section called "Character Classes" later in this chapter.

Symbolic Character Classes: There are several character classes that are used so frequently that they have a symbolic representation. The period metacharacter stands for a special character class that matches all characters except the newline. The rest are \d, \D, \s, \S, \w, and \W. These are mentioned in Table 8.7 earlier and are discussed in the section "Character Classes" later in this chapter.

Anchors: The caret (^) and the dollar sign ($) metacharacters are used to anchor a pattern to the beginning and the end of the searched string. The caret is always the first character in the pattern when used as an anchor unless the alternation metacharacter is used. For example, m/^one/; only matches if the searched string starts with the sequence of characters, *one*. The dollar sign is always the last character in the pattern when used as an anchor. For example, m/(last|end)$/; matches only if the searched string ends with either the character sequence *last* or the character sequence *end*. The \A and \Z metasequences are also used as pattern anchors for the beginning and end of strings.

Quantifiers: There are several metacharacters that are devoted to controlling how many characters are matched. For example, m/a{5}/; means that five *a* characters must be found before a true result can be returned. The *, +, and ? metacharacters and the curly braces are all used as quantifiers. See the section "Quantifiers" later in this chapter for more information.

Pattern Memory: Parentheses are used to store matched values into buffers for later recall. I like to think of this as a form of pattern memory. Some programmers call them back-references. After you use m/(fish|fowl)/; to match a string and a match is found, the variable *$1* holds either *fish* or *fowl* depending on which sequence was matched. See the section "Pattern Memory" later in this chapter for more information.

Word Boundaries: The \b metasequence matches the boundary between a space and the first character of a word or between the last character of a word and the space. The \b matches at the beginning or end of a string if there are no leading or trailing spaces. For example, m/\bfoo/; matches *foo* even without spaces surrounding the word. It also matches *$foo* because the dollar sign is not considered a word character. The statement m/foo\b/; matches *foo* but not *foobar*, and the statement m/\bwiz/; matches *wizard* but not *geewiz*. See the section "Character Classes" later in this chapter for more information about word boundaries.

The \B metasequence matches everywhere except at a word boundary.

Quoting Metacharacters: You can match metacharacters literally by enclosing them in a \Q..\E sequence. This lets you avoid using the backslash character to escape all metacharacters, and makes your code easier to read.

Extended Syntax: The *(?...)* sequence lets you use an extended version of the regular expression syntax. The different options are discussed in the section "Example: Extension Syntax" later in this chapter.

Combinations: Any of the preceding components can be combined with any other to create simple or complex patterns.

Patterns are powerful because you don't always know in advance the value of the string for which you are searching. If you need to match the first word in a string that is read in from a file, you probably have no idea how long it might be; therefore, you need to build a pattern. You might start with the \w symbolic character class, which matches any single alphanumeric or underscore character. So, assuming that the string is in the *$_* variable, you can match a one-character word like this:

```
m/\w/;
```

If you need to match both a one-character word and a two-character word, you can do this:

```
m/\w|\w\w/;
```

This pattern says to match a single word character or two consecutive word characters. You could continue to add alternation components to match the different lengths of words that you might expect to see, but there is a better way.

You can use the + quantifier to say that the match should succeed only if the component is matched one or more times. It is used this way:

```
m/\w+/;
```

If the value of *$_* is *AAA BBB*, then *m/\w+/;* will match the *AAA* in the string. If *$_* is blank, full of whitespace, or full of other non-word characters, an undefined value will be returned.

The preceding pattern lets you determine if *$_* contains a word, but does not let you know what the word is. In order to accomplish that, you need to enclose the matching components inside parentheses. For example:

```
m/(\w+)/;
```

By doing this, you force Perl to store the matched string into the *$1* variable. The *$1* variable can be considered as pattern memory.

This introduction to pattern components describes most of the details you need to know in order to create your own patterns or regular expressions. However, some of the components deserve a bit more study. The next few sections look at character classes, quantifiers, pattern memory, pattern precedence, and the extension syntax. Then, the rest of the chapter is devoted to showing specific examples of when to use the different components.

Character Classes

A character class defines a type of character. The character class *[0123456789]* defines the class of decimal digits, and *[0-9a-f]* defines the class of hexadecimal digits. Notice that you can use a dash to define a range of consecutive characters. Character classes let you match any of a range of characters; you don't know in advance which character is matched. This capability to match non-specific characters is what metacharacters are all about.

You can use variable interpolation inside the character class, but you must be careful when doing so. For example:

```
$_ = "AAABBBCCC";
$charList = "ADE";
print "matched" if m/[$charList]/;
```

displays

```
matched
```

This is because the variable interpolation results in a character class of *[ADE]*. If you use the variable as one end of a character range, you need to ensure that you don't mix numbers and digits. For example:

```
$_ = "AAABBBCCC";
$charList = "ADE";
print "matched" if m/[$charList-9]/;
```

results in the following error message when executed:

```
/[ADE-9]/: invalid [] range in regexp at test.pl line 4.
```

Though the range *[ADE-9]* is invalid, *[0-9a-f]*, which includes the hexadecimal range, is clearly valid. Make sure you understand the difference.

At times, it's necessary to match on any character except for a given character list. Complementing the character class with the caret does this. For example:

```
$_ = "AAABBBCCC";
print "matched" if m/[^ABC]/;
```

displays nothing. This match returns true only if a character other than *A*, *B*, or *C* is in the searched string. If you complement a list with just the letter *A*:

```
$_ = "AAABBBCCC";
print "matched" if m/[^A]/;
```

then the string *"matched"* is displayed because *B* and *C* are part of the string—in other words, a character other than the letter *A*.

Perl has shortcuts for some character classes that are frequently used. Here is a list of what I call symbolic character classes:

\w   This symbol matches any alphanumeric character or the underscore character. It is equivalent to the character class *[a-zA-Z0-9_]*.

\W   This symbol matches every character that the \w symbol does not. In other words, it is the complement of \w. It is equivalent to *[^a-zA-Z0-9_]*.

\s   This symbol matches any space, tab, or newline character. It is equivalent to *[\t \n]*.

\S   This symbol matches any non-whitespace character. It is equivalent to *[^\t \n]*.

\d   This symbol matches any digit. It is equivalent to *[0-9]*.

D\   This symbol matches any non-digit character. It is equivalent to *[^0-9]*.

You can use these symbols inside other character classes, but not as endpoints of a range. For example, you can do the following:

```
$_ = "\tAAA";
print "matched" if m/[\d\s]/;
```

which displays:

```
matched
```

because the value of *$_* includes the tab character.

<table>
<tr><td>**TIP**</td><td>Metacharacters appearing inside the square brackets that define a character class are used in their literal sense. They lose their metameaning. This might be a little confusing at first. In fact, I have a tendency to forget this when evaluating patterns.</td></tr>
</table>

<table>
<tr><td>**NOTE**</td><td>I think that most of the confusion regarding regular expressions lies in the fact that each character of a pattern can have several possible meanings. The caret could be an anchor, could be a caret, or could be used to complement a character class. Therefore, it is vital that you decide which context any given pattern character or symbol is in before assigning a meaning to it.</td></tr>
</table>

Quantifiers

Perl provides several different quantifiers that let you specify how many times a given component must be present before the match is true. They are used when you don't know in advance how many characters need to be matched. Table 8.8 lists the different quantifiers that can be used.

Table 8.8 *The Six Types of Quantifiers*

Quantifier	Description
*	The component must be present zero or more times.
+	The component must be present one or more times.
?	The component must be present zero or one time.
{n}	The component must be present *n* times.
{n,}	The component must be present at least *n* times.
{n,m}	The component must be present at least *n* times and no more than *m* times.

If you need to match a word whose length is unknown, you need to use the + quantifier. You can't use an * because a zero-length word makes no sense. So, the match statement might look like this:

```
m/^\w+/;
```

This pattern matches *QQQ* and *AAAAA* but not "" or *BBB*. In order to account for the leading whitespace, which might or might not be at the beginning of a string, you need to use the asterisk (*) quantifier in conjunction with the \s symbolic character class in the following way:

```
m/\s*\w+/;
```

> Be careful when using the * quantifier because it can match an empty string, which might not be your intention. The pattern /b*/ matches any string—even one without any *b* characters.   **TIP**

At times, you might need to match an exact number of components. The following match statement is true only if five words are present in the *$_* variable:

```
$_ = "AA AB AC AD AE";
m/^(\w+\W+){5}$/;
```

In this example, we are matching components with at least one character followed by zero or more whitespace characters. The {5} quantifier is used to ensure that this combination of components is present five times.

The * and + quantifiers are greedy. They match as many characters as possible. This might not always be the behavior that you need. You can create non-greedy components by following the quantifier with a *?*.

Use the following file specification in order to look at the * and + quantifiers more closely:

```
$_ = '/user/Jackie/temp/names.dat';
```

The regular expression .* matches the entire file specification. This can be seen in the following small program:

```
$_ = '/user/Jackie/temp/names.dat';
m/.*/;
print $&;
```

This program displays:

```
/user/Jackie/temp/names.dat
```

You can see that the * quantifier is greedy. It matched the whole string. If you were to add the *?* modifier to make the .* component non-greedy, what do you think the program would display?

```
$_ = '/user/Jackie/temp/names.dat';
m/.*?/;
print $&;
```

This program displays nothing because the smallest number of characters that the * matches is zero. If we change the * to a +, the program displays:

```
/
```

Next, let's look at the concept of pattern memory, which lets you keep bits of matched string around after a match is complete.

Pattern Memory

Matching an arbitrary number of characters is fine, but without the capability to find out what was matched, you would not find patterns to be very useful. Perl lets you enclose pattern components inside parentheses in order to store the string that matches the components into pattern memory. You might also hear *pattern memory* referred to as *pattern buffers*. This memory persists after a match statement is finished executing so that you can assign the matched value to another variable.

You saw a simple example of this earlier, after the component descriptions. That example looked for the first word in a string and stored it into the first buffer, *$1*. The following small program:

```
$_ = "AAA BBB CCC";
m/(\w+)/;
print("$1\n");
```

displays:

```
AAA
```

You can use as many buffers as you need. Each time you add a set of parentheses, another buffer is used. If you want to find all the words in a string, you need to use the /g match option. In order to find all the words, you can use a loop statement that loops until the match operator returns false.

```
$_ = "AAA BBB CCC";

while (m/(\w+)/g) {
    print("$1\n");
}
```

The program displays:

```
AAA
BBB
CCC
```

If looping through the matches is not the right approach for your needs, you can create an array consisting of the matches, like this:

```
$_ = "AAA BBB CCC";
@matches = m/(\w+)/g;
print("@matches\n");
```

The program displays

```
AAA BBB CCC
```

Perl also has a few special variables to help you determine what matches and what does not. These variables occasionally save you from having to add parentheses to find information.

$+   This variable is assigned the value that the last bracket match matched.

$&   This variable is assigned the value of the entire matched string. If the match is not successful, $& retains its value from the last successful match.

$`   This variable is assigned everything in the searched string that is before the matched string.

$'   This variable is assigned everything in the search string following the matched string.

TIP

If you need to save the value of the matched strings stored in pattern memory, make sure to assign them to other variables. Pattern memory is local to the enclosing block and lasts only until another match is done.

Pattern Precedence

Pattern components have an order of precedence just as operators do. If you see the following pattern:

```
m/a|b+/
```

it's difficult to tell if the pattern should be:

```
m/(a|b)+/   # match either the"a" character repeated one
            # or more times or the "b" character repeated
            # one or more times.
```

or

```
m/a|(b+)/   # match either the "a" character or the "b"
            # character repeated one or more times.
```

The order of precedence shown in Table 8.9 is designed to solve problems like this. By looking at the table, you can see that quantifiers have a higher precedence than alternation. Therefore, the second interpretation is correct.

Table 8.9 *The Pattern Component Order of Precedence*

Precedence Level	Component
1	Parentheses
2	Quantifiers
3	Sequences and anchors
4	Alternation

> You can use parentheses to affect the order in which components are evaluated because they have the highest precedence. However, unless you use the extended syntax, you are affecting pattern memory. **TIP**

Extension Syntax

The regular expression extensions are a way to significantly add to the power of patterns without adding a lot of metacharacters to the proliferation that already exists. If you use the basic *(?...)* notation, you can greatly extend the regular expression capabilities.

At this time, Perl recognizes five extensions. These vary widely in functionality—from adding comments to setting options. Table 8.10 lists the extensions and gives a short description of each.

Table 8.10 *Five Extension Components*

Extension	Description
(?# TEXT)	This extension lets you add comments to your regular expression. The *TEXT* value is ignored.
(?:...)	This extension lets you add parentheses to your regular expression without causing a pattern memory position to be used.
(?=...)	This extension lets you match values without including them in the *$&* variable.
(?!...)	This extension lets you specify what should not follow your pattern. For example, */blue(?!bird)/* means that *bluebox* and *bluesy* are matched, but not *bluebird*.

Table 8.10 *Five Extension Components (Cont'd)*

Extension	Description
(?sxi)	This extension lets you specify an embedded option in the pattern rather than adding it after the last delimiter. This is useful if you are storing patterns in variables and using variable interpolation to do the matching.

By far the most useful feature of extended mode, in my opinion, is the ability to add comments directly inside your patterns. For example, would you rather a see a pattern that looks like this:

```
# Match a string with two words. $1 is the
# first word. $2 is the second word.
m/^\s+(\w+)\W+(\w+)\s+$/;
```

or one that looks like this:

```
m/
        (?# This pattern matches any string with two)
        (?# and only two words in it. The matched words)
        (?# are available in $1 and $2 if the match)
        (?# is successful.)

    ^       (?# Anchor this match to the beginning)
            (?# of the string)

    \s*     (?# skip over any whitespace characters)
            (?# use the * because there may be none)

    (\w+)   (?# Match the first word, we know it's)
            (?# the first word because of the anchor)
            (?# above. Place the matched word into)
            (?# pattern memory.)

    \W+     (?# Match at least one non-word)
            (?# character, there may be more than one)

    (\w+)   (?# Match another word, put into pattern)
            (?# memory also.)

    \s*     (?# skip over any whitespace characters)
            (?# use the * because there may be none)
```

```
$          (?# Anchor this match to the end of the)
           (?# string. Because both ^ and $ anchors)
           (?# are present, the entire string)
           (?# needs to match the pattern. A)
           (?# sub-string that fits the pattern does)
           (?# not match.)
/x;
```

Of course, the commented pattern is much longer, but it takes the same amount of time to execute. In addition, it is much easier to maintain the commented pattern because each component is explained. When you know what each component is doing in relation to the rest of the pattern, it becomes easy to modify its behavior when the need arises.

Extensions also let you change the order of evaluation without affecting pattern memory. For example:

```
m/(?:a|b)+/;
```

matches either the *a* character repeated one or more times or the *b* character repeated one or more times. The pattern memory is not affected.

At times, you might like to include a pattern component in your pattern without including it in the *$&* variable that holds the matched string. The technical term for this is a *zero-width positive look-ahead assertion*. You can use this to ensure that the string following the matched component is correct without affecting the matched value. For example, if you have some data that looks like this:

```
David    Veterinarian 56
Jackie   Orthopedist 34
Karen Veterinarian 28
```

and you want to find all veterinarians and store the value of the first column, you can use a look-ahead assertion. This does both tasks in one step. For example:

```
while (<>) {
    push(@array, $&) if m/^\w+(?=\s+Vet)/;
}

print("@array\n");
```

This program displays:

```
David Karen
```

Let's look at the pattern with comments added using the extended mode. In this case, it doesn't make sense to add comments directly to the pattern because the pattern is part of the *if* statement modifier. Adding comments in that location would make the comments hard to format. So let's use a different tactic.

```
$pattern = '^\w+       (?# Match the first word in the
string)

            (?=\s+    (?# Use a look-ahead assertion to
match)
                      (?# one or more whitespace characters)

            Vet)      (?# In addition to the whitespace,
make)
                      (?# sure that the next column starts)
                      (?# with the character sequence "Vet")
            ';

while (<>) {
    push(@array, $&) if m/$pattern/x;
}

print("@array\n");
```

Here we use a variable to hold the pattern and then use variable interpolation in the pattern with the match operator. You might want to pick a more descriptive variable name than *$pattern*, however.

TIP

> Although the Perl documentation does not mention it, I believe you have only one look-ahead assertion per pattern, and it must be the last pattern component.

The last extension that we'll discuss is the *zero-width negative assertion*. This type of component is used to specify values that shouldn't follow the matched string. For example, using the same data as in the previous example, you can look for everyone who is not a veterinarian. Your first inclination might be to simply replace the *(?=...)* with the *(?!...)* in the previous example.

```
while (<>) {
    push(@array, $&) if m/^\w+(?!\s+Vet)/;
}

print("@array\n");
```

Unfortunately, this program displays:

```
Davi Jackie Kare
```

which is not what you need. The problem is that Perl is looking at the last character of the word to see if it matches the *Vet* character sequence. In order to correctly match the first word, you need to explicitly tell Perl that the first word ends at a word boundary, like this:

```
while (<>) {
    push(@array, $&) if m/^\w+\b(?!\s+Vet)/;
}

print("@array\n");
```

This program displays:

```
Jackie
```

which is correct.

> There are many ways of matching any value. If the first method you **TIP**
> try doesn't work, try breaking the value into smaller components
> and match each boundary. If all else fails, you can always ask for
> help on the *comp.lang.perl.misc* newsgroup.

Pattern Examples

In order to demonstrate many different patterns, this section departs from the standard prose format of the book. Instead, a pattern-matching situation is contained in the left columns of Tables 8.11, 8.12, 8.13, and 8.14. The right column holds a possible solution and some comments explaining how the pattern works. In all of these examples, the string to search is the *$_* variable.

Table 8.11 lists many examples showing how the matching operator can be used.

Table 8.11 *Examples of the Perl Matching Operator*

How Do I...	Answer
find repeated non-newline characters in a string like the *AA* in *ABC AA ABC:*	`m/(.)\1/;` This pattern uses pattern memory to store a single character and a back-reference to repeat the first character. Use the back-reference twice to match three repeated characters.
find the first word in a string:	`m/^\s*(\w+)/;` After this statement, *$1* holds the first word in the string. Any whitespace at the beginning of the string is skipped by the \s* metacharacter sequence. Then the \w+ metacharacter sequence matches the next word. Note that the ' —which matches zero or more—is used to match the whitespace because there might not be any. The + —which matches one or more—is used for the word.
find the last word in a string:	``` m/ (\w+) (?# Match a word, store its) (?# value into pattern memory) [.!?]? (?# Some strings might hold a) (?# sentence. If so, this) (?# component matches zero or) (?# one punctuation) (?# characters) \s* (?# Match trailing whitespace) (?# using the * because there) (?# might not be any) $ (?# Anchor the match to the end) (?# of the string) /x; ``` After this statement, *$1* holds the last word in the string. You need to expand the character class, *[.!?]*, by adding more punctuation.

Table 8.11 *Examples of the Perl Matching Operator (Cont'd)*

How Do I...	Answer
know there are only two words in a string:	`m/^(\w+)\W+(\w+)$/x;` After this statement, *$1* holds the first word and *$2* holds the second word, assuming that the pattern matches. The pattern starts with a caret and ends with a dollar sign, which means that the entire string must match the pattern. The *\w+* metacharacter sequence matches one word. The *\W+* metacharacter sequence matches the whitespace between words. You can test for additional words by adding one *\W+(\w+)* metacharacter sequence for each additional word to match.
know there are only two words in a string while ignoring leading or trailing spaces:	`m/^\s*(\w+)\W+(\w+)\s*$/;` After this statement, *$1* holds the first word and *$2* holds the second word, assuming that the pattern matches. The *\s** metacharacter sequence matches any leading or trailing whitespace.

assign the first two words in a string to *$one* and *$two* and the rest of the string to *$rest*:	`$_ = "This is the way to San Jose.";`
	
	`$word   = '\w+'; # match a whole word.`
	
	`$space  = '\W+'; # match at least one character`
	`                 # of whitespace`
	
	`$string = '.*';  # match any number of anything`
	`                 # except for the newline character.`
	
	`($one, $two, $rest) = (m/^($word) $space ($word) \`
	`$space ($string)/x);`
	
	After this statement, *$one* holds the first word, *$two* holds the second word, and *$rest* holds everything else in the *$_* variable. This example uses variable interpolation to, hopefully, make the pattern easier to read. This technique also emphasizes which metasequence is used to match words and whitespace. It lets the reader focus on the whole of the pattern rather than on the individual pattern components by adding a level of abstraction.

Table 8.11 *Examples of the Perl Matching Operator (Cont'd)*

How Do I...	Answer	
determine if *$_* contains a legal Perl variable name:	`$result = m/`	
	`^`	`(?# Anchor the pattern to the)` `(?# start of the string)`
	`[\$\@\%]`	`(?# Use a character class to)` `(?# match the first character)` `(?# of a variable name)`
	`[a-z]`	`(?# Use a character class to)` `(?# ensure that the)` `(?# character of the name is a)` `(?# letter)`
	`\w*`	`(?# Use a character class to)` `(?# ensure that the rest of the)` `(?# variable name is either an)` `(?# alphanumeric or an)` `(?# underscore character)`
	`$`	`(?# Anchor the pattern to the)` `(?# end of the string. This)` `(?# means that for the pattern)` `(?# to match, the variable name)` `(?# must be the only value in)` `(?# $_.)`
	`/ix;`	`# Use the /i option so that` `# the search is case-` `# insensitive and use the /x` `# option to allow extensions.`

After this statement, *$result* is true if *$_* contains a legal variable name and false if it does not.

Table 8.11 *Examples of the Perl Matching Operator (Cont'd)*

How Do I...	Answer	
determine if *$_* contains a legal Perl variable name:	`$result = m/`	
	`^`	`(?# Anchor the pattern to the)` `(?# start of the string)`
	`[\$\@\%]`	`(?# Use a character class to)` `(?# match the first character)` `(?# of a variable name)`
	`[a-z]`	`(?# Use a character class to)` `(?# ensure that the character)` `(?# of the name is a letter)`
	`\w*`	`(?# Use a character class to)` `(?# ensure that the rest of)` `(?# the variable name is either)` `(?# an alphanumeric or an)` `(?# underscore character)`
	`$`	`(?# Anchor the pattern to the)` `(?# end of the string. This)` `(?# means that for the pattern)` `(?# to match, the variable name)` `(?# must be the only value in)` `(?# $_.)`
	`/ix;`	`# Use the /i option so that` `# the search is case-` `# insensitive and use the /x` `# option to allow extensions.`

After this statement, *$result* is true if *$_* contains a legal variable name and false if it does not.

Table 8.11 *Examples of the Perl Matching Operator (Cont'd)*

How Do I...	Answer
| determine if $_ contains a legal integer value: | ```
$result = m/
            (?# First check for just numbers in
            (?# $_)
  ^         (?# Anchor to the start of the
            (?# string)
  \d+       (?# Match one or more digits)
  $         (?# Anchor to the end of the
            (?# string)
  |         (?# or)
            (?# Now check for hexadecimal
            (?# numbers)
  ^         (?# Anchor to the start of the
            (?# string)
  0x        (?# The "0x" sequence starts a
            (?# hexadecimal number)
  [\da-f]+  (?# Match one or more
            (?# hexadecimal characters)
  $         (?# Anchor to the end of the
            (?# string)
  /i;
```<br><br>After this statement, *$result* is true if *$_* contains an integer literal and false if it does not. |
| match all legal integers in *$_*: | ```
@results = m/^\d+$|^0[x][\da-f]+$/gi;
```<br><br>After this statement, *@result* contains a list of all integer literals in *$_*. *@result* contains an empty list if no literals were found. |
| match the end of the first word in a string: | ```
m/\w\W/;
```<br><br>After this statement is executed, *$&* holds the last character of the first word and the next character that follows it. If you want only the last character, use pattern memory, *m/(\w)\W/;*. Then *$1* is equal to the last character of the first word. If you use the global option, `@array = m/\w\W/g;`, then you can create an array that holds the last character of each word in the string. |
```

Table 8.11 *Examples of the Perl Matching Operator (Cont'd)*

How Do I...	Answer
match the start of the second word in a string:	`m/\W\w/;` After this statement, *$&* holds the first character of the second word and the whitespace character that immediately precedes it. While this pattern is the opposite of the pattern that matches the end of words, it does not match the beginning of the first word! This is because of the \W metacharacter. Simply adding a * metacharacter to the pattern after the \W does not help, because then it would match zero non-word characters and therefore match every word character in the string.

match the filename in a file specification:	`$_ = '/user/Jackie/temp/names.dat';`
	`m!^.*/(.*)!;`
	
	After this match statement, *$1* holds *names.dat*. The match is anchored to the beginning of the string, and the .* component matches everything up to the last slash because regular expressions are greedy. Then the next *(.*)* matches the filename and stores it into pattern memory. You can store the file path into pattern memory by placing parentheses around the first .' component.

match two prefixes and one root word, like "rockfish" and "monkfish":	`m/(?:rock|monk)fish/x;` The alternative metacharacter is used to say that either *rock* or *monk* followed by *fish* needs to be found. If you need to know which alternative was found, then use regular parentheses in the pattern. After the match, *$1* holds either *rock* or *monk*.

Table 8.11 *Examples of the Perl Matching Operator (Cont'd)*

How Do I...	Answer
search a file for a string and print some of the surrounding lines:	(see code below)

```
# read the whole file into memory.
open(FILE, "<fndstr.dat");
@array = <FILE>;
close(FILE);

# specify which string to find.
$stringToFind = "A";

# iterate over the array looking for the
# string.
for ($index = 0; $index <= $#array; $index++) {
    last if $array[$index] =~ /$stringToFind/;
}

# Use $index to print two lines before
# and two lines after the line that contains
# the match.
foreach (@array[$index-2..$index+2]) {
    print("$index: $_");
    $index++;
}
```

There are many ways to perform this type of search, and this is just one of them. This technique is only good for relatively small files, because the entire file is read into memory at once. In addition, the program assumes that the input file always contains the string that you are looking for.

Table 8.12 shows how the substitution operator can be used.

Table 8.12 *Examples of the Perl Substitution Operator*

How Do I...	Answer
remove whitespace from the beginning of a string:	`s/^\s+//;` This pattern uses the \s predefined character class to match any whitespace character. The plus sign means to match zero or more whitespace characters, and the caret means match only at the beginning of the string.
remove whitespace from the end of a string:	`s/\s+$//;` This pattern uses the \s predefined character class to match any whitespace character. The plus sign means to match zero or more whitespace characters, and the dollar sign means match only at the end of the string.

add a prefix to a string:	`$prefix = "A";`
	`s/^(.*)/$prefix$1/;`
	
	When the substitution is done, the value in the *$prefix* variable is added to the beginning of the *$_* variable. Variable interpolation and pattern memory are combined to do this. Of course, you might also consider using the string concatenation operator—for example, *$_ = "A" . $_;*—which is probably faster.

add a suffix to a string:	`$suffix = "Z";`
	`s/^(.*)/$1$suffix/;`
	
	When the substitution is done, the value in the *$suffix* variable is added to the end of the *$_* variable. Variable interpolation and pattern memory are combined to do this. Of course, you might also consider using the string concatenation operator—for example, *$_ .= "Z";*—which is probably faster.

Table 8.12 *Examples of the Perl Substitution Operator (Cont'd)*

How Do I...	Answer
reverse the first two words in a string:	`s/^\s*(\w+)\W+(\w+)/$2 $1/;` This substitution statement uses the pattern memory variables *$1* and *$2* to reverse the first two words in a string. You can use a similar technique to manipulate columns of information, to manipulate the last two words, or even to change the order of more than two matches.
duplicate each character in a string:	`s/\w/$& x 2/eg;` When the substitution is done, each character in *$_* is repeated. If the original string was *"123abc"*, the new string would be *112233aabbcc*. The *e* option is used to force evaluation of the replacement string. The *$&* special variable is used in the replacement pattern to reference the matched string, which is then repeated by the string repetition operator.
capitalize all words in a sentence:	`s/(\w+)/\u$1/g;` When the substitution is done, each character in *$_* has its first letter capitalized. The */g* option means that each word—the *\w+* metasequence—is matched and placed in *$1*. Then it is replaced by *\u$1*. The *\u* capitalizes whatever follows it; in this case, it's the matched word.

Table 8.12 *Examples of the Perl Substitution Operator (Cont'd)*

How Do I...	Answer
insert a string between two repeated characters:	(see code below)

```
$_       = "!!!!";
$char    = "!";
$insert = "AAA";

s{
        ($char)        # look for the specified
                       # character.

        (?=$char)      # look for it again, but don't
                       # include it the matched
                       # string, so the next search
}                      # also finds it.
{
        $char . $insert  # concatenate the
                         # specified character
                         # with the string to
                         # insert.

}xeg;                  # use extended mode, evaluate
                       # the replacement pattern, and
                       # match all possible strings.

print("$_\n");
```

This example uses the extended mode to add comments directly inside the regular expression. This makes it easy to relate the comment directly to a specific pattern element. The match pattern does not directly reflect the originally stated goal of inserting a string between two repeated characters. Instead, the example was quietly restated. The new goal is to substitute all instances of *$char* with *$char . $insert*, (e.g. the $insert variable appended to the $char variable) if *$char* is followed by *$char*. As you can see, the end result is the same. Remember that sometimes you need to think outside the box.

Table 8.12 *Examples of the Perl Substitution Operator (Cont'd)*

How Do I...	Answer

perform two levels of variable substitution in the replacement pattern:	`s/(\$\w+)/$1/eeg;`
	
	This is a simple example of secondary variable interpolation. If *$firstVar* = "*AAA*" and *$_* = '*$firstVar*', then *$_* would be equal to *AAA* after the substitution is made. The key is that the replacement pattern is evaluated twice. This technique is very powerful. It can be used to develop error messages used with variable interpolation.
	
	`$errMsg = "File too large";`
	`$fileName = "DATA.OUT";`
	`$_ = 'Error: $errMsg for the file named`
	`$fileName';`
	`s/(\$\w+)/$1/eeg;`
	`print;`
	
	When this program is run, it displays:
	
	`Error: File too large for the file named`
	`DATA.OUT`
	
	The values of the *$errMsg* and *$fileName* variables are interpolated into the replacement pattern as needed.

Table 8.13 shows how the translation operator can be used.

Table 8.13 *Examples of the Perl Translation Operator*

How Do I...	Answer
count the number of times a given letter appears in a string:	`$cnt = tr/Aa//;` After this statement executes, *$cnt* holds the number of times the letter *a* appears in *$_*. The *tr* operator does not have an option to ignore the case of the string, so both uppercase and lowercase need to be specified.
turn off the high bit for every character in *$_*:	`tr [\200-\377] [\000-\177];` This statement uses the square brackets to delimit the character lists. Notice that spaces can be used between the pairs of brackets to enhance readability of the lists. The octal values are used to specify the character ranges. The translation operator is more efficient—in this example —than using logical operators and a loop statement. This is because creating a simple lookup table can do the translation.

Table 8.14 contains some examples of how the **split** function can be used. For more detailed information about the **split** function, see your Perl documentation.

Table 8.14 *Examples of Perl's split Function*

How Do I...	Answer

split a string into words:	`s/^\s+//;`
	`@array = split;`
	
	After this statement executes, *@array* is an array of words. Before splitting the string, you need to remove any beginning whitespace. If this is not done, **split** creates an array element with the whitespace as the first element in the array, and this is probably not what you want.

Table 8.14 *Examples of Perl's **split** Function (Cont'd)*

How Do I...	Answer

split a string contained in *$line* into words:	`$line =~ s/^\s+//;`
	`@array = split(/\W/, $line);`
	
	After this statement executes, *@array* contains an array of words.

split a string into characters:	`@array = split(//);` After this statement executes, *@array* contains an array of characters. **split** recognizes the empty pattern as a request to make every character into a separate array element.
split a string into fields based on a delimiter:	`@array = split(/:/);` After this statement executes, *@array* contains an array of strings consisting of the values between the delimiters—the delimiter being the colon character for this example. If there are repeated delimiters—(e.g. two colons in a row like this "::") then an empty array element is created. Use /:+/ as the delimiter to eliminate the empty array elements.

Tcl

There are four main uses for regular expressions in Tcl:

- The **glob** function—Used to find filenames that match a pattern.

- The **string match** function—Used to find text that matches a pattern.

- The **regexp** function—Used to find text that matches a pattern. **regexp** has more powerful metacharacters than a string match has.

- The **regsub** function—Used to replace text that matches a pattern.

Each of these functions is described in its own section.

The glob Function

The **glob** function is a handy way to create a list of files whose names match a pattern. Listing 8.4 shows how to process all files in a directory (compare it to Listing 8.2).

Listing 8.4 *tcl_glob—Using the Tcl **glob** Command to Process All Files in a Directory*

```
#!/usr/bin/tcl

foreach file [glob *] {
  puts "$file is being processed."
}
```

Here is an example of this script in action:

```
% chmod +x tcl_glob
% ls
foo.c      bar.c      david
% ./tcl_glob
foo.c is being processed.
bar.c is being processed.
david is being processed.
```

The **glob** function accepts multiple patterns as arguments. This can frequently make your life easier. Listing 8.5 shows how to create a list of text filenames from the *project_a* and *project_b* directories and all text files in the current directory.

Listing 8.5 *tcl_glob_multi—Using the Tcl **glob** Command With Multiple Patterns*
```
#!/usr/bin/tcl

set filelist [glob {{project_{a,b}/*.txt} {*.txt}]
puts $filelist
```

Here is an example of this script in action:

```
% chmod +x tcl_glob_multi
% ./tcl_glob_multi
project_a/one.txt  project_b/two.txt readme.txt
```

This example uses curly braces around the pattern to avoid Tcl's command substitution. In fact, it's always a good idea to enclose your patterns in curly braces.

Table 8.15 lists the metacharacters used by the **glob** function.

Table 8.15 *Metacharacters for Tcl's* **glob** *Function*

Metacharacter(s)	Metameaning
?	The question mark matches any single character.
*	The asterisk matches zero or more of any character.
[ ]	Square brackets create a character list. All characters inside the square brackets are used to match or not match a single character. For example, *[xyz]* matches either *x*, *y*, or *z* but not *xx*, *xy*, or any other combination. Character lists only match a single character regardless of how many characters are in the list. You can use *[a-e]* as shorthand for *[abcde]*.
{ }	Curly brackets are used for pattern expansion. For example, *x{y,z}* matches either *xy* or *xz* and no other text. It is very useful when dealing with directories.

The string match Function

When you only need to find a basic pattern in some text, you can use the **string match** function. It uses nearly the same metacharacters as Bash uses for its filenames. Table 8.16 lists the metacharacters you can use with the **string match** function.

Table 8.16 *Metacharacters for Tcl's* **string match** *Function*

Metacharacter	Metameaning
?	The question mark matches any single character.
*	The asterisk matches zero or more of any character.
[ ]	Square brackets create a character list. All characters inside the square brackets are used to match or not match a single character. For example, *[xyz]* matches either *x*, *y*, or *z* but not *xx*, or *xy* or any other combination. Character lists only match a single character regardless of how many characters are in the list. You can use *[a-e]* as shorthand for *[abcde]*.

The **string match** function is typically used as part of the conditional expression of an **if** statement:

```
if [string match {f*} $file] {
  puts "$file starts with an f"
}
```

You could also assign the return value of the **string match** function to a variable:

```
set options "color, fixed, logging, maxsize"
set pattern {*log*}
set options_lc [string tolower $options]

set is_logging_set [string match $pattern $options_lc]
```

This example shows three things:

1. You can store patterns inside variables and then pass those variables to the **string match** function. This might help to improve program documentation and keep your source code tidy.

2. You don't need to explicitly test for the whole word you're looking for. This example uses the pattern *log* to allow the user leeway in specifying the option. Therefore, the following strings would match: *turn_log_on*, *logging_on*, and *log_on*.

3. You can use the **string tolower** function to eliminate the problem of needing to check for both uppercase and lowercase patterns.

If the *log_on=true* pattern is found inside the *options* variable, then *is_logging_set* gets a value of *1*; otherwise, it gets a value of *zero*.

The regexp Function

The **regexp** function works almost exactly like the **m//** function in Perl. It allows for a wider variety of metacharacters than the **string match** function. Table 8.17 lists the metacharacters used by the **regexp** function.

Table 8.17 *Metacharacters for Tcl's* ***regexp*** *Function*

Metacharacter	Metameaning
^	This metacharacter—the caret—matches the beginning of a string. It is one of two pattern anchors—the other anchor is the $ metacharacter.
.	This metacharacter—the period—matches any character.
$	This metacharacter matches the end of a string. It is one of two pattern anchors—the other anchor is the ^ metacharacter.
|	This metacharacter—called *alternation*—lets you specify two values that can cause the match to succeed. For example, *a|b* means that the target variable must contain the *a* or *b* character for the match to succeed.
[]	The square brackets let you create a character class. For example, *[abc]* evaluates to true if any of *a*, *b*, or *c* is contained in the target string.
()	The parentheses let you affect the order of pattern evaluation and act as a form of pattern memory.
*	The asterisk quantifier forces the previous component to be matched zero or more times.
+	The plus quantifier forces the previous component to be matched one or more times.
?	The question mark quantifier forces the previous component to be matched zero or one times.

All of the metacharacters in Table 8.17 have the same meanings as Perl's metacharacters. Rather than reproduce the same material in this section, I'll focus on how the **regexp** function is different.

The ? denotes optional components.

The **regexp** function uses this syntax:

```
regexp ?switches? pattern target ?match? ?subMatch ...?
```

There are three switches usable by **regexp**:

-nocase   This option causes uppercase characters in the target to
            be treated as lowercase characters.

-indices   This option affects the *match* and *subMatch* variables.
            Instead of containing the actual text that was matched,
            the *match* and *subMatch* variables contain a list of the
            starting and ending indices of the matched text.

--   This option (two dashes in a row) indicates that there
            are no more options. This can be useful if your pattern
            starts with a dash.

The **regexp** function returns *1* if a pattern can be matched, and a
zero if it cannot.

The *match* variable, if specified, is assigned the value of the text
that matches the pattern. If the *-indices* option is used, the *match*
variable contains the starting and ending indices of the matched
text. For example:

```
% tcl
tcl>set target "Time and Again"
tcl>regexp {^.} $target match
1
tcl>puts $match
T
```

The *match* variable is assigned the value *T* because the ^. pattern matches the first character of the target.

The *subMatch* variables, if specified, are assigned any text that
matches parenthesized subexpressions. If the *-indices* option is
used, the *match* variable contains the starting and ending indices of
the matched text. For example:

```
% tcl
tcl>set target "Time and Again"
tcl>regexp {^(.)(.)} $target match subMatch1 subMatch2
1
tcl>puts $match
T
tcl>puts $subMatch1
T
tcl>puts $subMatch2
i
```

Let's take a quick look at an example using the *-indices* options:

```
% tcl
tcl>set target "Time and Again"
tcl>regexp -indices {^..} $target match
1
tcl>puts $match
0 1
```

NOTE   You can use any variable names for the *match* and *subMatch* param-
          eters to **regexp**. *match* and *subMatch* were used in these examples
          simply to distinguish between the two types of values returned.

The regsub Function

The **regsub** function is used to replace a pattern in text. It uses
the same metacharacters as the **regexp** function. Please look at
Table 8.17 for a list of metacharacters usable by the **regsub** function.

The **regsub** function uses this syntax:

```
regsub ?switches? pattern target replacement newVariable
```

The ?
denotes
optional
components.

There are three switches usable by **regsub**:

-nocase   This option causes uppercase characters in the target to
            be treated as lowercase characters.

-all   This option replaces all matched text in the target
            string. Without this option, only the first matched text
            is replaced. This option is equivalent to the /g option in
            Perl.

--   This option (two dashes in a row) indicates that there
            are no more options. This is useful if your pattern
            starts with a dash.

The **regsub** function returns a count of the number of times the
pattern was matched and replaced.

The *newVariable* variable is assigned the result of replacing *pattern* with *replacement* in target. The *target* variable is not changed.
If no replacements were made, then *newVariable* becomes the same
as *target*.

Let's look at a simple example of **regsub**:

```
% tcl
tcl>set target "aaa bbb ccc"
tcl>set pattern {bbb}
tcl>set rep {zzz}
tcl>set count [regsub $pattern $target $rep newVariable]
tcl>puts $newVariable
aaa zzz ccc
tcl>puts $count
1
tcl>set target "aaa bbb ccc bbb"
tcl>set count [regsub -all $pattern $target $rep
newVariable]
tcl>puts $newVariable
aaa zzz ccc zzz
tcl>puts $count
2
```

The second call to **regsub** replaces both instances of *bbb* in the *target* variable.

Like Perl's *m//* and *s///* operators, the **regsub** function makes use of pattern memory. **regsub** lets you enclose pattern components inside parentheses in order to store the string that matches the components into pattern memory. You can use pattern memory as one of the components of the replacement pattern.

The character sequence \0, when used in the replacement string, gets replaced with the whole matched text. The \n character sequence gets replaced with the nth parenthesized sub-expression. For example:

```
% tcl
tcl>set target "aaa bbb ccc bbb"
tcl>set pattern {bbb}
tcl>set rep {z\0z}
tcl>regsub $pattern $target $rep newVariable
1
tcl>puts $newVariable
aaa zbbbz ccc
```

Summary

As you've seen, pattern matching is a useful, but complex, subject. Bash uses pattern matching mainly for filenames. Perl has integrated pattern matching and uses patterns in many different ways.

Tcl's patterns are more sophisticated than Bash's, but not quite up to Perl's level.

Bash

The Bash section shows you how pattern matching can be used to search for filenames. Table 8.1 lists the meaning for the *?*, ***, *[]*, and *()* metacharacters. The shell interprets these metacharacters before any applications see them unless they are prefixed with a backslash or are placed inside single quotes.

Bash also has some little-used pattern matching available for use with variables, as shown in Table 8.2. The patterns let you prune either the beginning or end of a variable's value. This ability might be valuable when you only need the first or last part of a string.

The **case** command uses filename metacharacters to determine which command block to execute.

And, finally, metacharacters can be used with the **for** command to create a list of filenames to iterate over.

Perl

The Perl section introduces you to regular expressions or patterns, regular expression operators, and the binding operators. There are three regular expression operators—*m//*, *s///*, and *tr///*— used to match, substitute, and translate. They use the *$_* variable as the default operand. The binding operators, =~ and *!~*, are used to bind the regular expression operators to a variable other than *$_*.

While the slash character is the default pattern delimiter, you can use any character in its place. This feature is useful if the pattern you are working with contains the slash character. If you use an opening bracket or parenthesis as the beginning delimiter, use the closing bracket or parenthesis as the ending delimiter. Using the single quote as the delimiter turns off variable interpolation for the pattern.

The matching operator has six options: */g*, */i*, */m*, */o*, */s*, and */x*. These options are described in Table 8.4. I've found that the */x* option is very helpful for creating maintainable, commented programs. The */g* option, used to find all matches in a string, is also very useful. And, of course, the capability to create case-insensitive patterns using the */i* option is crucial in many cases.

The substitution operator has the same options as the matching operator and one more—the /e option. The /e option lets you evaluate the replacement pattern and use the new value as the replacement string. If you use backticks as delimiters, the replacement pattern is executed as a Unix command, and the resulting output becomes the replacement string.

The translation operator has three options: /c, /d, and /s. These options are used to complement the match character list, delete characters not in the match character list, and eliminate repeated characters in a string. If no replacement list is specified, the number of matched characters is returned. This is handy if you need to know how many times a given character appears in a string.

The binding operators are used to force the matching, substitution, and translation operators to search a variable other than $_. The =~ operator can be used with all three of the regular expression operators, while the !~ operator can be used only with the matching operator.

Quite a bit of space is devoted to creating patterns, and the topic deserves even more space. This is easily one of the more involved features of the Perl language. One key concept is that a character can have multiple meanings. For example, the plus sign can mean a plus sign in one instance (its literal meaning), but can also mean to match something one or more times in another (its metameaning).

Regular expression components can be combined in an infinite number of ways. Table 8.7 lists most of the metameanings for different characters. Pattern matching also consists of character classes, alternation, quantifiers, anchors, pattern memory, word boundaries, and extended components.

The last section of the chapter is devoted to presenting numerous examples of how to use regular expressions to accomplish specific goals. Each situation is described, and a pattern that matches that situation is shown. Some commentary is given for each example.

Tcl

Tcl's use of patterns is almost as pervasive as Perl's. Tcl uses patterns for filename matching (the **glob** function), for simple pattern matching (the **string match** function), for advanced pattern matching (the **regexp** function), and for pattern replacement (the **regsub** function).

The **glob** function creates a list of files whose names match a specified pattern. The list can be directly processed using the **foreach** command or passed to a procedure for processing. Table 8.15 shows the metacharacters used by the **glob** function.

The **string match** function lets you search for basic patterns. Table 8.16 shows the metacharacters you can use.

The **regexp** function uses many of the same metacharacters as Perl's matching operator. Table 8.17 shows the available metacharacters.

The **regsub** function, like Perl's substitution operator, lets you replace one pattern with another. It uses the same metacharacters as the **regexp** function.

The next chapter, "Examining the Tools," introduces you to many of Unix's more popular commands. Each chapter section covers a different Unix command, complete with syntax and examples.

Examining the Tools

This chapter provides a reference for some of the more commonly used and useful shell commands. Unlike many other references, it won't present arcane X Windows commands or system adminis-trivia. The commands in this chapter are those you'll use day in and day out. Their features and syntax need to become second nature in order for you to become truly productive.

While some Unix commands are quite simple—the **mv** command, for example—nearly all of them have valuable options and features that might not be immediately obvious. When I first learned Unix—some 16 years ago—few of the reference books had examples. They consisted of lists of command options and a minimum amount of information about what each option does. Commands were rarely shown in combination with other commands—the way they are used by experienced Unix users. In the ensuing 16 years, the documentation hasn't gotten much better. Yes, it is more comprehensive, but not more understandable. In this chapter, I hope to remedy that situation.

The tools described in this chapter, and the many others that are available, comprise one of Unix's biggest advantages over other operating systems. Recently, I needed to manipulate a 17MB text file in DOS. Without the aid of tools such as **csplit**, **grep** and **cut**, I had to write all of the information extraction routines from scratch. The project took much longer than it would have if Unix were the operating system used for the project.

Table 9.1 *Commands and Their Page Numbers*

Command	Page	Description
[ ]	390	Performs file tests and evaluates expressions.
basename	297	Removes the directory and, optionally, the suffix from a filename.
clear	302	Erases the terminal screen.
cat	298	Displays one or more files.
cksum	300	Calculates a file's checksum.
col	302	Filters reverse movement characters (like backspaces).
cp	303	Copies files.
csplit	306	Splits a file into pieces using context as the spilt criterion.

Table 9.1 *Commands and Their Page Numbers (Cont'd)*

Command	Page	Description
cut	310	Displays one or more sections from each line of input.
date	313	Displays and sets the system time.
diff	316	Finds differences between two files.
echo	319	Displays its own parameters. For example, *echo "Press Enter to Continue."* displays the "Press Enter to Continue." message on the computer screen.
env	321	Runs a command in a subshell with a modified environment.
expr	322	Evaluates an expression and sends the result to *STDOUT.*
eval	325	Generates and executes command lines on the fly.
false	326	Returns an exit value of *1* to indicate failure.
find	326	Examines directory trees—evaluates an expression for every file encountered.
fgrep	340	Searches through files for fixed-string patterns of text.
grep	340	Searches through files for patterns of text.
groff	346	Formats documents.
head	356	Displays the beginnings of files.
info	357	Displays online documentation.
join	358	Merges two files based on a common field.
kill	362	Sends a signal to one or more processes.
less	363	Displays files one page at a time.
mv	365	Renames or moves files.

Table 9.1 *Commands and Their Page Numbers (Cont'd)*

Command	Page	Description
nl	367	Prepends each input line with a number before outputting it.
ps	368	Reports process statistics.
pstree	372	Reports process lists using a tree format.
rm	376	Deletes files.
sort	377	Sorts, merges, or verifies the alphabetic order of input lines.
split	383	Splits a file into pieces using size as the split criterion.
strings	384	Displays the printable characters in a binary file.
tail	386	Displays the ends of files.
tee	388	Reads from *STDIN* and writes to both *STDOUT* and one or more other files.
test	390	Performs file tests and evaluates expressions.
tr	396	Translates or deletes characters.
troff	346	Formats documents. For details see the **groff** command.
true	401	Returns an exit value of *0* to indicate success.
tty	401	Displays the name of the terminal connected to *STDIN*.
type	402	Displays information about commands.
uname	403	Displays system information.
uniq	404	Removes repeated lines from sorted input.
wc	406	Counts the number of characters, words, and lines in a file.
who	407	Displays information about who is logged on to the system.

Table 9.1 *Commands and Their Page Numbers (Cont'd)*

Command	Page	Description
write	409	Sends a terminal message to a logged-on user.
xargs	410	Builds and executes command lines.

The rest of this chapter looks at each command in alphabetical order.

> Many of the options shown in this chapter are only available with **NOTE**
> Bash. Since Bash is freely available and runs on nearly all computer
> platforms, you've probably already installed it on your computers. If
> not, some of the options mentioned in this chapter won't work for
> you.

The basename Command

Synopsis:

basename removes the directory and, optionally, the suffix from a filename.

Syntax:

```
basename filename [suffix]
```

Description:

The **basename** command comes in handy when you need to remove the directory information from a filename. The *suffix* parameter can be used to remove suffixes from filename, but only when the *suffix* parameter matches the suffix of filename. Here are a few examples:

basename can also remove suffixes from non-filenames.

```
% basename "/home/medined/test.dat"
test.dat
% basename "/home/medined/test.dat" ".dat"
test
% basename "Newark, NJ" ",NJ"
Newark
```

The last example shows that you can use the **basename** command on text other than filenames. This feature might solve a thorny problem for you some day.

The cat Command

Synopsis:

cat (short for concatenate) copies one or more files to *STDOUT.*

Syntax:

```
cat [options] [file...]
```

Description:

The **cat** command reads the files on the command line and sends their contents to *STDOUT.* If no files are listed on the command line, *STDIN* is used. At first glance, it might not seem very useful, but it does have a few good options. Additionally, **cat** is frequently used to combine two or more files in order to pipe the combination to some other command for processing.

Table 9.2 shows the options that are available with the **cat** command.

Table 9.2 *Options for the* **cat** *Command*

Option	Description
-b or --number-nonblank	Prepends a number to all nonblank output lines.
-E or --show-ends	Appends a dollar sign ($) to all lines.
--help	Displays a help message.
-n or --number	Prepends a number to all output lines.
-s or --squeeze-blank	Combines multiple blank lines into one.
-T or --show-tabs	Displays tab characters as ^I. The ^I notation is used because the tab character is equivalent to ASCII code 9 and I is the ninth letter of the alphabet.
-v or --show-nonprinting	Displays all control characters, except for the linefeeds and tabs, using the caret (^) notation and characters with their high-bit set using the M- notation.
--version	Displays a version message.

Let's use the file in Listing 9.1 for sample data.

Listing 9.1 *cat.dat—A Datafile Used to Demonstrate the cat Command*

```
Monday morning when I answered the door there were


twenty-one new real estate agents there, all in

horrible polyester gold jackets. They came swarming
in and scattered to every corner of my great dry-
rotted California manse. Several of them had video
cameras. What a thing to wake up to.
```

This paragraph begins the science fiction novel, "The Hacker and the Ants," by Rudy Rucker.

You can't see it in Listing 9.1, but the first line contains two tab characters. Let's use the *--show-tabs* option to display them and the *--show-ends* option to see if any extra spaces are present at the end of the lines.

```
% cat --show-tabs --show-ends cat.dat
Monday^Imorning when^II answered the door there were$
$
$
twenty-one new real estate agents there, all in $
$
horrible polyester gold jackets. They came swarming$
in and scattered to every corner of my great dry-$
rotted California manse. Several of them had video$
cameras. What a thing to wake up to.$
```

I've bolded the tab characters that appear on the first line of output to make them easier to spot. You should also notice that there is an extra space at the end of the fourth line.

If this data file were many lines long, the *--number* option would definitely come in handy:

```
% cat --show-tabs --show-ends --number cat.dat
     1  Monday^Imorning when^II answered the door there were$
     2  $
     3  $
     4  twenty-one new real estate agents there, all in $
     5  $
     6  horrible polyester gold jackets. They came swarming$
     7  in and scattered to every corner of my great dry-$
     8  rotted California manse. Several of them had video$
     9  cameras. What a thing to wake up to.$
```

If you're only looking for trailing spaces, that's an awful lot of output to wade through. Let's use the **grep** command to filter it:

```
% cat --show-ends --number cat.dat | grep " [$]$"
     4  twenty-one new real estate agents there, all in $
```

This command filters the output from **cat** through **grep**. The pattern that **grep** is looking for is a space followed by a dollar sign followed by the end of the line. The first dollar sign was placed inside square brackets (to form a character class consisting of only one character) in order to prevent **grep**'s interpreting it as a meta-character.

The **grep** command is discussed later in this chapter in its own section. However, if you've skipped ahead and then come back here, you might be wondering why I didn't use the [:space:] character class as part of the filter pattern. Good question. Let's try it:

```
% cat --show-ends --number cat.dat | grep "[[:space:]][$]$"
     2  $
     3  $
     4  twenty-one new real estate agents there, all in $
     5  $
```

The special [:space:] character class matches the empty string at the beginning of lines in addition to matching the space character that we were filtering for.

The cksum Command

Synopsis:
   cksum calculates the checksum of a file.

Syntax:
   ```
   cksum [--help | --version] [file..]
   ```

Description:
   The **cksum** command was originally intended to make sure that files transferred from one system to another weren't corrupted in the process. This test requires the checksum to be calculated on the original system, calculated again on the destination system, and the two figures compared. If the checksums were the same, the files were assumed to have transferred intact.

I've included the **cksum** command in this reference chapter because it comes in handy when you need to check files or directories for tampering. By determining the checksum of a directory or file and comparing it to an old checksum, you can tell if the file has been changed.

cksum reads from *STDIN* if no filenames are specified on the command line. When one or more filenames are specified, **cksum** displays the checksum, the number of bytes in the each file, and the filename.

The first step to using **cksum** to check for tampering is to create a baseline file:

```
% mkdir /cksum
% cksum /bin/* > /cksum/bin.cksum
% cat /cksum/bin.cksum
2967046608 2088 /bin/arch
919332943 62692 /bin/ash
2817380754 151496 /bin/ash.static
...
```

Once the baseline file is created, you—at any time in the future—can quickly determine if any of the checksummed files have changed using this command:

```
% cksum /bin/* | diff - /cksum/bin.cksum
4c4
< 890459061 138812 /bin/awk
---
> 890459061 138812 /bin/awk
```

The output clearly shows that the */bin/awk* file has been renamed. All output lines that begin with a > character belong to the baseline file. The **diff** command is documented in its own section of this chapter.

If someone had replaced the *awk* file with another, the output might look like this:

```
% cksum /bin/* | diff - /cksum/bin.cksum
4c4
< 2165160898 29 /bin/awk
---
> 890459061 138812 /bin/awk
```

This output shows that both the contents of the file and its size have been altered.

The clear Command

Synopsis

> **clear** erases the terminal screen.

Syntax

```
clear
```

Description:

The **clear** command uses the *terminfo* database to determine how to clear the terminal. This command is useful immediately before displaying messages or process results that the user needs to read.

The col Command

Synopsis

> **col** filters backward movement characters (like backspaces).

Syntax

```
col [options]
```

Description:

vi is a popular text editor. To exit, type :q, or if you've changed the file, type :q! to exit without saving the changes.

The **col** command filters backward movement characters (like backspaces) and, optionally, converts whitespace into tabs where possible. Many terminals need the character sequence B^HB in order to display in bold. The **man** command is a good example of this technique:

```
% man col
col(1) ... UNIX Reference Manual ...    col(1)

NAME
        col - filter reverse ...
...
```

Let's look under the covers to see what is actually sent to the terminal:

```
% man col > man.out
% vi man.out
col(1) ... UNIX Reference Manual ...    col(1)

N^HNA^HAM^HME^HE
```

```
        c^Hco^Hol^Hl - filter reverse ...
...
```

The ^*H* notation that you see in the above example represents a backspace character. The display interprets *N^HN* as a request to display a bold letter **N**.

The **col** command can be used to remove those backspace characters:

```
% col -b < man.out > col.out
% vi col.out
col(1) ... UNIX Reference Manual ...   col(1)

NAME
      col - filter reverse ...
...
```

When the *-b* option is used, **col** removes the backspace character and the character in front of it.

Table 9.3 shows some of the options available with the **col** command.

Table 9.3 *Some Options of the col Command*

Option	Description
-b	Filters out all backspace characters and the character immediately preceding each backspace character.
-x	Suppresses the conversion of spaces into tabs.

The cp Command

Synopsis:

> **cp** copies files.

Syntax:

> ```
> cp [options] source destination
> ```

Description:

The **cp** command can be used in two ways. What it does depends on the *DESTINATION* parameter. If *destination* is a filename, that filename becomes the name of the copied file. If the destination is a directory, the source file is copied into the new directory using its old filename. When pattern-matching metacharacters are used, more than one file can be copied into the destination directory at a time.

Table 9.4 shows the options available with the **cp** command.

Table 9.4 *Options for the cp Command*

Option	Description
`-a` or `--archive`	Preserves as much as possible of the structure and attributes of the original files.
`-b` or `--backup`	Creates backup copies of any files about to be overwritten. Related options are *--suffix* and *--version-control*.
`-d` or `--no-dereference`	Preserves the hard link relationships between source files and copies symbolic links instead of the files they point to.
`-f` or `--force`	Removes existing destination files.
`--help`	Displays a help message.
`-i` or `--interactive`	Asks for confirmation before overwriting existing destination files.
`-l` or `--link`	Creates hard links to the source files instead of copying them.
`-P` or `--parents`	Creates a directory hierarchy under the destination directory by appending the path of the source files to the destination directory. For example, *cp --parents /home/medined*.dat backup_dm* copies the data files into the *./ backup_dm/home/medined* directory. Any intermediate directories are created as needed.
`-p` or `--preserve`	Makes sure that the new copies have the same owner, group, permissions, and timestamps as the source files.

Table 9.4 *Options for the cp Command (Cont'd)*

Option	Description
-R or -r or --recursive	Recursively copies directories. The *-r* option copies non-directories as if they were regular files.
-S or --suffix *SUFFIX*	Defines the suffix to be used when creating backup files with the *–b* option. The default is a tilde (~). You can also set the *SIMPLE_BACKUP_SUFFIX* variable. The command-line option overrides the variable.
-s or --symbolic-link	Creates symbolic links to the source files instead of copying them. All source files must start with a slash (i.e., they must be absolute filenames).
-u or --update	Only copies files whose modification time is newer than existing destination files. This typically results in only copying changed files.
-V *TYPE* or -version-control *TYPE*	Controls the type of backup files that are made. *TYPE* can be numbered, existing, or simple. The existing type of backup makes a numbered backup file if a simple backup file already exists. The numbered and simple options do the obvious thing. You can set a default type of backup using the *VERSION_CONTROL* variable.
-v or --verbose	Displays the name of each source file before copying it.
--version	Displays version information.
-x or --one-file-system	Skips source subdirectories that are on a different filesystem from the one that the copy started from. This option is useful to avoid copying files from mounted disks—such as a floppy disk or CD-ROM.

The **cp** command is too simple for me to include examples. I only include it in this chapter so that you can become aware of its options, especially the *--update* and *--recursive* options.

The csplit Command

Synopsis:

csplit breaks a file into pieces using context as the split criterion.

Syntax:

```
csplit [options] infile pattern...
```

Description:

The **csplit** command can be used to split up a file based on number of lines, a pattern, or a series of patterns. An error occurs if the specified pattern can't be found in the input. When an error occurs, all output files are removed, unless this behavior is overridden by the *--keep-files* option. After every pattern on the command line has been matched, any leftover input is stored in the last output file.

Let's take a look at how **csplit** is used. Listing 9.2 contains the text file used in the examples. Each record (a record is a grouping of information) is delimited by two at (@) signs. The examples show how to create files that each contain one record.

Listing 9.2 *csplit.dat—A Data File Used to Demonstrate the* **csplit** *Command*

```
1
#/#@@
2
@@
3
@@
```

In order to make it easy to see the output filenames, the following commands were issued in a directory that only contains *csplit.dat*:

```
% csplit csplit.dat 2
2      <- The number of bytes written to xx00.
13     <- The number of bytes written to xx01.
% ls
csplit.dat xx00 xx01
```

```
% cat xx00
1
% cat xx01
#/#@@
2
@@
3
@@
% csplit csplit.dat 2 3
2      <- The first split happens at line 2.
3      <- The second split happens at line 3.
10     <- Everything else goes into the last file.
% ls
csplit.dat xx00 xx01 xx02  <- The old files are
                               overwritten.
% rm xx*
% csplit csplit.dat '/@@/'
2
13
% cat xx00
1
% cat xx01
#/#@@   <- The line containing the matched pattern
2       <- always starts the new output file. Even though
@@      <- the pattern was at the end of the line, the whole
3       <- line is in the new output file.
@@
% rm xx*
% # The next command adds a repeat count
% # and specifies a prefix for the output file.
% csplit --prefix rec csplit.dat '/@@/' '{*}'
2
7
5
3
% ls rec*
rec00 rec01 rec02 rec03
% cat rec00
1
% cat rec01
#/#@@
2
% cat rec02
@@
3
% cat rec03
@@
% rm rec* xx*
```

```
% # The following command ignores the second
% # record in the input file.
% csplit.dat csplit.dat '/@@/' '%@@%' '/@@/'
2
5
3
% cat xx00
1
% cat xx01
@@              <- This is the third record, indicating
3               <- that the second record was skipped.
% cat xx02
@@
```

The above examples show that the **csplit** command has great flexibility. They used three methods to control the context split:

- Line Number—The exact line number(s) at which to split can be specified on the command line.

- Pattern—Using the *'/PATTERN/' ['{n|*}']* notation, you can specify a regular expression to control the splits. The entire line containing the pattern starts a new output file. The optional *'{n|*}'* notation means to look for the pattern *n* times or, if the asterisk is specified, look for the pattern until the end of the input.

- Anti-Pattern—Using the *'%PATTERN%' ['{n|*}']* notation, you can specify a section of file to ignore. **csplit** ignores from the line containing the anti-pattern to the next pattern found. The optional *'{n|*}'* notation means to look for the pattern *n* times or, if the asterisk is specified, look for the pattern until the end of the input.

Unlike what I've shown in the examples in this book, you can also use non-identical patterns in the same command line. For example, the first split can happen on a pattern like *'/@@END OF DATA@@/'* and other splits can be controlled by *'/@@END OF RECORD@@/'*.

Using the options shown in Table 9.5, you have even more flexibility and control.

Table 9.5 *Options for the* ***csplit*** *Command*

Option	Description
`-f=`*PREFIX* or `--prefix=`*PREFIX*	Specifies a prefix for the output files.
`-b"`*SUFFIX*`"` or `--suffix=`*SUFFIX*	Specifies a suffix format for the output files. The format can use any one of the *d*, *i*, *u*, *o*, *x*, or *X* format specifiers understood by C's **printf** function. For example, the option *--suffix-format=*`"%d"` creates a suffix that does not use leading zeroes. The format specifier letters stand for *decimal*, *integer*, *unsigned integer*, *octal*, *hexadecimal*, and *uppercase hexadecimal*, respectively.
`--help`	Displays a help message.
`-k` **or** `--keep-files`	Keeps output files when an error is encountered.
`-n`*NUM_DIGIT* or `--digits=`*NUM_DIGIT*	Specifies the number of digits used in the suffix. Normally, only two digits are used. This option is ignored if the *--prefix* option is also used.
`-s` **or** `-q` **or** `--silent` **or** `--quiet`	Suppresses the display of the file size for each output file.
`--version`	Displays the version information.
`-z` **or** `--elide-empty-files`	Suppresses the creation of *zero-length* files. If the command-line pattern marks the beginning of records instead of the end, the first output file is normally *zero-length*. This option prevents that file from being created.

The cut Command

Synopsis

cut displays one or more sections from each line of input.

Syntax

```
cut {section_specifiers} [options] [file...]
```

Description:

The first section on a line is numbered 1.

The **cut** command looks at each line of input, chops each line into sections, and then displays those sections specified on the command line. If no files are listed on the command line, *STDIN* is used.

Table 9.6 shows how sections are specified.

Table 9.6 *Section Specifiers for the* **cut** *Command*

Section Specifier	Description
-b*LIST* or --bytes *LIST*	Displays the bytes located in the positions specified by the *LIST* parameter. For example, *--bytes 1-3* displays only the first three bytes of each line. Note that the *--bytes* specifier needs a space before the *LIST* parameter.
-c*LIST* or --characters *LIST*	Displays the characters located in the positions specified by the *LIST* parameter. For example, *--characters 1-3* displays only the first three bytes of each line. Note that the *--characters* specifier needs a space before the *LIST* parameter.
-f*LIST* or --fields *LIST*	Displays the fields specified by *LIST*. A field is delimited by the beginning of a line, the end of a line, and the *DELIMITER* specified by the *-d/--delimiter* option. The default delimiter is a tab character. Note that the *--fields* specifier needs a space before the *LIST* parameter.

NOTE   A distinction is made between bytes and characters because of international character sets. For now, assume the two options perform the same actions.

You can use several different notations to form the *LIST* parameter:

- Use commas for non-contiguous sections. For example, to select sections four and seven, use -*f4,7*.

- Use range notation for contiguous sections. For example, to select sections two, three, and four, use –*b2-4*.

- Use *n-* notation to select from section *n* to the end of the line.

Table 9.7 shows the options that are available with the **cut** command.

Table 9.7 *Options for the **cut** Command*

Option	Description
-d*DELIMITER* or --delimiter *DELIMITER*	Specifies the delimiter used by the -*f*/--*fields* specifier. The default delimiter is a tab character.
--help	Displays a help message.
-n	Unused for now. Intended to be used when international character sets are supported.
-s or --only-delimited	Used in conjunction with the -*f*/--*fields* specifier to eliminate lines that don't contain the field delimiter character.
--version	Displays version information.

The **cut** command is excellent when used with fixed-length fields and records. For example, if you have a data file, as shown in Listing 9.3, describing a typical family:

Listing 9.3 *cut.dat—A Data File Used to Demonstrate the **cut** Command*

```
Robert   Male    Husband
Barbara  Female  Wife
Peter    Male    Son
Richard  Male    Son
```

You can easily use the **cut** command to display information from any of the columns. The following command views the second column:

```
% cut -b9-14 cut.dat
Male
Female
Male
Male
```

Once you've determined the section of information that you need, the **pipe** command can be used for further processing. For example, to generate a list of the unique values in a section:

```
% cut -b9-14 cut.dat | sort | uniq
Female
Male
```

Let's briefly turn our attention to the *--fields* option before moving on to the **echo** command. The *--fields* option works in conjunction with the *--delimiter* option to virtually chop each input line into sections, based on the *end-of-field* delimiter. Let's see how this works:

```
% cut -delimiter=" " --fields 1 cut.dat
Robert
Barbara
Peter
Richard
```

That's seems pretty straightforward. Let's try looking at the second column:

```
% cut -delimiter=" " --fields 2 cut.dat

Female

Male
```

What happened? Why didn't all four lines of input produce output? The answer lies in how **cut** defines the *end-of-field* delimiter. The *end-of-field* delimiter can only be a single character. Therefore, when there is more than one space between the words, **cut** sees more than two fields.

The **tr** command can solve this problem by collapsing multiple spaces into one space:

```
% cat cut.dat | \
> tr " " --squeeze-repeats | \
> cut -delimiter=" " --fields 2
Male
Female
Male
Male
```

Now the **cut** command performs as expected. Notice that the **cat** command is needed to pipe the *cut.dat* file into the **tr** command. **cat** is needed because **tr** only reads from *STDIN*—not from a file specified on the command line.

The date Command

Synopsis
> **date** displays and sets the system time.

Syntax
```
date [format]
```

Description:

The **date** command can either display or set the system time. Because this book is devoted to programming and not to system administration, only the time display format specifiers are shown in Table 9.8. The format specifiers are only used when a + is the initial character of the *FORMAT* parameter.

date has two options that are useful for displaying information, as shown in Table 9.8.

Table 9.8 *Display Options for the* **display** *Command*

Option	Description
`-d` *DATE +FORMAT* or `--date` *DATE +FORMAT*	Displays *DATE* using the format specified by the *FORMAT* parameter. This option can be very powerful because it understands some natural language phrases. For example, use *date --date 'yesterday'* to display yesterday's date.
`-u` **or** `--universal`	Displays the Greenwich Mean Time.

Table 9.9 shows the format specifiers used by **date**.

Table 9.9 *Display Format Specifiers for the **date** Command*

Specifier	Description
%a	Abbreviated weekday name
%A	Full weekday name
%b	Abbreviated month name
%B	Full month name
%c	Date and time
%C	Century
%d	Day of month (always two digits)
%D	Month/day/year (eight characters)
%e	Day of month (leading zero blanked)
%h	Abbreviated month name
%H	24-hour-clock hour (two digits)
%I	12-hour-clock hour (two digits)
%j	Julian day number (three digits)
%k	12-hour-clock hour (leading zero blanked)
%l	24-hour-clock hour (leading zero blanked)
%m	Month number (two digits)
%M	Minute (two digits)
%n	newline character
%p	AM/PM designation
%r	Hour:minute:second AM/PM designation
%R	Hour:minute
%S	Second (two digits)
%t	tab character

Table 9.9 *Display Format Specifiers for the **date** Command (Cont'd)*

Specifier	Description
%T	Hour:minute:second
%U	Sunday-based week number (two digits)
%w	Day number (one digit, Sunday is 0)
%W	Monday-based week number (two digits)
%x	Date
%X	Time
%y	Last two digits of year
%Y	Year in full
%Z	Time zone abbreviation
%+	Default output format
-	The *dash* specifier tells **date** not to pad numeric fields with zeros. For example, instead of displaying *01*, **date** would display *1*.
_	The *underscore* specifier tells **date** to pad numeric fields with spaces.

The exact format of some of these specifiers is determined by the locale of your computer. If you need more detailed information, please see the **date** man page.

Here are some examples of the **date** command:

```
% date
Sun Jun 14 19:51:01 EDT 1998
% date '+%B'
June
% date '+%Y_%j'   <- This format is excellent
1998_165          <- for sorting by date and,
                  <- therefore good for filenames.
% date --date '2 days ago' '+%d-%m-%y'
13-06-98          <- The European format, day first.
% date --date '2 days' '+%b %d, %Y'
Jun 18, 1998      <- A nice international format.
```

You can easily use **date** to create filenames based on the current date:

```
run_process >> `date '+%Y_%j.log'`
```

This command creates a log file with a four-digit year and the Julian date. This technique has two nice features: The files sort correctly in directory listings, and a new log file is automatically created every day when the redirection is performed.

The diff Command

Synopsis:

   diff finds differences between two files.

Syntax:

```
diff [options] from to
```

Description:

   The **diff** command is used extensively by Unix programmers to determine what has changed between two versions of a file. Programmers usually focus their attention on source code files. However, you can be much more creative. I've used **diff** to monitor whole directories (as explained in the **cksum** section of this chapter).

   If either the *FROM* or *TO* parameters are directory names, **diff** handles them in a special way. If only *FROM* is a directory, then **diff** compares the file named *FROM/TO* (i.e., the file in the *from* directory with the same name as the destination file) to the file named *TO*. For example, (cd /home/medined; diff /home/harry .bashrc) compares */home/medined/.bashrc* to */home/harry/ .bashrc*. If both *FROM* and *TO* are directories, then **diff** compares each of the files in one directory to the corresponding files (based on their names) in the other directory, in alphabetical order. If you need the comparison to walk the directory hierarchy, use the *-- recursive* option.

   If there are no differences between the compared files, **diff** will not display any output at all (unless you use the *–s* option).

   Table 9.10 shows some of the options available with the **diff** command. The options that are not shown mostly deal with creating and maintaining different versions of C source code. Therefore, they're not relevant to this book.

Table 9.10 *Options for the diff Command*

Option	Description
`-a` or `--text`	Treats all files as text by comparing them line by line.
`-b` or `-w` or `--ignore-all-space` or `--ignore-space-change`	Ignores changes that involve spaces, tabs, and newlines.
`-B` or `--ignore-blank-lines`	Ignores changes that involve inserting or deleting blank lines.
`-C NUM_LINES` or `--context[=NUM_LINES]`	Displays *NUM_LINES* of context around the changed line. If *NUM_LINES* is not specified, the default value is three.
`-d` or `--minimal`	Uses an alternative, slower algorithm to find smaller sets of changes.
`-i` or `--ignore-case`	Ignores differences that result from changes from lowercase to uppercase and vice versa.
`-I PATTERN` or `--ignore-matching-lines=PATTERN`	Ignores changes that result from inserting or deleting lines that match *PATTERN*.
`-L LABEL` or `--label=LABEL`	Uses *LABEL* instead of the filename in the output.
`-q` or `--brief`	Reports only whether files are different, not the details.
`-r` or `--recursive`	When comparing directories, recursively compares any subdirectories found.
`-s` or `--report-identical-files`	Reports when two files are identical.

Table 9.10 *Options for the **diff** Command (Cont'd)*

Option	Description
`--suppress-common-lines`	Suppresses the display of common lines when using the side-by-side format.
`-v` **or** `--version`	Displays version information.
`-x PATTERN` **or** `--exclude=PATTERN`	When comparing directories, ignores files and subdirectories whose base-names match *PATTERN*.
`-X FILE` **or** `--exclude-from=FILE`	When comparing directories, ignores files and subdirectories whose base-names match patterns read from *FILE*.
`-y` **or** `--side-by-side`	Displays difference in a side-by-side format.

Here are some examples of the **diff** command in action:

```
% # Use the echo to quickly create two files.
% echo -e "1\n2\n3" > diff1.dat
% echo -e "1\n2\n3" > diff2.dat
% # Compare the two files.
% diff diff1.dat diff2.dat
%        <- No output equals no differences.
% diff --report-identical-files diff1.dat diff2.dat
Files diff1.dat and diff2.dat are identical.
% # Add a space to beginning of line one.
% echo -e " 1\n2\n3" > diff2.dat
1c1
< 1
---
> 1
% diff --ignore-all-space diff1.dat diff2.dat
%        <- No output.
% # Change all the lines.
% echo -e "A\nB\nC" > diff2.dat
% diff diff1.dat diff2.dat
1,3c1,3
< 1
< 2
```

```
< 3
- - -
> A      <- The lines starting with > are from
> B      <- the TO file on the command line.
> C
```

The echo Command

Synopsis:
   echo displays its parameters, separated by spaces, to *STDIN*.

Syntax:
   echo [options] [parameters]

Description:
   The **echo** command is one of the workhorses of Bash scripts. It
can be used to display prompts or messages to a user or to perform
variable substitution when providing input to another command
or program through a pipe.
   Table 9.11 shows the options that are available with the **echo**
command.

Table 9.11 *Options for the echo Command*

Option	Description
-e	Enables the interpretation of the following backslash sequences: \a bell \b backspace \c suppress trailing newline (same as the –n option) \f formfeed \n newline \r carriage return \t horizontal tab \v vertical tab \\ backslash \nnn the character whose ASCII code is nnn in octal.
-E	Disables the interpretation of backslash sequences. The –E option is used on systems where the echo interprets the sequences by default.

Table 9.11 *Options for the echo Command (Cont'd)*

Option	Description
-n	Doesn't print a trailing newline. This option is mostly used when prompting for user input.

The **echo** command, while very simple to use, has quite an important role in Bash scripts. It serves as the link between your script and the user. Whenever you need to communicate information to the user of your script, **echo** is probably the command to use.

One of the most basic ways to use **echo** is to create a prompt for the user, using the following lines of code in a script:

```
echo -n "Enter a command: "
read USER_COMMAND
echo "Thanks for the '$USER_COMMAND' command!"
```

These lines of code result in this display:

```
Enter a command: ls -l
Thanks for the 'ls -l' command!
```

The above example also shows that **echo** performs variable substitution. You can use all of the variable notations with the **echo** command.

FRI

You can read about variable notations in the "Variable Substitution" section of Chapter 2 and the "Metacharacters for Variables" section in Chapter 8.

The *–e* option is mostly used when you want to display tabs and newlines. For example:

```
% echo -e "$USER,\n\tYour account has expired."
medined,
        Your account has expired.
```

The *nnn* backslash sequence of the *–e* option is rarely used. However, you might need to create text that ends with a zero character to pipe into a program or to use an unusual field separator character:

```
echo -e "Robert\000Male\000Husband\000"
echo -e "Robert\100\101Male\100\101Husband\100\101"
```

The first line shows how to create zero-ended text fields. The second line shows how to create fields that end with the characters 64 and 65 (*100* and *101* when expressed in octal).

The \nnn notation uses base 8 numbering instead of the more widely used base 10.

The env Command

Synopsis

env runs a command in a subshell with a modified environment.

Syntax

```
env [options] [name=value...] [command [args]]
```

Description:

The **env** command starts a subshell whose environment depends on the command-line parameters that you specify. You can make new or changed environment variables available by using the *NAME=VALUE* notation. Setting a variable equal to the empty string ("") is not the same as using the *--unset* option.

If no *COMMAND* is specified, the subshell's environment is displayed.

Table 9.12 shows the options that are available with the **env** command.

Table 9.12 *Options for the **env** Command*

Option	Description
--help	Displays a help message.
- or -i or --ignore-environment	Starts the subshell with an empty environment.
-u *NAME* or --unset *NAME*	Unsets the variable called *NAME* so the subshell won't see it.
--version	Displays version information.

The expr Command

Synopsis

expr evaluates an expression and sends the result to *STDOUT.*

Syntax

```
expr expression
```

Description:

The expressions used in **expr** commands can be very complex. Some of them involve regular expressions. The simpler expressions evaluate arithmetic expressions, like this:

```
% n=`expr 12 + 34`
% echo $n
46
% n=`expr $n + 1`
% echo $n
47
```

The first **expr** command assigns the results of *12+34* to the variable *n*. The second **expr** command increments *n* by one. More examples are shown after Table 9.13—which shows all of the operators that can be used with **expr**.

Table 9.13 *Operators for the expr Command*

Operator	Description
\(*op1* \)	Returns the result of evaluating *op1*.
op1 | *op2*	Returns *op1* if *op1* is not null or *0*. Otherwise *op2* is returned.
op1 & *op2*	Returns *op1* if both operands are not null and not *0*. Otherwise *0* is returned.
op1 = *op2* *op1*!= *op2* *op1* > *op2* *op1* >= *op2* *op1* < *op2* *op1* <= *op2*	Returns *1* if the expression evaluates as true, *0* otherwise. These operators perform their normal functions of *equals, not equals, greater than, greater than or equal to, less than, less than or equal to.*

Table 9.13 *Operators for the **expr** Command (Cont'd)*

Operator	Description
`op1 + op2` `op1 - op2`	Returns *op1 plus op2* or *op1 minus op2* depending on the operator.

`op1 \* op2`
`op1 / op2`
`op1 % op2`
	Returns *op1 times op2* or *op1 divided by op2* or *op1 mod op2* depending on the operator.

`op1: PATTERN` or `match op1 PATTERN`	Returns the number of characters that match *PATTERN* or *0*. The *PATTERN* is automatically anchored to the beginning of *op1*.
`op1 : \( PATTERN \)` `match op1 \( PATTERN \)`	Returns the substring of *op1* that matches *PATTERN* or null. The *PATTERN* is automatically anchored to the beginning of *op1*.
`substr op1 POSITION LENGTH`	Returns the substring that begins at *POSITION* and is *LENGTH* long. If the *POSITION* or *LENGTH* parameters are negative or non-numeric, a null string is returned.
`index op1 CHARLIST`	Returns the first position in *op1* where a character in *CHARLIST* was found.
`length op1`	Returns the length, in characters, of *op1*.

Using **expr** to evaluate arithmetic expressions is quite straight-forward. So let's move directly to looking at the *substr* and *index* operations:

```
% op1='The Cat in the Hat'
% expr substr $op1 5 3
expr: syntax error        <- Forgot the quotes!
% expr substr "$op1" 5 3
Cat
% expr substr "$op1" 5 9999
Cat in the Hat            <- Use a large length to
                          <- return the rest of op1.
```

```
% expr index "$op1" 'A'
0                               <- The index operator is
                                <- case-sensitive.
% expr index "$op1" 'Aa'
6                               <- Returns the position of the
                                <- first letter a or A.
```

Now it's time for examples that use the *match* operator. First, let's extract the basename without any extension:

```
% filespec='/home/medined/foobar.txt'
% filename=`expr $filespec : '.*/\(.*\)\.' '|' $filespec`
% echo $filename
foobar
```

The pattern in the above command line is '.*/\(.*\)\.'. The only way to understand patterns is to pick them apart piece by piece:

- .*/—matches zero or more characters until a slash is found.

- \(.*\)—tells **expr** to display whatever matches the pattern inside the parentheses.

- \.—matches a single period (the start of the extension).

The '|' *$filespec* part of the command displays the original filename if it doesn't match the pattern. Alternatively, you might want to return a string like "Incompatible Filespec" to indicate an error condition.

By slightly changing the pattern, you can extract just the extension:

```
% extension=`expr $filespec : '.*\(\..*\)' '|' $filespec`
% echo $extension
.txt
```

The only difference between the last two patterns is the location of the \. notation. You can go a step further and remove the period altogether from the output by placing the \. in front of the parentheses:

```
% extension=`expr $filespec : '.*\.\(.*\)' '|' $filespec`
% echo $extension
txt
```

The eval Command

Synopsis

eval generates and executes command lines on the fly.

Syntax

```
eval [parameters...]
```

Description:

The **eval** command concatenates its parameters and then executes the resulting command. Its exit value is the exit value of the command that is executed, or *0* if no parameters are supplied.

Perhaps the only reason to use the **eval** command is to force a second round of variable substitution. For example, simply executing a command with variables on the left side of an assignment command looks like this:

Chapter 5, "Controlling the Shell," has a section called "Using eval."

```
% mm='Jun'
% dd='15'
% $mm$dd="John's Birthday"
bash: Jun16=John's Birthday: command not found
```

Bash performs the variable substitution correctly, but tries to find a command called **Jun16=John's Birthday** instead of interpreting the command correctly.

The **eval** command fixes this problem at the expense of simplicity:

```
% eval "$mm$dd=\"John's Birthday\""
% echo $Jun15
John's Birthday
% eval "echo \$$mm$dd"
John's Birthday
```

From this example, you can determine that *\$$mm$dd* evaluates to *$Jun15* because when either is displayed with the **echo** command, it has the same value: *John's Birthday.*

The backslash characters are needed to prevent certain characters from interfering in the first round of variable substitution. For example, without the backslash *\$$mm$dd* would be seen as the variable *$$* followed by the text *mm* followed by the variable *$dd*, which is not what is intended.

The false Command

Synopsis:
false exits with a value of *1*, indicating failure.

Syntax:
```
false
```

The fgrep Command

See the "The grep Command" section.

The find Command

Synopsis
find examines directory hierarchies, evaluating an expression
for every file found.

Syntax
```
find [path...] [expression]
```

Description:
The **find** command examines directory trees evaluating expression for every file that is encountered. The main concept behind the
find command is not to locate files—it is to evaluate the expression.
However, one important use of the evaluation might be to display
filenames that match the specified criteria (i.e., the expression).

NOTE   The default path is the current directory. The default expression is
-print. Therefore a simple **find** command with no parameters
resembles the **ls** command because the *-print* option always
returns true.

You can examine multiple directory trees by specifying more
than one path. Therefore, **find** looks for one the following characters—a dash, a parenthesis, a comma, or an exclamation mark—to
determine the start of the expression parameter. If no expression is
given, the default action is *-print*.

I think that **find** is one of the more complex commands available
in Unix. It takes five tables to list all of its features. This means that
there's a lot of stuff to learn. The following tables briefly describe

the options, tests, and actions that you can use. Following the tables are several examples that let you see the **find** command in action.

The *expression* is evaluated left to right, and you can use any operators shown in Table 9.14.

Table 9.14 *Operators for the find Command*

Operator	Description
`(expression)`	Anything inside parentheses is evaluated first.
`! expression` or `not expression`	Returns true if *expression* is false.

`expression1 expression2`
`expression1 -a expression2`
`expression1 -and expression2`
	Returns true if both *expression1* and *expression2* are true. If *expression1* is false, then *expression2* is never evaluated.

`expression1 -o expression2` `expression1 -or expression2`	Returns true if either *expression1* or *expression2* is true. If *expression1* is true, then *expression2* is never evaluated.
`expression1, expression2`	Returns the value of *expression2*. Both expressions are always evaluated.

Expressions can be made of clauses that consist of options, tests, or actions. Each clause is connected by an operator to the next clause. If no operator is specified, the *and* operator is assumed.

Options affect the entire **find** command, not the processing of individual files. Therefore, they always return true so that they don't hinder the evaluation of an expression. Tests can return either true or false. And actions, like *–print*, have side effects and can also return true or false.

If no operator is specified between find command clauses, the and operator is assumed.

Table 9.15 lists the options available with the **find** command and briefly describes them.

Table 9.16 lists the tests available with the **find** command and briefly describes them.

Table 9.15 *Options Available with the **find** Command*

Option	Description
-daystart	Measures times from the beginning of today rather than from 24 hours ago. This option affects the *–amin, -atime, -cmin, -ctime, -min,* and *-mtime* tests.
-depth	Processes the contents of each directory before the directory itself.
-follow	Dereferences symbolic links when needed. This option implies the *–noleaf* option.
-help or --help	Prints a summary of the **find** command-line usage.
-maxdepth N	Descends at most *N* levels below the paths listed on the command line. If *N* is zero, the tests and actions are only applied to the command line arguments.
-mindepth N	Applies to tests and actions at all levels of the directory tree except those at depths less than *N*. For example, if *N* is 1, all files except those on the command line are processed.
-mount or -xdev	Forces **find** to ignore directories that belong to other filesystems. For example, the *–mount* option would ignore the */mnt/floppy* directory for searches starting at the root directory.
-noleaf	Increases the speed of searching filesystems that do not follow Unix conventions—like CD-ROM, MS-DOS, and AFS volume mount points. Please see the **man** page for more information.
--version	Displays the version number of the **find** command.

NOTE Remember to use operators between tests and actions when they are needed. The *–or* operator is especially useful.

Table 9.16 *Tests Available with the **find** Command*

Test	Description
`-amin N`	True if a file was last accessed N minutes ago.
`-anewer FILE`	True if a file was last accessed more recently than *FILE* was modified.
`-atime N`	True if a file was last accessed $N*24$ hours ago. Please note that saying a file was last accessed 48 hours ago is not really the same as saying two days ago. The word "day" generally means midnight to midnight. Think carefully about what you need to test for.
`-cmin N`	True if a file's status was last changed N minutes ago.
`-cnewer FILE`	True if a file's status was last changed more recently than *FILE* was changed.
`-ctime N`	True is a file's status was last changed $N*24$ hours ago.
`-empty`	True if a file is empty and either a regular file or a directory.
`-false`	Always false.
`-fstyle TYPE`	True if a file is on a filesystem of the type called *TYPE*. The *%F* directive of the *–printf* option can be used to display filesystem names for each file. For example, *find / -printf "%f\t%F\n"* displays two columns of information. The first column is the filename and the second is the filesystem type.
`-gid N`	True if a file belongs to the group whose ID is N.
`-group NAME`	True if a file belongs to the group whose name is *NAME*.
`-inum N`	True if a file has inode number N.

Table 9.16 *Tests Available with the* **find** *Command (Cont'd)*

Test	Description
-links *N*	True if a file has *N* links.
-lname *PATTERN* and -ilname *PATTERN*	True if a file is a symbolic link whose contents match *PATTERN*. The *-ilname* test is case-insensitive.
-mmin *N*	True if a file's data was last modified *N* minutes ago.
-mtime *N*	True if a file's data was last modified *N*24* hours ago.
-name *PATTERN* and -iname *PATTERN*	True if the basename of a file matches *PATTERN*. Basenames are the path with leading directories removed. For example, the basename of */home/medined/test.dat* is *test.dat*. The *–iname* test is case-insensitive. If you need to match a directory name, use the *–path* test.
-newer *FILE*	True if a file was modified more recently than *FILE*.
-nouser	True if a file's numeric user ID does not exist in the system's password file.
-nogroup	True if a file's numeric group ID does not exist in the system's password file.
-path *PATTERN* and -ipath *PATTERN*	True if a directory matching *PATTERN* is found. When searching for subdirectories of the current directory, use *./storage* instead of simply *storage*. The *-ipath* test is case-insensitive.
-perm *MODE*	True if a file's permission bits are equivalent to *MODE*. You can use *octal* or *symbolic* notation for *MODE*. Use *–MODE* to test that all of the permission bits *MODE* are set and use *+MODE* to test if any of the permission bits *MODE* are set.

Table 9.16 *Tests Available with the find Command (Cont'd)*

Test	Description
`-regex PATTERN` and `-iregex PATTERN`	True if a file's path matches *PATTERN*. For example, search for *./m*/t** to match all the files starting with the letter t in all of the directories starting with the letter m. The *–iregex* test is case-insensitive.
`-size N [bckw]`	True if a file uses *N* units of space. You can optionally test for blocks using *b* after *N*, bytes using a *c* after *N*, kilobytes using a *k* after *N*, or two-byte words using a *w* after *N*. Indirect blocks are not counted but unallocated blocks in sparse files are counted.
`-true`	The *–true* test always returns true.
`-type C` and `-xtype C`	True if file is of type C, where C can be *b* for block files, *c* for character files, *d* for directories, *p* for named pipes, *f* for regular files, *l* for symbolic links, and *s* for sockets. The *–xlink* test is identical to *–type* unless the file is a symbolic link. Here's the complex part: If a file is a symbolic link and the *–follow* option is not used, the test is true if the link points to a file of type C. If the *–follow* option is used, then the test is true only if C is *l*.
`-uid N`	True if the file's numeric user ID is *N*.
`-used N`	True if file was last accessed *N* days after its status was last changed.
`-user USERNAME`	True if file is owned by *USERNAME*. You can use either the text or numeric user ids.

Table 9.17 lists the actions available with the **find** command and briefly describes them.

Table 9.17 *Actions Available with the* find *Command*

Action	Description
`-exec COMMAND \;` and `-ok COMMAND \;`	This action executes the *COMMAND* parameter in the starting directory, returning true if the exit value of *COMMAND* is *0*. The *–ok* action asks for confirmation before executing *COMMAND*. The *–ok* action is *HIGHLY RECOMMENDED* when you are developing your **find** command. Notice that the ; character is a separate parameter of the **find** command. All text between the **–exec** and ; is considered to be *COMMAND*. The notation *{}* is replaced by the current file everywhere it appears in *COMMAND*. At times, you might need to use the backslash or quotes to stop variable and command substitution. *BE VERY CAREFUL WHEN USING THIS ACTION!* It can easily destroy files and perform in unexpected ways. Make sure you know what files will be found before executing any commands.
`-ls` and `-fls` *FILE*	This action displays information about a file in *ls –dils* format. The default block size is 1K, but can be overridden using the *POSIXLY_CORRECT* variable so that 512-byte blocks are used. The *–fls* action writes the information into a file called FILE.
`-print` and `-fprint` *FILE*	This action prints the full filename to *STDOUT*. The *–fprint* action writes the full filename to *FILE*. If *FILE* already exists, it is overwritten.

Table 9.17 *Actions Available with the find Command (Cont'd)*

Action	Description
`-print0` and `-fprint0` *FILE*	This action prints the full filename followed by a null character to *STDOUT*. The *–fprint0* action writes the output to *FILE*. If *FILE* already exists, it is overwritten. Some programs (mainly C-based) might need to see string input terminated by nulls.
`-printf` *FORMAT* and `-fprintf` *FILE FORMAT*	This action has many, many options. Basically, it displays information that you specify in the *FORMAT* parameter. For example, using a *FORMAT* of "*%f %a*" displays the file's name and the last time it was accessed. The *%f* and *%a* options are called format specifiers. The *–printf* action does not end its display with a newline. Use the \n format specifier if a newline is needed. The \n and the other specifiers are detailed in Table 9.18. The *–fprintf* action writes the information into a file called *FILE*.
`-prune`	This complex action causes the **find** command to ignore the current directory as long as the *–depth* action is not active. Examples of the *–prune* action can be found after the Format Specifier table in the text. If *–prune* is the only action on the command line, the *–print* action is performed on all files for which the expression is true.

If you'd like more information about using *–printf,* please look in a C or C++ language reference guide. The guide should explain how to specify field widths and precisions; these topics are beyond the scope of this book.   **NOTE**

Table 9.18 lists the specifiers available with the *–printf* action and briefly describes them.

Table 9.18 *Format Specifiers Usable with the –printf Action*

Specifier	Description
\a	This specifier rings the display's alarm bell.
\b	This specifier displays a backspace character.
\c	This specifier ends the current file's output and flushes the output device's queue.
\f	This specifier displays a formfeed character.
\n	This specifier displays a newline character.
\r	This specifier displays a carriage return character.
\t	This specifier displays a tab character.
\v	This specifier displays a vertical tab character.
\\	This specifier displays a backslash.
%%	This specifier displays a percent sign character.
%a	This specifier displays the file's last access time.
%A_K	This specifier displays the file's last access time in various formats as determined by K. There are many formats and not all of them are available on all systems; you'll need to experiment. Rather than create another table, I'll mention them all here. Time fields: @, seconds since 01/01/1970 00:00:00 GMT; H, hour from 00-23; I, hour from 01-12; k, hour from 0-23; l, hour from 1-12; m, minute from 00-59; p, AM or PM; r, time in hh:M:S AM format; S, second from 00-61; T, time in 24-hour format--hh:M:S; X, time in local format; Z, time zone or blank if undeterminable. Date fields: a or h, abbreviated weekday name Sun-Sat; A, full weekday name; b, abbreviated month name Jan-Dec; B, full month name; c, date and time; d, day of month; D, date M/D/Y; j, day of year; m, month; U, week number with Sunday as first day of the week; w, day of week; W, week number with Monday as first day of the week; x, date in local format; y, last two digits of the year; Y, four-digit year.

Table 9.18 *Format Specifiers Usable with the –printf Action (Cont'd)*

Specifier	Description
%b	This specifier displays the file's size in 512-byte bytes.
%c	This specifier displays the time of the file's last status change.
%C_K	This specifier displays the time of the file's last change in various formats as determined by K. Please see the %A specifier for details about K.
%d	This specifier displays the file's depth in a directory tree. A depth of zero means that the file is in one of the directories specified on the command line.
%f	This specifier displays the file's name without leading directories. For example, *perl* would be displayed—not */bin/local/perl*.
%F	This specifier displays the type of filesystem the file is in.
%g	This specifier displays the file's group name. The numeric group ID is displayed if the file has no group name.
%G	This specifier displays the file's numeric group ID.
%h	This specifier displays the file's path. For example, */bin/local* would be displayed for the */bin/local/perl* file.
%H	This specifier displays the path specified on the command line under which the file was found.
%i	This specifier displays the file's inode number in decimal notation.
%k	This specifier displays the file's size in 1k blocks.
%l	This specifier displays the object of the file's symbolic link or an empty string if there is no link.
%m	This specifier displays the file's permission bits in octal notation.
%n	This specifier displays the number of hard links to the file.
%p	This specifier displays the file's name.
%P	This specifier displays the file's name and the path specified on the command line under which the file was found.

Table 9.18 *Format Specifiers Usable with the –printf Action (Cont'd)*

Specifier	Description
%s	This specifier displays the file's size in bytes.
%t	This specifier displays the file's last modification time.
%T_K	This specifier displays the file's last modification time in various formats as determined by *K*. Please see the *%A* specifier for details about *K*.
%u	This specifier displays the file's user name, or the numeric user ID if the file's user has no name.
%U	This specifier displays the file's numeric user ID.

Now that you've read the brief descriptions of the **find** command's features, let's look at some examples. In order to run these examples yourself, you need to run the following commands to create a directory structure and sample files:

```
$ mkdir finddir
$ cd finddir
$ echo "test" > one.txt
$ echo "test" > two.txt
$ echo "test" > three.txt
$ mkdir dir1
$ cp *.txt dir1
$ ls -l
total 4
drwxr-xr-x  2 root     ...  1024 May 31 00:28 dir1
-rw-rw-r--  1 medined  ...     5 May 31 00:24 one.txt
-rw-rw-r--  1 medined  ...     5 May 31 00:24 three.txt
-rw-rw-r--  1 medined  ...     5 May 31 00:24 two.txt
$ ls -l dir1
total 3
-rw-rw-r--  1 medined  ...     5 May 31 00:28 one.txt
-rw-rw-r--  1 medined  ...     5 May 31 00:28 three.txt
-rw-rw-r--  1 medined  ...     5 May 31 00:28 two.txt
```

We'll use these directories and files to demonstrate the **find** command. All of the following commands are run in the *~/finddir* directory.

The most basic use for the **find** command is to determine which directory a file is located in:

```
% find two.txt
two.txt
```

This looks quite simple. The **find** command is obviously looking in the current directory and not looking in the *dir1* subdirectory. Just as obvious, the *–print* action is being used as the default.

Now let's see what happens if we explicitly tell **find** to look in the current directory:

```
% find . two.txt
.
./one.txt
./two.txt
./three.txt
./dir1
./dir1/one.txt
./dir1/three.txt
./dir1/two.txt
two.txt
```

Why were so many files displayed? The answer is not obvious. However, the display offers a clue. Notice that both *./two.txt* and *two.txt* are displayed. But aren't these the same file? Yes, they are. Remember what the **find** command does: It evaluates expressions. Because no expression was specified, the default action of *–print* was performed for each file under the command-line path parameters.

If you need to find all instances of a given filename used somewhere in a directory structure, the *–name* test comes in handy:

```
% find -name "two.txt"      <- the current directory is the
./two.txt                   <- default path.
./dir1/two.txt
```

Finding all files except for a given filename means that you want to print the filename when *–name "two.txt"* is false, so the *–or* operator is needed:

The find command is frequently used to generate a list of files.

```
% find -name "two.txt" -or -print
.
./one.txt
./three.txt                 <- ./two.txt is missing.
./dir1
./dir1/one.txt
./dir1/three.txt            <- ./dir1/two.txt is missing.
```

When you need to list all files except for those in a given directory, the *–prune* action comes into play:

```
% find -path "./dir1" -or -print
.
./one.txt          <- list all files except those
./two.txt          <- in the dir1 subdirectory.
./three.txt
```

You can combine the *–name* test and the *–prune* action in order
to stop **find** from looking in certain directories. The following
example looks for all files starting with the letter t in all subdirectories except for *dir1*:

```
% find -path "./dir1" -prune -or -name "t*" -print
./two.txt
./three.txt
```

With the **find** command, you can use very complex search criteria. There is no easy way for me to show you all of the possibilities;
you'll just have to experiment. Instead, let's look at how the *–printf*
action is used:

```
% (echo "Depth Path"
> find dir1 -printf "%d      %h/%f\n")
Depth Path
0/dir1
1       dir1/one.txt
1       dir1/two.txt
1       dir1/three.txt
```

This example displays the depth of the file in the directory tree
and its path and name.

I sometimes use the **find** command to locate all files with world-
executable permissions:

```
% # create some executable files for the find
% # command to find.
% chmod 001 two.txt dir1/three.txt
% # look for only files(-type f) with
% find . -type f -perm -001 -printf "%P\n"
two.txt
dir1/three.txt
```

When a minus sign is placed in front of the *–perm* parameter,
the parameter is *bitwise ANDed* with the current file's permission

list. If the parameter was –*010*, files that were group-executable would be found.

Using **find** to generate lists of files is all well and good, but now let's look at something really exciting! You can use **find** to automatically generate command lines—saving you tons of time and effort.

This idea and the command line used in the example were generously suggested by Phil Howard (philh@best.com), whom I met in the #cgi IRC channel. Phil has been a great help in clarifying some of the concepts behind the Bash commands.

NOTE

One of my friends from IRC, Phil Howard, has worked with the **find** command for many years. He frequently uses it to construct command lines. For example:

```
% dir2="backup"
% find dir1 -type d -printf "mkdir -p '${dir2}/%P'\n" -o \
> ! -type d -printf "mv '%p' '${dir2}/%p'\n"
mkdir -p 'backup/'
mv 'dir1/one.txt' 'backup/dir1/one.txt'
mv 'dir1/two.txt' 'backup/dir1/two.txt'
mv 'dir1/three.txt' 'backup/dir1/three.txt'
```

This **find** command copies all of the files from the *dir1* directory into a backup directory named by the *dir2* variable. The command also creates any subdirectories that are needed. There are two main clauses to this command:

```
-type d -printf "mkdir -p '${dir2}/%P'\n"
```

and

```
! -type d -printf "mv '%p' '${dir2}/%p'\n"
```

The first clause is activated when a directory is found because of the –*type d* test. The second clause is activated when any other type of file is found because of the *! -type d* test. The %*p* and %*P* format specifiers display the file's name and path, respectively.

NOTE   Notice that this example did not actually execute the commands
that are generated. *Make sure you verify the commands before taking
the next step—actually running them!* You can execute the generated command lines by piping the output directly to the shell:

```
find [path] [expressions] | sh
```

The grep Command

Synopsis

grep and **fgrep** search input files for lines that match a given
pattern.

Syntax

```
grep [options] pattern [files...]
```

Description:

The **grep** command is a favorite of many programmers. It is frequently used to locate variable names in source files or to find
records in text-based databases. **grep**'s many options are quite
powerful and well worth the time it takes to become familiar with
them.

If you haven't used patterns (also called regular expressions)
before, please read Chapter 8, "Pattern Matching."

By default, **grep** displays input lines that match the pattern
parameter. If no files are specified or the – notation is used, then
grep reads from *STDIN*.

The **fgrep** command interprets the pattern parameters as a
series of fixed strings, delimited by newlines, any of which can be
matched.

The **grep** command can exit with the following values:

- *0*—matches were found.

- *1*—no matches were found.

- *2*—there were syntax errors in the pattern, unreadable input
  files, or other errors.

Using the *–v* parameter inverts the sense of the exit values. The exit value is *0* if no matches were found and *1* if matches were found.

Table 9.19 shows the options that are available with the **grep** command and its variants.

Table 9.19 *Options for the grep Command*

Option	Description
`-A NUM_LINES` or `--after-context=NUM_LINES`	Displays *NUM_LINES* number of lines after the line(s) matching the pattern parameter. For example, if the matching line(s) is the first line of a four-line record, setting *NUM_LINES* to four lets you display all records that contain the pattern parameter.
`-B NUM_LINES` or `--before-context=NUM_LINES`	Displays *NUM_LINES* number of lines before the line(s) matching the pattern parameter. For example, if the matching line(s) is the last line of a four-line record, setting *NUM_LINES* to four lets you display all records that contain the pattern parameter.
`-b` or `--byte-offset`	Displays the byte offset of the line(s) matching the pattern parameter.
`-C` or `--context`	Displays two lines before and two lines after the line(s) matching the pattern parameter. These extra lines hopefully provide some context for the matching line(s).
`-c` or `--count`	Displays the number of matching lines instead of the lines themselves. The *–c* option is sometimes used in conjunction with the *–v* option to display the number of non-matching lines.

Table 9.19 *Options for the* **grep** *Command (Cont'd)*

Option	Description
-e *PATTERN* or --regexp=*PATTERN*	Uses *PATTERN* as the pattern to be matched. This option is mainly used for patterns that begin with a dash (-) character.
-F or --fixed-strings	Interprets the pattern parameter as a series of fixed strings, delimited by newlines, any of which can be matched.
-f FILE or --file=FILE	Reads the pattern to be matched from a file. This option is useful when you have complex patterns or if you need to run **grep** from the command line and don't want to keep retyping the pattern parameter.
-h or --no-filename	Forces **grep** not to display the filenames associated with matching lines when multiple files are searched.
-i or --ignore-case	Ignores case distinction in both the pattern parameter and the input files.
-L or --files-without-match	Displays the filename of each input file that doesn't contain the pattern parameter.
-l or --files-with-matches	Displays the filename of each input file that contains the pattern parameter.
-n or --line-number	Prefixes each line of output with the line number.
-q or --quiet	Suppresses all normal output.
-s or --silent	Suppresses error messages about nonexistent or unreadable files.
-V or --version	Displays **grep**'s version number to *STDOUT.*

Table 9.19 *Options for the* **grep** *Command (Cont'd)*

Option	Description
-v or --revert-match	Displays all lines that don't match the pattern parameter.
-w or --word-regexp	Displays only lines whose matching text forms whole words. Words are formed by letters, digits, and underscores.
-x or --line-regexp	Displays only lines whose matching text is exactly one whole line.
-NUM_LINES	Displays *NUM_LINES* number of lines before and after the line matching the pattern parameter. These extra lines hopefully provide some context for the matching line(s).

Chapter 8 covers many aspects of pattern matching. However, the **grep** command does have some unique named classes of characters:

- \w—matches one alphanumeric character.

- \W—matches one non-alphanumeric character.

- [:alnum:]—matches one alphanumeric character.

- [:alpha:]—matches one alphabetic character.

- [:cntrl:]—matches one control character.

- [:digit:]—matches one numeric character.

- [:graph:]—matches one graph character.

- [:lower:]—matches one lowercase letter.

- [:print:]—matches one printable character.

- [:punct:]—matches one punctuation character.

- *[:space:]*—matches a space, a tab, a newline, and the empty string at the beginning of a line.

- *[:upper:]*—matches one uppercase letter.

- *[:xdigit:]*—matches one hexadecimal character (0-9 and A-F).

- \<—matches an empty string at the beginning of a word.

- \>—matches an empty string at the end of a word.

- \b—matches an empty string at the edge of a word.

- \B—matches an empty string not at the edge of a word.

You can invert the sense of any of these character classes using this notation:

```
[^[class]]
```

For example *[^[:xdigit:]]* matches one non-hexadecimal character.

grep is a deceptive command. When you first look at it, it might seem quite simple—after all, searching files for text is a common task. However, the many options that are available make **grep** quite powerful. Let's look at some examples using the data file in Listings 9.4 and 9.5 as our input files.

Listing 9.4 *grep1.dat—A Data File Used to Demonstrate the **grep** Command*

```
Paul    Male    Husband
Mindy   Female  Wife
Rachel  Female  Daughter
Sara    Female  Daughter
```

Listing 9.5 *grep2.dat—Another Data File Used to Demonstrate the **grep** Command*

```
Bill    Male    Husband
Cheryl  Female  Wife
Foo     Male    Son
Bar     Male    Son
```

Our first example looks for all the males in the *grep1.dat* file:

```
% grep "male" grep1.dat
Mindy    Female Wife
Rachel   Female Daughter
Sara     Female Daughter
```

It that the result that you expected? Probably not. **grep** found exactly what we asked for—the lines matching the lowercase text **male**. What we really want is for the **grep** command to ignore the case and intelligently look for the word *male*, like this:

```
% grep --ignore-case "\<male\>" grep1.dat
Paul     Male   Husband
```

The *--ignore-case* option forces **grep** to ignore the case of both the pattern and the input file. The \< and \> backslash sequences match the beginning and end of a word, respectively.

Because humans can only be male or female, you can use the *--revert-match* to find all of the females listed the in *grep1.dat* file:

```
% grep --revert-match --ignore-case "\<male\>" grep1.dat
Mindy    Female Wife
Rachel   Female Daughter
Sara     Female Daughter
```

If we assume that the first-born child is always listed right after the wife in the file, you can extract the name of the first-born child like this:

```
% grep --ignore-case --after-context=1 "wife" grep1.dat | \
> grep --ignore-case "son|daughter" | \
> cut -d" " -f1
Rachel
```

This example uses two **grep** commands linked together by a pipe. The first **grep** command filters the input file, so that only the lines containing the wife's name and the line following it are left. The second **grep** command filters the file even more, so that only lines with either the text "son" or the text "daughter" are left. Finally, the **cut** command displays the first column.

The *--count* option comes in handy at times. It counts the number of lines that match the pattern or, when used with *--revert-match,* counts the number of lines that don't contain the pattern. The following example shows how many men are listed in *grep1.dat*:

```
% grep --count --ignore-case "<\male\>" grep1.dat
3
% numMen=`grep --count --ignore-case "<\male\>" grep1.dat`
% echo "There are $numMen men in the file."
There are 3 men in the file.
```

As shown in the second command, you can assign the number of men to a variable using a backticked string.

The groff Command

Synopsis

groff formats text files using a tag-based language.

Syntax

```
groff [options] [file...]
```

Description:

The **groff** command accepts text files as input and formats the contexts as specified by tags embedded in the text. The embedded tags are similar, in concept, to HTML. However, unlike HTML, **groff** provides a much greater level of control over what your document looks like.

groff is a newer version of troff.

At first glance, **groff** might not seem like a command that shell programmers need to know about. However, let me tell you a short story about a pharmaceutical company. Every year this company needed to create an annual report listing all of the pharmaceutical compounds in their database and their hazard ratings. A couple of years ago, a programmer wrote a program to generate an HTML report that showed the required information and allowed people to view the report at any time through their web browsers. There were several problems with this solution:

- The report needed to be printed, not viewed. Each year the report was printed, copied 20 times, and distributed in an annual review meeting.

- The report was more than 1,600 pages long! Even though only 800 compounds were in the database, HTML's lack of whitespace control and pagination control resulted in a lot of pages with only one or two lines on them.

- No table of contents page was included. HTML's lack of pagination implies that it can't produce a table of contents.

- It seemed to take forever for the web browser to load the 3MB document.

I used **groff** to shrink the report to 800 pages, add a table of contents, and automatically print the report upon request. **groff** neatly solved all of the problems and vastly improved the efficiency of the process. Oh, and shrinking the report to 800 pages—that saved more than 32 reams of paper!

A full examination of the **groff** command is beyond the scope of this book. This section is designed to give you a basic understanding of the command and how the tags work.

Before looking at the options, let's see some tags. To save space in this book, these examples show input to the **groff** command in the form of inline input. Normally, you would create a file to hold the input text.

```
% groff -Tascii >g.out <<EOT
> This is line one.
> This is line two.
> EOT                    <- The end if in-place input.
% cat g.out
This is line one.  This is line two.
...                     <- The rest of the file consists
                        <- of blank lines.
```

Essentially, **groff** ignores the formatting of the input file, replacing the existing format with its own. In this case, no tags were found in the input, so no formatting was applied.

Now let's add some newlines:

```
% groff -Tascii >g.out <<EOT
> This is line one.
> .sp
> This is line two.
> .sp 2
> This is line three.
> EOT
% cat g.out
This is line one.
                        <- Produced by .sp
```

```
This is line two.
                            <- Two blank lines produced
                            <- by .sp 2
This is line three.
...
```

One of the nice features of **groff** is that it knows what a page is. A page has a height and width and is blank unless text or graphics are printed on it. Therefore, **groff** always creates full pages—which is why the examples have so many blank lines. The blank lines pad the output so that it is a full page.

The *.br* tag lets you start a new line without also creating a blank line:

```
% groff -Tascii >g.out <<EOT
> This is line one.
> .br
> This is line two.
> EOT
% cat g.out
This is line one.
This is line two.
...
```

The tag language used by **groff** is primitive but complete. It even has variables, although they are called *registers* by **groff**. Register names are one to three letters long. For example, the *.j* register holds the alignment and *.ce* holds the number of lines to be centered. Some of the registers that **groff** uses are described in Table 9.20.

Table 9.20 *Some of the Registers Used by groff*

Register	Description
%	Holds the current page number.
dw	Holds the day of the week.
dy	Holds the day of the month.
ln	Holds the current output line number. This number is reset to zero for each new page.
mo	Holds the current month.
pn	Holds the next page number.

Table 9.20 *Some of the Registers Used by* ***groff*** *(Cont'd)*

Register	Description
yr	Holds the last two digits of the year.
.$	Holds the number of parameters passed to a macro.
.c	Holds the current input line number.
.j	Holds the text alignment mode. The \n.j notation displays the number assigned to the current alignment mode, which can be used as an offset into this list: *l, r, c, b, n*. For example, if \n.j displays a *3*, the current alignment mode is *c*, or centered.

groff's registers are the same as variables in other computer languages. Some of **groff's** registers are read-only.

I nearly always use **groff** with the *-me* option. This option loads macros.   **NOTE**

groff macros are the same as functions. Macros are usually used as a shorthand way of specifying a format. For example, the *.(c* macro begins a centered block, and *.)c* ends the block.

Table 9.21 shows some of the most frequently used tags. Tags that begin with a period are called requests and must be placed on separate lines. Tags beginning with a slash are called escapes and can be placed anywhere in the input text—except, perhaps, inside of requests.

Table 9.21 *Some of the Tags for the* ***groff*** *-me Command*

Tag	Description
.ad *MODE*	Enables text alignment mode and sets the current alignment to *MODE*, which can be *l, r, c, b* or *n*. These parameters stand for left, right, center, and both. The *b* and *n* parameters both signify justification to both margins. If used without a parameter, the last alignment used is enabled.

Table 9.21 *Some of the Tags for the groff -me Command (Cont'd)*

Tag	Description
.aln *ALIAS REGISTER*	Creates an alias for a register.
.af *REGISTER FORMAT*	Changes the display format for a register. The options for *FORMAT* are: *1, 001, I, i, A,* and *a.* The default is *1* which displays the value of *REGISTER* as a decimal number. *001* pads the number to whatever width is needed. *0001* pads to four positions while *01* pads to two positions. *I* and *i* display the value as uppercase or lowercase Roman numerals. And, finally, *A* and *a* display the value as uppercase and lowercase letters.
.as *ABBREV TEXT*	Appends text to the two-letter abbreviation.
.bp *PAGE_NUMBER*	Begins a new page. The *PAGE_NUMBER* parameter lets you specify the number of the new page.
.br	Breaks a line.
.bu	Starts a new bulleted paragraph.
.ce *NUMLINES*	Centers, horizontally, *NUMLINES* lines. If you don't know how many lines need to be centered, use a large number like 1,000. You stop centering by using the *.ce 0* tag. Unlike the *.ad c* tag, which also centers text, *.ce* does not almost perform the text-fill function.
.de *NAME CMDLIST*	Defines a macro. A **groff** macro is equivalent to a Bash function—both store a series of commands for later use.

Table 9.21 *Some of the Tags for the* **groff** *-me Command (Cont'd)*

Tag	Description
`.ds ABBREV TEXT`	Defines a two-letter abbreviation for *TEXT*. The *TEXT* parameter is delimited by the end of the line, therefore you can't place comments on the same line as the *.ds* tag. When the *(notation is used, the abbreviation is expanded. This tag lets you create templates—by defining fields at the top of a document. For example, *.ds au David Medinets* could be used to define the author of a document. Later in the document the *(au tag might be used to display the author's name in the document's footer. The *TEXT* parameter can include tags.
`.hl`	Draws a horizontal line the width of the page.
`.in AMOUNT`	Controls the left indentation. For example, *.in 2i* produces a two-inch margin, while *.in +.5i* indents an additional half-inch. Use negative amounts to return the margin to normal.
`.fi`	Enables text filling.
`.fr [R|I|B|BI/P]`	Changes the current font. If a parameter is specified, the fonts correspond to *Times Roman, Italic, Both, Bold Italic,* or *Previous.* If no parameter is given, the previous font is used.
`.ll AMOUNT`	Controls the line length. Changing the length line by *-.5i* has the effect of indenting the right-hand margin. Using a positive amount undoes the indentation.

Table 9.21 *Some of the Tags for the **groff** -me Command (Cont'd)*

Tag	Description
.ls *NUMBER*	Controls the line spacing. The default is single spacing.
.lt *LENGTH*	Controls the length of the title line.
.na	Disables text alignment.
.nf	Disables text filling.
.np	Starts a new numbered paragraph.
.nr *REGISTER VALUE INCR*	Assigns *VALUE* to *REGISTER*. If specified, the *INCR* parameter specifies the amount to increment the register by when the \n+ tag is used.
.pn *PAGE_NUMBER*	Changes the page number of the next page.
.pnr	Lists all of the currently defined registers and their values to *STDERR*. You might use this tag and process the file using this command line: groff -me 2>register.out >groff.out INPUTFILE. When the command is finished, the file *register.out* holds the register list.
.pp	Starts a new paragraph with the first line indented.
.rj *NUMLINES*	Right-justifies *NUMLINES* lines. If you don't know how many lines need to be centered, use a large number like 1,000. You stop justification by using the *.rj 0* tag. Unlike the *.ad r* tag, which also justifies text, *.rj* does not perform the text-fill function.
.rr *REGISTER*	Removes a register.
.rrn *REGISTER1 REGISTER2*	Renames register *1* to register *2*.

Table 9.21 *Some of the Tags for the groff -me Command (Cont'd)*

Tag	Description
`.sp AMOUNT`	Displays blank vertical space. Normally, *AMOUNT* is the number of lines to leave blank (the default is one line). However, you can also use inches (1.5i) or centimeters (1.5c).
`.tl 'LEFT'CENTER'RIGHT'`	Displays a title on the page. **groff** replaces the % character with the page number. For example, a short title might be `.tl 'Written by DMM'Shell Programming Tools'Page %'`.
`.(c and .)c`	Begins and ends a centered block of text.
`.(f and .)f`	Begins and ends a footnote. Footnotes are displayed at the end of the page they appear on.
`.(q and .)q`	Begins and ends a major quote block of text. This displays a text block with indentation on both sides.
`\*(ABBREV`	Expands the two-letter abbreviation.
`\#`	Lets you place comments inside the input text. Anything between the `\"` tag and the next linefeed is ignored by **groff**. Placing comments on separate lines is a good idea.
`\f[R|I|B|BI|P]`	Changes the current font. If parameters are specified, the fonts correspond to *Times Roman, Italic, Both, Bold Italic,* or *Previous*. If no parameter is given, the previous font is used. The \f notation is used for changing fonts in the middle of a line. For example, the next \fB*word*\fP is bolded.
`\gREGISTER`	Displays the current format associated with a register. The *.af* tag sets the format.

Table 9.21 *Some of the Tags for the **groff -me** Command (Cont'd)*

Tag	Description
\p	Causes a line break without regard to text alignment.
\n+	Huh?
\nREGISTER	Displays the value of the register called REGISTER. If the register is two characters long, use the \n(notation. For example, \n(yr displays the last two digits of the current year, and \na displays the value contained in register a.

Very few of the options to **groff** are good for everyday use. Many of them involve graphic concepts beyond the scope of this book. However, Table 9.22 describes the options I use most often.

Table 9.22 *A Partial List of Options for the **groff** Command*

Option	Description
-h	Displays a help message.
-me	Loads a package of macros designed to ease formatting. This package is partly documented by the **man me** command.
-TDEVICE	Prepares the output for a specific device. The default is usually postscript. However, you can also specify *ascii* to prepare the output for further text processing or viewing. Check the **groff** man page for more output options.
-tbl	Loads a package of macros designed to help you create tables.
-z	Displays only error messages.

Before taking our leave of the **groff** command, we'll look at the *-me* option in action:

```
% groff -me -Tascii << EOF
> .tl 'A groff Example'by David Medinets'Page %'
> .sp 2
> .pp
> This is an example of a paragraph that begins
> with a small indent. Like any paragraph, when
> needed the text automatically wraps to the
> next line.
> .(f
> 1 - This is the first footnote.
> .)f
> .(f
> 2 - This is the second footnote.
> .)f
> .bu
> This is a bulleted item.
> .bu
> This is another bulleted item.
> .hl
> .np
> This paragraph begins with a number. Unlike
> the pp paragraph it has no beginning
> indentation.
> .np
> This is the second numbered paragraph.
> EOT
...    <- blank lines that are
       <- part of the header.

A groff Example       by David Medinets              Page 1

     This   is   an   example of a paragraph that begins with a
small indent. Like any paragraph, when needed the text auto-
matically wraps to the next line.

 o This is a bulleted item.
 o This is another bulleted item.
_____


(1)    This paragraph begins with a number.  Unlike  the  pp
       paragraph it has no beginning indentation.

(2)    This is the second numbered paragraph.
```

```
...    <- many blank lines that make
       <- up the bulk of the page.
```

```
1 - This is the first footnote.
2 - This is the second footnote.
```

Although the various tags and registers of the **groff** command are complex, there isn't another command that can produce such tightly controlled output. I was only able to scratch the surface in this section. If you need to produce output from your programs, spending some time to become familiar with **groff** is well worth it.

The head Command

Synopsis

head displays the beginning of files.

Syntax

```
head [options] [file...]
```

Description:

By default, the **head** command displays the first 10 lines of each file specified on the command line. If no files are specified, *STDIN* is read. When more than one file is specified, a header is used to separate the files. For example:

```
% head --lines 2 grep1.dat grep2.dat
==> grep1.dat <==      <- header line.
Paul   Male    Husband
Mindy  Female  Wife

==> grep2.dat <==      <- header line.
Bill Male    Husband
Cheryl Female  Wife
```

Table 9.23 shows the options for the **head** command.

Table 9.23 *Options for the head Command*

Option	Description
`-c NUM[b|k|m]` or `--bytes NUM[b|k|m]`	Displays the first NUM bytes in each of the specified files. You can optionally specify NUM in blocks of 512 bytes, one kilobyte, or one megabyte by using the *b*, *k*, or *m* suffixes.
`-NUM` or `-n NUM` or `--lines NUM`	Displays the first NUM lines of a file.
`--help`	Displays a help message about **head**'s features.
`-q` or `--quiet` or `--silent`	Suppresses the display of filename header lines.
`-v` or `--verbose`	Always displays filename header lines.
`--version`	Displays **head**'s version information.

The most useful option in my experience is *--lines*. It frequently comes in handy when I only need to process the first one or two lines of a file.

The info Command

Synopsis

info displays online documentation.

Syntax

```
info [options] [nodename...]
```

Description:

The **info** command starts up GNU's extensive hypertext documentation system. This command is included in this chapter because you need to know about it. Most people are familiar with Unix's man pages, but the info hypertext system is at least as extensive and more up-to-date.

Each nugget of information in the system is called a *node*. Use the **info info "Getting Started"** command to learn about how to get around inside the system.

Table 9.24 shows the options available with the **info** command.

Table 9.24 *Options of the info Command*

Option	Description
`--directory` *DIRECTORY*	Adds *DIRECTORY* to the **info** command's search path.
`-f` *FILENAME*	Specifies which information file to view. For example, **info -f info** displays an introduction to the **info** command. If no *-n* option is specified, the top node in the file is displayed.
`-n` *NODENAME*	Specifies which node (each file usually has several nodes) to view. For example, **info -f info -n "Getting Started"** displays information about what keys are active inside the info hypertext system.
`-o` *FILE*	Sends the requested information to a file instead of the terminal.
`-h` ·	Displays a brief summary of **info**'s options.
`--version`	Displays version information.

The join Command

Synopsis
   join merges two files based on a common field.

Syntax
```
join [options] file1 file2
```

Description:
   Back in the days before relational databases become ubiquitous, the **join** command made it easy to combine one set of records with another—even though each set resided in a different file. Listings 9.6, 9.7, and 9.8 hold three data files you can use when experimenting with **join**.

The data files used by the **join** command must be pre-sorted. If you need to sort information, read the section called "The sort Command" in this chapter. **NOTE**

Listing 9.6 *jnames.dat—A Datafile of Names*

```
001 Barry
002 Mario
003 John
004 Harry
005 Dorothy
006 Jackie
```

Listing 9.7 *jsalaries.dat—A Datafile of Salaries*

```
001 132500
002 80000
003 45000
004 75000
005 90000
```

Listing 9.8 *jhiredt.dat—A Datafile of Hire Dates*

```
001 04/12/1989
002 06/23/1994
003 12/12/1997
004 11/17/1997
005 02/06/1998
006 07/20/1995
```

These three files are linked because the initial field on each line has a common number. The *003* associated with *John* in *jnames.dat* is also associated with a salary of *45000* in *jsalaries.dat*. The **join** command performs this association task for you:

```
% join jnames.dat jsalaries.dat
001 Barry 132500
002 Mario 80000
003 John 45000
004 Harry 75000
005 Dorothy 90000
```

Input lines that aren't pairable—i.e., that don't have corresponding entries in the other file—aren't displayed normally. The *-a FILE* option can be used to display the unpaired information:

```
% join -a1 jnames.dat jsalaries.dat
001 Barry 132500
002 Mario 80000
003 John 45000
004 Harry 75000
005 Dorothy 90000
006 Jackie
```

If you need to join three files together, first join two files and then join the third using a pipe:

NOTE The *dash* filename tells a command to read from *STDIN* instead of a file. Some commands normally only read from files. The *dash* filename lets these commands be used with pipes.

```
% join -a1 jnames.dat jsalaries.dat | \
> join - jhiredt.dat
001 Barry 132500 04/12/1989
002 Mario 80000 06/23/1994
003 John 45000 12/12/1997
004 Harry 75000 11/17/1997
005 Dorothy 90000 02/06/1994
006 Jackie 07/20/1995
```

Notice that a dash is used in the second **join** command to indicate that its first file should be read from *STDIN*.

The *-o* option lets you rearrange the order that the fields display in. For example, you can display just the hire date and name fields using this command line:

```
% join -a1 jnames.dat jsalaries.dat | \
> join -o2.2,1.2 - jhiredt.dat
04/12/1989 Barry
06/23/1994 Mario
12/12/1997 John
11/17/1997 Harry
02/06/1994 Dorothy
07/20/1995 Jackie
```

The field list uses *file.field* notation with commas as field delimiters. In this last example, the first file has three fields (number, name, and salary), while the second file has only two fields (number and hire date). By using *2.2,1.2* as the field list, we see that only the hire date and name fields are displayed.

If you need to add column headings, try this technique:

```
% echo "Hire Date  Name"; \
% echo "---------------"; \
% join -a1 jnames.dat jsalaries.dat | \
> join -o2.2,1.2 - jhiredt.dat
Hire Date  Name
---------------
04/12/1989 Barry
06/23/1994 Mario
12/12/1997 John
11/17/1997 Harry
02/06/1994 Dorothy
07/20/1995 Jackie
```

You can use the **grep** command to select just the information you need. For example, the following command displays only the line associated with *Barry* and *Harry*:

```
% join -a1 jnames.dat jsalaries.dat \
> join - jhiredt.dat \
> grep -i "[BH]arry"
001 Barry 132500 04/12/1989
004 Harry 75000 11/17/1997
```

Using the **cut** command, you can be even more selective. The following command displays only the salary for *Mario*:

```
% join -a1 jnames.dat jsalaries.dat \
> join - jhiredt.dat \
> grep --ignore-case "Mario" \
> cut --delimiter " " --fields 3
80000
```

By combining the various Bash commands, you can create a powerful data retrieval system.

Table 9.25 shows some of the options available with the **join** command.

Table 9.25 *Some Options of the **join** Command*

Option	Description
-a [1|2]	Displays a line for each unpairable line in the file specified, in addition to the normal output.
-e *STRING*	Replaces empty output fields with *STRING*.

Table 9.25 *Some Options of the **join** Command (Cont'd)*

Option	Description
`-j1 FIELD` or `-1 FIELD`	Joins on a specific field of file *1*. By default, the join is performed using the first field.
`-j2 FIELD` or `-2 FIELD`	Joins on a specific field of file *2*. By default, the join is performed using the first field.
`-j FIELD`	Joins both files using the same field number.
`-o FIELDLIST`	Displays only the fields specified in *FIELDLIST*. The field list uses *file.field* notation with commas as field delimiters. For example, *2.4,1.1,2.1* displays three fields—the fourth field from file *2*, the first field from file *1*, and the first field from file *2*.
`-t CHARACTER`	Specifies the field delimiter for both file *1* and file *2*.
`-v [1|2]`	Displays a line for each unpairable line in the file specified, instead of the normal output.
`--help`	Displays help information.
`--version`	Displays version information.

The kill Command

Synopsis

> **kill** sends a signal to one or more processes.

Syntax

```
kill [options] [pid...]
```

Description:

The **kill** command lets you stop a never-ending process (the normal use), or you can use **kill** to test the error handling of your scripts or programs. For example, what would happen to your mission-critical application if it suddenly was sent an I/O error signal?

You can use the **kill -l** command to get a list of signals that your Unix system understands. For my Linux system, here is the result:

```
% kill -l
 1) SIGHUP      2) SIGINT    3) SIGQUIT    4) SIGILL
 5) SIGTRAP     6) SIGIOT    7) SIGBUS     8) SIGFPE
 9) SIGKILL    10) SIGUSR1  11) SIGSEGV   12) SIGUSR2
13) SIGPIPE    14) SIGALRM  15) SIGTERM   17) SIGCHLD
18) SIGCONT    19) SIGSTOP  20) SIGTSTP   21) SIGTTIN
22) SIGTTOU    23) SIGURG   24) SIGXCPU   25) SIGXFSZ
26) SIGVTALRM  27) SIGPROF  28) SIGWINCH  29) SIGIO
30) SIGPWR
% kill -l 23
SUGURG
```

The signal to be sent can be specified four ways:

- -s *SIGNAL_NAME* (with or without the SIG prefix)

- -s SIGNAL_NUMBER

- -*SIGNAL_NAME* (with or without the SIG prefix)

- -SIGNAL_NUMBER

You can determine what processes are currently running by using the **ps** command. See "The ps Command" section for more information about **ps**.

The less Command

Synopsis

less displays a file one page at a time.

Syntax

```
less [options] [filename...]
```

Description:

The **less** command is surprisingly complex for a command whose only job is to display files. Part of the complexity arises because, while displaying a file, you can move forward and backward through its content.

The keys used while viewing documents are well documented by **less** itself. While viewing a document, press the **h** key to view the internal help information. You can also read the information available via the **info less** command.

There are many options used by **less**. However, none of them aid in programming the shell, so I won't describe them here.

Two items that I would like to mention are how to search for text while viewing a file and how to move from one file to another when you've specified more than one file on the command line:

- Searching for text is accomplished using the / key. After pressing /, enter a regular expression that matches the text you need to find. (Regular expressions are described in Chapter 8, "Pattern Matching.")

- Moving from one file to another is done using either *:n* (for the next file) or *:p* (for the previous file).

The man Command

Synopsis
   man displays online documentation.

Syntax
```
man [options] name
```

Description:
   The **man** command searches directories for a documentation file that matches *NAME*. This search is controlled by the *MANPATH* variable. Once a documentation file is found, it is displayed using the software specified by the *PAGER* variable or the -*P* option.

   The techniques that **man** uses to find and display information are unimportant to most people. If you are curious, start with the **man man** command and then explore the **groff** command.

   The manual pages that **man** searches are broken up into nine categories:

1. User Commands

2. System Calls

3. Library Functions

4. Special Files

5. File Formats

6. Games

7. Miscellaneous

8. Administration and Privileged Commands

9. Kernel Reference Guide

Table 9.26 shows some of the options available with the **man** command.

Table 9.26 *Some Options of the* **man** *Command*

Option	Description
-a	Displays all manual pages that match the name on the command line instead of just the first matching page.
-h	Displays a help message.
-k	Displays the titles of all **man** pages that refer to the name on the command line.
-P *PAGER*	Specifies which pager program should be used to display the manual page. The **less** command is used by default.
-S *SECTION_LIST*	Specifies which manual sections should be searched. For example, **man -S 1 chmod** and **man -S 2 chmod** display different pages—assuming, of course, the library man pages are installed on your system.
--version	Displays version information.

The **man** pages have a lot of useful information. However, some of it might be outdated. When looking for information, try the **info** command first. Then, if that fails, try the **man** command.

The mv Command

Synopsis

mv renames or moves files.

Syntax

```
mv [options] original_filename new_filename
mv [options] filelist target_directory
```

Description:

The **mv** command has two functions:

- Moving files from one directory into another—done when the last parameter on the command line is a directory.

- Renaming files—done when there are only two filenames on the command line.

The **mv** command, like the **cp** command, only affects regular files. Therefore, you might want to use the **find** command and its –*type f* option to build a list of files to move.

When using **mv** in a script, use the –*force* option to avoid having the **mv** command prompt the user to confirm overwriting files.

Table 9.27 shows the options for the **mv** command.

Table 9.27 *Options for the mv Command*

Option	Description
-b or --backup	Makes backup copies of files about to be over-written by the moved files.
-f or --force	Overwrites files without warning—useful inside shell scripts.
-i or --interactive	Requests confirmation before overwriting any file.
-S or --suffix *SUFFIX*	Defines the suffix to be used when creating backup files with the –*b* option. The default is a tilde (~). You can also set the *SIMPLE_BACKUP_SUFFIX* variable. The command-line option overrides the variable.
-u or --update	Only moves files that are newer than existing files.
-v or --verbose	Displays the name of each moved file.

Table 9.27 *Options for the mv Command (Cont'd)*

Option	Description
`-V TYPE` or `-version-control TYPE`	Controls the type of backup files that are made. *TYPE* can be numbered, existing or simple. The existing type of backup makes a numbered backup file if a simple backup file already exists. The numbered and simple options do the obvious thing. You can set a default type of backup using the *VERSION_CONTROL* variable.
`--help`	Displays a help message about **mv**'s features.
`--version`	Displays **mv**'s version information.

The **mv** command is pretty straightforward and is included here because everyone takes it so much for granted that they never bother looking at the documentation. For example, before looking at Table 9.27, did you know that the **mv** command could create backup files automatically?

The nl Command

Synopsis
   nl prepends a number to each line of input before displaying it.

Syntax
```
nl [options] [file...]
```

Description:
   The **nl** command works almost exactly like the **cat** command, except a line number is prepended to each line before the line is output. This seemingly unimportant behavior is very helpful when combined with the **grep** command:

```
% grep "@@" csplit.dat
##@@
@@
@@
% nl csplit.dat | grep "@@"
     2 ##@@
     4 @@
     6 @@
```

This combination of commands helps you to get an idea of where, in the input file, the pattern you're looking for resides. In this case, it is every two lines. Adding the **wc** command into the mix might be even more useful:

```
% nl csplit.dat | grep "@@"; wc -l csplit.dat
     2 ##@@
     4 @@
     6 @@
     6 csplit.dat
```

Using **wc** also lets you know how long the input file is—giving you an even clearer picture of where the pattern is located.

nl does more than simply prepending a line number to each page; it also understands the concept of a logical page, complete with header and footer sections. However, I believe this functionality strays away from this book's focus on programming. If you're curious about how to use **nl** to format pages, I encourage you to use the **info nl** command so you can read the online documentation.

The ps Command

Synopsis

ps reports process statistics.

Syntax

```
ps [options] [pid...]
```

Description:

I mainly use the **ps** command to determine process id numbers (PIDs) and terminal (TTY) numbers. However, **ps** has a lot more utility than that. You can also see cpu time, page faults, and a host of other information.

Information about each process is displayed on a row of the **ps** output. Each row contains columns. And each column relates directly to specific statistics describing the process. For example, the *PID* column tells you the Process ID, and the *PPID* tells you the Parent's Process ID.

By default, **ps** displays information about the Process ID (PID), Terminal Number (TTY), Status (STAT), CPU Time (TIME), and the command the process is running (COMMAND).

The output of the **ps** command is normally truncated after 80 characters—so each process only takes one line of your terminal display. However, the *w* command-line option lets you extend the output lines. Each *w* used on the command line extends the maximum length of output lines by another line. However, since **ps** only uses as many lines as needed, blank lines will not be displayed. So **ps wwww-wwww** is ok to use if you're unsure how many lines the output needs.

If you only need information about a specific process or a list of processes, you can specify it or them by typing PID on the command line.

At first glance, the **ps** command doesn't have too much to do with programming; it is more like a system administration command. It's included in this chapter for three reasons. For one, other entries reference it and, therefore, it needs to be here. For another, you can combine it with **grep** and **awk** to extract useful information. Finally, I found the manual pages to be unclear.

The *h* command-line option is handy when using **ps** inside scripts because it eliminates the default header line. After all, because you already know which column you need to extract information from, the header line only gets in the way.

Table 9.28 lists most of the options available for the **ps** command. The options dealing with sorting the output are not shown.

> Unlike most Unix commands, the **ps** command shouldn't include a dash (-) in front of the its command-line options. You can simply place the options one after another. For example, **ps af** displays processes for all users in a tree structure.   **NOTE**

Table 9.28 *Options for the ps Command*

Option	Description
a	Displays information about the processes for all users.
c	Displays the command name for each process instead of the full directory path to the command and the parameter used on the command line. For example, instead of displaying **ps fj**, only **ps** would be shown.

Table 9.28 *Options for the ps Command (Cont'd)*

Option	Description
e	Displays the environment variables available to each process.
f	Alters the COMMAND column of information so the parent-child relationship is apparent. This is not too useful for shell programming. If you need to determine the parent of a process inside your script, use the PPID column.
h	Suppresses the display of a header line.
j	Adds the PPID, PGID, SID, TPGID, and UID columns to the default list.
l	Adds the FLAGS, UID, PPID, PRI, NI, SIZE, RSS, WCHAN, and STA columns to the default list.
m	Adds the MAJFLT, MINFLT, TRS, DRS, SIZE, SWAP, RSS, SHRD, LIB, and DT columns to the default list. Combine -m and -p to get the number of memory pages.
n	Changes the display of various statistics to display numbers instead of text. For example, user ids are shown instead of usernames. The TTY and WCHAN columns are also affected.
r	Only displays information about running processes.
s	Displays information about signals—adds the UID, SIGNAL, BLOCKED, IGNORED, and CATCHED columns to the default list.
S	Adds the cpu time and page faults of child processes to the statistics of their parent processes.
tN	Displays information about processes connected to a specific terminal. For example, *t1* displays only processes using */dev/tty1*.
u	Displays information about users—adds the USER, %CPU, %MEM, SIZE, RSS, and START columns to the default list.
v	Displays information about virtual memory—adds the PAGEIN, TSIZ, DSIZ, RSS, LIM, and %MEM columns to the default list.
x	Displays information without controlling the terminal.

Descriptions of each column can be found using the **man proc** command; little would be accomplished by repeating them here. However, let me show you some quick examples of the output from **ps** so you can become more familiar with the command.

```
% ps
PID TTY STAT TIME COMMAND
 1512   2 S    0:00 /bin/login -- medined
 1634   2 S    0:00 -bash
 1773   2 R    0:00 ps
% # Display information without a header line.
% ps h
 1512   2 S    0:00 /bin/login -- medined
 1634   2 S    0:00 -bash
 1773   2 R    0:00 ps
% # Display information for all users.
% ps a
PID TTY STAT TIME COMMAND
  204  a0 S    0:00 gpm -t ms
  219   1 S    0:00 /bin/login -- medined
  222   4 S    0:00 (mingetty)
  223   5 S    0:00 (mingetty)
  224   6 S    0:00 (mingetty)
  227   1 S    0:00 -bash
  814   1 S    0:00 pppd connect ...
 1512   2 S    0:00 /bin/login -- medined
 1634   2 S    0:00 -bash
 1777   2 R    0:00 ps a
 1739   3 S    0:00 /bin/login -- kathy
 1740   3 S    0:00 -bash
 1753   3 S    0:00 lynx http://www.affy.com
% # Show the child-parent relationships between processes.
% ps af
PID TTY STAT TIME COMMAND
  204  a0 S    0:00 gpm -t ms
  219   1 S    0:00 /bin/login -- medined
  227   1 S    0:00  \_ -bash
  222   4 S    0:00 (mingetty)
  223   5 S    0:00 (mingetty)
  224   6 S    0:00 (mingetty)
  814   1 S    0:00 pppd connect ...
 1512   2 S    0:00 /bin/login -- medined
 1634   2 S    0:00  \_ -bash
 1778   2 R    0:00     \_ ps af
 1739   3 S    0:00 /bin/login -- kathy
 1740   3 S    0:00  \_ -bash
 1753   3 S    0:00      \_ lynx http://www.affy.com
```

```
% # Show information about the users who
% # are running the Lynx application.
% ps ua | grep "lynx"
kathy     1753  0.0  3.8  2048  1196  ...
% # Use the cut commnd to extract just the
% # username column.
% ps ua | grep "lynx" | awk '{print $1}'
kathy
```

You can use the **awk** command to extract any single column or combination of columns from the output of **ps**. For example, the filter *awk '{print $1 " " $3 }* displays the first and third columns.

The pstree Command

Synopsis

pstree displays process names using a tree format.

Syntax

```
pstree [options] [pid|user]
```

Description:

I like the **pstree** command better than the **ps** command for learning which processes are running on a system and how they relate to one another. This is because the **ps** command shows a lot of extraneous information, while the **pstree** command only shows the process name—the focus of the command is narrower.

By default, the beginning of the displayed tree starts with the *init* process—the first process started when Linux is booted. You can change the starting point by specifying a PID or username on the command line.

Normally, a series of identical processes (like the *getty* process that monitors TTYs) is shown on one line of the tree, along with a number showing how many of the processes exist. For example, *4*[getty]* means that four getty processes are running.

Table 9.29 lists the options available for the **pstree** command

Table 9.29 *Options for the* ***pstree*** *Command*

Option	Description
-a	Shows the command lines of processes in the tree. Processes that are swapped out are shown in parentheses.
-c	Suppresses the compaction of identical processes.
-G	Draws the tree using VT100 line-drawing characters.
-h	Highlights the current process and its children.
-l	Uses long lines when displaying the tree. Normally, lines are truncated to the display width.
-n	Sorts processes by PID instead of by name.
-p	Displays the PIDs of each process.
-u	Displays the username of the process if the username of the parent is different—see the example following this table.
-U	Displays the table using Unicode characters.
-V	Displays version information.

Here is the **pstree** command in action:

```
% # The default pstree command.
% pstree
init-+-atd
     |-crond
     |-gpm
     |-inetd
     |-kerneld
     |-kflushd
     |-klogd
     |-kswapd
     |-login---bash---man---sh---less
     |-login---bash---pstree
     |-login---bash---lynx
     |-lpd
     |-3*[mingetty]
     |-netscape-commun---netscape-commun
     |-sendmail
     |-syslogd
     `-update
```

```
% # This command shows the command lines for each process.
% pstree -a
init
 |-atd
 |-crond
 |-gpm -t ms
 |-inetd
 |-kerneld
 |-(kflushd)
 |-klogd
 |-(kswapd)
 |-login -- medined
 |   `-bash
 |       `-man pstree
 |           `-sh -c /bin/gunzip\040-...
 |               `-less -is
 |-login -- medined
 |   `-bash
 |       `-pstree -a
 |-login -- kathy
 |   `-bash
 |       `-lynx http://www.affy.com
 |-(lpd)
 |-(mingetty)
 |-(mingetty)
 |-(mingetty)
 |-netscape-commun /usr/doc/HTML/index.html
 |   `-netscape-commun
 |-sendmail
 |-syslogd
  `-update
% # This next command highlights the current process, the
% # one running the pstree command, and shows when the
% # username of a child is different from its parent.
% pstree -hpu
init
  |- atd(144)
  |-crond(155)
  |-gpm(204)
  |-inetd(167)
  |-kerneld(23)
  |-kflushd(2)
  |-klogd(133)
  |-kswapd(3)
  |-login(219)---bash(227)
  |-login(1512)---bash(1634,medined)---pstree
  |-login(1739)---bash(1740,kathy)---lynx(1753)
  |-lpd(178)
```

```
 |-mingetty(222)
 |-mingetty(223)
 |-mingetty(224)
 |-netscape-commun(2041)---netscape-commun(2050)
 |-sendmail(192)
 |-syslogd(124)
 `-update(226)
% # The next command shows how pstree can be restricted
% # to showing information about a single user.
% pstree -a kathy
bash
 `-lynx http://www.affy.com
```

The read Command

Synopsis

read gets one line of input from *STDIN*.

Syntax

```
read [-r] [variable_name...]
```

Description:

The **read** command can be quite versatile because it can read both from the keyboard and from files.

The **read** command is also described, with more examples, in **FRI** the "Reading Input" section of Chapter 5, "Controlling the Shell."

With no parameters, the command simply reads from *STDIN* and stores one line of input in the *REPLY* variable. If you supply variable names, Bash stores each word of input in its corresponding variable, with any leftover words being assigned to the last variable.

Bash uses the *IFS* variable to determine where words start and end; when getting input from the user, you rarely need to change *IFS*. However, if you redirect *STDIN* to come from a file, you might need to change *IFS* to recognize different end-of-field delimiter characters. Chapter 5, in the "Reading Input" section, has examples of changing *IFS* to use different delimiters.

The *-r* option indicates that the backslash (\) character does not perform its normal line-continuation function. For example:

```
% read
Line One \
Line Two
```

```
% echo $REPLY
Line One Line Two
% read -r
Line One \
% echo $REPLY
Line One \
```

Notice that *REPLY* does not contain a newline after the first **read** command. The backslash character essentially hides the following newline from the **read** command.

The rm Command

CAUTION   The rm command is very, very dangerous! Never use the command **rm *** unless you really sure it's the right thing to do! And never, under any circumstances, issue the command **rm *..**

Synopsis
   rm deletes files.

Syntax
```
rm [options] [file...]
```

Description:

The **rm** command deletes files and directories. It rarely asks for permission. Therefore, I recommend you create an alias that turns on the interactive option whenever **rm** is used. However, your system administrator might have already taken care of creating this alias. Use the **alias** command to find out:

```
% alias
alias rm='rm -i'
```

TIP   Creating an alias that maps **rm -i** to **rm** is usually a good idea. On my system, I use the command, **alias rm='rm -i'**, to accomplish this.

If your system displays an alias that looks like the one above, you don't need to worry. Otherwise, add **alias rm='rm -i'** to your *.bash_profile* file or contact your system administrator for advice.

You can use the *--recursive* option to delete a directory:

```
% mkdir temp
% echo "test" > temp/temp.out
% rm -ri temp
rm: descend directory 'temp'? y
rm: remove 'temp/temp.out'? y
rm: remove directory 'a'? y
```

Table 9.30 shows the options for the **rm** command.

Table 9.30 *Options for the **rm** Command*

Option	Description
-d or --directory	Unlinks directories instead of deleting them. Don't use this option unless you are an experienced system administrator, because it can cause you to lose information unintentionally.
-f or --force	Suppresses any confirmation requests.
--help	Displays help information.
-i or --iteractive	Seeks confirmation before deleting each file. Highly recommended.
-r or -R or --recursive	Deletes subdirectories and the files associated with them.
-v or --verbose	Displays the name of each file before it is deleted.
--version	Displays version information.

The sort Command

Synopsis

sort arranges input lines into alphabetical order (or numerical if you use an option), merges files, or simply checks for alphabetical order.

Syntax

```
sort [options] [file...]
```

Description:

The **sort** command, without any command-line parameters, reads lines of input from *STDIN* until an end-of-file character (^D) is received, and then arranges the lines in alphabetical order before sending them to *STDOUT*.

There are three main ways to use the **sort** command:

- to sort—This is the default usage. All input lines are rearranged until they are in alphabetical order.

- to merge—This usage (the *-m* option) merges two or more sorted files into one sorted file. Because the input files are pre-sorted, this mode is faster than simply concatenating all input files and sorting the resulting file.

- to verify sortedness—This usage (the *-c* option) checks to see if all input lines are already in alphabetical order. If not, an error message is displayed (*disorder on filename*) and **sort** ends with an exit value of *1*.

Table 9.31 shows the options available with the **sort** command. Options that are set globally can be overridden when the same option is used with a specific sort key. If no sort keys are specified, global options affect the comparison of entire input lines.

Table 9.31 *Options for the* **sort** *Command*

Option	Description
-b	Ignores leading blanks when finding sort keys in each line. This option can be specified globally or for each sort key.
-c	Verifies that the input lines are already in sorted order.
-d	Sorts in phone directory order. All characters except letters, digits, and blanks are ignored.
-f	Ignores case when sorting by folding lowercase letters into their uppercase equivalents.
--help	Displays a help message.

Table 9.31 *Options for the* **sort** *Command (Cont'd)*

Option	Description
-i	Ignores characters outside the ASCII range (32 to 126 inclusive) when sorting.
-k POS1 [,POS2]	Specifies a sort field (also called a key field) within each input line. The field begins at POS1 and extends to, but does not include, POS2. All fields and character positions are numbered starting with 1 when using the -k option.
-M	Looks for three-letter month abbreviations at the beginning of input lines and sorts in a logical manner (i.e., "*Jan*" is before "*Feb*"). Valid abbreviations are sorted before invalid ones. Initial whitespace (spaces and tabs) is ignored.
-m	Merges two or more sorted input files.
-n	Looks for a number at the beginning of input lines and sorts accordingly (i.e., this option provides a numerical sort).
-o FILENAME	Writes the sorted output to FILENAME instead of to STDIN. FILENAME can also be one of the input files; **sort** handles this situation correctly.
-r	Reverses the order of the sort. For example, reverse alphabetical order is "Z" to "A".
-s	Eliminates the last-ditch comparison by machine-collating sequence that **sort** performs when comparison by key fields determines that input lines are the same. In other words, if the key fields on two or more input lines are the same, the lines are left in the same relative order.
-T DIRNAME	Specifies a temporary directory for **sort** to use. This option overrides the TMPDIR environment variable. If no temporary directory is specified, */tmp* will be used.

Table 9.31 *Options for the **sort** Command (Cont'd)*

Option	Description
-t *DELIMITER*	Defines the *end-of-field* delimiter used when finding **sort** keys. Normally **sort** creates fields where there is a transition between non-whitespace and whitespace. For example, the input file *David 35 Author* has three fields; however, the second and third fields have extra leading spaces. The delimiter character is not considered to be part of any field.
-u used with -c	Checks that no consecutive pair of input lines are duplicates of each other.
-u	Causes, when not used with -c, only the first of a series of duplicate lines to be displayed. In order words, all output lines are guaranteed to be unique.
--version	Displays **sort**'s version information.
+*POS1* [-*POS2*]	Specifies a sort field (also called a key field) within each input line. The field begins at *POS1* and extends to, but does not include, *POS2*. All fields and character positions are numbered starting with zero, using the +*POS* notation. However, using the +*POS* notation is discouraged. Please use the -*k* option instead.

Just in case you haven't been exposed to key fields before, let's quickly review. Key fields are used by **sort** to compare two input lines. If no key field is defined, the entire line is essentially considered to be one big key field. Let's use the file in Listing 9.9 to explore the key field concept.

Listing 9.9 *sort1..dat—A Data File Used to Demonstrate the **sort** Command*

```
1 AC BB CC
2 AB CC DD
3 CA BB CC
4 BE DD EE
5 BD AA AA
```

The *sort1.dat* file has four fields (or columns) per line. By default, **sort** arranges the lines based on the leftmost field. If two lines have identical leftmost fields, then the next field is examined—and so on until **sort** decides which line should come first in the sorted output.

You can force **sort** to base its comparison on a different field order using the *-k* option. For example, the following command sorts on the second field:

```
% sort -k2 sort1.dat
2 AB CC DD
1 AC BB CC
5 BD AA AA
4 BE DD EE
3 CA BB CC
```

Notice that the second column, the sort key, is shown in bold for easy reference. This was only done for illustration purposes; the **sort** command doesn't have this feature.

You can also **sort** on a subfield. For example:

```
% sort -k2.3 sort1.dat
3 CA BB CC
2 AB CC DD
1 AC BB CC
5 BD AA AA
4 BE DD EE
```

The above command line sorts on the second characters of the second field. Why the command needs .3 instead of .2 is unclear to me. But, hey, it works and that's what counts.

The various sort key options can be appended to the *-k* option to modify the sort behavior. For example, to sort in reverse order, use the *r* option.

```
% sort -k2.3r sort1.dat
4 BE DD EE
5 BD AA AA
1 AC BB CC
2 AB CC DD
3 CA BB CC
```

The *-b* option comes in handy if your input files aren't in nice neat rows. Listing 9.10 shows such a file.

Listing 9.10 *sort2..dat—A Datafile Used to Demonstrate the* **sort**
Command

```
1    AC BB CC
2 AB    CC DD
3 CA   BB CC
4 BE DD   EE
5 BD   AA AA
```

Sorting *sort2.dat* on the second column doesn't quite work:

```
% sort -k2 sort1.dat
1    AC BB CC
2 AB    CC DD
5 BD   AA AA
4 BE DD   EE
3 CA   BB CC
```

This command didn't work properly because **sort**, by default,
doesn't understand multiple spaces or tabs between fields. Using
the *-b* option fixes the situation:

```
% sort -k2 sort1.dat
2 AB    CC DD
1    AC BB CC
5 BD   AA AA
4 BE DD   EE
3 CA   BB CC
```

If you actually want to eliminate the extra spaces, use the **tr**
command:

```
% cat sort1.dat | \
> tr --squeeze-repeats " " | \
> sort -k2 sort1.dat
2 AB CC DD
1 AC BB CC
5 BD AA AA
4 BE DD EE
3 CA BB CC
```

The **sort** command is quite useful. However, when sorting large
files, make sure you have adequate temporary disk space.

The split Command

Synopsis

split breaks a file into pieces using size as the split criterion.

Syntax

```
split [options] [infile] [outfile]
```

Description:

The **split** command, by default, creates as many 1,000-line files as needed to hold the contents of the input file specified on the command line or *STDIN* (if no input file is specified). You can use the options shown in Table 9.32 to change the size of the output files.

*The **split** command can be used to break large files into pieces small enough to fit onto diskettes.*

Table 9.32 *Options for the **split** Command*

Option	Description
`-NUM` or `-1 NUM` or `--lines=NUM`	Limits the size of the output files to *NUM* lines.
`-b NUM[b|k|m]` or `--bytes=NUM[b|k|m]`	Limits the size of the output files to *NUM* bytes or you can specify a block size of 512 bytes, 1 kilobyte, or 1 megabyte using the *b*, *k*, or *m* suffixes respectively.
`-C NUM[b|k|m]` or `--line-bytes=NUM[b|k|m]`	Stuffs as many lines as possible into output files that are limited to *NUM* bytes or you can specify a block size of 512 bytes, 1 kilobyte, or 1 megabyte using the *b*, *k*, or *m* suffixes respectively.
`--help`	Displays a help message.
`--version`	Displays the version information.

Using the **split** command is quite straightforward. Each time an output file is created, a suffix is appended to its name to make it unique. The first suffix is *aa*, the second is *ab*, and the rest of the suffixes continue the pattern (*ac*, *ad*, and so forth).

The strings Command

Synopsis

strings displays the printable characters in a binary file.

Syntax

```
strings [options] [filename...]
```

Description:

The **strings** command peeks inside binary files looking for printable sequences of characters. The printable characters in compiled programs are rarely encrypted. Therefore, I once was able to use **strings** to find the Oracle database name and user id that a program was using when the original source code was lost—something my system administrator didn't think was possible.

By default, **strings** looks for any printable sequence longer than three characters. This is controllable by the *--bytes* option. **strings** limits its search of object files to the initialized and loaded sections. If you don't know what the initialized and loaded sections are, don't worry—simply use the *--all* option.

Table 9.33 *Options for the strings Command*

Option	Description
`-a` or `--all`	Scans the entire file for strings.
`-f` or `--print-file-name`	Prepends the filename to each string that is found.
`--help`	Displays a help message.
`-v` or `--version`	Displays the version information.
`-n LENGTH` or `--bytes=LENGTH`	Tells **strings** to look for printable sequences that are at least *LENGTH* characters long.
`-o` or `-t [o	x	d]` or `--radix=[o	x	d]`	Displays the location of each string using octal, hexadecimal, or decimal notation.

Let's use the **strings** command to find out what files the *date* program uses:

```
% strings /bin/date | grep "/"
/lib/ld-linux.so.2
/usr/share/locale
  %%D    date (mm/dd/yy)
  %%x    locale's date representation (mm/dd/yy)
```

By filtering the output of the **strings** command with the **grep** command, only those strings that contain a slash are displayed. Some of the displayed lines don't deal with files, but you can easily ignore them.

Searching more than one file at a time is simple. All you need to do is add the second filename to the command line:

```
% strings /bin/date /bin/date | grep "/"
/lib/ld-linux.so.2
/usr/share/locale                     .
  %%D    date (mm/dd/yy)
  %%x    locale's date representation (mm/dd/yy)
/lib/ld-linux.so.2
>/t[j/
/usr/share/locale
//DIRED//
//SUBDIRED//
```

Now there's a problem. How do you know which line belongs to which file? Looking at Table 9.33 provides the answer, the *--print-file-name* option. Let's try it:

```
% strings --print-file-name /bin/date | grep "/"
/bin/date: /lib/ld-linux.so.2
/bin/date: __gmon_start__
...
```

Interestingly enough, using the *--print-file-name* option causes the previous technique to fail because the full path of each file is displayed on each line. This prevents **grep** from filtering any lines, because they all have slashes in them.

Connecting to the */bin* directory before running the **strings** command solves this problem:

```
% (cd /bin; strings --print-file-name date ls | grep "/")
date: /lib/ld-linux.so.2
date: /usr/share/locale
date:   %%D    date (mm/dd/yy)
date:   %%x    locale's date representation (mm/dd/yy)
ls: /lib/ld-linux.so.2
ls: >/t[j/
```

```
ls: /usr/share/locale
ls: //DIRED//
ls: //SUBDIRED//
```

The *--radix* option comes in handy if you need to know the exact location of each string:

```
% (cd /bin; \
> strings --print-file-name --radix=x date ls | \
> grep "/")
date:   d4 /lib/ld-linux.so.2
date: 3727 /usr/share/locale
date: 3df5   %%D   date (mm/dd/yy)
date: 40d9   %%x   locale's date representation (mm/dd/yy)
ls:   d4 /lib/ld-linux.so.2
ls: 31a1 >/t[j/
ls: 591b /usr/share/locale
ls: 5964 //DIRED//
ls: 596e //SUBDIRED//
```

You can glean quite a bit of inside knowledge by peeking into program files. For example, because both the *date* and *ls* files have the */lib/ld-linux.so.2* string at location *d4*, it's a safe bet that the *d4* location is part of some program header section.

The tail Command

Synopsis

tail displays the end of files.

Syntax

```
tail [options] [file...]
```

Description:

Being roughly the opposite of the **head** command, the **tail** command displays the *last* lines of each specified file, by default. If no files are specified on the command line, then *STDIN* is used. When more than one file is specified, a header is used to separate the files, for example:

```
% tail --lines 2 grep1.dat grep2.dat
==> grep1.dat <==      <- header line.
Rachel Female  Daughter
Sara   Female  Daughter

==> grep2.dat <==      <- header line.
```

```
Foo    Male    Son
Bar    Male    Son
```

Table 9.34 shows the options for the **tail** command.

Table 9.34 *Options for the tail Command*

Option	Description
`+NUM`	Starts displaying input lines beginning at line *NUM*.
`-c NUM[b│k│m]` or `--bytes NUM[b│k│m]`	Displays the first *NUM* bytes in each of the specified files. You can optionally specify *NUM* in blocks of 512 bytes, one kilobyte, or one megabyte by using the *b*, *k*, or *m* suffixes.
`-f` or `--follow`	Displays the end of a file and then waits for more input. This option is very useful to watch log files.
`-n NUM` or `--lines NUM`	Displays the last *NUM* lines of a file. This option is useful to see the latest messages in a log file.
`-q` or `--quiet` or `--silent`	Suppresses the display of filename header lines.
`-v` or `--verbose`	Always displays filename header lines.
`--help`	Displays a help message.
`--version`	Displays **tail**'s version information.

The **tail** command can be used to monitor the content being appended to a file when the *--follow* option is used. One creative way of using this option is to run a command as a background process while watching its standard output. For example:

```
% find / >/filelog.out 2>filelog.out &
[1] 396
% tail --follow filelog.out
find: /var/spool/cron: Permission denied
-1.10/addon/00index.txt
...
```

This example redirects both *STDOUT* and *STDERR* to a log file called *filelog.out* and runs the **find** command in the background. In this case, the **find** command locates all files and displays their filenames. The **tail** command monitors the output. This technique lets you save all of **find**'s output, while still being able to view that output while the command is still running.

Using this technique of viewing a command's output and still logging it isn't too useful when only the **find** command is being used. However, if the command being monitored is a web server or some other type of service program, the technique becomes much more important.

You can choose to display lines from the middle of a file by using a combination of the **tail** and **head** commands. Listing 9.11 shows a datafile we can use for experimenting.

Listing 9.11 *tail..dat—A Datafile Used to Demonstrate the **tail** Command*

```
1
2
3
4
5
```

The following line of code displays the third line:

```
% tail +3 tail.dat | head -1
3
```

And this line of code displays three lines starting with line two:

```
% tail +2 tail.dat | head -3
2
3
4
```

The tee Command

Synopsis

tee reads from *STDIN* and writes to both *STDOUT* and one or more other files.

Syntax

```
tee [options] [file...]
```

Description:

The **tee** command does two things at once. It performs the same function as the | character (sending the *STDOUT* of one process to the *STDIN* of another). However, **tee** also can send the *STDOUT* to one or more files listed on the command line. The *--append* option is used when existing files shouldn't be overwritten.

The following lines demonstrate **tee**:

```
% # Create some files to work with.
% echo "demo" > file1
% echo "demo" > file2
% echo "demo" > file3
% # Sort the filenames in reverse order
% ls file* | tee ls.lst | sort -r
file3
file2
file1
% # Display the output from ls file*
% cat ls.lst
file1
file2
file3
```

This example shows that the output of the **ls file*** command is saved in the *ls.lst* file. You can use **tee** as many times as needed in the same command line. For example, here is an example that uses **tee** twice:

```
% # Sort the filenames in reverse order but only
% # display the first file in the list.
% ls file* | tee ls.lst | sort -r | tee -a ls.lst head -1
file3
% cat ls.lst
file1           <- output from
file2           <- the first tee
file3           <- command.
file3             <- output from
file2             <- the second tee
file1             <- command.
```

Table 9.35 shows the options for the **tee** command.

Table 9.35 *Options for the tee Command*

Option	Description
`-a` or `--append`	Appends to the specified files rather than overwriting them. Files that don't exist will be created.
`-i` or `--ignore-interrupts`	Ignores interrupt signals.
`--help`	Displays a help message.
`--version`	Displays **tee**'s version information.

The test Command

Synopsis

> **test** performs file tests and evaluates expressions.

Syntax

```
test expression
```

Description:

The **test** command evaluates the expression on the command line and returns an exit value of either *0* (success) or *1* (failure), depending on the result of the evaluation. Table 9.36 shows the operators available for the **test** command. Some of them, like *-e*, are designed to be used with only one operand, which is usually a filename. Other operators, like *-o*, need two operands, typically two subexpressions.

NOTE   Use double quotes around any text arguments so that Bash can ignore any spaces that happen to be part of the text.

When using the square bracket notation, be sure to add spaces after the first bracket and before the second. For example, *[expr]* is correct, but *[expr]* is not.

Table 9.36 *Operators for the* **test** *Command*

Operator	Description
-b *DEVICE*	Returns true if *DEVICE* is block oriented.
-c *DEVICE*	Returns true if *DEVICE* is character oriented.
-d *DIRECTORY*	Returns true if *DIRECTORY* is a directory.
-e *FILENAME*	Returns true if *FILENAME* exists.
FILE1 -ef *FILE2*	Returns true if *FILE1* and *FILE2* have the same device and inode numbers.
-f *FILENAME*	Returns true if *FILENAME* is a regular file.
-g *FILENAME*	Returns true if *FILENAME* has its *set-group-id* or *SGID* bit turned on. Turning on the *SGID* bit means that the person running the executable file has the same rights as the file's real owner. In this case, the person running the executable file becomes a temporary member of what-ever group the real owner belongs to.
-G *FILENAME*	Returns true if *FILENAME* is owned by the effective group id.
-k *FILENAME* | *DIRECTORY*	Returns true if *FILENAME* or *DIREC-TORY* has its sticky bit turned on. The interpretation of the sticky bit is system-dependent. However, many systems inter-pret it as follows: If the sticky bit is set on a directory, files inside the directory may be renamed or removed only by the owner of the file, the owner of the directory, or superuser. This feature was added to keep ordinary users from deleting other users' files from the */tmp* directory.

Table 9.36 *Operators for the **test** Command (Cont'd)*

Operator	Description
`-L FILENAME`	Returns true if *FILENAME* is a symbolic link.
`-n STRING`	Returns true if *STRING* has a non-zero length.
`FILE1 -nt FILE2`	Returns true if *FILE1* has been modified more recently than *FILE2*. This operator is the opposite of *-ot*.
`-O FILENAME`	Returns true if *FILENAME* is owned by the effective user id.
`FILE1 -ot FILE2`	Returns true if *FILE2* has been modified more recently than *FILE1*. This operator is the opposite of *-nt*.
`-p FILENAME`	Returns true if *FILENAME* is a named pipe. Named pipes are similar to the pipes used to connect the *STDOUT* of one command to the *STDIN* of another. The difference is that pipes created with the | notation are nameless and temporary; they only last for the lifetime of the command line that contains them. Named pipes can last as long as needed and are generally created by programs rather than by Bash.
`-r FILENAME | DIRECTORY`	Returns true if *FILENAME* or *DIRECTORY* is readable by the current user.
`-s FILENAME`	Returns true if *FILENAME* has a file size larger than zero.

Table 9.36 *Operators for the* **test** *Command (Cont'd)*

Operator	Description
-S *FILENAME*	Returns true if *FILENAME* is a socket. Sockets are used for communication between a client program and a server program. The whatis.com web site—*http://whatis.com*—has definitions of many terms, including the term socket.
-t *FILE_DESCRIPTOR*	Returns true if *FILE_DESCRIPTOR* is opened on a terminal.
-u *FILENAME*	Returns true if *FILENAME* has its *set-user-id* or *SUID* bit turned on. Turning on the *SUID* bit means that the person running the executable file has the same rights as the file's real owner. In this case, the person running the executable file temporarily becomes the real owner.
-w *FILENAME | DIRECTORY*	Returns true if *FILENAME* or *DIRECTORY* is writeable by the current user.
-x *FILENAME*	Returns true if *FILENAME* is executable by the current user.
-z *FILENAME*	Returns true if *FILENAME* has a file size of zero.
STRING1 = STRING2	Returns true if *STRING1* and *STRING2* are equal.
STRING1 != STRING2	Returns true if *STRING1* and *STRING2* are not equal.
! *EXPRESSION*	Returns true if *EXPRESSION* evaluates to false and false if *EXPRESSION* evaluates to true.

Table 9.36 *Operators for the **test** Command (Cont'd)*

Operator	Description
EXPR1 -a *EXPR2*	Returns true if both *EXPR1* and *EXPR2* evaluate to true.
EXPR1 -o *EXPR2*	Returns true if either *EXPR1* and *EXPR2* evaluate to true.
STRING1 != *STRING2*	Returns true if *STRING1* and *STRING2* are not equal.
ARG1 -eq *ARG2*	Returns true if *ARG1* and *ARG2* are equal. This operator is used for integer expressions.
ARG1 -ne *ARG2*	Returns true if *ARG1* and *ARG2* are not equal. This operator is used for integer expressions.
ARG1 -lt *ARG2*	Returns true if *ARG1* is less than *ARG2*. This operator is used for integer expressions.
ARG1 -le *ARG2*	Returns true if *ARG1* is less than or equal to *ARG2*. This operator is used for integer expressions.
ARG1 -gt *ARG2*	Returns true if *ARG1* is greater than *ARG2*. This operator is used for integer expressions.
ARG1 -ge *ARG2*	Returns true if *ARG1* is greater than or equal to *ARG2*. This operator is used for integer expressions.
--help	Displays a help message.
--version	Displays **test**'s version information.

Let's take a look at some examples of the **test** command:

```
% # Is the floppy disk a block device? YES
% (test -b /dev/fd0; echo $?)
0
% # Is the hard disk a block device? NO
% (test -b /dev/hd0; echo $?)
1
% # Have I spelled my home directory correctly? NO
% (test -d /hme/medined; echo $?)
1
% # Create two files.
% echo "FILE1" > file1
% echo "FILE2" > file2
% # Test the modification times.
% # Is file1 newer? NO
% (test file1 -nt file2; echo $?)
1
% # Is file1 older? YES
% (test file1 -ot file2; echo $?)
0
% # The ~ notation is valid and is a directory.
% (test -d ~; echo $?)
0
% # test can handle strings quite well.
% # Is $USER empty? NO
% (test -n $USER; echo $?)
0
% # Is $USER equal to "medined"? YES
% (test $USER = "medined"; echo $?)
0
% # Is $USER equal to "MEDINED"? NO,
% # The test is case-sensitive.
% (test $USER = "MEDINED"; echo $?)
1
% # Is the current user my wife or myself?
% test $USER = "medinek" -o $USER = "medined"
% echo $?
0
% # test can also handle positive and negative integers.
% (test 5 -eq "5"; echo $?)
0
% # As a special case, you can use -l STRING, the length
% # of STRING, in place of one or more integer arguments.
% (test 5 -eq -l "12345"; echo $?)
0
```

```
% # Is the username is longer than 8 characters? NO
% (test -l $USER -gt 8; echo $?)
1
```

The tr Command

Synopsis

tr translates characters into other characters or deletes characters.

Syntax

```
tr [options] charset1 [charset2]
```

Description:

The **tr** command copies *STDIN* to *STDOUT*. However, along the way, the command-line options determine what filter effect, if any, is performed. The length of *CHARSET1* and *CHARSET2* should always be the same length; each character in *CHARSET1* should have an equivalent character in *CHARSET2*.

Normally, **tr** is used to convert all instances of one character to another. For example, all instances of the letter *A* might be changed to the letter *C*. You can convert more than one character at a time. *CHARSET1* and *CHARSET2* specify which characters are converted and what they are converted into. Examples of the **tr** command are shown after Table 9.37.

tr performs translation when both *CHARSET1* and *CHARSET2* are specified and the *--delete* option is not. Each input character that matches a character in *CHARSET1* is translated to the corresponding character in *CHARSET2*. Non-matching characters are not translated.

tr can also be used to squeeze repeated sequences of characters into single characters. I use this feature quite frequently to remove extra spaces in my files.

The **tr** command is picky about which backslash sequence it understands in *CHARSET1* and *CHARSET2*. If you use a backslash sequence that is not shown in Table 9.37, an error message will be displayed.

Table 9.37 *Backslash Sequences Used with the **tr** Command*

Backslash Sequence	Description
\a	The alarm or *CTRL-G* character.
\b	The backspace or *CTRL-H* character.
\f	The formfeed or *CTRL-L* character.
\n	The newline or *CTRL-J* character.
\r	The carriage return or *CTRL-M* character.
\t	The tab or *CTRL-I* character.
\v	The vertical tab or *CTRL-K* character.
\nnn	Any character specified in octal.
\\	The backslash character.

In addition to simple backslash sequences and regular characters, you can use any of the following notations in *CHARSET1* and *CHARSET2*:

- Ranges—The notation *m-n* expands to all characters from *m* to *n*, inclusive. The character *m* must sort before *n* or an error message is generated. For example, *D-G* expands to *D,E,F,G*.

- Repeated characters—The notation *[c*n]* creates *n* repetitions of *c* character in *CHARSET2*. If you need to replace characters *A, B* with the character *1* and the character *C* with the character *2* you could use *tr* `"ABC"` `"[1*2]2"`. The notation *[c*]* repeats character *c* as many times as needed to make *CHARSET1* and *CHARSET2* the same length. The *[c*n]* notation does not need to appear at the end of *CHARSET2*. Please see the examples shown in the text after Table 9.38.

- Character classes—The character class notation, *[:class:]*, provides an easy-to-remember way to specify types of characters. Only the *upper* and *lower* classes expand in ascending order. The *upper* and *lower* classes are valid in *CHARSET2* only if the opposite class is specified in *CHARSET1* (resulting in case conversion) unless the *--delete* or *--squeeze-repeats* options are both used. If both *--delete and --squeeze-repeats* are used, then any class can be used in *CHARSET2*. The following classes are valid:

- *[:alnum:]*—Matches letters and digits.

- *[:alpha:]*—Matches alphabetical characters.

- *[:blank:]*—Matches spaces, tabs, and newlines.

- *[:cntrl:]*—Matches control characters.

- *[:digit:]*—Matches numerical characters.

- *[:graph:]*—Matches all printable characters except the space character.

- *[:lower:]*—Matches lower-case letters.

- *[:print:]*—Matches printable characters.

- *[:punct:]*—Matches punctuation characters.

- *[:space:]*—Matches spaces, tabs, vertical tabs and newlines.

- *[:upper:]*—Matches uppercase letters.

- *[:xdigit:]*—Matches one hexadecimal character (0-9 and A-F).

- Equivalence classes—This notation, *[=c=]*, is intended to support international character sets but is not fully implemented.

  Table 9.38 shows the options for the **tr** command.

Table 9.38 *Options for the tr Command*

Option	Description
`-c` or `--complement`	Replaces all of the characters in the input that don't match *CHARSET1* with the last character of *CHARSET2*. There is an example of this option in the text after this table.
`-d` or `--delete`	Deletes all characters in *CHARSET1* from the input lines. *CHARSET2* is not used with this option.

Table 9.38 *Options for the* **tr** *Command (Cont'd)*

Option	Description
`--help`	Displays a help message.
`-s or --squeeze-repeats`	Looks for repeated instances of the characters specified in *CHARSET1* and, if found, replaces them with a single instances of the repeated character. For example, *aaabbb* becomes *abbb* if *CHARSET1* includes *a*. If both *--delete* and *--squeeze-repeats* are specified, the deletions are done first. If *--squeeze-repeats* is specified in conjunction with translation, the translation is done first. Then **tr** looks for repeated instances of characters specified in *CHARSET2*.
`--version`	Displays **sort**'s version information.

Listing 9.12 contains the datafile used in the **tr** examples.

Listing 9.12 *tr..dat—A Datafile Used to Demonstrate the* **tr** *Command*

```
ABC DEF GHI
ABC DEF GHI
AAA BBB CCC
```

Let's start by translating all *A*s to *Z*s. The changes wrought by the **tr** command are shown in bold for illustration purposes only; you won't see bolded characters on your display.

```
% tr "A" "Z" < tr.dat
ZBC DEF GHI
ZBC DEF GHI
ZZZ BBB CCC
```

You can convert the three lines into one line by removing the newline characters:

```
% tr --delete "\n" < tr.dat; echo
ABC DEF GHIABC DEF GHIAAA BBB CCC
```

The **echo** command is used so that the next shell prompt appears on its own line instead of the same line as the output. Try the above command without the added **echo** to see what happens.

Translating several characters into the same character is quite easy:

```
% tr "ABC" "[Z*]" < tr.dat
ZZZ DEF GHI
ZZZ DEF GHI
ZZZ ZZZ ZZZ
```

Translating *A* and *B* characters to *Y* while translating *C* and *D* characters to *Z* looks like this:

```
% tr "ABCD" "YYZZ" < tr.dat
YYZ ZEF GHI
YYZ ZEF GHI
YYY YYY ZZZ
```

Translating uppercase letters into lowercase letters is best done by using character classes:

```
% tr "[:upper:]" "[:lower:]" < tr.dat
abc def ghi
abc def ghi
aaa bbb ccc
```

You need to be a little careful when using the *--complement* option. Its behavior takes a little getting used to. The *--complement* option translates into *CHARSET2* all input characters *except* those listed in *CHARSET1*.

For example, let's see how to change all characters except *A*s into *Z*s:

```
% tr --complement "A" "Z" < tr.dat
AZZZZZZZZZZZAZZZZZZZZZZZAAAZZZZZZZZ
```

It looks like too much was translated! Even the space and newline characters were translated into Zs. Probably not your original intent. Here is another attempt:

```
% tr --complement "A \n" "Z" < tr.dat
AZZ ZZZ ZZZ
AZZ ZZZ ZZZ
AAA ZZZ ZZZ
```

The *--squeeze-repeats* option is repeated in examples throughout this chapter and in chapter 12, "Customizing the Tools," so only two short examples are given here:

```
% tr --squeeze-repeats "BC" < tr.dat
ABC DEF GHI
ABC DEF GHI
AAA B C
```

Only those characters listed in *CHARSET1* are affected by the *--squeeze-repeats* option unless translation is also done. When translation is done, only the characters listed in *CHARSET2* are affected—as shown below:

```
% tr --squeeze-repeats "BC" "ZZ" < tr.dat
AZ DEF GHI
AZ DEF GHI
AAA Z Z
```

The first and second lines are affected because the character sequence *ABC* is first translated into *AZZ* and then the two *Z*s are squeezed into one.

The true Command

Synopsis

true exits with a value of *0*, indicating success.

Syntax

```
true
```

The tty Command

Synopsis

tty displays the name of the terminal connected to *STDIN*.

Syntax

```
tty [options]
```

Description:

The **tty** command is one of the simpler Unix commands—it just lets you know which terminal the current process is using for *STDIN*. Occasionally, you might only need to know if the *STDIN* is connected to a tty or not (*STDIN* might have been redirected to a file). In this case, you must examine the exit value:

- *0—STDIN* is a tty.

- *1—STDIN* is not a tty.

- *2*—Incorrect parameters were given to the **tty** command.

- *3*—A write error occurred.

Table 9.39 shows the options for the **tty** command.

Table 9.39 *Options for the tty Command*

Option	Description
`--help`	Displays a help message.
`-s` or `--silent` or `--quiet`	Stops **tty** from generating output. This option is used when only the exit value is needed.
`--version`	Displays **tty**'s version information.

The type Command

Synopsis

    type displays system information.

Syntax

```
type [options] name [name...]
```

Description:

    The **type** command, by default, displays information about each *NAME* on the command line. **type** reports that some commands are hashed (for example, the **ls** command)—this means that Bash already knows where the command is located and that the *PATH* variable is not needed.

    type has three options:

- The *-all* option displays all of the directories that contain an executable file called *NAME*. This includes aliases and functions when the *-path* option is not used.

- The *-type* option displays *alias, keyword, function, builtin,* or *file* depending on what kind of command you specified on the command line. Keywords are shell reserved words, like **for** and **while**. The term "builtin" means those commands that are intrinsic to Bash, like **type** itself. If *NAME* can't be found, nothing is displayed and the exit value is *1*, otherwise the exit value is *0*.

- The *-path* option displays the name of the file that would be executed for the *NAME* command or nothing if there is no file associated with *NAME*.

The uname Command

Synopsis

uname displays system information.

Syntax

```
uname [options]
```

Description:

The **uname** command, by default, displays the operating system name. On my system it looks like this:

```
% uname
Linux
```

This result might not seem too exciting. However, if you're working on more than one type of system, you might need to know the operating system in order to determine which commands to run and what directories to use.

Table 9.40 lists the options usable with the **uname** command.

Table 9.40 *Options for the **uname** Command*

Option	Description
`-a` or `--all`	Displays all of the information **uname** knows about.
`--help`	Displays a help message.
`-m` or `--machine`	Displays the hardware type.
`-n` or `--nodename`	Displays the computer's network node hostname.

Table 9.40 *Options for the **uname** Command (Cont'd)*

Option	Description
`-r` or `--release`	Displays the operating system's release information.
`-s` or `--sysname`	Displays the operating system's name. This is the default action if no options are specified.
`-v`	Displays the operating system's version information.
`--version`	Displays a version message.

The output from the **uname --all** command looks like this:

```
Linux localhost.localdomain 2.0.32 #1
Wed Nov 19 00:46:45 EST 1997 i586 unknown
```

The uniq Command

Synopsis

uniq removes repeated lines from sorted input.

Syntax

```
uniq [options] [input_file] [output_file]
```

Description:

The **uniq** command reads from *STDIN* or *INPUT_FILE*, filters the information, and then outputs to *STDOUT* or *OUTPUT_FILE*. The different filtering actions are controlled by the options listed in Table 9.41.

Table 9.41 *Options for the **uniq** Command*

Option	Description
`-c` or `--count`	Displays the number of times each line is repeated as well as the line itself. Every line will have a minimum count of 1.
`-d` or `--repeated`	Displays only repeated lines.

Table 9.41 *Options for the **uniq** Command (Cont'd)*

Option	Description
`-f` *NUM_FIELDS* or `--skip-fields=`*NUM_FIELDS* or `-`*NUM_FIELDS*	Skips *NUM_FIELDS* before checking input lines for uniqueness. Fields are delimited by any number of spaces and tabs. If both *--skip-fields* and *--skip-chars* options are used, the fields are skipped first.
`--help`	Displays a help message.
`-s` *NUM_CHARS* or `--skip-chars=`*NUM_CHARS* or `+`*NUM_CHARS*	Skips *NUM_CHARS* before checking input lines for uniqueness. If both *--skip-fields* and *--skip-chars* options are used, the fields are skipped first.
`-u` or `--unique`	Displays only unique lines. This means that repeated lines are not sent to the output file.
`-w` *NUM_CHARS* or `--check-chars=`*NUM_CHARS*	Specifies the number of characters to check for uniqueness. Normally, the entire line (except the skipped section) is checked.
`--version`	Displays a version message.

Listing 9.13 contains the data file used in the **uniq** examples.

Listing 9.13 *uniq..dat—A Datafile Used to Demonstrate the **uniq** Command*

```
01 12345 67890
02 12345 67890
03 12345 22222
03 12345 22222
04 11111 22222
```

Our first example shows how **uniq** filters the test datafile when no parameters are specified:

```
% uniq uniq.dat
01 12345 67890
02 12345 67890
03 12345 22222    <- Notice the duplicate 03 line has
04 11111 22222    <- been removed.
```

The *-unique* option removes all traces of repeated or duplicate lines:

```
% uniq -unique uniq.dat
01 12345 67890    <- Notice all of the 03 lines have
02 12345 67890    <- been removed.
04 11111 22222
```

The *-repeated* option is the opposite of the *-unique* option. Only one copy of each duplicated line is output:

```
% uniq -repeated uniq.dat
03 12345 22222
```

When you need **uniq** to ignore the beginning of input lines, you can use the *--skip-fields* option:

```
% uniq --skip-fields=1 uniq.dat
01 12345 67890
03 12345 22222
04 11111 22222
```

The *--check-chars* option limits the number of characters checked for uniqueness:

```
% uniq --skip-fields=1 --check-chars=5 uniq.dat
01 12345 67890
04 11111 22222
```

Line *03* was not output because both *01* and *03* have *12345* in the second field and the *--check-chars* option limited the check for uniqueness to the second field.

The wc Command

Synopsis

wc counts the number of characters, words, and lines in a file.

Syntax

```
wc [options] [filename...]
```

Description:

The **wc** command is a handy utility when you need to quickly determine the size of a file. If no filenames are specified on the command line, **wc** reads from *STDIN*. When multiple files are specified, a line is appended to the output with cumulative counts.

By default, the totals for bytes, words, and lines are displayed. However, you can be more selective by using the options shown in Table 9.42. By combining options, you can display any combination of counts.

Table 9.42 *Options for the wc Command*

Option	Description
-c or --bytes or --chars	Displays only the number of bytes in the file.
-w or --words	Displays only the number of words in the file. A word is defined as alphabetical characters delimited by whitespace.
-l or --lines	Displays only the number of lines in the file.
--help	Displays a help message.
--version	Displays a version message.

The who Command

Synopsis

who displays information about who is logged on to the system.

Syntax

```
who [options] [filename | am i]
```

Description:

The **who** command normally displays the login name, terminal name, login time, and remote hostname or X display for each account logged into the system.

If you specify a *FILENAME* on the command line, **who** gets the user information from that file instead of its default location.

The command **who am i** displays data about the current user.

Table 9.43 lists the options usable with the **who** command.

Table 9.43 *Options for the who Command*

Option	Description
`--help`	Displays a help message.
`-H` or `--heading`	Displays column titles.
`-i` or `-u` or `--idle`	Displays the amount of time each user has been idle. A period in the time column means the user was active in the last minute, whereas **old** in the time column means the user was inactive for more than 24 hours.
`-m`	Displays information about the current user.
`-q` or `--count`	Displays the usernames of users who are logged on and how many there are.
`-s`	Does nothing; it's ignored.
`--version`	Displays a version message.
`-w` or `-T` or `--mesg` or `--message` or `--writeable`	Displays a column indicating if the user accepts terminal messages. A plus sign (+) indicates that terminal messages are being accepted. A minus sign (-) indicates they are not. A question mark (?) indicates a problem with the user's terminal.

Here are some examples of the **who** command:

```
% who --heading
USER      LINE      LOGIN-TIME      FROM
medined   tty1      Jun  2 20:08
root      tty2      May 31 00:26
harry     tty4      Jun 10 12:32
% who --count
medined root harry
# users=3
% who am I -H
USER      LINE      LOGIN-TIME      FROM
localhost.localdomain!medined  tty1      Jun  2 20:08
```

```
% who --heading --idle --message
USER     MESG  LINE     LOGIN-TIME     IDLE   FROM
medined  +     tty1     Jun  2 20:08      .
root     -     tty2     May 31 00:26 00:31
harry    +     tty4     Jun 10 12:32   old
```

The write Command

Synopsis

write sends terminal messages to a logged-on user.

Syntax

```
write user [ttyname]
```

Description:

The **write** command is used by system administrators to send messages about backups and system shutdowns to specific users. It can also be useful inside your scripts to send messages to terminals that aren't connected to the script via *STDOUT*. For example, Listing 9.14 shows how to send a message in a script.

Listing 9.14 *sndmsg.sht—How to Use **write** Inside a Shell Script*

```
write medined tty1 << END
This is a test message.
END
```

When this script is run, the output looks like this on *medined*'s terminal:

```
Message from root@localhost.localdomain on tty2 at 16:01
...
This is a test message.
EOF
```

The xargs Command

Synopsis

xargs builds and executes command lines.

Syntax

```
xargs [options] [command [initial-parameters]]
```

Description:

The **xargs** command is used to circumvent some limitations on the length of command lines. It does this by calling a command many times with a single parameter instead of one time with many parameters. In other words, instead of executing:

```
ls grep1.dat grep2.dat tr.dat
```

you could use **xargs** to execute:

```
ls grep1.dat
ls grep2.dat
ls tr.dat
```

If you imagine a longer command with three hundred filenames instead of just three, you can see how the command line might get a tad too long for the shell to handle.

xargs reads *STDIN* to generate a list of parameters. Parameters are delimited by spaces (however, if spaces are inside quotes or preceded by a backslash, **xargs** ignores them). Blank lines are ignored.

xargs has the following possible exit values:

- *0*—success.

- *1*—unknown reason for failure.

- *123*—if any instance of the executed command exited with a value between 1 and 125.

- *124*—if the command exited with status 255.

- *125*—if the command is killed by a signal.

- *126*—if the command can't be run.

- *127*—if the command isn't found.

Table 9.44 lists the options usable with the **xargs** command.

Table 9.44 *Options for the xargs Command*

Option	Description
`--eof=`*DELIMITER* or `-e`*DELIMITER*	Defines the *end-of-file* string. When the *end-of-file* string is encountered in the input, no further processing is done. The default delimiter is the underscore character (_). If the *--eof* option is present without the *DELIMITER* being specified, then **xargs** stops looking for an *end-of-file* string.
`--exit` or `-x`	Exits the current command line if the maximum command-line length is exceeded. The *-size* option specifies the maximum command-line length.
`--help`	Displays a help message.
`--interactive` or `-p`	Requests confirmation from the user before running each command line. This option implies the *--verbose* option.
`--max-args=`*NUM_ARGS* or `-n `*NUM_ARGS*	Uses at most *NUM_ARGS* per command line. Fewer than *NUM_ARGS* will be used if using *NUM_ARGS* exceeds the maximum command-line length specified in the *--max-chars* option. If the *--exit* option is specified and the maximum command-line length is exceeded using *NUM_ARGS*, then **xargs** exits.
`--max-chars=`*MAX_CHARS* or `-s `*MAX_CHARS*	Specifies that each command line can be at most *MAX_CHARS* long. The default maximum characters is as long as Unix can handle, up to 20,000 characters.
`--max-lines=`*NUM_LINES* or `-l`*NUM_LINES*	Uses at most *NUM_LINES* nonblank input lines per command. This option implies the *--exit* option.

Table 9.44 *Options for the **xargs** Command (Cont'd)*

Option	Description
`--max-procs=`*NUM_PROCS* or `-P `*NUM_PROCS*	Runs up to *NUM_PROCS* processes at once. If *NUM_PROCS* is zero, as many processes as possible are used. The *--max-args* option is frequently used in conjunction with *--max-procs* to ensure that multiple processes are started.
`--no-run-if-empty` or `-r`	Prevents the command from running if the input is empty or all blanks. Normally, the command is run at least once.
`--null` or `-0`	Uses a null or zero byte as the delimiter when determining the list of parameters present in the input. No other characters have any special meanings. Additionally, the *--eof* parameter, if present, is ignored. Frequently used in conjunction with the *-print0* option of the **find** command.
`--replace=`*REPLACE_STR* or `-i`*REPLACE_STR*	Provides a mechanism of substitution into the command that gets executed. All instances of *REPLACE_STR* in the *initial_parameters* section of the command line are replaced with the parameters found in *STDIN*. Using this option implies the *--exit* and *--max-lines=1* options. If *REPLACE_STR* is omitted, curly braces({}) are used.
`--verbose` or `-t`	Displays each command line to *STDERR* before executing it.
`--version`	Displays a version message.

In order to demonstrate the **xargs** command, the data file in Listing 9.15 will be used.

Listing 9.15 *xargs.dat—A Datafile Used to Demonstrate the **xargs***
Command
```
grep1.dat
grep2.dat
tr.dat
```

The following examples show the **xargs** command in action:

```
% cat xargs.dat | xargs
grep1.dat grep2.dat tr.dat
% cat xargs.dat | xargs --verbose
/bin/echo grep1.dat grep2.dat tr.dat  <- executed command.
grep1.dat grep2.dat tr.dat            <- output of command.
% cat xargs.dat | xargs --verbose --max-args=1
/bin/echo grep1.dat    <- executed command
grep1.dat
/bin/echo grep2.dat    <- executed command
grep2.dat
/bin/echo tr.dat       <- executed command
tr.dat
```

The last example shows exactly how the **xargs** command
works. When you set the maximum parameters per generated command and turning on the *--verbose* option, each parameter parsed
from the input file is revealed.

The *--replace* option lets you insert the current filename into
whatever command **xargs** is executing. For example:

```
% cat xargs.dat | \
> xargs --verbose --replace wc --bytes {}
wc --bytes grep1.dat    <- command
    91 grep1.dat
wc --bytes grep2.dat    <- command
    81 grep2.dat
wc --bytes tr.dat       <- command
    36 tr.dat
```

The example shows that the curly braces on the command line
are replaced by the different parameters that **xargs** generates.

Summary

This chapter introduces you to many of the Unix commands that
I've found useful over the years. Unfortunately, I don't have the
space in this book to cover them all. The more commands you're

familiar with, the better you'll be able to meet the programming challenges that lie ahead of you.

Chapter 10, "Portability Issues," is the next chapter. It compares the Bash, Perl, and Tcl programming languages to show you their similarities and differences.

Portability Issues

This chapter addresses the portability issues between Bash, Perl, and Tcl. Additionally, cross-platform issues are discussed that relate to the different Unix, Microsoft, and Apple operating systems. First, a Bash script is developed under Unix and converted into Perl and Tcl. Then a task-level comparison of the three languages is presented so you can convert your own scripts as needed. Finally, the chapter looks at cross-platform portability.

Let's develop a script to see how we might port a simple CGI script written in Bash into Perl or Tcl. If you're not familiar with CGI, don't worry. The discussion is focused on the low-level mechanics of the three languages. The higher-level concepts of CGI and HTML are ignored.

NOTE   CGI stands for *Common Gateway Interface*—the protocol used by web servers to communicate information to programs running on the server machine. Here's a quick synopsis: In order to communicate with the CGI program, the web server creates a group of exported environment variables, then the CGI program is started. The CGI program reads the environment variables as needed and generates a file (i.e., writes to *STDOUT*) that the web server sends to the web client (generally a web browser like Netscape).

The script we'll work on was developed to provide a quick-and-dirty filter for a web-based threaded discussion board. It will create a web page that only contains the latest messages.

Before we jump into the script, let's quickly review the discussion board application. The board simulates a graphical news reader, organizing posts to the board by topic, like so:

```
* dates - Jen 5/08/98 (1)
      o Re: dates - tim 5/09/98 (0)
  * And then there's boulder - Dan 5/07/98 (1)
      o Re: And then there's boulder - tim 5/07/98 (0)
  * Hows about Eugene - Dan Talayco 5/07/98 (0)
  * RV rental - tim 5/03/98 (0)
  * driveaways - tim 5/02/98 (2)
      o Re: driveaways - Christine 5/11/98 (1)
          + Re: driveaways - tim 5/11/98 (0)
```

These dates are shown in month, day, year order.

As you can see, new entries don't necessarily appear at the top of the board; sometimes they appear in the middle (the last two entries, shown in bold, are also the newest). Because the new posts are not marked, they can be a little hard to spot. And that is a usability problem. Most people only want to see the newest messages.

To solve this problem, we can write a script that reads through the HTML file that contains the entries and extracts only the lines that contain the current date, displaying any such new posts in its own web page. The basic approach uses the following steps:.

> HTML, or *Hypertext Markup Language*, is the lingua franca of the   **NOTE**
> Web. It defines the structure and content of a web document.
>
> All communication between web servers and web clients starts
> with HTTP headers. HTTP, or *Hypertext Transport Protocol*, lets the
> servers and clients know what kind of request is being made and
> what kind of response has been generated.

1. Spit out a standard HTTP header and some initial HTML for the page.

2. Get the current date and store it in a variable.

3. Make sure that the date is formatted as the dates appear on the board page (i.e., with no leading zeros in the number for the month), like this: `5/02/98`.

4. Search through the board page line by line and print out any lines that contain today's date.

5. Print out a little more HTML to finish off the web page.

As it turns out, this task is shockingly easy to perform using Bash. Listing 10.1 shows how it's done.

Listing 10.1 *filter.sh—Filter Out Today's Messages from the Rest Using Bash*

```
#!/usr/local/bin/bash

# The Messages are stored in the file assigned
# to filterfile.
filterfile="board.html"

# Step 1: Display the Initial HTML
cat << EOHEADER
Content-type: text/html

<head>
<title>filtered output</title>
</head>
<body>
<h1>Today's Posts</h1>
EOHEADER
```

```
# Step 2: Get the Current Date
today=$(date +%m/%d/%y)

# Step 3: Remove leading zero
today=${today#0}

# Step 4: Display Today's Posts
grep -e $today $filterfile

# Step 5: Display Closing HTML
cat << EOFOOTER
<br><br>
<hr>
<a href = board.html>
  Back to main message board
</a>
</body>
EOFOOTER
```

Even in this short script, we can see a few "idioms" that are specific to Bash: command substitution—*$(date +%m/%d/%y)*—vari-
able substitution with some string-formatting thrown in (i.e.,
${today#0}, which strips off the leading zero), and file handling,
which Bash basically leaves to the operating system.

NOTE   I could have used backticks instead of the command substitution.
The end result would have been the same.

Let's rewrite this thing in Perl. First, we need to let the web
server know that the script is written in Perl, and set up a variable
to hold the name of the file we want to process:

```
#!/usr/local/bin/perl

$filterfile = "wwwboard.html";
```

NOTE   We don't really need to set up *$filterfile* at all—we could simply plug
the file's name into the open function call—but setting up this variable at the top of the script makes it easier to modify the script to
work with a new HTML file later.

Now it's time for step 1 of the master plan. It's easy to print out
a multiline block of text in Perl, so we don't need to store the text

in a separate file. Rather, we'll just print out the whole HTTP/
HTML header with a single print statement, like so:

```
# Notice the semi-colon in the print statement? That's
# new, Bash didn't need one.
print <<EOHEADER;
Content-type: text/html

<head>
<title>filtered output</title>
</head>
<body>
<h1>Today's Posts</h1>
EOHEADER
```

Next, we'll do steps 2 and 3: Get the current date with a call to
the Unix **date** command, and format it. Perl's backtick substitution
is *nearly* the same as the shell's command substitution, so we can
replace the shell script's:

```
today=$(date +%m/%d/%y)
```

with:

```
$today = `date +%m/%d/%y`;
```

Here's another important difference between Bash and Perl:
Bash strips the newline from the result, whereas Perl retains it.
(After all, it was there when system returned its result, right?)
Because the newline screws up matching later on, we'll need to
remove it with Perl's elegant **chomp** function:

```
chomp $today;
```

Perl doesn't offer a ready equivalent of the shell's variable substitution. (Recall that in the shell, *${<command>#<character>}*
strips the leading *<characters>* from the variable's value.) Fortunately, there are plenty of other ways to format text with Perl.
We'll use regular expression substitution to see if the date has a
leading zero and, if it does, snip it off:

```
$today =~ s/^0//;
```

Now comes the real core of the script, step 4 of the master plan.
The shell doesn't really have the tools to handle sophisticated pattern matching, so it passes off the task of finding instances of the

The ^ pattern matching metacharacter, in Perl, matches the beginning of the string. Therefore, ^0 matches a zero at the beginning of the $today variable.

current name to **grep**. Of course, we could make a system call to **grep** from Perl, but that would be cheating, and would make our Perl script non-portable to Windows or Mac OS environments. Fortunately, we can simulate **grep** in a few lines of Perl. We simply open up the *messages* file and run through it line by line, printing out the lines if they yield a regular expression match:

```
open FILTER, $filterfile;
while (<FILTER>) {
        print if m#$today#;
}
close FILTER;
```

NOTE   The diamond operator (<>) reads a single record of input—usually a line of text.

I used the # as a delimiter in the regular expression statement above, because I know with absolute certainty that my regular expression contains a few slashes. See Chapter 6, "Using Perl," for information about alternate delimiters.

Finally, we need to replace the shell's **cat** command that outputs the closing HTML. As with the opening HTTP/HTML code, we can kick this out with a single **print** function call, like so:

```
print <<EOFOOT;
<br><br>
<hr>
<a href = board.html>Back to main message board</a>
</body>
EOFOOT
```

For your reading convenience, the complete Perl script is repeated in Listing 10.2.

Listing 10.2 *filter.pl—Filter Out Today's Messages From the Rest Using Perl*

```
#!/usr/local/bin/perl

$filterfile = "wwwboard.html";

print <<EOH;
Content-type: text/html
```

```
<head>
<title>Filtered Output</title>
</head>
<body>
<h1>Today's Posts</h1>
EOH

$today = `date +%m/%d/%y`;
chop $today;
$today =~ s/^0//;

open FILTER, $filterfile;
while (<FILTER>) {
      print if m#$today#;
}
close FILTER;

print <<EOFOOT;
<br><br>
<hr>
<a href = board.html>
  Back to main message board
</a>
</body>
EOFOOT
```

The Tcl implementation of the script is surprisingly similar to the Perl version. Again, we start by telling the server that we're using Tcl, and we also set up a variable to hold the name of the HTML file:

```
#!/usr/local/bin/tclsh

set filterfile wwwboard.html
```

Next, we'll write out the opening header. Tcl's **puts** function is nearly the same as Perl's **print**. There is only one difference—**puts** appends a newline by default—but because we're working with HTML, we don't really need to worry about newlines. As with Perl, we can use a single command to write the whole header:

Notice that Tcl doesn't use an assignment operator, while both Bash and Perl do.

```
puts {Content-type: text/html

<head>
<title>Filtered Output</title>
</head>
<body>
<h1>Today's Posts</h1>
}
```

*Like the
shell, and
unlike Perl,
Tcl strips the
newline from
the results of
the system
call.*

Now, we need to make a system call to **date**, and put the results into a variable. Tcl provides a special function, called **exec**, for executing system calls. We'll use Tcl's command substitution to stand in for the shell's version of command substitution and Perl's backticks:

```
set today [exec date +%m/%d/%y]
```

CAUTION Be careful with *exec* on Windows! It really doesn't do what you'd expect at all. (See the "Tcl Under Windows" section, later in this chapter, for more details.)

Step 3 of the master plan is to format the date string by removing the leading zero. Tcl's variable substitution doesn't offer an equivalent for the shell's fancy strip-leading-characters substitution, but it does offer a built-in function, **string trimleft,** that neatly accomplishes the same result—removing the first character:

```
set today [string trimleft $today 0]
```

NOTE The **string trimleft** function removes any instances of its second parameter from the beginning of its first parameter. In this example, all zero characters are removed from the start of *$today*.

In step 4, it's time to write our **grep**-surrogate in Tcl. It's easy, and it's nearly equivalent to the Perl procedure, if a little wordier:

```
set myfile [open $filterfile]
while {![eof $myfile]} {
    gets $myfile line
    if [regexp $today $line] {puts $line}
}
close $myfile
```

Finally, we write out the closing HTML. Once again, we can use a single **puts** function call:

```
puts {
<br><br>
<hr>
<a href = board.html>Back to main message board</a>
</body>
}
```

That, as they say, is that. Listing 10.3 holds the Tcl script in its uninterrupted glory.

Listing 10.3 *filter.tcl—Filter Out Today's Messages from the Rest Using Tcl*

```
#!/usr/local/bin/tclsh

set filterfile wwwboard.html

puts {Content-type: text/html

<head>
<title>filtered output</title>
</head>
<body>
<h1>Today's Posts</h1>
}

set today [exec date +%m/%d/%y]
set today [string trimleft $today 0]

set myfile [open $filterfile]
while {![eof $myfile]} {
    gets $myfile line
    if [regexp $today $line] {puts $line}
}
close $myfile

puts {
<br><br>
<hr>
<a href = board.html>
  Back to main message board
</a>
</body>}
```

Command Equivalents Between Scripting Languages

The following subsections summarize some common programming "idioms"—writing output to the screen, reading from a file, and so on—and show how each of these idioms is implemented in Bash, Perl, and Tcl.

File I/O

Task: **Open the file *myfile.txt* and put the first line in the variable *line*.**

Bash: `read line < myfile.txt`

Perl:
```
open INFILE, "myfile.txt";
$line = $_;
```

Tcl:
```
set infile [open myfile.txt]
gets $infile line
```

Task: **Close the file *myfile.txt*.**

Bash: n/a

Perl: `close INFILE;`   `# assuming that the file was`
                             `# assigned the filehandle INFILE`

Tcl: `close $infile;`   `# assuming that the file code was`
                             `# stored in the variable infile`

Task: **Read through the file *myfile.txt* and process each line.**

Bash:
```
{
while read line
    do
        # process the variable called line
    done
} < myfile.txt
```

Perl:
```
open INFILE, "myfile.txt";
while (<>) {
    # process $_;
}
close INFILE;
```

Tcl:
```
set infile [open myfile.txt]
while {![eof $infile]} {
    gets $infile line
    # process the variable line
}
close $infile
```

Task: **Open the file *output.txt* and write the contents of variable *x* to the file.**

Bash:
```
echo $x > output.txt
```

Perl:
```
open OUTFILE, ">output.txt";
print OUTFILE $x;
close OUTFILE;
```

Tcl:
```
set infile [open myfile.txt]
puts $infile $x
close $infile
```

Task: **Append the contents of the variable *x* to the end of file *myfile.txt* (assuming file exists—check first!).**

Bash:
```
echo $x >> output.txt
```

Perl:
```
open OUTFILE, ">>output.txt";
print OUTFILE $x;
close OUTFILE;
```

Tcl:
```
set infile [open myfile.txt a]
puts $infile $x
close $infile
```

Task: **Open a pipe to the ls command and read the first line into the variable line.**

Note that Perl uses different pipe character positions for reading and writing, but Tcl puts the pipe in front in either case.

Bash: n/a

Perl:
```
open MYPIPE, "ls |";
$line = $_;
close MYPIPE;
```

Tcl:
```
set mypipe [open "|ls"]
gets $mypipe x    ;# you can almost hear Popeye
                  # saying this. . .
close $mypipe;
```

Task: **Open a pipe to the sendmail command and send the contents of the variable *x* to the pipe:**

Bash: n/a

Perl: ```
open MYPIPE, "|sendmail";
print MYPIPE $x;
close MYPIPE;
```

Tcl:  ```
set mypipe [open "|sendmail"]
puts $mypipe $x;
close $mypipe;
```

Variable Types

Task: Store the scalar value "Hello, World" in the variable *x*.

Bash: `x="Hello, World"`

Perl: `$x = "Hello, World"`

Tcl: `set x "Hello, World"`

Task: Store the three-element list *do, re, mi* in the variable *notes*.

Bash: `notes="do re mi"`

Perl: ```
@notes = ("do", "re", "mi");
    or
@notes = split "do re mi";
```

Tcl:  `set notes "do re mi"`

**Task:    Store the value "Hello, World" in a new associative array *greetings* using the index *standard*.**

Bash:  n/a

Perl:  ```
%greetings = ("standard", "Hello, World");
    or
$greetings{"standard"} = "Hello, World";
```

Tcl: `set greetings(standard) "Hello, World"`

Task: Display the value of the variable *x*.

Bash: `echo $x`

Perl: `print $x;`

Tcl: `puts $x;`

Task: **Display the second element of the list stored in the list variable *notes*.**

Bash: `echo $notes | cut -c 2`

Perl: `print @notes[2];`

Tcl: `puts [lindex $notes 2]`

Task: **Display the contents indexed with *standard* of hash *greeting*.**

Bash: n/a

Perl: `print $greetings{"standard"};`

Tcl: `puts $greetings("standard");`

Task: **Dump the contents of the of hash *greeting*, without sorting or formatting.**

Bash: n/a

Perl: `print %greetings;`

Tcl: `array get greetings`

Looping Commands

Task: **Repeat a command or block exactly 10 times.**

Bash: n/a. Workaround:

```
declare -i x=1
while [  $x  > 10 ]
      do
           # your statements here
           x=$x+1
      done
```

Perl:
```
for (x = 1; x <= 10; x++) {
    # your statements here
}
```

Tcl:
```
for {set x 1} {$x <= 10} {incr x} {
    # your statements here
}
```

Task: Repeat a block of commands for each element in the list
**   *mylist*.**

Bash:
```
for x in $mylist
do
    # your statements here
done
```

Perl:
```
foreach x @mylist {
    # your statements here
}
```

Tcl:
```
foreach x $list {
    # your statements here
}
```

Task: Repeat a block of code while the variable *x* is less than 10.

Bash:
```
while [ $x  < 10 ]    do
    # be sure to change x somewhere in here!
done
```

NOTE   Be sure to use the **declare -i** command, so that Bash knows that x is an integer, or your loop won't end!

Use the **test** command, rather than square brackets, if you're doing a *while* loop at the Bash prompt.

Perl:
```
while ($x < 10) {
    # be sure to change x somewhere in here!
}
```

Tcl:
```
while {$x < 10} {
    # be sure to change x somewhere in here!
}
```

Decision Commands

Task: **Execute a statement if the variable *x* matches the string *foo*, otherwise execute an alternative statement.**

Bash:
```
if  $x = "foo"
then
     # your statements here
else
     # some other statements
fi
```

Perl:
```
if ($x eq "foo") {
     # your statements here
} else {
     # some other statements
}
```

Tcl:
```
if [string match $x foo] {
     # your statements here
} else {
     # some other statements
}
```

Task: **Execute one of several commands, based on the value of the variable *x*.**

Bash:
```
case $x in
    pattern )
        statement ;;
    pattern2 )
        statement ;;
    pattern3 ) ;;
        statement ;;
    * )
esac
```

Perl: No exact equivalent to the "classic" *case* or *switch* statements. In the opinion of Larry Wall (the creator of Perl), workarounds are just as easy and elegant:

```
CASE: {
    if ($x ~= /pattern1/) {statement; last CASE; }
    if ($x ~= /pattern2/) {statement; last CASE; }
    if ($x ~= /pattern3/) {statement; last CASE; }
    if (/.*/)             {statement; last CASE;}
}
```

```
Tcl:    switch <expression> {
            pattern1 {statement}
            pattern2 {statement}
            pattern3 {statement}
            default {statement}
        }
```

NOTE   Tcl also has a similar but obsolete function called **case**. Don't use it.

Portability Across Platforms

Sometimes, you need to convert your scripts for use on another platform. Fortunately, both Perl and Tcl have been ported to both the Mac and Windows platforms, and, because the ports have been around for a few years, many of the significant problems have been worked out.

Bash

Bash has been ported to the Windows platform. However, documentation is scarce, and I'm a little hesitant to suggest it as a solution. It's probably safer to rewrite your Bash scripts in Perl or Tcl: There's plenty of freely available documentation and a fair-sized user base for each "foreign" port. If you're still curious about Bash under Windows, take a look at *http://sourceware.cygnus.com/cygwin/*.

Perl and Windows 32

Perl has been around on Windows for quite a while now. In fact, ActiveState, the major provider of Perl tools and Perl support under Windows, provides several different flavors of Windows Perl: a basic distribution, Perl for ISAPI™ a version for use with Microsoft's IIS server software, and "PerlScript," a version of Perl that can been used with Microsoft products that support ActiveX scripting components. (The IIS server and Microsoft Internet Explorer are two such applications.) ActiveState also sells a commercial visual debugger for Perl that functions in a similar way to the visual debuggers commonly found in C++ and Java IDE tools.

Perl is deeply rooted in Unix, and there are plenty of Perl commands that just don't make much sense in the context of the Windows 95 and NT operating systems. (Henceforth, I shall refer to Windows 95 and Windows NT as simply "Windows.") For example, there s a whole family of commands for dealing with inter-process communication—i.e., programs communicating with or controlling other programs—but Windows has its own proprietary methods for dealing with these issues. Similarly, Windows handles security and file access privileges in its own way, and it's impossible to map the Unix model onto Windows.

Table 10.1 shows the Perl functions not available in the Windows environment.

Table 10.1 *Perl Functions NOT Available in Windows*

Function	Description
`getnetbyname, getnetbyaddr, getnetent, getprotoent, getservent, sethostent, setnetent, setprotoent, setservent, endhostent, endnetent, endprotoent, endservent, socketpair`	Functions to handle basic network operations.
`msgctl, msgget, msgrcv, msgsnd, semctl, semget, semop, shmctl, shmget, shmread, shmwrite`	Functions to handle interprocess communications.
`ioctl`	Function to manipulate the properties of devices, especially terminals. Not especially portable across Unixes, and doesn't make sense on Windows, where devices aren't treated like files.
`chroot`	Function to change root for current process.
`fcntl`	Function for file locking and multithreading.
`link, lstat, readlink, symlink`	Function to handle symbolic links.
`umask`	Function used for file permissions.

Table 10.1 *Perl Functions NOT Available in Windows (Cont'd)*

Function	Description
`getpgrp, getppid, getpriority, getpwnam, getgrnam, getpwuid, getgrgid, getpwent, getgrent, setpwent, setgrent, endpwent, endgrent, setpgrp`	Functions for security and userid handling.
`fork, setpriority, times, wait, waitpid`	Functions for Unix multitasking.
`alarm`	Function used when scripts need to send signals to themselves. Windows doesn't support signals.
`dump`	Function used to create a core dump.
`syscall`	Function used to make a system function call.

In most cases, Perl for Windows warns you when you try to use a function that isn't supported. However, Perl for Windows can't warn you about **link, readlink, symlink,** and **syscall,** so pay special attention to these functions.

TIP

Here's a great way to sharpen your Perl skills: Write a little script that cycles through the forbidden commands, and **greps** a Perl file against each function to make sure it's portable. It's a breeze, really—the hardest part is typing in the forbidden functions, which is a good way to learn them anyway.

Commands that are normally passed to Unix—via functions like **system** and **exec,** or by "backticking"—are supported by Perl for Windows. Of course, Windows won't be able to make anything of a Unix command that you send it, but it *will* be able to execute any DOS command that you pass. In other words, the following Unix-based line yields an error under Windows:

```
C:\Perl\bin> perl -e "$x = `ls`; print $x"
Bad command or file name
```

but the DOS-based equivalent works fine:

```
C:\Perl\bin> perl -e "$x = `dir`; print $x"

 Volume in drive C has no label
 Volume Serial Number is 2872-10EA
 Directory of C:\Perl\bin

 .            <DIR>         05-23-98 10:47p .
 ..           <DIR>         05-23-98 10:47p ..
 CMD32   EXE        41,472  03-13-98  9:46a Cmd32.exe
 PERL    EXE        87,040  03-13-98  9:46a Perl.exe
 [. . . and so on . . .]
```

Let's take a look at the filtering CGI that we wrote in the first section of this chapter, and see if we can adapt it for use on a Windows-based server. Take a gander back at Listing 10.2. The first line:

```
#!/usr/local/bin/perl
```

is obviously wrong, unless you have an extremely funny-looking Windows file system. Depending on the web server package that you use, you can modify or delete this line. Check your web server's documentation to make sure. (As far as Perl is concerned, it's a comment, so you don't really need to do anything to make the line Perl-friendly.)

Everything else in the script looks pretty good, except for the system call:

```
$today = `date +%m/%d/%y`;
chop $today;
$today =~ s/^0//;
```

In fact, DOS does have a command called **date**. However, when we run the script at the DOS prompt, it hangs:

```
C:\Perl\bin> perl filter.pl
Current Date is Wed 05-27-1998
Enter new date (mm-dd-yy):
```

Unfortunately, the DOS **date** command doesn't just deliver date information, it also prompts the user to set a new date. There's no command switch or other means to simply get the date without a prompt. (If this strikes you as short-sighted, it is.)

Fortunately, we can rewrite the **date** system call in Perl fairly easily. The following two lines replace the three lines of code above:

```
@timelist = localtime(time);
$today = (@timelist[4] + 1) . "/" .
    @timelist[3] . "/" . @timelist[5];
```

MacPerl

Perl has also been ported to the Mac. In some ways, such a port seems bizarre: Larry Wall sometimes refers to Perl as a "distillation of Unix," and there are those (present company excluded) who think of the Mac's command-line-less interface as the antithesis of Unix. Still, MacPerl makes a lot of sense. First, MacPerl is handy for system administration tasks that aren't especially easy under a graphical interface—such as renaming all of the files in a folder or grepping through several different files for a search term. Second, plenty of web development takes place on Macs (where all the nice tools are), and there are plenty of test servers running under Mac OS.

The Mac OS has its own models for security and multitasking, and it's nonsensical to try to map Unix concepts (like permissions and inter-process communications) onto Mac ideas. Thus, there are some Unix-based Perl functions that simply aren't implemented in MacPerl.

Table 10.2 shows the Tcl functions not available in the MacPerl environment, according to the most recent documentation.

Table 10.2 *Perl Functions NOT Available in MacPerl*

Function	Description
crypt	This function encrypts a file.
exec	This function executes a built-in system program.
chroot, getlogin, getpgrp, setpgrp, getppid, getpw*, getgr*, setgr*, endgren, endpwe, umask	These functions get (or set) user and security information.
fork, kill	These functions are process-related.

Table 10.2 *Perl Functions NOT Available in MacPerl (Cont'd)*

Function	Description
link	This function deals with symbolic links (unfortunately, this doesn't work with Mac OS aliases). The good (or bad) news: MacPerl treats aliases as ordinary files.
msg*, shm*	These functions deal with interprocess communications.
syscall	This function makes calls to system functions.
alarm, wait, waitpid	These functions are simply not implemented.
dump	This function dumps the system core.

Although not mentioned in the documentation, the following functions are presumably not supported in MacPerl:

system: calls a Unix built-in program.

sem: deals with interprocess communication.

The MacPerl documentation also includes the following information about nonstandard behavior of certain Perl functions under Mac OS. These functions are shown in Table 10.3.

Table 10.3 *Perl Functions That Are DIFFERENT in MacPerl*

Function	Description
chmod	The meaning of the mode of files is different between Unix and Mac.
chown	The meaning of file ownership is different between Unix and Mac.
exit	This function needs to be accompanied by *MacPerl::Quit* in order for it to do what you expect.

Table 10.3 *Perl Functions That Are DIFFERENT in MacPerl*

Function	Description
fcntl	The meaning of file controls is system specific. Try using the *POSIX.pm* module, which provides a useful interface.
ioctl	The meaning of input/output controls is system specific. Try using the *POSIX.pm* module, which provides a useful interface.
time	The beginning of time for Mac uses January 1, 1904, which is different from Unix's beginning of time.

The most significant difference between standard Perl and MacPerl is support for system calls. The Mac just doesn't have a command-line interface, so there's no Unix-like (or DOS-like) language for communicating with the operating system. Consequently, Perl code that makes system calls—via **exec, system,** backticking, or opening a pipe, rather than via a file—just won't work on a Mac.

TIP

There is a software that adds a command line to the Mac—the MPW (*Macintosh Programmer's Workshop*) Shell, distributed (freely) by Apple. There's a special build of MacPerl that allows you to pass commands to the MPW tools. See *http://devworld.apple.com/dev/tools/mpw-tools/about_mpw.html* for details.

NOTE

Don't forget that there's a good chance that the next implementation of the Mac OS will have a Unix kernel, and it's not completely crazy to imagine that future versions of MacPerl will be wholly compatible with the standard Perl distribution. Keep your fingers crossed.

Let's rewrite our filtering CGI for MacPerl. The first line of the script notifies the operating system that the script is to be executed by Perl:

```
#!/usr/local/bin/perl
```

You can simply delete this line. If you want to use the script as a CGI with a MacHTTPd-compatible web server, such as WebSTAR or the Web Sharing system software bundled with Mac OS 8.x, perform the following steps:

1. Open the script with MacPerl.

2. Chose File|Save As from the MacPerl menu.

3. Pick "CGI Script" from the pull-down menu at the bottom of the Save As dialog box.

As we look at the rest of the script, the only obvious problem is the line with the system call:

```
$today = `date +%m/%d/%y`;
chop $today;
$today =~ s/^0//;
```

Fortunately, we can rewrite the system call in Perl, in exactly the same way we rewrote it for Windows. The following two lines replace the three lines above:

```
@timelist = localtime(time);
$today = (@timelist[4] + 1) .
    "/" . @timelist[3] . "/" . @timelist[5];
```

By now, you're probably thinking that we (meaning I) should have figured out the date in Perl in the first place, rather than using a backticked string to get the date from the operating system. You're absolutely right, and if I had written the script from scratch in Perl, rather than porting the Bash script as lazily as possible, that's exactly what I would have done.

Tcl Under Windows

Tcl has been ported to the Windows 95 and Windows NT platforms. As I mentioned in Chapter 6, "Using Tcl," Tcl's proponents sometimes call Tcl the "cross-platform scripting language"; in fact, *all but one core Tcl command has been implemented in Tcl 8.0 for Windows.* In the real world, there are some important platform-specific issues, but basically it's easy to move Tcl Unix scripts to a Windows machine.

The function that you need to worry about is **exec**. When you run **exec** under Unix, you invoke the system's built-in commands, like so:

```
% exec ps
PID  TT  STAT      TIME COMMAND
 8645  pv  Is     0:00.00  (tclsh)
 8651  pv  R      0:00.00  (bash)
 8723  pv  R+     0:00.00  (ps)
```

exec does work under Windows, but it works in a strange way. You can't **exec** a Windows built-in command directly, such as:

```
% exec dir
couldn't execute "dir": no such file or directory
```

Similarly, you can't open a pipe to one of DOS's built-in commands:

```
% set mypipe [open "|dir"]
couldn't execute "dir": no such file or directory
```

The problem is that the Tcl interpreter (or maybe DOS) is looking for a file to execute, and there's no *dir.exe* or *dir.com* file to run. There *is* a way to handle this problem: Let me warn you right now that it's pretty ugly. Let's say that you want to open a pipe to **dir**. Tcl needs a file to run, so we'll give it one:

```
set batchfilename "dir.bat"

;# create a new DOS batch file on the fly
;# then add the DOS command to the batch file
set mybatch [open $batchfilename w]
puts $mybatch dir
close $mybatch

;# open a pipe to the batch file's process
;# then read the first line from the pipe
set mypipe [open "|$batchfilename"]
gets $mypipe line

# do more stuff with the process here
close $mypipe

;# clean up…only works under Tcl 8.0 or later
file delete $batchfilename
```

You are right to cringe when you see this. Note that I haven't added any error-trapping to handle files or processes that can't be opened, or wrapped this up in a procedure, as I probably would in a serious script. In the real world, you might never need to work with a DOS built-in command, but it is possible.

The **exec** function under Tcl for Windows doesn't care what kind of file it's executing. You can **exec** an application, such as:

```
% exec mirc32.exe
```

as easily as you can **exec** a command file that outputs text. Executing a graphical application, like the *mIRC chat* program, causes the Tcl interpreter to block (i.e., wait patiently) until the chat program is finished. If you **exec mirc32.exe** at the tclsh prompt, you won't get another prompt until you quit *mIRC*; if you **exec** from within a script, your script will pause when *mIRC* launches, and resume when *mIRC* is finished.

Let's take a quick look at that filter CGI script from the first section of this chapter and see how portable it is to Tcl. (See Listing 10.3 for the whole script.) Remember that the first line is actually a message to Unix; the pound sign (#) at the beginning of the line causes Tcl to treat it as a comment. Depending on your web server application software, you might need to edit or remove this line. Check your software's documentation to be sure.

```
#!/usr/local/bin/tclsh
```

Otherwise, the only problem with the script is the **exec** function:

```
set today [exec date +%m/%d/%y]
```

Woe to the Tcl hacker who opens a pipe to a graphical application! You can't send anything to the application, and you won't get anything out of it except a -1 when the application quits.

As you saw earlier in this section, **exec** requires a file to run, and there's no *date.exe* or *date.com* file—support for the command is built right into DOS. In any case, the DOS **date** command doesn't quite suit our needs. As you saw in the Perl for Windows section, the DOS **date** command prompts the user for a new date. Because the web server software is the user of this particular script, the prompt will never be answered.

Fortunately, we can rewrite the Unix **date** command in Tcl without much fuss. Tcl provides a handy **clock format** function that renders the current time as a date. The following line of code replaces the preceding **exec**-based line:

```
set today [clock format [clock seconds] -format %D]
```

That's it—our CGI has been ported to Windows.

Tcl Under Mac OS

Finally, let's look at Tcl under Mac OS. In many ways, tclsh and Wish *are* a kind of command-line interface for Mac OS. MacPerl is cool, but it's mostly useful for writing and compiling scripts; if you use the Wish console to navigate the Mac, you might feel—if only in passing—that you're using Unix on the anti-Unix box.

Tcl lives up to its cross-platform ambitions on the Mac: Every core Tcl command is implemented under Mac OS, except for **exec**. As I mentioned in the MacPerl section, there's no Macintosh command-line interface, so **exec** makes no sense on the Mac.

NOTE   The Mac does have its own native scripting language, called Apple-Script, and the Mac port of Tcl includes a module that allows Tcl scripts to execute or communicate with AppleScript. (This module adds its own set of commands, rather than allowing access to AppleScript via exec and pipes.) Of course, you'll need to know a little something about AppleScript, which is a topic too large to cover in this chapter. For more information on getting started with Mac scripting, see *http://applescript.apple.com/default.html*.

The biggest problem with using Tcl on the Mac is Mac filenames. Unfortunately, the Mac OS allows filenames to contain a slash. If you want to refer to a file or folder that contains a slash in its name, such as:

```
cd {Tcl/Tk Folder}
```

the Tcl interpreter assumes that you want a directory called *Tk Folder* that's a subdirectory of a directory called *Tcl*. As far as the interpreter is concerned, a directory with the name *Tcl/Tk* is unthinkable. There isn't an elegant way to address this problem in every situation; you'll need to figure out solutions to individual problems on a case-by-case basis.

What about our filtering CGI from the beginning of the chapter? Unfortunately, I cannot in good faith recommend that you write CGIs in Tcl on the Mac. To date, there isn't a good mechanism to pass information (such as the contents of the *$ENV* variable) from a MacHTTPd-compatible server to a Tcl script. It is theoretically possible, using AppleScript as the glue between the server and tclsh, but it's a non-trivial task. I suggest that you use MacPerl for your Mac CGI needs. (If you're serious about running Tcl-based CGIs on a Mac, you should probably start by writing your own homebrewed web server in Tcl. Really. See Laurent DeMailly's work at *http://hplyot.obspm.fr/~dl/wwwtools.html.*)

Summary

In this chapter, you learn about the basic issues that you face when you port scripts from one language to another. We look at a case study of a simple CGI script ported from Bash to both Perl and Tcl.

Perl has been ported to Windows. Although certain functions, such as those that handle security issues and multitasking, are not supported under Windows, it's fairly easy to port Perl scripts to Windows. System calls (via **system**, **exec**, backticking, and pipes) can be used to invoke DOS's built-in commands.

Tcl has also been ported to Windows. All of the core Tcl commands are supported under Windows. The behavior of **exec** (and pipes) is a little peculiar: **exec** must execute a file, rather than a DOS command. You can work around this restriction by writing DOS commands to a batch file and executing the file.

Perl has been ported to the Mac in the form of MacPerl. Many security and multitasking commands are not supported under Mac OS, and there is no means to invoke operating system commands (because there aren't any to invoke!)

There's also a Mac port of Tcl. The only core Tcl command that is not supported on the Mac is **exec.** It's especially important to be careful about Mac filenames that contain slashes (/) when you're working with Tcl on the Mac OS.

Chapter 11, "Debugging Concepts," introduces you to both syntax and logic errors. It shows how to distinguish between them and how to prevent some of them from ever appearing in your code.

Debugging Concepts

This chapter introduces you to the many types of errors that arise when you create scripts. The two basic types of problems are *syntax errors* and *logic errors*. Syntax errors reflect incorrectly formed statements—missing spaces, too many parentheses, and so forth. Logic errors are all but impossible to guard against. Logic errors result when you want to count to 10 and, instead, you only count to 9 because you use a *less than* operator instead of a *less than or equal to* operator.

Logic errors are quite numerous and hard to predict. My best advice regarding logic errors is to keep your statements as simple as possible. When using Perl, avoid the **++** and **--** (*pre-increment and post-increment* operators). Additionally, both Perl and Tcl use a single equal sign for assignment and *two* equal signs in conditional expressions; for programmers who use more than one language, equal signs can be a source of continuing frustration.

The most common type of error is the typo. You might have entered a curly brace instead of a square brace or spelled "name" as "nane." Frequently, programmers forget to use end-of-line delimiters like the semi-colon in Perl or the slash line-continuation character in Bash.

Syntax Errors

The *syntax* of a programming language is the set of rules for creating legal, well-formed statements in the language, and when you break the rules, Bash or Perl or Tcl can't decipher your code. They display error messages describing what they think the problem is and on what approximate line the error resides.

Syntax errors are the easiest kind of error to make when you're writing a script, and they're the easiest kind of error to fix. They are the easiest in the sense that you are *absolutely positive something is wrong*—after all, the script interpreter tells you so. However, knowing that something is wrong and knowing what that something is are two different kettles of fish.

There are a million different ways to make syntax mistakes in a script. Here are a few common examples, which represent just a few ways that you can mess up your script if you're not paying attention.

Improper Form

Form is important. In English, you need to make sure that the words in a sentence are in a certain order: *you that English, sure are a need make the words in in in a certain sentence order to* just doesn't make sense, even though it contains the same words as the first part of the sentence. Similarly, the script's interpreter expects commands to be structured in a certain way.

For example, consider Tcl's **puts** function. If you look at **puts**'s syntax in the Tcl documentation, you see the following:

```
puts ?-nonewline? ?channelId? string
```

In other words, the Tcl interpreter expects the word **puts** to be followed by a list of one to three words: possibly the word *?-none-wline?*, possibly a word that indicates the name of a channel (i.e., the file or pipe that will receive the string), and certainly the string to be output. If a **puts** function call in your script is followed by anything other than one to three words, the Tcl interpreter complains that your command has improper form:

```
% puts hello, crazy little world;
wrong # args:
    should be "puts ?-nonewline? ?channelId? string"
```

If you've read Chapter 7, "Using Tcl," you know you can use quotes or brackets to group text into a single "word," so the interpreter can figure out what to do with your string:

```
% puts "hello, crazy little world"
hello, crazy little world
```

Punctuation can be important, too, when you're working with Perl. For example, when you're working with **if/then** constructions, Perl expects you to wrap up the expression—the thing that gets evaluated as true or false to see if the commands are executed—in parentheses, like so:

```
if ($x) {
  print "foo\n"
}
```

In the example above, the expression is simply the name of the variable *$x*. If the variable's value is not zero or undefined, the subsequent block of code is executed. If you forget to surround the expression with parentheses (which is easy to do if the expression is just a variable name), the Perl interpreter complains that it doesn't understand the command. Let's say that you execute the incorrect parenthesis-less code shown in Listing 11.1:

Listing 11.1 *iftest.pl—An Incorrect Snippet of Perl Code*

```
#!/usr/bin/perl

if $x {
    print "foo\n"
}
```

Here's what happens when you run the script:

```
% perl -w iftest.pl
syntax error at iftest.pl line 2, near "if $x "
Execution of iftest.pl aborted due to compilation errors.
```

What is the bottom line? You really need to have some documentation handy for your language of choice. And you need to look at the expected format for each of the commands you use. After a while, you'll know the forms of the functions that you use all of the time (like **puts** and **if**) but, even so, years from now, when you are a high-rollin' Perl or Tcl consultant, you will find yourself looking up the proper syntax for seldom-used commands.

Missing and Misplaced Command Separators

Perl uses a semicolon to mark the end of each Perl statement. In a one-line program (or in the last line of the program), you don't need to worry about separators. However, if you forget the semicolon anywhere else in the script, Perl will let you know. When you run the script shown in Listing 11.2, you'll see a Perl error message.

Listing 11.2 *bughunt.pl—An Incorrect Snippet of Perl Code*

```
#!/usr/bin/perl

print "hello, world\n"
print "hello, again\n"
```

Running this script looks like this:

```
% perl bughunt.pl
syntax error at bughunt.pl line 2, near "print"
Execution of bughunt.pl aborted due to compilation errors.
```

Yes, the mistake actually occurs in line 1 of the code, and yes, Perl tells you the error occurs in line 2. That's the way that compilers work, sometimes. Don't take every compiler message literally.

This is also one of the biggest sources of frustration with syntax errors—the inexactness of the error messages.

Tcl uses line-ends as command separators, so you don't need to worry about remembering to append a semicolon to the end of every line. However, you *do* need to worry about putting a command separator at the end of every line. Breaking a line of code for legibility's sake causes the Tcl interpreter to return a cryptic error message. Listing 11.3 shows a Tcl script with an incorrect line break.

Syntax error messages are rarely exact. Frequently, the error is one or two lines before the line number in the message.

Listing 11.3 *bughunt.tcl—An Incorrect Snippet of Tcl Code*

```
set mystring
  "boy, this is really a long string!"
```

Running this script looks like this:

```
% tclsh bughunt.tcl
can't read "mystring": no such variable
```

Tcl thinks line 1 is a complete instruction and that you are asking for the value of the variable *mystring*. Because the *mystring* variable hasn't been created yet, the interpreter can't return the value of the variable. (Strictly speaking, this isn't a syntax error, because **set mystring** is a legal command, albeit not really the command that you had in mind.) And, even though it doesn't warn you, the Tcl interpreter also thinks that you intend *boy* as some sort of bizarre procedure name, and unless you have created a procedure called *boy* for your own nutty reasons, the interpreter will return an error for the second line.

> **NOTE**
>
> If you really need to put a Tcl command on two lines, end the first line with a backslash (\)—Tcl's line-continuation character. The Tcl interpreter replaces the \<*return*> sequence with a space, so the line doesn't end, as far as the interpreter is concerned.

Misspelled Words

Unfortunately, spelling counts in the world of programming. A simple typo can cause Perl or Tcl to return an error. For example:

```
% perl -e "primt 'goodbye, robert'"
String found where operator expected at -e
  line 1, near "primt 'goodbye, robert'"
       (Do you need to predeclare primt?)
syntax error at -e line 1, near
  "primt 'goodbye, robert'"
Execution of -e aborted due to compilation errors.
```

or

```
bash> tclsh
% Puts "goodbye, robert"
invalid command name "Puts"
```

Sometimes, as in the Tcl example, the error message is pretty easy to figure out: *puts* has been misspelled *Puts*, and the Tcl interpreter doesn't know what *Puts* means, even if it's immediately obvious to any human who looks at the code (remember, Tcl and Perl are case sensitive!)

Sometimes, as in the Perl example, the error message might seem a little cryptic—unfortunately, you'll see different kinds of cryptic messages on different occasions. (And if you misspell a variable's name, the interpreter won't catch the problem at all, but the typo will probably cause you problems when you're running the script.) The moral: Be extra careful about spelling, and when you see a funny-looking error message, do a quick check for spelling mistakes.

Unbalanced Pairs

Lots of things in scripts are paired up. Ordinarily, every left parenthesis must have its right parenthesis, every left bracket its right bracket, each opening double quote its closing double quote, and so on. This is an easy rule to follow in a simple construction, such as:

```
print %myarrary{$myindex};
```

or

```
puts [lindex $mystring 0]
```

However, after you've been programming for a while, you'll find yourself typing baroque constructions, such as:

```
set itemnumber \
  [expr int(floor(rand()*[llength $biglist]))]
```

Suddenly, it's not so clear that each left bracket has its own right bracket. It's easy to leave out something somewhere in code like the line above, and if you do, the interpreter will return an error:

```
bash> tclsh
% set biglist "snap crackle pop"
% set itemnumber \
[expr int(floor(rand()*[llength $biglist])]
syntax error in expression "int(floor(rand()*3)"
```

It's probably not immediately clear to you that the second Tcl line of code is missing a right parenthesis. Once again, there's really no substitute for being careful and making sure that every bracket and parenthesis has its mate. However, you should be pleased to learn that there are special "programmer's editors" that can check for bracket/parenthesis symmetry and—if it doesn't drive you nuts—beep whenever you type a line with unbalanced pairs. Take a look at your favorite shareware/freeware web site for information about the latest editors.

Runtime Errors

After you've fixed the syntax errors in your script, the real work of debugging begins. A script that makes perfect syntactic sense to a Perl or Tcl interpreter might still not do what you want it to do; in fact, it might do something really stupid or (if you're not careful) really dangerous. For example, consider this perfectly legal and simple-looking Perl script:

```
% perl -e '$x = 1; print $X'

%
```

You might think—at least I thought, in my innocent years—that this script would print out the number 1. However, it prints out nothing at all, not even an error message. What's going on here? Remember, Perl is case sensitive, so when we set the value of $x, the variable $X remains undefined. Perl doesn't mind printing out an undefined value, so it prints nothing. By the way, the proper form of this code is:

```
% perl -e '$x = 1; print $x'
```

Here's another example: the infamous and nefarious infinite loop. Take a look at the following Tcl code:

```
for {set x 1} {$x != 10} {set x [expr $x + 2]} {
    puts $x
}
```

The idea here is that the loop prints out the odd numbers between 1 and 10. Let's walk through this code step by step and see why it doesn't stop. When the **for** statement starts, it initializes the value of the variable x to 1. Next, it evaluates the test part of the command, to make sure that the value of x is not equal to 10. It's not, so the body of the loop is executed, which prints out the value of x. Finally, after the loop is executed, the interpreter executes the next part of the command, which adds 2 to the value of x, making it 3.

You can probably see where this is heading. Now the value of x is 3, so the body is executed and x is incremented by 2 to 5. At the next test, x is still not equal to 10, so the body is executed and x is incremented to 7. At the next test, x doesn't equal 10, so the body is executed and x is incremented to 9. The test is performed again, and x doesn't equal 10, so the body is executed and x is incremented to 11. At this point, it's clear that x will never be equal to 10, because it's already more than 10, and we're adding to its value at the end of every loop.

The problem here is the test portion of the **if** command. Tests that make sure that x equals 10, or that x does not equal 10, are not very robust tests. We can rewrite this snippet of code so that the loop stops when x is more than 10:

```
for {set x 1} {$x <= 10} {set x [expr $x + 2]} {
    puts $x
}
```

You will never run out of opportunities to make fresh new mistakes of this nature. My best advice is that you should stay calm and analyze the error messages and your code closely for errors. If it takes more than 15 minutes to find the syntax problem, get up and take a short walk to clear your head.

Meltdowns

It's sometimes easy to forget that the Bash, Perl, and Tcl interpreters are software distributions and, like all software, might contain their own bugs that manifest themselves even if your own code is completely error free. There's very little you can do about such errors, other than submit a bug report via the appropriate channels and try to rewrite your software around the problem. Such bugs might cause your script to return bizarre or unexpected results or, on the Mac OS or Windows platforms, might cause the Perl or Tcl application (or the whole machine) to go down.

Fortunately, such problems are rare, and patches and fixes appear with startling promptness. In fact, I am not aware of any unfixed bugs in the current distributions of Bash, Perl, or Tcl.

Debugging Techniques

In the real world, programmers spend more time debugging programs than writing the code in the first place. If you're banging out little scripts for your own personal quick-and-dirty use, you probably don't need to make your scripts flawless. However, you will still need to fix problems when your scripts misbehave.

Bash Debugging

Shell scripts are generally small. But you can still run into problems while creating them. To help you, Bash provides a few options through its **set** command.

The **set -u** command turns on unbound variable flagging. Here is a demonstration of its use:

```
% echo $bookName

% set -u
% echo $bookName
bash: bookName: unbound variable
% bookName='Shell Programming Tools'
% echo $bokName
bash: bokName: unbound variable
% echo $bookName
Shell Programming Tools
```

The **set +x** command turns on expanded command display. After all of the variables have been expanded, each command line is output to *STDERR* right before execution. Listing 11.4 holds the short script used to demonstrate the **set +x** command.

Listing 11.4 *x.pl—An Incorrect Snippet of Perl Code*

```
#!/usr/bin/perl

for n in 1 2 3
do
  echo "$n is ok."
done
```

The following interactive session shows the **set +x** command in action. The italicized lines are the ones generated because of the **set +x** command.

```
% chmod +x x.sh
% set +x
% ./x.sh
+x.sh
++ [ -f /etc/bashrc ]
++ . /etc/bashrc
+++ PS1=[\u@\h \W]\$
+++ PATH=/usr/local/bin:/bin:/usr/bin:...
++ echo 1 is ok.
1 is ok.
++ echo 2 is ok.
2 is ok.
++ echo 3 is ok.
3 is ok.
```

You can create a log file of the command lines being executed with redirection:

```
% ./x.sh 2>x.log
% cat x.log
++ [ -f /etc/bashrc ]
++ . /etc/bashrc
+++ PS1=[\u@\h \W]\$
+++ PATH=/usr/local/bin:/bin:/usr/bin:...
++ echo 1 is ok.
++ echo 2 is ok.
++ echo 3 is ok.
```

The command lines displayed by the **set +x** command have all variables and all file wildcards expanded. This feature helps track down problems in wildcard expansion—you can make sure that the filename you need to refer to is in the list.

```
% ls *.dat
+ ls f1.dat input.dat xargs.dat
f1.dat input.dat xargs.dat
```

Although the "Generic Debugging" section discusses the importance of using display statements when debugging, this technique is so essential that it bears repeated mention here.

Many Bash commands are dangerous, even a seemingly innocuous one like **chown**. Changing the owner associated with a file doesn't seem like a major problem. Usually, it's not. However, when you accidentally change the owner of a system file, all of a sudden you might not be able to login to your system or start it up after a shutdown.

Because of the danger involved, I highly recommend using the **echo** command to give yourself a chance to catch typing errors when executing potentially dangerous commands—especially when you are using the root user account.

Let me give you a good example of why you might want to use the **echo** command. Perhaps you need to remove all of the files beginning with a period from the current directory. You'd use **rm .***, right? Wrong. And here's why:

```
% echo rm .*
ls . .. .Xdefaults .bash_history
.bash_logout .bash_profile .bashrc
```

See those two periods displayed as the second file in the expanded list of files? Those two periods mean the parent directory. And if you had executed **rm .*** for real, a disaster might have happened.

Perl Debugging

When you're debugging Perl scripts, one of the most valuable tools at your disposal is the *-w* switch. You can also use the strict module.

Turning on Warnings

Perl stratifies its warning messages into several different "levels," as shown in Table 11.1, below.

TIP   ALWAYS USE THE -w OPTION! I can't emphasize this point enough. In fact, I've gotten in the habit of using *#!/usr/bin/perl -w* as the first line of every Perl script that I write—no matter how small or large.

Table 11.1 *The Different Levels of Perl's Error Messages*

Level Code	Description
(W)	A warning message, not printed out unless Perl is invoked with the *-w* switch.
(D)	A deprecation, not printed out unless Perl is invoked with the *-w* switch. (A deprecation marks something that was supported in an old version of Perl that is being phased out in modern and "official" Perl.)
(S)	A severe warning message, which will always be printed.
(F)	A fatal warning, which will always be printed and will cause your script to fail.
(P)	A panic warning, which suggests that something wrong is going on inside Perl. In theory, you'll never see a panic warning.
(X)	A fatal warning, which will always be printed.
(A)	An alien message, generated by another program. For example, an error message generated by Bash or tclsh if you generate an error in a backticked command.

Perl's optional warnings can tell you a lot about what's happening in a malfunctioning script. For example, let's take another look at the do-nothing script from the last section:

```
% perl -e '$x = 1; print $X'

%
```

Remember the problem here? Because Perl is case sensitive, *$x* and *$X* are completely different variables. If you run this script with the *-w* switch, Perl's optional warnings try to tell you that something seems wrong:

```
% perl -w -e '$x = 1; print $X'
Name "main::X" used only once: possible typo at -e line 1.
Name "main::x" used only once: possible typo at -e line 1.
Use of uninitialized value at -e line 1.

bash>
```

Now, Perl doesn't say "Hey, I'm case sensitive, $x isn't the same as $X," but its warning messages do provide some valuable clues about the nature of the problem.

If you find the standard Perl warnings a little too terse, you can use the diagnostics module that comes with most Perl distributions to get a more detailed description of the problem. To do so, you'll need to add the line *use diagnostics;* near the top of your script, as shown in Listing 11.5.

Listing 11.5 *pbug.pl—Using the Perl Diagnostics Module*

```
#!/usr/bin/perl

use diagnostics;

$x = 1;

print $X;
```

Using the diagnostics module enables warnings even if you don't explicitly use the *-w* option when you run Perl. Execute the script in Listing 11.5 and you see a detailed message in place of the standard warning.

```
% perl pbug
Name "main::X" used only once: possible typo at pbug line 5
(#1)

  (W) Typographical errors often show up as unique
  variable names. If you had a good reason for having
  a unique name, then just mention it again somehow to
  suppress the message.  The use vars pragma is provided
  for just this purpose.
```

```
Name "main::x" used only once: possible typo at pbug line 3
(#1)

Use of uninitialized value at pbug line 5 (#2)
```

> (W) An undefined value was used as if it were
> already defined. It was interpreted as a "" or
> a 0, but maybe it was a mistake. To suppress this
> warning assign an initial value to your variables.

If you are truly desperate for feedback from your script, you can use the *verbose* option with the diagnostics module, like this:

```
use diagnostics -verbose;
```

The *verbose* option simply displays the Perl man page, which describes the levels of error messages listed in Table 11.1, before it responds to particular messages. It does not cause Perl to provide more detailed responses or descriptions for individual messages.

NOTE   Some Perl distributions might not include the standard Perl libraries, or might store the libraries in a peculiar location. Check with
your system administrator (or the *readme* file that came with your
copy of Perl) for details.

Being Strict With Your Code

Chapter 6, "Using Perl," barely touches on the topic of modules. Perl modules dramatically increase the scope of what can be done with Perl. They also can be used to change Perl's behavior. This section discusses the *strict* module, which does two things:

- Forces you to use the **my** function to declare all variables. When all variables have a local scope, you avoid problems associated with unintentionally changing the value of a variable in a function.

- Ensures that you can't use accidental symbolic dereferencing. This topic was not covered in Chapter 6, "Using Perl," because it is relatively advanced. If you're not working with references or object-oriented programming techniques, you won't need to worry about this feature of the strict module.

When the strict module is used, your script won't compile if the preceding two rules are violated. For example, if you tried to run the script in Listing 11.6:

Listing 11.6 *strict1.pl—Using Perl's Strict Module*

```
#!/usr/bin/perl -w

use strict;

$foo = {};
$bar = 5;

print "$foo\n";
print "$bar\n";
```

You would receive these error messages:

```
Global symbol "foo" requires
  explicit package name at test.pl line 5.
Global symbol "bar" requires
  explicit package name at test.pl line 6.
Execution of strict.pl aborted due to compilation errors.
```

In order to eliminate the messages, you need to declare *$foo* and *$bar* as local variables, as shown in Listing 11.7.

Listing 11.7 *strict2.pl—Using Perl's Strict Module and the my()*
Function

```
#!/usr/bin/perl -w

use strict;

my($foo) = { };
my($bar) = 5;

print "$foo\n";
print "$bar\n";
```

Generic Debugging

The most ancient and time-honored way to handle debugging is to use a language's display function (i.e., **echo**, **print**, and **puts** for Bash, Perl, and Tcl, respectively) to print to the screen a description of the task that the script is currently performing. By watching these messages as the program runs, you can make sure the program is doing what you think it is doing.

Suppose, for example, you're working on a little Tcl script that reads through a text file line by line and puts each line into a variable. Perhaps you have plans to use the variable later in your script, but the details are unimportant.

Let us say, for the sake of working through an example, that you want to use the file shown in Listing 11.8 as your input file.

Listing 11.8 *myinput.txt—A Datafile for Testing Purposes*

```
inky
dinky
doo
```

Listing 11.9 holds a Tcl script that reads the input files and appends each input line to a variable called *biglist*. When the whole input file has been read, *biglist* should hold the entire input file—without any of its linefeeds.

Listing 11.9 *tbug.tcl—A Tcl Script with a Logic Error*

```
#!/usr/bin/tclsh

set inputfile "myinputfile.txt"
set infile [open $inputfile]

while {![eof $infile]} {
    gets $infile line
    set biglist $line
}
close $infile

puts $biglist
```

Running this script looks like this:

```
% tclsh tbug.tcl
doo
```

The last line of the script, *puts $biglist*, was intended to print out the complete contents of the text file, but instead it only returns the last line of the text file.

Could it be that the script is somehow skipping over some of the lines in the file, i.e., we have misused the **gets** function? Are we reading in the information, but losing it somewhere along the way? We don't really know. In order to get an idea of what's going on inside that **while** command, we'll add a little **puts** function call to monitor the situation. Add the bold line of the following code to your version of *tbug.tcl*.

```
while {![eof $infile]} {
    gets $infile line
    puts "I just read '$line'"
    set biglist $line
}
```

Now, we re-run the script:

```
% tclsh tbug.tcl
I just read 'inky'
I just read 'dinky'
I just read 'doo'
doo
```

From this output, we can conclude that the script appears to read the text file correctly. Let's add another **puts** line to see what's happening to the *biglist* variable inside the body of the **while** command. Add the bold line of the following code to your version of *tbug.tcl*.

```
while {![eof $infile]} {
    gets $infile line
    puts "I just read '$line'"
    set biglist $line
    puts "biglist = '$biglist'"
}
```

When we re-run the script, here's what we see:

```
% tclsh tbug.tcl
I just read 'inky'
biglist = 'inky'        <- the output is displayed in
I just read 'dinky'     <- bold face for your convenience.
biglist = 'dinky'       <- Your script's output will not
I just read 'doo'       <- be in bold.
biglist = 'doo'
doo
```

Ah-ha. The *while* loop isn't adding the newline to the end of *biglist*—it's clobbering the old value of *biglist*, and replacing it with the value of the latest line. We shouldn't be using *set* at the end of the loop, we should be using *lappend*! Try adding the bold line of

the following code (and remove the *set* line) to your version of
tbug.tcl—this is the last time, I swear!

```
while {![eof $infile]} {
    gets $infile line
    puts "I just read '$line'"
    lappend biglist $line
    puts "biglist = '$biglist'"
}
```

Now run it:

```
% tclsh tbug.tcl
I just read 'inky'
biglist = 'inky'
I just read 'dinky'
biglist = 'inky dinky'
I just read 'doo'
biglist = 'inky dinky doo'
inky dinky doo              <- Finally, the correct output!
```

Now that you've fixed the program, you can go in and remove
the diagnostic messages—the extra *puts* statements. If you're not
completely sure that you're finished with the debugging process,
"comment them out" by adding a hash at the beginning of each
line, like so:

```
#   puts "I just read '$line'"
```

Even though the line is valid, the interpreter treats it as a comment and ignores it.

Debugging Tools

The *-w* switch and *echo/print/puts* technique can only take you so
far through the debugging process. At some point, if you've got a
complex script with a lot of problems (or at least a few subtle
ones), you might want to use a dedicated debugging tool.

If you're using Perl, you already have an excellent tool—the
command-line debugger that's built into Perl. If you're a Perl user
on the Windows platform, you might also wish to investigate the
handy visual debugger that has been released as a commercial software package by ActiveState software. (You can find more information on their web site at *http://www.ActiveState.com.*)

If you're building scripts in Tcl and you're on the Unix platform, you have several options. Although there is no debugger
built into the core Tcl distribution, there are several freely available extensions to Tcl that provide debugging services. One of the
most common Tcl-based applications, Expect, includes a Tcl interpreter and is installed on many Unix systems. There are also many
visual debuggers for Tcl based on Tcl/Tk, including one called
Tuba. (Information about Tuba can be found on its web site at
http://www.doitnow.com/~iliad/Tcl/tuba/.)

Perl

Perl provides an interactive environment that lets you execute
your script's statements one at a time. This environment is called a
debugger. If necessary, you can display the lines of your script, view
or alter variables, and even execute entirely new statements.

You start the debugger by using the *-d* command-line option.
The following line

```
perl -w -d test.pl
```

starts the debugger and loads the script called *test.pl*. If you want
to invoke the debugger with no script, you need to perform a small
bit of magic, like this:

```
perl -d -e "1;"
```

I say this is a bit of magic because this book doesn't discuss all of
the different command-line options available for Perl. There are
simply too many of them. The *-e* option tells Perl to execute a single Perl statement. In this case the statement is *1;*, which basically
means do nothing. It does, however, stop the interpreter from looking for the name of a script file on the command line.

When the debugger starts, your screen should look something
like this:

```
Loading DB routines from perl5db.pl version 1
Emacs support available.

Enter h or 'h h' for help.

main::(-e:1):   1;
  DB<1>
```

This message tells you that the debugger (*DB*) routines have been loaded. The *DB<1>* is a prompt that indicates that the debugger is waiting for input. The line number inside the angle brackets is the *current execution line*. The current execution line is that linethe debugger waits to execute.

One of the features of the debugger is the capability to insert *breakpoints* into your script. A breakpoint is an instruction that tells the debugger to stop, to display a prompt, and to wait for input. When the debugger first starts, there are no breakpoints defined for your program.

You can use any of the commands listed in Table 11.2 while using the debugger. While these commands are not demonstrated because of space considerations, you can't hurt anything by experimenting with any or all of the commands on your own.

Table 11.2 *The Debugger Commands*

Command	Description
Commands That Control Actions:	
a ACTION	This command tells the debugger to perform **ACTION** just before the current execution line is executed. Optionally, you can specify a line number. For example, *a 10 print("$numFiles");* executes the *print* statement before line 10 is executed. If line 10 is inside a loop, the action is performed each time through the loop.
A	Deletes all actions.
L	Lists all breakpoints and actions.
< ACTION	Forces the debugger to execute **ACTION** each time the debugger prompt is displayed. This command is great if you need to print the value of certain values each time you are prompted by the debugger.
> ACTION	Forces the debugger to execute **ACTION** after every debugger command you issue.

Table 11.2 *The Debugger Commands (Cont'd)*

Command	Description
Commands That Involve Breakpoints:	
b	Sets a breakpoint at the current execution line. You can specify a line where the breakpoint should be set. For example, *b 35* sets a breakpoint at line 35. You can also create a conditional breakpoint. For example, *b 35 $numLines == 0* causes the debugger to stop at line 35 only if *$numLines* is equal to zero. Watch conditions can also be attached to functions; just use the function name instead of a line number.
d	Deletes the breakpoint from the current execution line. If you specify a line number, the breakpoint is deleted from that line.
D	Deletes all breakpoints.
L	Lists all breakpoints and actions.
Commands That Display Information:	
l	Lets you print out parts of your script. There are several flavors of this command that you can use: • Using a plain **l** displays about 10 lines of your script. • Using **l 5+4** displays 4 lines of your script, starting with line 5. • Using **l 4-7** displays lines 4 through 7 of your script. • Using **l 34** displays line 34 of your script. • Using **l foo** displays roughly the first 10 lines of the **foo** function.
L	Lists all breakpoints and actions.
p EXPR	Prints the result of evaluating **EXPR** to the display. It is a shorthand way of saying *print DB::OUT (EXPR)*.
S	Lists all function names that are defined. The list will include any function defined in modules as well as those in your script.

Table 11.2 *The Debugger Commands (Cont'd)*

Command	Description
T	Prints a *stack trace*. A stack trace displays a list of function calls and the line number where the calls were made.
V	Lists all variables that are currently defined from all packages and modules that are loaded. A better form of this command is **V PACKAGE** or **V PACKAGE VARLIST,** where **PACKAGE** is the name of a loaded package or module and **VARLIST** is a currently defined variable in **PACKAGE**. When specifying variable names, don't use the $, @, or % type specifiers.
w *LINE*	Displays about 10 lines centered around *LINE*. For example, if you use *w 10*, lines 7 to 16 might display.
X	Lists all variables in the current package. If you have stepped into a function that is in package *foo*, the variables in package *foo* are displayed, not those in *main*. You can also specify exactly which variables to display if needed. When specifying variable names, don't use the $, @, or % type specifiers.
-	Displays about 10 lines of your script that are before the current line. For example, if the current display line is 30, this command might display lines 19 to 29.
Commands That Control Execution:	
s	Steps through the lines in your script one at a time and into any user-defined function that is called. While single stepping is slow, you see exactly how your code is being executed.
n	Executes the next statement in your script. Although all function calls are executed, it does not follow the execution path inside a function. This command enables you to move more quickly through the execution of your script than simply using the **s** command. An example of this is shown in the "Examples: Using the **n** Command" section later in this chapter.
r	Executes the rest of the statements in the current function. The debugger pauses for input on the line following the line that made the function call.

Table 11.2 *The Debugger Commands (Cont'd)*

Command	Description
c *LINE*	Executes the rest of the statements in your script, unless a breakpoint is found before the script ends. You can optionally use this command to create a temporary break by specifying a line number after the **c**. I think of this command as **c**ontinue until *LINE*.
NO COMMAND	Pressing the Enter key without specifying a command will make the debugger repeat the last **n** or **s** command that was used. This feature makes it a little easier to single step through your script.
Commands That Work With the Debugger Command History:	
!	Redoes the previous command. You can also specify the number of the previous command to execute. Use the **H** command to get a list of the previous commands. If you specify a negative number, like *! -2*, the debugger counts backwards from the last executed command.
H	Lists all the debugger commands you have issued. Only commands that cause action are saved in the command history. This means that the **l** and **T** commands are not saved. You can limit the history viewed by specifying a negative number. For example, **H -5** displays the last five commands you have issued.
Miscellaneous Commands:	
f *FILENAME*	Causes the debugger to switch to *FILENAME*. The file specified must have already been loaded via the *use* or *require* statements. Please note that some of the documentation that accompanies the Perl interpreter might indicate that **f** is the **finish** command. It used to be; however, the *finish* functionality is now accomplished by the **r** command.
q	Quits the debugger. You can also use the *Ctrl+D* key sequence under Unix and the *Ctrl+Z* key sequence under DOS and Windows.

Table 11.2 *The Debugger Commands (Cont'd)*

Command	Description
t	Toggles trace mode on and off. Trace mode, when on, displays each script line as it is being executed. I don't recommend this option except for very short programs, because the lines are displayed so quickly that you won't be able to read them.
/pattern/	Searches for *pattern* in the currently loaded file. If *pattern* is found, the current display line is changed to the line where *pattern* was found.
?pattern?	Searches backward for *pattern* in the currently loaded file. If *pattern* is found, the current display line is changed to the line where *pattern* was found.
=	Displays any aliases that are currently defined. You can also use it to create aliases. See the section "Examples: Creating Command Aliases" later in this chapter for more information about aliases and the = command.
COMMAND	Any text that is not recognized as an alias or a debugger command is executed as a Perl statement. See the section "Examples: Using the Debugger as an Interactive Interpreter" later in this chapter for more information about executing Perl statements inside the debugger.

As you can see, the debugger has quite a few commands to choose from, and it is very powerful. Few programmers need all of the functionality that the debugger has. If you learn to display script lines, use breakpoints, and display variables, you'll be well on your way to solving any problem that might arise.

Tcl/Expect

Let's say you're using Tcl to write a little utility that searches through a file for lines of a certain length. For example, if you call this utility *fl* (for line length), and you're interested in lines containing exactly 10 characters in the file named *fl.dat*, you'd use:

```
% fl 10 fl.dat
```

and the *fl* utility would return lines such as:

```
1234567890
1111111111
```

but not

```
123456789012345
```

or

```
2222222222222211
```

The script in Listing 11.10 is *almost* right.

Listing 11.10 *fl.tcl—Another Tcl Script with a Logic Error*

```
#! /usr/bin/tclsh

if {$argc != 2} exit

set magiclength [lindex $argv 0]
set myfilename [lindex $argv 1]

set infile [open "$myfilename"]
while {![eof $infile]} {
  gets $infile line
  if {[string length line] == $magiclength}
    {puts $line}
}
close $infile
```

However, if you run it, you'll find that it usually returns nothing. Sometimes, however, it might return *all* of the lines in the file, regardless of length. Can you spot the mistake? If you're a seasoned Tcl programmer, the error might be easy to find. If you can't see the problem right away, though, you might want to run the script through a debugger to see what's happening.

Listing 11.11 shows a version of *fl.dat* you can use for your testing.

Listing 11.11 *fl.dat—A Data File for the fl.tcl Script*

```
1234567890
11111111111111
1234567890
222222222222222
```

Regrettably, Tcl does not have its own debugger. (The Scriptics company is planning a final release of its TclPro development environment that should include a visual debugger.) However, the freely available (and widely distributed) *Expect* application, which uses Tcl as its scripting language, contains a debugger that you can use with your Tcl scripts.

TIP

> To make sure you have Expect on your system, type **which expect** at the shell prompt. If Expect is not installed, point your preferred web browser at *http://expect.nist.gov* for more information.

To debug *fl.tcl*, invoke Expect using the *-D* switch with a value of *1*:

```
% expect -D 1 fl.tcl 10 fl.dat
1: if {$argc != 2} exit
dbg1.0>
```

As you can see, the Expect debugger displays the *dbg1.0>* prompt. For the record, the first 1 in "1.0" shows the level of the stack, and the second 1 is simply the number of the current command in the history of the current Expect session. You'll also notice that the first command in the script (the **if** command) appears above the prompt. This is the command that Expect executes next when you ask Expect to execute a command. Typing **s** at Expect's debugger prompt executes this command:

NOTE

> A stack holds the temporary information that gets passed from caller to callee as functions are executed within programs. Each time one function calls another, and then that function calls another, the stack gets deeper. As functions end and control is returned to the caller, the stack gets shallower.

```
dbg1.0> s
1: lindex $argv 0
dbg1.1>
```

The debugger has executed the *if* statement and, finding the expression false, moved along to the next line. Continue stepping until the prompt says *dbg1.3>*.

At any point along the way, we can execute any command that we like, exactly as if we were typing in commands at the tclsh prompt. Let's make sure that *magiclength* has been read in correctly from the command line:

```
1: lindex $argv 1
dbg1.3> set magiclength
10
dbg1.4>
```

Now, let's skip another two steps to make sure that the filename has been read in correctly:

```
dbg1.4> s
1: lindex $argv 1
dbg1.5> s
1: open "$myfilename"
dbg1.6> set myfilename
f1.tcl
```

Everything seems to be in order so far. Now it's time to loop through the datafile and read in the lines of text:

```
dbg1.10> s
2: eof $infile
dbg2.11> s
2: gets $infile line
dbg2.12> s
2: if {[string length line] == ...
dbg2.13> s
3: string length line
dbg3.14> s
2: eof $infile
dbg2.15>
```

At this point, we should expect the script to print out the first line of the text file—assuming, of course, that the first line is 10 characters long, and that 10 is the argument for *fl* that we used when we invoked the debugger.

Because we expect some results here, and we don't see anything, we should take a closer look at this line. A-ha! I forgot to use variable substitution on the variable *line* in the embedded **string length** function: The complete if statement should read:

```
if {[string length $line] == $magiclength} {
   puts $line
}
```

For want of a single dollar sign, the script failed—the interpreter is evaluating the length of the literal string "line" rather than the value of the variable called "line." (Substitution is the essence of Tcl!) In order to test our theory, let's start the debugger again and change the value of *magiclength* to four, to see if the interpreter yields a match:

Tcl's exit function stops the debugger.

```
% expect -D 1 fl.tcl 10 fl.dat
1: if {$argc != 2} exit
dbg1.0> s
1: lindex $argv 0
dbg1.1> s
1: lindex $argv 0
dbg1.2> s
1: lindex $argv 1
dbg1.3> set magiclength
10
dbg1.4> set magiclength 4
4
dbg1.5> s
1: lindex $argv 1
dbg1.6> s
1: open "$myfilename"
dbg1.7> s
1: open "$myfilename"
dbg1.8> s
1: while { ! [ eof $infile ] } {
     gets $infile line
     if { [ string length ...
dbg1.9> s
1: eof $infile
dbg1.10> s
2: gets $infile line
dbg2.11> s
2: if {[string length line] == ...
     puts $line
  }
dbg2.12> s
2: string length line
dbg2.13> s
3: puts $line
dbg3.14> s
1234567890          <- The input line is displayed!
1: eof $infile
dbg1.15>
```

Well, that did it. We can exit the debugger and make the appropriate changes to our source code.

Table 11.3 summarizes Expect's debugging commands.

Table 11.3 *Expect's Debugging Commands*

Level Code	Description
s	step into procedure
n	step over procedure
r	return from procedure
b	breakpoint
c	continue
w	show stack
u	move scope up
d	move scope down
h	help
<\r>	repeat last debugger command

Summary

This chapter presents an overview of the many types of errors you can encounter as you create scripts. No programmer that I've ever heard of writes perfect scripts more than a few lines long. Just remember, as you make your own mistakes, that you're in good company.

Debugging generally has two phases. The first phase involves fixing any syntax or typographical errors you introduced into your program while entering the code. For example, in Perl you might not have added a semi-colon to the end of a line, or you might have used **elseif** instead of **elsif**. Every programming language has its own unique blend of easy-to-make typing mistakes.

Sometimes, typographical errors aren't revealed until your script has started running. These errors are called runtime errors. Runtime errors include the classic division by zero error and using incorrect variable names, like using a variable called *shipping-Books* instead of *Shipping_Books*.

After the relative ease of fixing the syntax errors comes phase two—finding and fixing logic errors. In Bash, you can use the **set -u** and **set +x** command to turn on unbound variable flagging and expanded command display. I also recommend the use of the **echo** command to verify the command-line variable and filename expansion before running any potentially dangerous command.

Perl has three main techniques for catching bugs. The *-w* command-line option, the strict module, and the **print** statement. The *-w* option tells Perl to look for some dangerous situations, like variables that are only used once. The strict module does a few things, the most important being that it requires you to declare all variables before they are used. And the last technique, the **print** statement, is ubiquitous across all computer languages. Simply place **print** statements at strategic locations throughout your code to display status messages and the value of important variables.

Tcl doesn't have Perl's ability to turn on extra levels of warning messages, but using the **puts** function to display variables and monitor the progress of your program is very helpful.

The Perl interactive debugger can be very useful, although I have a feeling that most Perl programmers don't use it enough. Its many commands and its ability to interactively display variables, call functions, and change the values of variables make it invaluable when creating larger and more complex scripts.

The Tcl/Expect combination produces an interactive debugger similar to Perl's. You can use it to single step through your script, display the value of variables, and change the variable's value on-the-fly.

Chapter 12, "Customizing the Tools," gives you a chance to use all of these debugging techniques when you try out the sample scripts provided. The scripts are shown in more than one language so you can compare and contrast how the languages are similar and how they are different.

Chapter 12, "Customizing the Tools," investigates how Bash, Perl, and Tcl can be used to perform everyday tasks. You see new tools created through custom scripts. Each custom script is developed using two or more languages so you can form your own opinion about which language is best for each task.

Customizing the Tools

This chapter combines the concepts from Section 1 and the tools from Chapter 9 into usable scripts. The scripts are developed using two or more of the three languages mentioned in Section 1: Bash, Perl, and Tcl. By seeing all three languages in action, you'll get a feel for how much they have in common—and where their differences are. You'll also be able to form your own opinion about which scripting tasks are best handled by each language.

Most of the scripts in this chapter are heavily commented. There-fore, you won't have to move between the text and the listings to understand what the scripts are doing. Important elements and techniques of the scripts are specifically mentioned in the text fol-lowing each listing.

A Better find Command

Some Unix administrators frown on users who search entire direc-tory hierarchies when looking for files. Indiscriminately searching the entire disk leads to disk contention as the system tries to balance the needs of the search program with the needs of the other users.

Listing 12.1 contains the *nfind.sh* script, which checks its first argument to see if it is a slash character—indicating that the file search should start at the root directory. If the slash is found, then the user is asked for confirmation.

NOTE The **find** command is not actually executed in the *nfind.sh* script to make it easier to test and debug. Instead, the **echo** command is used to display **find** commands that would normally be executed.

Listing 12.1 *nfind.sh—Using **test** and **read** to Limit Searching Entire Disk Hierarchies*

```
#!/bin/bash

# First, let's cover the case of no parameters.
if [ $# = 0 ]
then
  echo find
  exit
fi

# Now we check the first parameter for a slash
# which indicates the search begins at the ROOT
# directory.
if [ "$1" = "/" ]
then
  # Ask the user to confirm his command.
  echo "Are You Sure You Want to Start Searching at ROOT?"
  echo "  Enter 'Y' to continue, anything else cancels."
  read
```

```
else
  # If not searching from the root, run the command.
  echo find $@
  exit
fi

# Test for capital Y and lower-case y. If the
# user confirmed the command, execute it.
if [ "$REPLY" = "Y" -o "$REPLY" = "y" ]
then
  echo find $@
  exit
fi

# If this point has been reached, then the user
# wants to cancel. Print a message to provide
# feedback.
echo "Canceling Search."
echo "Good thing I asked, no?"
```

Here is an example of this script in action:

```
% chmod +x nfind.sh
% ./nfind.sh              <- no parameters.
find
% ./nfind.sh . test.dat   <- with parameters
find . test.dat
% ./nfind.sh / test.dat   <- from the ROOT.
Are You Sure You Want to Start Searching at ROOT?
  Enter 'Y' to continue, anything else cancels.
Y
find / test.dat
% ./nfind.sh / test.dat
Are You Sure You Want to Start Searching at ROOT?
  Enter 'Y' to continue, anything else cancels.
n
Canceling Search.
Good thing I asked, no?
```

This example shows the following techniques:

- How to determine if no parameters are given on the command line.

- How to query the user for a confirmation.

- How to use the **echo** command to aid script testing.

One of the keys to quickly developing this type of script is to speed up the edit-test-change development cycle. For this example, I used the **echo** command to display the shell command that would normally be executed. This avoids the sometimes lengthy wait for the commands to complete before being able to move to the change phase of the development cycle.

Now let's take a look at the same **nfind** command written in Perl, as shown in Listing 12.2.

NOTE   The **find** command is not actually executed in the *nfind.pl* script to make it easier to test. Instead, Perl's **print** function is used to display the result of the shell **echo** command, which displays the **find** command that would normally be executed.

FRI   You can read about *STDIN* (standard input) in Chapter 5, "Controlling the Shell."

FRI   You can read about Perl's *m//* operator in Chapter 8, "Pattern Matching."

Listing 12.2 *nfind.pl—Using Perl to Implement the **nfind** Command*

```perl
#!/usr/bin/perl -w

# Evaluating an array in a scalar context returns the
# number of elements in the array.

# Perl stores script parameters in an array called ARGV.
if (scalar(@ARGV) == 0) {
  print `echo find`;
  exit;
}

# Unlike the shell, the first element of the parameter list is
# not the name of the script. Instead the first element is the
# first parameter. And the first element of a Perl array has
# an index of zero.
if ($ARGV[0] eq '/') {
  print "Are You Sure You Want to Start Searching at ROOT?\n";
```

```
  print "  Enter 'Y' to continue, anything else
cancels.\n";

  # The <STDIN> notation reads a single line from STDIN.
  $REPLY = <STDIN>;
}
else {
  print `echo find @ARGV`;
  exit;
}

# The i option of Perl's matching operator means that case
# is ignored. So m/y/i matches both Y and y.
if ($REPLY =~ m/y/i) {
  print `echo find @ARGV`;
  exit;
}

# Notice that Perl needs newlines explicitly added to the
# print statements.
print "Canceling Search.\n";
print "Good thing I asked, no?\n";
```

Here is an example of this script in action:

```
% chmod +x nfind.pl
% ./nfind.pl              <- no parameters.
find
% ./nfind.pl . test.dat  <- with parameters
find . test.dat
% ./nfind.pl / test.dat  <- from the ROOT.
Are You Sure You Want to Start Searching at ROOT?
  Enter 'Y' to continue, anything else cancels.
Y
find / test.dat
% ./nfind.pl / test.dat
Are You Sure You Want to Start Searching at ROOT?
  Enter 'Y' to continue, anything else cancels.
n
Canceling Search.
Good thing I asked, no?
```

By comparing Listing 12.1 and 12.2, you can see that Bash scripts and Perl scripts contain a lot of the same logic structures.

Listing 12.3 shows how to use Tcl to create the **nfind** command.

NOTE   The **find** command is not actually executed in the *nfind.tcl* script to
               make it easier to test. Instead, Tcl's **puts** function is used to display
               the result of the shell **echo** command, which displays the **find** com-
               mand that would normally be executed.

Listing 12.3 *nfind.tcl—Using Tcl to Implement the **nfind**
Command*

```tcl
#!/usr/bin/tcl

# Tcl uses the $argc variable to determine the number
# of parameters to the script.
if {$argc == 0} {
  puts [echo find];
  exit;
}

# You can't directly access array elements in Tcl. You must
# use the lindex command.
if {[lindex $argv 0] == "/"} {
  puts "Are You Sure You Want to Start Searching at ROOT?";
  puts "  Enter 'Y' to continue, anything else cancels.";
  gets stdin REPLY
} else {
  puts [echo find $argv];
  exit;
}

# Tcl uses a string match command when doing regular
# expression testing.
if [string match {[Yy]} $REPLY] {
  puts [echo find $argv];
  exit;
}

# Notice that Tcl does not need newlines added to
# puts statements.
puts "Canceling Search.";
puts "Good thing I asked, no?";
```

Here is an example of this script in action:

```
% chmod +x nfind.tcl
% ./nfind.tcl              <- no parameters.
find
```

I won't reproduce the other test conditions for this script. The output is identical to that of Listings 12.1 and 12.2.

Now that you've had a chance to see all three languages (Bash, Perl, and Tcl) performing the same task, have you formed any opinions? The rest of the chapter shows more scripts using the three languages. Some show Bash and Perl, some show Bash and Tcl. This chapter gives you the chance to become tri-lingual.

A Better write Command

The **write** command lets you send a message to another user's terminal. In order to run the **write** command, you need to know the user's username and, perhaps, their terminal name. After specifying the username, you simply type in your message and then, on a separate line, enter the *end-of-file* character, *Ctrl-D*. When the *end-of-file* character is received by the **write** command, the message is sent—to appear seconds later on the display of the recipient.

In order to demonstrate some shell scripting techniques, let's make the **write** command a bit more user-friendly. One improvement might be to provide a list of usernames for the sender to select from. A refinement on this theme would be to provide a list of terminal names if the recipient is logged in to more than one terminal.

When beginning to create a script, I like to start at the most basic level and work my way from simple to more complex. Our first improvement to the **write** command is to provide a list of usernames. By perusing the **man** pages that come with Unix, I found the **who** command:

```
% whoami
medined
% who
medined    tty1      Jun  2 20:08
root       tty2      May 31 00:26
medined    tty3      Jun  2 20:08
kathy.medinets tty4     Jun 2 22:38
medined    tty5      Jun  2 22:44
```

The **whoami** command displays the username of the user running the login shell. In this case, I was using my *medined* user account. The **who** command does indeed display a list of current users—just what we need. However, the list is not easy to read and contains the username of the person running the **who** command. Additionally, some usernames are repeated, the list is not sorted, and the columns are unaligned.

We can change all of these problems using various shell commands.

First, we'll remove the name of the person running the **who** command from the list of users. This makes sense, because people don't usually need to send messages to themselves:

```
% who | grep --revert-match `whoami`
root      tty2      May 31 00:26
kathy.medinets tty4      Jun 2 22:38
```

By sending the output of the **who** command through the **grep** command and rejecting any lines that contain the owner of the login shell, we get a shorter list of users.

The grep command is discussed in Chapter 9, "Examining the Tools." All of the other commands used to create the nwrite script are also discussed in Chapter 9.

Is this really the list we want to present to the user of the **write** command? Probably not. For example, one person might have "lent" his userid to another, and perhaps the "real" person is on a computer in the lecture hall building and the borrower is working on a computer in a dorm room. In this scenario, a message sender might indeed want to send a message to himself!

So what we really need to do is remove only the line containing the terminal name of the sender. After a little more searching of the Unix manual, I found the **tty** command:

```
% tty
/dev/tty1
```

This command returns the terminal name of the shell—in this case, */dev/tty1*. However, there is a complication. Only the last part of the terminal name is displayed by the **who** command, so we can't simply use the output of the **tty** command in place of the **whoami** command in the **grep --revert-match** command.

Getting rid of the */dev/* in the output from **tty** requires using the variable name metacharacters, as mentioned in Chapter 8, "Regular Expressions." For example:

```
% termid=`tty`
% termid=${termid#/dev/}
% echo $termid
tty1
```

```
% who | grep --revert-match $termid
root       tty2      May 31 00:26
medined  tty3      Jun  2 20:08
kathy.medinets tty4      Jun 2 22:38
medined  tty5      Jun  2 22:44
```

Now the output of the **who** command is filtered, so that the line containing **tty1** is not displayed.

This display is still disorganized. Let's only display the first column, so that the user is not distracted or confused by the other extraneous information. The **cut** command is a good choice for manipulating columns of text:

```
% who | \
> grep --revert-match $termid | \
> cut -d" " -f1
root
medined
kathy.medinets
medined
```

This list is starting to look good. Let's try to eliminate the duplicate names. Perhaps the **uniq** command could work:

```
% who | \
> grep --revert-match $termid | \
> cut -d" " -f1 | \
> uniq
root
medined
kathy.medinets
medined
```

Hmm... Using the **uniq** command didn't work. Back to the man pages for more information. Ah ha, the **uniq** command requires a sorted list:

```
% who | \
> grep --revert-match $termid | \
> cut -d" " -f1 | \
> sort | \
> uniq
kathy.medinets
medined
root
```

Now the list looks even better. Just one more adjustment to make. The list should display horizontally instead of vertically, so that less screen space is used and more names can be displayed. Even though the **xargs** command is not designed for this purpose, it can be used:

```
% who | \
> grep --revert-match $termid | \
> cut -d" " -f1 | \
> sort | \
> uniq | \
> xargs
kathy.medinets medined root
```

By now, it should be abundantly clear that one of Bash's strengths is the ability to string together lists of commands in a lot of different ways.

Listing 12.4 contains the final *nwrite.sh* script. In addition to displaying a horizontal list of usernames, it requests the terminal name if the recipient name is logged in more than once.

Listing 12.4 *nwrite.sh—Creating a User-Friendly **write** Command with Bash*

```
#/bin/bash

echo "nwrite: Please enter a user's name from this list:"

# The tty command returns the device name of the terminal
# associated with the shell.
termid=`tty`

# The pound sign metacharacter removes matching characters
# from the front of the variable's value. /dev/ttyx turns
# into ttyx
termid=${termid#/dev/}

# The who command displays a list of the current users. The
# other commands:
#    remove lines containing the current terminal name.
#    eliminate all but the first column
#    sort the lines
#    remove duplicate entries
#    display the list horizontally instead of vertically.
who | \
  grep --revert-match $termid | \
```

```
  cut -d" " -f1 | \
  sort | \
  uniq | \
  xargs

# The -n option of the echo command tells echo not to print
# an ending newline - so the prompt and the input remain on
# the same line.
echo -n "> "

# The read command gets a line of input from STDIN. In this
# instance, the input line is placed into the NWRITE_USERNAME
# variable.
read NWRITE_USERNAME

# The -count option of the grep command displays the number
# of matched lines.
numTerminals=`who | \
  grep --revert-match $termid | \
  grep --count $NWRITE_USERNAME`

if [ $numTerminals -gt 1 ]
then
    echo "nwrite: Please select the terminal for $NWRITE_USERNAME:"

    # In order to display the list of terminals for a particular
    # username, we need to display the second column of the who
    # command. But the cut command has a problem determining
    # columns when columns are separated by more than one space
    # character. Therefore, the tr command is used to eliminate
    # repeated spaces.
    who | \
      grep --revert-match $termid | \
      grep $NWRITE_USERNAME | \
      tr --squeeze-repeats ' ' | \
      cut -d" " -f2 | \
      xargs
    echo -n "> "
    read NWRITE_TTY
else
    # If the selected user is only logged in once, extract the
    # terminal name from the who command using grep, tr, and cut.
    NWRITE_TTY=`who | \
      grep --revert-match $termid | \
      grep $NWRITE_USERNAME | \
      tr --squeeze-repeats ' ' | \
      cut -d" " -f2`
fi
```

```
echo "Please type your message now. Remember to end your"
echo "message by typing Ctrl-D on a blank line."

# After all the preparation work is done, the original
# write command can now be invoked.
write $NWRITE_USERNAME $NWRITE_TTY

# The -e option of the echo command lets it interpret
# escape sequences. For example, the \n sequence displays
# a newline.
echo -e "\nYour message has been sent!\n"
```

Here is an example of this script in action:

```
% chmod +x nwrite.sh
% ./nwrite.sh
nwrite: Please enter a user's name from this list:
kathy.medinets medined root
> kathy.medinets
Please type your message now. Remember to end your message
by typing Ctrl-D on a blank line.
This is a test message.
Ctrl-D

Your message has been sent!

% ./nwrite.sh
nwrite: Please enter a user's name from this list:
kathy.medinets medined root
> medined
nwrite: Please select a TTY for that user:
tty1 tty5
> tty5
Please type your message now. Remember to end your message
by typing Ctrl-D on a blank line.
This is a test message.
Ctrl-D

Your message has been sent!
```

This short script introduced you to many shell commands. The
cut, echo, grep, read, sort, tr, tty, uniq, who, write, and **xargs**
commands were used by the *nwrite.sh* script—in total, 11 different
commands. These wonderfully varied commands are both the
strength and weakness of Bash. They are a strength because, when
they have become second nature, you can perform amazing feats of
programming. On the other hand, the large number of commands

is daunting to new programmers. Many of Bash's commands are only lightly documented, and some aren't documented at all.

To some programmers, the Perl programming language is a better option. Let's recreate the **nwrite** command using Perl and see what changes occur in the script.

From the user's point of view, the first thing the script does is display a list of usernames from which a selection needs to be made. What the user doesn't know is that their own terminal has been removed from the list—in effect, removing their own name if they are only logged into one terminal.

Before we can remove the user's terminal from the list, we first need to know what it is. The *nwrite.sh* script used the following two lines to determine this information:

```
termid=`tty`
termid=${termid#/dev/}
```

Let's look at how this task can be handled in Perl:

```
($termid) = `tty` =~ m!/dev/(.*)!i;
```

The *m!!* portion of this statement looks for the text after */dev/* in the output of the **tty** command. Notice that, in this case, the matching operator is using alternative delimiters. Normally, slashes are used to delimit patterns. However, because slashes are part of the pattern, an alternative is needed.

The *$termid* variable is inside parentheses because the =~ operator returns an array of elements that matches the specified pattern. Parentheses are used, on the left side of an assignment operator, to assign elements of an array to scalar variables. In this situation, we're only interested in the first element of the array, so only one variable is inside the parentheses.

Now we can use the *$termid* variable to remove the user's terminal from the output of the **who** command. We then create a list of the usernames that are left. In order to create the list, we'll need to loop through the output of the **who** command, extract the user and **tty** names, then store those elements into a hash or associative array:

```
# loop through each line of output from the who command.
foreach $line (`who`) {

  # If the output line mentions the current users tty,
  # ignore it.
  next if $line =~ m/$termid/i;

  # Extract the user and tty information.
  ($username) = $line =~ m/(.+?)\s;
  ($tty)      = $line =~ m/.+?\s(.+?)\s/;

  # Use the username as the key half of a key/value
  # entry in a hash variable called list_usernames. Each
  # time the same username is encountered, the value half
  # of the entry is incremented. This results in the value
  # half of the entry always knowing how many times each
  # username is encountered in the input.
  $hash_usernames{$username}++;

  # The hash entries created here link the tty and the
  # username.
  $hash_ttys{$username} = $tty;
}
```

All of the information has been assembled to create the first prompt of the *nwrite* script, except for the fact that the list of user-names is stuck in a hash variable that is not too easy to display. Let's create a sorted list of usernames from the *hash_usernames* variable, display the first prompt, and request some input from the user:

```
# The keys function returns a list of the key half of
# the key-value hash entries. And the sort function
# returns a sorted version of the array passed to it.
@list_sorted_usernames = sort(keys(%hash_usernames));

print "nwrite: Please enter a user's name from this
list:\n"
print "@list_sorted_usernames\n"
print "> ";

# The <STDIN> notation reads a single line of input
# from the standard input - the keyboard in this case.
$NWRITE_USERNAME = <STDIN>;

# The chomp function removes the trailing newline from
# the line of input because the $/ variable is set to
# the newline character by default.
chomp($NWRITE_USERNAME);
```

Now that we know the user to whom the message should be sent (the sendee), it's time to find out the name of the target **tty**. If the user is only logged in once, then his entry in the *hash_usernames* variable has a value of one. Otherwise, *nwrite.pl* needs to present a list of **tty** names to the user:

```
if ($hash_usernames{$NWRITE_USERNAME} == 1) {
  $NWRITE_TTY = $hash_ttys{$NWRITE_USERNAME};
}
else {

  #Empty the hash_ttys variable so it can be reused.
  undef %hash_ttys

  # loop through each line of output from the who command.
  for $line (`who`) {

    # Ignore all lines except those related to the sendee.
    next unless ($line =~ m/$NWRITE_USERNAME/i);

    # Black magic is happening on this next line. See the
    # text for an explanation.
    $hash_ttys{($line =~ m//+?\s+(.+?)\s/)[0]} = 1;
  }
  @sorted_list_ttys = sort(keys(%hash_ttys));

  print "nwrite: Select the terminal for
$NWRITE_USERNAME\n";
  print "@sorted_list_ttys\n";
  print "> ";
  $NWRITE_TTY = <STDIN>;
  chomp($NWRITE_TTY);

}
```

You've seen most of the techniques used in this section of the script before, except for the line labeled "black magic." Let's look at that line more closely:

```
$hash_ttys{($line =~ m//+?\s+(.+?)\s/)[0]} = 1;
```

Whenever you need to explore a line of complex code, always start in the middle. In this case, the inner piece is `$line =~ m// +?\s+(.+?)\s/`. I'm sure you already recognize this as the way to extract the second column, or the **tty** name, from the **who** line of output.

The next part to look at is *(...)[0]*, where the ... part is the pattern match piece from the last paragraph. In order to explain this notation, I need to digress for a moment to discuss the difference between evaluating an array variable in an array context versus in a scalar context. When an array variable is viewed in an array context, Perl sees a list of elements. When an array variable is viewed in a scalar context, Perl sees the number of elements. For example, *(1, 2, 3)* is an array. When viewed in a scalar context, it has the value of three—the number of elements in the list.

Many Perl functions know the context in which they are being evaluated. In a scalar context, the matching operator returns the number of matches that are found. However, in an array context, a list of the matching text is returned. You can create an array context by surrounding an expression with parentheses. Then, using the *[n]* notation, you can access the nth element of the returned array. Now, we know what the *(...)[0]* notation does—it extracts the first matching text that was found.

The rest of the "black magic" line is easy. The *$hash_ttys{...}* = *1;* notation creates a key-value entry in the *hash_ttys* hash variable. In essence, a marker (the value of 1) is placed for each **tty** name found. After all the processing is done, a list of the **tty** names can be retrieved using the **keys** function.

The rest of the code snippet asks the user to select from the **tty** list.

The *nwrite.pl* script is nearly finished. The only piece left is to run the **write** command so the user can enter the message that needs to be sent. The piece is shown at the end of Listing 12.5.

Listing 12.5 *nwrite.pl—Creating a User-friendly **write** Command with Perl*

```
#/bin/perl

($termid) = `tty` =~ m!/dev/(.*)!i;

# loop through each line of output from the who command.
foreach $line (`who`) {

  # If the output line mentions the current users tty,
  # ignore it.
  next if $line =~ m/$termid/i;
```

```perl
    # Extract the user and tty information.
    ($username) = $line =~ m/(.+?)\s/;
    ($tty)      = $line =~ m/.+?\s(.+?)\s/;

    # Use the username as the key half of a key/value
    # entry in a hash variable called list_usernames. Each
    # time the same username is encountered, the value half
    # of the entry is incremented. This results in the value
    # half of the entry always knowing how many times each
    # username is encountered in the input.
    $hash_usernames{$username}++;

    # The hash entries created here link the tty and the
    # username.
    $hash_ttys{$username} = $tty;
}

# The keys function returns a list of the key half of
# the key-value has entries. And the sort function
# returns a sorted version of the array passed to it.
@list_sorted_usernames = sort(keys(%hash_usernames));

print "nwrite: Please enter a user's name from this
list:\n"
print "@list_sorted_usernames\n"
print "> ";

# The <STDIN> notation reads a single line of input
# from the standard input - the keyboard in this case.
$NWRITE_USERNAME = <STDIN>;

# The chomp function removes the trailing newline from
# the line of input because the $/ variable is set to
# the newline character by default.
chomp($NWRITE_USERNAME);

if ($hash_usernames{$NWRITE_USERNAME} == 1) {
    $NWRITE_TTY = $hash_ttys{$NWRITE_USERNAME};
}
else {

    #Empty the hash_ttys variable so it can be reused.
    undef %hash_ttys

    # loop through each line of output from the who command.
    for $line (`who`) {
```

```
# Ignore all lines except those related to the sendee.
next unless ($line =~ m/$NWRITE_USERNAME/i);

# Extract the tty name and create an entry for
# it in the hash_ttys variable.
$hash_ttys{($line =~ m//+?\s+(.+?)\s/)[0]} = 1;
}
@sorted_list_ttys = sort(keys(%hash_ttys));

print "nwrite: Select the terminal for
$NWRITE_USERNAME\n";
print "@sorted_list_ttys\n";
print "> ";
$NWRITE_TTY = <STDIN>;
chomp($NWRITE_TTY);

}

echo "Please type your message now. Remember to end your
message"
echo "by typing Ctrl-D on a blank line."
`write $NWRITE_USERNAME $NWRITE_TTY`

echo -e "\nYour message has been sent!\n"
```

Running the *nwrite.pl* looks exactly like *nwrite.sh*, so you don't need to see it in action. Instead, let's look at the different strengths of the two languages, Bash and Perl.

NOTE   I can't resist making a comment here. Do you remember back in high school when the homework assignments asked you to compare and contrast two things? Did you hate those assignments as much as I did? And yet, over 20 years later, here I am. Comparing and contrasting Bash and Perl... Life is funny, eh?

Bash uses a series of commands to first filter output and then select the relevant information. Perl uses a loop statement and pattern matching to select relevant information. However, Perl has the advantage of array and hash variables. Array and hash variables effectively give Perl complex long-term memory, while Bash has only scalar memory to hold information.

Every good programmer learns to recognize patterns in their code. These patterns can be used as the building blocks for future scripts. The more building blocks you have, of all shapes and sizes, the more productive you become.

From the Bash script you can find these building blocks:

- Extract a suffix when the prefix doesn't change:

```
termid=${VARIABLE#PREFIX}
```

- Filter out input lines that contain a pattern:

```
grep --revert-match "PATTERN"
```

- Filter out newlines from input—effectively changing a list of items that displays vertically into a horizontal list:

```
xargs
```

- Filter out repeated lines from input:

```
sort | uniq
```

- Remember the number of times a pattern is matched:

```
VARIABLE=`COMMAND | grep --count "PATTERN"`
```

- Extract the first column of input—provided the first column ends with a space character:

```
cut -d" " -f1 | \
```

- Extract the second column of space-character delimited input:

```
tr --squeeze-repeats ' ' | cut -d" " -f2
```

From the Perl script you can find mostly the same building blocks. This makes sense, because the two scripts perform the same function.

- Extract a suffix when the prefix doesn't change:

```
($VARIABLE) = TARGET_STRING =~ m!PREFIX(.*)!i;
```

- Filter out input lines that contain a pattern:

```
foreach $line (INPUT_ARRAY) {

  next if $line =~ m/PATTERN/i;

  # Process lines

}
```

In this example, Perl's main advantages are its array and hash variables. They give Perl long-term memory of complex information.

Notice that the pattern shown here uses generic variable names; only items in uppercase need to be changed in order to use them. Using a naming convention aids in reusability.

- Filter out newlines from input—effectively changing a list of items that displays vertically into a horizontal list:

```
foreach $line (INPUT_ARRAY) {

  chomp($line);

  # Process lines

}
```

- Filter out repeated lines from input:

```
foreach $line (INPUT_ARRAY) {

  $hash_lines{$line} = 1;

}

@list_VARIABLE = keys(%hash_lines);
```

- Remember the number of times a pattern is matched:

```
VARIABLE = TARGET_STRING =~ m/PATTERN/i;
```

- Extract the first column of input—provided the first column ends with a space character:

```
foreach $line (INPUT_ARRAY) {

  push(@list_VARIABLE, $($line =~ m/(.+?)\s/)[0]);

}
```

- Extract the second column of space-character delimited input:

```
foreach $line (INPUT_ARRAY) {

  push(@list_VARIABLE, $($line =~ m/.+?\s(.+?)\s/)[0]);

}
```

I call these little snippets of functionality *CodeBits*. You can find more CodeBits at my web site, *http://www.CodeBits.com.*

A "Safe" delete Command

One of the major causes of headaches for system administrators is that users unintentionally delete files and don't have backup copies to restore. Instead, the administrator winds up having to find the backup tape from the night before and spend 10 minutes or more restoring the lost file.

In order to combat this problem, let's develop an alternative to the **rm** command. In fact, let's disable the **rm** command altogether. Listing 12.6 shows my copy of the *letclbashrc* file. If you don't have access to the *letclbashrc* file, you can append it to the *.bash_profile* file in your home directory. The shell function that replaces the **rm** shell command is shown in bold.

Listing 12.6 *letclbashrc—Disabling the rm Command*

```
# /etc/bashrc
...

# Create a rm function that does nothing.
# This should help users keep out of mischief.
rm () {
  echo "Please use the delete command."
}
```

Listing 12.6 creates a shell function that gets called whenever a user tries to use the **rm** command. The shell function's only job is to point them towards the **delete** command we're about to create.

In order for users to be able to restore their own files, the files need to be stored in a subdirectory of their home directory. Let's use *.trash* as the directory name so it won't show up in normal directory listings.

The first step of the new **delete** function should be to check for the *.trash* directory:

```
delete () {
  if [ ! -d ~/.trash ]; then
    mkdir ~/.trash
  fi
}
```

Now that we know the directory exists, files can be moved there instead of being deleted:

```
delete () {
  if [ ! -d ~/.trash ]; then
    mkdir ~/.trash
  fi

  mv --force $@ ~/.trash
}
```

This shell function works fine, but it can be improved. What if the user doesn't enter a filename? Let's add an error message:

```
delete () {
  if [ ! -d ~/.trash ]; then
    mkdir ~/.trash
  fi

  if [ $# eq 0 ]; then
    echo "Please specify a filename to remove."
  else
    mv --force $@ ~/.trash
  fi
}
```

After adding the **delete** function to the */etc/bashrc* file or the *~/.bash_profile* file, you need to use the **source** command to make Bash understand the changes:

```
% source /etc/bashrc
```

or

```
% source .bash_profile
```

Here is the new **delete** function in action:

```
% # First create some files and directories to test with.
% echo "test" > aaa
% echo "test" > aab
% mkdir dda
% mkdir ddb
% echo "test" > dda\aaa
% echo "test" > dda\aab
% ls -p
aaa  aab  dda/  ddb/
% delete *
% ls -p
% ls -p .trash
aaa  aab  dda/  ddb/
```

Let's add one more refinement to the **delete** function—requesting a confirmation before moving the files, as shown in Listing 12.7.

Listing 12.7 */etc/bashrc—Disabling the **rm** Command*

```
delete () {
  if [ ! -d ~/.trash ]; then
    mkdir ~/.trash
  fi

  if [ $# eq 0 ]; then
    echo "Please specify a filename to remove."
  else
    echo "You are about to delete these files: $@"
    echo -n "Are you sure about this? Enter 'y' for yes. "
    read
    if [ "$REPLY" = "y" ]; then
      mv --force $@ ~/.trash
    fi
  fi
}
```

While the **delete** function goes a long way towards preventing the user from deleting important files, it is not always effective. For example, if you try to delete a directory that has already been deleted, the **mv** command complains that it can't overwrite an existing directory.

You can improve upon this functionality by creating a house-keeping function to delete all trash files more than 30 days old. The housekeeping function might also monitor how large the trash directory is getting. If too many files are being stored, perhaps some need to be deleted to free up disk space.

A Limited-Use Login Shell

Your ability to control how Unix looks, feels, and reacts to users is unparalleled. I've heard stories about system administrators who create different environments depending on who is logging into the system. For example, when an engineer logs in, a short menu of technical programs is displayed. If a secretary logs in, a different menu of word-processing options is displayed.

The options that a user sees can be controlled by their entry in the */etc/passwd* file. Simply replace the */bin/bash* entry (the last field on the line) with the program you want the user to run upon login. This technique of limiting the user's choice has three advantages:

*Part of this section requires you to create user accounts. In order to do this, you must either log in as **root** or speak with your system administrator.*

- It reduces training costs because the Unix command line is never seen.

- It raises productivity because the opportunities for making time-consuming errors are reduced.

- It improves security because users never get a chance to poke around the system.

You can even create a single-use username. Let's create a user whose sole purpose is to run the **top** command. Add the following line to your */etc/passwd* file:

```
top::999:999:,,,,:/home/misc:/usr/bin/top
```

Now, log in using the *top* userid. Notice that no password is needed because the second field on the line is blank. After the login, the **top** command should immediately start.

Many Unix commands let you start subshells while they are running. For example, inside the *vi* editor you can use the command **:!ls -l** to run the **ls** command. I hope you already see the next step—running Bash in the subshell using the command **:!/bin/ bash**. If the user can get to a Bash command line, the effort you put into creating a limited-use login is wasted—assuming that security was your goal.

After you create a single-use login shell, the next logical step is to create a multiple-use shell. Listing 12.8 shows a script that helps users keep a diary up-to-date. Users can edit their diaries, list them to determine their file sizes, back them up on a daily basis, and log off.

Listing 12.8 *diary.sh—A Multiple-Use Login Shell Script*

```
#!/bin/bash

# Loop forever - the script exits when the user
# enters the logoff command.
while true
do
  # Clear the screen and display the menu of choices.
  clear
  echo    "Commands are: Edit, List, Backup, Logoff"
  echo -n "> "

  # Accept the user's choice and translate it
```

```
# to uppercase.
read command ARGUMENTS
COMMAND=`echo $command | tr '[:lower:]' '[:upper:]'`

# Use the case command to interpret the user's request
# and execute the requested command.
case $COMMAND in

   # The edit option prepends the current date
   # to the diary and a line of dashes to separate
   # entries, then opens the vi editor for the user.
   EDIT)
     (echo "`date '+%B %d, %Y'` Diary Entry"; \
      echo; \
      echo "-------------------";
      cat $USER.log) >> $USER.tmp
     rm $USER.log
     mv $USER.tmp $USER.log
     vi $USER.log
     ;;
   LIST)
     ls -l $USER.log
     ;;
   BACKUP)
     TODAY_DATE=`date '+%Y%m%d'`
     cp $USER.log "$USER-$TODAY_DATE.bak"
     ;;
   QUIT)
     exit
     ;;
  esac
  echo -n "Press Enter to Continue"
  read
done
```

This script is useful because it manages some of the file-handling details. Users never need to see a filename; this makes life easier.

I wanted to show you a diary script using Tcl, but while developing the script I discovered something about Tcl's **exec** command that prevented me from finishing. It turns out that **exec** doesn't let subprocesses have access to the screen or keyboard. Therefore, the **vi** command executes, but is both deaf (can't hear the keyboard) and dumb (can't display information). There might be a way to work around this limitation, but I'm not aware of it.

Instead of Tcl, Listing 12.9 contains a Perl version of the diary script, called *diary.pl*.

Listing 12.9 *diary.pl—A Multiple-Use Login Shell Script*

```perl
#!/usr/bin/perl

# Loop until the user enters a quit command.
while ( 1 ) {

  # The clear UNIX command outputs control characters
  # to clear the display. Those control characters need
  # to be printed in order for the display to see them.
  print `clear`;
  print "Commands are: Edit, List, quit\n";

  # Read a line of input from the keyboard.
  $command = <STDIN>;

  # Remove the newline from the end of the input line.
  chomp($command);

  # Translate all input characters to upper-case.
  $COMMAND = uc($command);

  # Perl doesn't have a case or switch statement, like
  # Bash and Tcl, but the if statement works fine.
  if ($COMMAND eq "EDIT") {

    # Read the whole diary file and store in into
    # the list_lines array variable.
    undef $/;
    open FILE, "$ENV{'USER'}.log";
    @list_lines = <FILE>;
    close FILE;
    $/ = "\n";

    # Create an array of month names. The qw notation
    # lets you avoid quotes and commas when only single
    # word array elements are needed.
    @months = qw(January  February  March
                 April     May       June
                 July      August    September
                 October   November  December
             );

    # The localtime function returns an array of 9
    # elements. For this script we only need three of them.
```

```
  ($day, $mon, $year) = (localtime())[3, 4, 5]

  # Perl starts counting years at 1900. So adding 1900 to
  # the year variable results in a four-digit year.
  $year += 1900;

  # Create a new log file with today's date on top.
  open FILE, ">$ENV{'USER'}.log";
  print FILE "$months[$mon-1] $day, $year Diary Entry\n";
  print FILE "\n";
  print FILE "-------------------\n";
  print FILE "@list_lines";
  close FILE;

  # Unlike using backticked strings, the system
  # command lets the sub-process access the terminal
  # and keyboard.

  # The $ENV{} notation lets Perl access individual
  # environment variables.
  system("vi $ENV{'USER'}.log");
}
elsif ($COMMAND eq "LIST") {
  print `ls -l $ENV{'USER'}.log`;
}
elsif ($COMMAND eq "QUIT") {
  exit;
}
print "Press Enter to Continue";
$temp = <STDIN>;
}
```

Now that the scripts are finished, it's time to find some building blocks:

- Translate all characters to uppercase:

  ```
  (Bash) tr '[:lower:]' '[:upper:]'

  (Perl) $NEW_VARIABLE = uc($VARIABLE)
  ```

- Prepend information to a file:

  ```
  (Bash) (echo "FIRST_LINE"; cat FILE_NAME) >> FILE_NAME.TMP
         rm FILE_NAME
         mv FILE_NAME.TMP FILE_NAME

  (Perl) ... The Perl code is over 4 lines long. See Listing 12.X
  ```

- Find the current date:

```
(Bash) $TODAYS_DATE = `date '+%B %d, %Y'`

(Perl) ($day, $mon, $year) = (localtime())[3, 4, 5]
       $year += 1900;
```

By this time, you should be seeing that Bash and Perl both have their own strengths and weaknesses. The simple task of adding information to the start of a file certainly highlights some of the differences. It took 11 lines of Perl code and only three lines of Bash code to perform this task. Likewise, it took more effort to generate the current date, complete with a month name, because Perl doesn't have the format specifiers that Bash's **date** command has.

One of the biggest advantages to using Perl or Tcl is portability. Most of the time your scripts work, without modification, on other platforms. However, if portability isn't one of your goals, you can use backticks to incorporate Bash statements in your Perl scripts. For example, you could replace these lines of Perl:

```
@months = qw(January February March
             April    May      June
             July     August   September
             October  November December
         );

($day, $mon, $year) = (localtime())[3, 4, 5]
$year += 1900;
print FILE "$months[$mon-1] $day, $year Diary Entry\n";
```

with the following lines of Perl:

```
$date_today = `date '+%B %d, %Y'`;
chomp($date_today);
print FILE "$date_today Diary Entry\n";
```

The decision on whether to use 100 percent Perl code or to mix Perl and Bash is yours.

What is the User's First Name?

The last section discussed how to create a login shell with limited functionality. This section shows how to extract the user's first name from the */etc/passwd* file. My computer always says "Hi, David! How's your day going?" when I log in.

The first step in this task requires filtering the password file so that only the line relating to the current user is shown. Filtering usually implies the **grep** command, and that's what we use here:

```
% grep "$USER" /etc/passwd
medined::500:500:David Medinets,,,,,:/home/medined:...
kathy::500:500:Kathryn,,,,,:/home/medined:...
```

Oops. I forgot that my wife and I share a home directory. The pattern used with **grep** needs to be changed so that only the start of the input lines is looked at:

```
% grep "^$USER" /etc/passwd
medined::500:500:David Medinets,,,,,:/home/medined:...
```

Much better. Now there is only one line to deal with. The next step involves extracting the fifth column where the columns are delimited by colons. Column extraction usually means using the **cut** command:

```
% grep "^$USER" /etc/passwd | \
  cut --delimiter=":" --fields=5
David Medinets,,,,,:/home/medined:...
```

Well, there's the first name that is needed. So let's perform a second extraction based on the space character:

```
% grep "^$USER" /etc/passwd | \
  cut --delimiter=":" --fields=5 | \
  cut --delimiter=" " --fields=1
David
```

Let's test this command line using the *kathy* userid:

```
% grep "^kathy" /etc/passwd | \
  cut --delimiter=":" --fields=5 | \
  cut --delimiter=" " --fields=1
Kathryn,,,,
```

Because no last name was specified in the password file, a *third* extraction needs to be done—this time based on the comma character:

```
% grep "^kathy" /etc/passwd | \
  cut --delimiter=":" --fields=5 | \
  cut --delimiter=" " --fields=1
```

```
    cut --delimiter="," --fields=1
Kathryn
```

Now that the hard part is done, all that is needed is to place the following lines at the end of the */etc/profile* file to display the greeting message:

```
FIRST_NAME=`grep "^$USER" /etc/passwd | \
  cut --delimiter=":" --fields=5 | \
  cut --delimiter=" " --fields=1 .
  cut --delimiter="," --fields=1`
```

```
echo -e "Hi $FIRST_NAME! How's your day going?\n"
```

The *-e* option lets **echo** recognize escape sequences, like the \n. In this case, an extra newline is displayed to separate the greeting message from the first shell prompt.

Perl and Tcl aren't really appropriate for this particular application. Both are relatively large programs and needlessly invoking them during the login process wastes computing resources.

On the other hand, knowing the user's first name can be handy at times other than during the login process. You might want to personalize your reporting program or error messages that are displayed. So it pays to explore how Perl and Tcl handle this task.

As always, we'll look at Perl before Tcl. Listing 12.10 contains a Perl script that stores the first name of the current user into a variable called *FIRST_NAME*.

Listing 12.10 *first.pl—Using Perl to Find the Current User's First Name*

```
#!/usr/bin/perl

open FILE, "/etc/passwd"

while (<FILE>) {
  if (m/^$ENV{'USER'}/) {
    ($FIRST_NAME) = split(/[\s,]/, (split(/:/))[4]);
    last;
  }
}

close FILE
```

The *first.pl* script makes use of Perl's *$_* special variable. Many of Perl's functions use the *$_* variable if no other variable is specified. For example, when a line of input is read using the *<FILE>* operation, that input line is stored in *$_*. When you use the *m//* operator, it looks for patterns using *$_* as the target string. Additionally, **split** breaks up the string in *$_* if no second parameter is supplied. The *$_* variable provides a nice way to streamline your code.

Perl's **split** function creates an array out of a string using a specified pattern as the delimiter. The heart of the *first.pl* script lies in the following line of code:

Many of Perl's functions and operators use the $_ variable by default.

```
($FIRST_NAME) = split(/[\s,]/, (split(/:/))[4]);
```

This line of code performs the following steps. First, it creates an array using the colon character as a delimiter. Then, using parentheses to create an array context and the *[n]* notation to specify an array element, it selects the fourth array element (which corresponds to the fifth column). Next, that element is split further using either whitespace or the comma character. The first element returned by the second **split** function is assigned to the *$FIRST_NAME* variable.

The following lines of code show each step as a single line of code—which is less efficient than placing everything on one line.

```
@list_fields    = split(/:/);
$user_info      = $list_fields[4];
@list_user_info = split(/[\s,]/, $user_info);
$FIRST_NAME     = $list_user_info[0];
```

The Tcl script, *first.tcl*, shown in Listing 12.11, is remarkably similar to *first.pl*. The only real difference is that Tcl tends to be more "wordy" than Perl, so the assignment to the *$FIRST_NAME* variable needs two lines to print within the page boundaries of this book.

Listing 12.11 *first.tcl—Using Tcl to Find the Current User's First Name*

```
#!/usr/bin/tcl

set FILE [open "/etc/passwd" r]
```

```
while { [gets $FILE line] >= 0} {
  if [regexp "^$env(USER)" $line] {
    set user_info [lindex [split $line :] 4]
    set FIRST_NAME [lindex [split $user_info { ,}] 0]
    break;
  }
}

close $FILE
```

Creating Proper Capitalization

One of the ways that I relax is to read the Usenet newsgroups looking for questions to answer. Recently, someone asked how to
change just the first letter of a word to uppercase. For example,
instead of a variable containing "david" it should contain
"David."

While the answer that I came up with it is not simple, it does
have the virtue of only using basic Bash commands.

The problem boils down to three steps: One, extract the first letter of the word; two, extract the rest of the word; and three, join
them back together.

Step 1: Extract the first letter of the word:

```
% name="david"
% first=`echo $name | cut -c1 | tr '[:lower:]' '[:upper:]'`
D
```

Step 2: Extract the rest of the word:

```
% rest=`echo $name | cut -c2-`
```

Step 3: Join the first letter back together with the rest of the
word:

```
% echo "$first$rest"
David
```

These steps are pretty simple, no? However, by trying different
variations, we can perhaps gain additional insight into how Bash
works.

Our first experiment is creating a shell script called *proper1.sh*.
This script, shown in Listing 12.12, lets you specify a word on the
command line that needs to be proper-cased.

Listing 12.12 *proper1.sh—Change the First Letter in Each Word of Input to Uppercase Using Bash*

```
#!/bin/bash

for word in $@
do
  first=`echo $word | cut -c1 | tr '[:lower:]' '[:upper:]'`
  rest=`echo $word | cut -c2-`
  echo "$first$rest"
done
```

Here is an example of this script in action:

```
% chmod +x proper1.sh
% proper1.sh This is a test.
This
Is
A
Test.
```

Hmm, the result is not quite what we need, is it? Displaying the words one per line isn't too user-friendly. Perhaps, using a variable to store the proper-cased words as the loop progresses would work. Listing 12.13 tries this technique.

Listing 12.13 *proper2.sh—Change the First Letter in Each Word of Input to Uppercase Using Bash*

```
#!/bin/bash

# Initialize the storage variable.
PROPER=""

for word in $@
do
  first=`echo $word | cut -c1 | tr '[:lower:]' '[:upper:]'`
  rest=`echo $word | cut -c2-`
  PROPER="$PROPER$first$rest"
done

echo $PROPER

% chmod +x proper2.sh
% ./proper2.sh This is a test
ThisIsATest
% proper2.sh This   is   a   test
ThisIsATest
```

Interestingly enough, the example shows a side effect that happens when Bash parses the command line into words—all of the whitespace between the words is removed. In order to get around this problem, I added a space to the assignment statement inside the *while* loop:

```
PROPER="$PROPER$first$rest "
```

Now the display is a little nicer:

```
% proper2.sh This   is   a   test
This Is A Test
```

We can learn one more thing from this exercise in creating proper-case strings. Let's create a single command line that only affects the first word. We already know how to extract the first letter and the rest of the word. Let's join them together in a sequential command list to see what happens:

```
% word="waswaldo"
% echo $word | cut -c1 | tr '[:lower:]' '[:upper:]'; \
> echo $word | cut -c2-
W
aswaldo
```

Bash displays a pesky newline right in the middle of our word! The problem could be with the **echo** command. After all, we know that **echo** always adds a newline. So let's use the *-n* option to stop this behavior:

```
% word="waswaldo"
% echo -n $word | cut -c1 | tr '[:lower:]' '[:upper:]'; \
> echo $word | cut -c2-
W
aswaldo
```

Adding the *-n* option didn't work. Therefore, the **cut** command must be adding the newline. The next logical step is to use the **tr** command to remove all newline characters:

```
% word="waswaldo"
% echo -n $word | \
> cut -c1 | \
> tr -d '\n' | \
> tr '[:lower:]' '[:upper:]'; \
> echo $word | cut -c2-
Waswaldo
```

That did the trick. Sometimes, solving a problem requires trial-and-error backed up by logic.

Using Tcl to proper-case a string is remarkably similar to using Bash. Listing 12.14 shows the *proper.tcl* script.

Listing 12.14 *proper.tcl—Change the First Letter in Each Word of Input to Uppercase Using Tcl*

```tcl
#!/usr/bin/tcl

# Initialize the storage variable.
set PROPER {};

foreach word $argv {
  set first [ string toupper [ string index $word 0 ]];
  set rest  [ string range $word 1 end]
  PROPER="$PROPER$first$rest "
}

puts $PROPER
```

The **string index** function returns a single character, in this case the first character that is located at position zero. The **string range** function returns a string value. In this example, the string starts at the second position and continues to the end of the *$word* variable.

Perl, being the Swiss Army knife of computer languages, actually has a built-in function to perform the proper-case operation. It's called **ucfirst**. Listing 12.15 shows the short Perl script needed to proper-case all command-line parameters.

Listing 12.15 *proper.pl—Change the First Letter in Each Word of Input to Uppercase Using Tcl*

```perl
#!/usr/bin/perl

# Initialize the storage variable.
undef $PROPER;

foreach $word (@argv) {
  $PROPER .= ucfirst($word) . " " ;
}

print "$PROPER\n";
```

Useful Information, Tips, and Warnings

This section is devoted to information, tips, and warnings that I can't fit neatly into one of the other sections in this book or that I feel bear repeating.

One of the important tasks a programmer can undertake involves molding the computing environment to better suit their everyday needs. This frequently involves creating aliases for commonly used commands. However, it could also involve using special commands to check disk quotas or automatically connect to remote disks when you log in.

When Bash starts up, it executes several files so that both system-wide or user-specific environment changes can be made. The following files are executed in order:

- */etc/profile*—Executed for all login shells.

- *~/.bash_profile* or *~/.profile*—Executed for all login shells. The *.profile* file is only executed if the *.bash_profile* file is not found.

Like most command interpreters, Bash has startup files that you can modify to create a customized environment.

- *~/.bashrc*—Executed for interactive non-login shells. For example, if you run the **:!/bin/bash** command inside the *vi* editor, you start an interactive non-login shell.

- *$ENV*—Executed for all shells, if it is set.

If you are new to Unix, consider placing the following lines of code at the start of all these files:

```
echo "The $0 file is being executed."
read     <- highly optional.
```

This technique lets you know exactly which files are being executed and when. Every time one of the files is executed, Bash displays the message from the **echo** command and then pauses. As you go about your daily activities, you'll discover exactly when and why the files are called.

When you log out, Bash executes a file called *.bash_logout*. This file is a good place to put backup and housekeeping routines.

I like to personalize my login shell by adding the following lines to my *~/.bash_profile* file:

```
# I add the . to the end of the PATH variable so
# that executable scripts in the current directory
# are found.
PATH="$PATH:."

# Setup the ls command to display filenames with
# controls to use question marks so they are easier
# to pick out of the listing. Also append a character
# to the end of the filename indicating its file type.
alias ls='ls --hide-control-chars -p'

# Make sure that the mv command asks before
# overwriting a file and displays the name of
# each file that gets moved.
alias mv='mv --interactive --verbose'

# Make sure that the rm command requests
# confirmation before deleting each file.
alias rm='rm --interactive'
```

I've mentioned how dangerous the . * pattern can be when used with the **rm** command, but it bears repeating. The . * pattern can delete files in the current directory, *and in directories higher up the directory tree*. Use caution when deleting files.

Counting Files

The next example shows you how to display the number of files in a directory. It's quite short:

```
# Note: The following command uses the digit one, not
# the letter el.
% ls -1 | wc --lines
19
% ls -1a | wc --lines
26
```

*Using the . * pattern can be very dangerous!*

The first command shows how many files without counting files that begin with a dot. The second command uses the *-a* option of **ls** to include the *dot* files in the count.

I include this example because I want to introduce you to directory handling in Perl and Tcl—and I need a lead-in example for the topic.

Both Perl and Tcl understand how to **glob**. This strange term relates to expanding pattern to determine filenames. When the

glob function is run, a list of files matching a pattern is returned. If the pattern is *.dat*, then a list of datafiles is returned. However, Perl and Tcl handle globbing slightly differently.

The following is an example of Perl's **glob** function. Please note the file called *nofile* does not exist.

```
% perl
@files = glob("nwrite.pl nofile");
print "@files\n";
^D
diary.pl nwrite.pl nofile
```

And now, here is Tcl's **glob** function:

```
% tcl
tcl> puts [ glob "*.pl" "nofile" ];
diary.pl nwrite.pl
tcl> puts [ glob "nofile" ];
Error: no files matched glob pattern "nofile"
tcl> puts [ glob -nocomplain "nofile" ];

tcl>
```

Perl expands any wildcards in the expression passed to it. It then returns an array based on the expanded expression. Filenames are not tested for existence; that's why the non-existent *nofile* file shows up in the *@files* array. Tcl, on the other hand, only returns the filenames of existing files. In fact, an error message is displayed if no files match the pattern you specify. You can avoid the error message by using the *-nocomplain* option.

The replace Command

I frequently see requests for a script to replace one batch of text with another on IRC channels and Usenet groups. To answer this need, Kristine Moncada was kind enough to create a script that used the Korn shell. I added a bit more error-checking and made sure the script works using the Bash shell.

Before you look at the *replace.sh* script, I'd like to point out one of Kristine's techniques I hadn't seen before:

```
[ $# -lt 2 ] && {
  echo "Usage: ... "
  exit 1
}
```

You might recall from Chapter 5, "Controlling the Shell," that *command1 && command2* is a command list. The second command executes only if the first command succeeds. You might also recall that the *{ command1; command2 }* notation indicates a compound command and that all of the commands inside the curly braces are executed in the current shell. A child shell is not used.

By using both techniques, you can simulate an **if..then** control statement. I know that Bash actually has an **if** statement, but every technique you learn moves you along the slippery slope to "expert programmer."

In order for the text replacement script to be flexible, it needs be able to search in a variety of different directories using a specific file extension or no file extension. This type of flexibility can be achieved using options on the command line.

The first step to recognizing command-line options is deciding how they need to be specified. Should the user use single-letter options or longer, more descriptive words? Let's focus on single-letter options for this example.

The next step is deciding which options to support and determining if they are optional. We've already talked about needing to specify a directory and file extension, so let's stick with those as command-line options. Using *-d* to specify a directory and *-e* to specify a file extension should work fine. It makes sense that the majority of replacements are done in the current directory, so the *-d* option should be optional. What about the *-e*? Well, a good default action, if no extension is specified, can be searching every file. Therefore, the *-e* option is optional also.

Let's take stock of the situation so far. The syntax of the *replace.sh* script looks like this:

```
replace.sh [-d=directory] [-e=extension] oldtext newtext
```

The last step is determining how to tell if a command-line option is specified. Remember that inside shell scripts, the options are stored in variables named n. So the four options are stored in $1, $2, $3, and $4. However, because the options are optional, the *oldtext* and *newtext* parameters might be stored in any of the four variables. For example, if only one option is specified, then *oldtext* and *newtext* will be in $2 and $3, respectively.

Regardless of how many options are specified, the options are stored in *$1* and *$2*. Because we know this fact won't change, that's a good place to start. The following lines of code strip off the endings of *$1* and *$2*, leaving just the text before the equals sign. If the variable has no equals sign (and therefore is not an option), then the whole value of *$1* and *$2* is retained.

```
option1=${1%%=*}
option2=${2%%=*}
```

NOTE   The *${variable%%pattern}* notation expands the pattern and then tries to find the longest matching text at the end of the variable's value. If a match is found, the matching text is deleted and the rest of the text is returned.

In order to see what the *option1* variable can be assigned, there are two test cases to be worried about—one where *$1* contains an option and one where *$1* does not. The following command-line session performs these tests using the *opt* variable, because the *$1* variable can only be used inside shell functions and scripts.

```
% opt="oldtext"
% echo ${opt%%=*}
oldtext
% opt="-d=directory"
% echo ${opt%%=*}
-d
```

Note that the *$1* variable can't be used on the command line.

These tests show that the evaluation of *${1%%=*}* produces the text that is needed—just the option letter. If *$1* doesn't contain an option letter, then comparing *$1* to *-d* or *-e* fails, indicating that no option was specified on the command line.

Because the *-d* and *-e* options are optional, the *oldtext* and *newtext* parameters might be found in any of positions one through four. There are at least two methods you can use to determine which positions are being used.

Let's look at the easy-to-understand, low-tech method first:

```
# If there are only two parameters, then
# oldtext and newtext must be in $1 and $2.
```

```
[ $# -eq 2 ] && {
  old=$1
  new=$2
}

# With three parameters, the oldtext and
# newtext parameters must be $2 and $3.
[ $# -eq 3 ] && {
  old=$2
  new=$3
}

# With four parameters, the oldtext and
# newtext parameters must be $3 and $4.
[ $# -eq 4 ] && {
  old=$3
  new=$4
}
```

I'm sure you see the pattern emerging: The *oldtext* and *newtext* parameters are always in the last two positions. Using this bit of insight, we can devise a complex, high-tech series of commands to always locate the last two parameters.

Step 1: Determine the position of the last parameter—the location of the *newtext* parameter. The $# variable holds the number of parameters, so it should be used:

```
newPos=$#
```

Step 2: Determine the position of the next-to-last parameter—the location of the *oldtext* parameter. Because *newPos* already holds the position of the last parameter, we can simply subtract one from it to get the position of the next-to-last parameter:

```
let oldPos=newPos-1
```

Step 3: Create a variable whose value is the name of the positional variable that contains the *newtext* parameter. For example, if there are three parameters, the $newVar variable should contain "$3":

```
newVar="$`echo $newPos"
```

Step 4: Do the same thing for the *oldtext* parameter:

```
oldVar="$`echo $oldPos`"
```

Step 5: Use the **eval** command to find out the value of the positional variables held in *$oldVar* and *$newVar*:

```
old=`eval echo $oldVar`
new=`eval echo $newVar`
```

The last step might be a little tricky to understand because the **eval** command is not used too often. Chapter 5, "Controlling the Shell," has a section called "The eval Command" that discusses it. But let me briefly go over the command. The **eval** command expands its parameters and then executes them. If you run the **replace.sh** command with this command line:

```
% replace.sh -d=dir -e=ext oldText newText
```

then *$oldVar* has a value of "*$4*" after step 4 is completed. If you only use a command line like:

```
old=`eval $oldVar`
```

Bash tries to execute a command called **oldText**. That is not the result needed. Instead, the text **oldText** needs to be sent to *STD-OUT* so that it can be assigned to the *$old* variable. That's where the **echo** command comes into play:

```
old=`eval echo $oldVar`
```

This line becomes `old="oldText"` after the backticked string is executed.

Finally, the explanation of the *replace.sh* script is finished. Listing 12.16 contains the full script.

Listing 12.16 *replace.sh—Replace Text in More Than One File Using Bash*

```
#!/bin/bash

# If there were less than two parameters on the
# command line, display a usage message.
[ $# -lt 2 ] && {
  echo -n "Usage: `basename $0` "
  ecgo "[-d=directory] [-e=extension] oldtext newtext"
  exit 1
}
```

```
# The next section of code sets default values
# in case command-line options are not used.
dir="."
ext=""
pattern="*"

# Extract the option letters, if any, from the
# command-line parameters.
option1=${1%%=*}
option2=${2%%=*}

# Test for the existence of the command-line options.
# If they exist, their values are stored in $dir
# and $ext. The order of the options should be irrelevant,
# meaning that the user can specify -d -e or -e -d.
# Therefore, both $1 and $2 needs to be tested for
# each option.
#
# Test for the -d option.
[ "$option1" = "-d" ] && {
  dir=${1#-d=}
}
[ "$option2" = "-d" ] && {
  dir=${2#-d=}
}

# Test for the -e option. Notice that
# the extension is combined with *. to
# create a pattern that the find command
# can use.
 [ "$option1" = "-e" ] && {
  pattern="*.${1#-e=}"
}
[ "$option2" = "-e" ] && {
  pattern="*.${2#-e=}"
}

# See the text above for an explanation of
# the next code section. Essentially it figures
# out where the oldText and newText parameters are
# and stores them in the old and new variables.
newPos=$#
let oldPos=newPos-1
newVar="$`echo $newPos"
oldVar="$`echo $oldPos`"
old=`eval echo $oldVar`
new=`eval echo $newVar`
```

```
# Check to make sure that the specified directory,
# if any, exists.
[ -d $dir ] || {
  echo "`basename $0`: $dir is not a directory!"
  exit 1
}

# Use the find command to generate a list of
# files. Then iterate over the list using the for
# command. Inside the loop, the sed command does
# the replacement saving the output to a temporary
# file. Then, the old file is overwritten and the
# temporary file is deleted.
for File in `find $dir -name "$pattern"`
do
  sed "s/$old/$new/g" $File > $File.zzzz
  cat $File.zzzz > $File && rm $File.zzzz
done
```

Now it's time to look at how Perl can handle the job of replacing text inside files. When porting from one language to another, I look at a program as a series of steps. Actually, that last sentence is a platitude. I always think of programs as carrying out steps in a process. However, when porting, *you* get to decide how much activity each step covers. For example, the beginning of the *replace* shell script can be seen as either:

```
# 1. Display an error message if the number of
#    parameters is less than 2.
```

   or

```
# 1. Determine the number of parameters
# 2. Display error if number is less than 2.
```

While these two options seem similar, the more detailed second option is better for porting purposes. It is better because it is easier to port simple blocks of code than integrated blocks of code. The less a code block does, the greater the chance the target language has an analog that can be used.

Small blocks of code reduce the amount of information needed at any one time during the porting process, helping to speed things along. Additionally, segmenting your code into logical steps helps you focus on how the new language handles a task rather than remaining in the mindset of the original language.

That said, I don't think we need to dwell on the subject of how to analyze a problem from a portability standpoint. I'm sure there are whole books devoted to that subject.

Instead, let's look at some of the some of the Perl techniques you'll need to use to create *replace.pl* (located, in full, in Listing 12.17).

Perl stores command-line options in an array called *ARGV*. The first or zeroeth element of *ARGV* holds the first command line. The *ARGV* array corresponds to shell's $*n* positional variables.

One of the first steps in the *replace.pl* script is to determine the number of parameters. By using the $#*arrayName* notation, you can determine how many elements are in an array. However, because Perl usually starts array indexes from zero, in order to keep your conditional expression the same between Bash and Perl, you need to add one to $#*ARGV*.

Checking the number of command-line parameters is straightforward. However, determining whether or not options are used on the command line is a bit tricky. The first command-line option is stored in $*ARGV[0]*. Using the following regular expression extracts the option letter and option argument in one step. The option letter is stored in the $*1* variable, and the option argument is stored in the $*2* variable. If the parameter doesn't contain an option, then $*1* and $*2* are empty.

Perl uses the value of the $[variable as the starting array index. Normally, this variable is set to zero. Please don't change it.

You might recall from Chapter 8, "Pattern Matching," that Perl uses the $*n* variables to store text that matches sub-patterns contained in parentheses. For example, the following code displays *BBB*:

```
$line = "aaaBBBaaa";
$line =~ m/a+(B+)a+/;
print "$1\n";
```

I like to think of the $*n* variables as a type of pattern memory. They say "Hey Perl! Please remember whatever matches the pattern inside these parentheses." Perl remembers the text that matches each set of parentheses in your pattern.

Time to continue with the replace Perl script. The following pattern-matching operation returns true if the first command-line parameter begins with a dash and has an equals sign as the third

character. As a side effect, the *$1* and *$2* variables are set because
of the parentheses in the pattern.

```
$ARGV[0] =~ m/^-(.)=(.*)/
```

A simple test of the *$1* variable lets you set the *$dir* or *$pattern*
variables:

```
if ($ARGV[0] =~ m/^-(.)=(.*)/) {
  $dir = $2           if $1 eq 'd';
  $pattern = "*.$2" if $1 eq 'e';
}
```

In order to test both the first and second variables for parameters, you could simply repeat the *if* statement again and change the
$ARGV[0] to *$ARGV[1]*. However, there is a more elegant technique available that uses a *foreach* statement:

```
foreach $iindex (0..1) {
  if ($ARGV[$iindex] =~ m/^-(.)=(.*)/) {
    $dir = $2           if $1 eq 'd';
    $pattern = "*.$2" if $1 eq 'e';
  }
}
```

Perl's *foreach* statement iterates over the elements of an array.
As you can see from the code snippet above, you can create an
array on the fly using Perl's range operator. The *0..1* notation creates an array with two elements, zero and one. The *$iindex* vari-
able is used as an array index into the *@ARGV* array variable.

Now that the command-line arguments have been identified, it's
time to verify that the specified directory exists:

```
unless (-d $dir) {
  print "$0: $dir is not a directory!\n";
  exit(1);
}
```

The *-d* directory test returns true if the specified directory exists,
and false otherwise. This code uses the *unless* statement, which is
the opposite of the *if* statement. When the conditional expression
evaluates to false, the statement block is executed—so the error
message is only displayed when the directory doesn't exist.

The options have been parsed and the directory has been
checked. Now it's time to initialize the *$old* and *$new* variables.

The text that needs replacing is stored in old, and the replacement text is stored in new. The Bash shell required six lines of code to accomplish this task, and those six lines of code involved the **eval** command, so they weren't simple. Here is how to grab the last two elements of an array in Perl:

```
$new = $ARGV[-1];   <- the last array element
$old = $ARGV[-2];   <- the next to last element
```

Yup, it's that simple. Perl's negative array subscripts can come in quite handy. However, Perl being Perl, there's also another technique you can use involving array slices:

```
($old, $new) = @ARGV[-2, -1];
```

Array slices let you specify exactly which elements of an array you'd like to extract and into which variables you'd like to store those elements. So in one line you can initialize the old and new variables:

```
@files = `find $dir -name "$pattern"`;
```

You've already seen backticked strings several times. This line of code executes the command inside the backticked string and stores the output in the *@files* array. Each line of output is a separate element of the array. Notice that variable interpolation does take place inside backticked strings. In case you've forgotten what variable interpolation means, let me refresh your memory. When variables are replaced by their values—inside double-quoted and backticked strings—they are said to be interpolated (and no, I don't know the origin of this word).

Our *replace* script is nearly complete. The only thing left to do is perform the replacement on each file in the *@files* array.

```
foreach $file (@files) {
  $buffer = readFile($file);
  $buffer =~ s/$old/$new/g;
  writeFile($file, $buffer);
}
```

This *foreach* loop couldn't be simpler. The contents of each file is stored in the $buffer$ variable, then the replacement is performed, using the *s///* operator, and the file is written. Behind the scenes, the *readFile* and *writeFile* routines do a little housekeeping, but not much.

If you need to
refresh your
memory
about Regu-
lar Expres-
sions and
Pattern
Matching,
turn to Chap-
ter 8.

The *readFile* routine looks like this:

```perl
sub readFile {
  my($filename) = shift;
  my($buffer);
  local($/) = undef;

  open(FILE, "<$filename")
    or die "Couldn't open $filename for reading: $!\n";
  $buffer = <FILE>;
  close(FILE);

  return($buffer);
}
```

Notice that the **shift** function is used to store the first parameter (the first element of the *@_ array)* into the *$filename* variable. Then the *$/* variable, which holds the end-of-record delimiter, is made undefined. Once the *$/* variable is undefined, Perl no longer understands the concept of a record, so the whole file is read at once.

The `$buffer = <FILE>;` line of code actually reads the file from disk. And the `return($buffer);` line of code tells Perl what is the return value for the function.

Using read-
File to read a
whole file
into memory
at once is
very conve-
nient, but
you need to
make sure
the files you
read aren't
too large.
Trying to
read a 10 mil-
lion byte file
into memory
is not usually
recom-
mended.

After reading a file and making the changes, it's time to write the file back to disk. The *writeFile* routines does this:

```perl
sub writeFile {
  my($filename, $buffer) = @_;
  local($/) = undef;

  open(FILE, ">$filename")
    or die "Couldn't open $filename for writing: $!\n";
  print FILE $buffer;
  close(FILE);
}
```

The *writeFile* routine doesn't introduce any new concepts. But you might not be familiar with how the **print** function is being used. By default, the **print** function sends output to *STDOUT*. However, if a file handle is specified as the first argument, the output is sent there.

Listing 12.17 shows the whole *replace.pl* script in one piece.

Listing 12.17 *replace.pl—Replace Text in More Than One File Using Perl*

```perl
#!/usr/bin/perl

# Perl starts array indexes at zero. So in order to
# make the conditional test of the if statement the
# same as in the Bash script, one needs to be added
# to the number of elements in the ARGV array.
$numParameters = $#ARGV + 1;

if ($numParameters < 2) {
  print "Usage: $0";
  print "[-d=directory] [-e=extension] oldtext newtext\n";
  exit(1);
}

# Because of the method used in the foreach loop in the
# next section to determine the parameters, the default
# values of the dir, ext, and pattern variables need to be
# set now.
$dir     = '.';
$pattern = '*';

# This section of code is explained in the text above
# this listing. The quick explanation is that the code
# loops through the first two parameters. If either one
# of the parameters is a valid option, the $dir or
# $pattern variables are set.

# Loop from zero to one.
foreach $iindex (0..1) {
  # extract the option letter and value.
  if ($ARGV[$iindex] =~ m/^-(.)=(.*)/) {
    # only set the variables if one of the options
    # were found.
    $dir     = $2      if $1 eq 'd';
    $pattern = "*.$2" if $1 eq 'e';
  }
}

# Make sure the directory exists.
unless (-d $dir) {
  print "$0: $dir is not a directory!\n";
  exit(1);
}
```

```perl
# Take advantage of Perl's negative indexes to
# grab the last and next-to-last command-line
# parameters.
$new = $ARGV[-1];
$old = $ARGV[-2];

# Capture the output from the find command into
# an array variable.
@files = `find $dir -name "$pattern"`;

# Iterate over the list of files (the files
# array variable), reading each file, performing
# the replacement, and then writing the file.
foreach $file (@files) {
  $buffer = readFile($file);
  $buffer =~ s/$old/$new/g;
  writeFile($file, $buffer);
}

# It's always a good idea to explicitly decide
# where your script file ends by using an exit
# statement.
exit;

# readFile - this function reads an entire file
# in one shot. The whole file is stored in the
# scalar variable passed as a parameter.
sub readFile {
  my($filename) = shift;
  my($buffer);
  # When the end-of-record variable is undefined, Perl
  # reads the whole file at once.
  local($/) = undef;

  # If the open function fails, the die function is
  # called, which displays the error message and terminates
  # the execution of the script.
  open(FILE, "<$filename")
    or die "Couldn't open $filename for reading: $!\n";

  # The next statement stores the whole file into
  # the $buffer variable.
  $buffer = <FILE>;

  close(FILE);

  return($buffer);
}
```

```
# writeFile - this function writes an entire file
# in one shot.
sub writeFile {
  my($filename, $buffer) = @_;
  # When the end-of-record variable is undefined, Perl
  # writes the whole file at once.
  local($/) = undef;

  open(FILE, ">$filename")
    or die "Couldn't open $filename for writing: $!\n";

  print FILE $buffer;

  close(FILE);
}
```

Tcl also does an admirable job at replacing text inside of files. Because of Tcl's quoting rules and particular viewpoint, it's worth looking closely at how Tcl can be used to implement *replace.sh*.

Tcl's approach to command-line parameters is similar to Perl's. However, instead of needing to determine how many parameters exist by examining the @*ARGV* array, you can simply use the *argc* Tcl variable. Another small difference is revealed when the name of the script itself is needed. Bash and Perl store the name of the currently executing script in *$0*; Tcl uses *argv0*.

> **NOTE** I usually refer to Bash and Tcl variable names without the initial dollar sign because that's how they are used in assignment statements. However, with Perl it seems better to always show the initial data type indicator—the $, @, or % characters. You can use whatever method you like. I haven't seen any "official" rules regarding this topic.

As a programmer who works with many languages, I frequently make mistakes that relate to how computer languages handle quotes. For me, Tcl is no exception. These typos invariably require several tries to fix. So let me point out one gotcha with Tcl. You might think that the following three lines of code are identical (except for the variable names, of course):

```
set a '.';
set b ".";
set c {.};
```

However, when you print them, they display like this:

```
$a='.'
$b=.
$c=.
```

As you can see, the single-quoted string displays differently from the double-quoted string and the string in curly braces.

Tcl has a **foreach** command that can be used to examine the first two command-line parameters. It looks like this:

```
foreach iindex {0 1} {
}
```

This **foreach** command iterates over a list of two elements. Therefore, it can be used to find the command-line options. Tcl stores the command-line parameters in the *argv* array.

I feel that, in some ways, Tcl's **regexp** function is more programmer-friendly than either Bash or Perl, because you can specify variables to hold the matching text. The syntax of the **regexp** function is:

```
regexp pattern target [whole_match] [submatches...]
```

If you specify a third parameter, whatever text is in *target* that matched the whole *pattern* is stored in the variable named by the third parameter. Submatches, created by using parentheses in *pattern*, are also optional.

Regular expressions are discussed in Chapter 8, "Pattern Matching."

The *replace.tcl* script uses the **regexp** function like this:

```
regexp {^\-(.)=(.*)} $parameter temp letter value;
```

The pattern used here is identical to the one used in the *replace.pl* script, except that the dash character needs to be escaped. The *parameter* variable holds the text that gets searched. In this situation, the text matching the whole pattern is not important, so it is ignored. The text matching the two submatches is stored in the *letter* and *value* variables, respectively.

Because the option letter is readily available in the *letter* variable, it's easy to test to see if the *d* or *e* option was specified:

```
if { $letter == "d" } {
  set dir "$value";
}
if { $letter == "e" } {
  set pattern "*.$value";
}
```

Notice that when an option is found, the *value* variable returned from the **regexp** function is used. There are no intermediary variables (like *$1* or *$2*) to worry about.

Once the options are determined, the script needs to find out if the specified directory exists. The existence of a directory is determined by using the **file isdirectory** function, which is used like this:

```
if [ file isdirectory $dir ] puts "dir exists";
```

However, when you need to test for non-existence—which is what our script needs—the conditional expression becomes a little more complex:

```
if { ! [ file isdirectory $dir ] } puts "no such dir";
```

The next step is determining the old text and the new, or replacement, text. Tcl doesn't have negative subscripts like Perl. But grabbing the last and next-to-last array elements isn't too painful. First, the subscript of the last element is determined. Then, the last element is assigned to the *new* variable. Finally, the subscript is decremented and the next-to-last element is assigned to the *old* variable.

```
set iindex [ expr [ llength $argv ] - 1 ];
set new [ lindex $argv $iindex ];
set iindex [ expr $iindex - 1 ];
set old [ lindex $argv $iindex ];
```

The **llength** function returns the length of a list (or array)—in this case the *argv* variable. However, in order to grab the last element, you need to subtract one. Using the **lindex** function is straightforward—simply specify which array and subscript to use. Notice that, unlike what we know to be true of Perl, using math in Tcl requires the **expr** function. Personally, I find this requirement a bit irksome, but at least it's consistent with the language's paradigm.

One of the earlier examples in this chapter needed to run the **vi** shell command inside a child process. Tcl couldn't run the **vi** command because of the way that subshells are handled—all output is collected and then returned as one unit to the called program. However, Tcl can handle running the **find** shell command just fine:

```
set files [ exec "find" "$dir" "-name" "$pattern" ];
```

The output lines from the **find** command are stored in the *files* array. Notice that each parameter of the **find** command is enclosed in quotes. This ensures that **find** sees three separate parameters instead of one parameter with three parts.

Remarkably enough, Tcl handles files in a very compact manner. I say remarkable because of Tcl's tendency towards long function names (for example, **string length** and **file isdirectory**). The following three lines of code read a whole file into memory:

```
set f [ open $file r ];
set inpBuffer [ read $f ];
close $f;
```

The first line opens the file in read-only mode. The second line reads the while file and stores it into the *f* variable. And the last line closes the file. It is very important to close files as soon as possible. This lets the operating system allocate file space and internal memory efficiently.

If you like to write dense code (a lot of function packs onto one line), you might be tempted to condense these three lines of code into two:

```
set inpBuffer [ read [ open $file r ] ];
close $f;
```

Can you spot the problem in these lines of code? The **close** function refers to the *f* variable, but it's no longer being defined! Therefore, in this case, creating dense code doesn't work.

The Bash and Perl versions of the *replace* script are inefficient because they rewrite *every* file they examine. I didn't mention this issue before, so that you could have a chance to figure it out on your own. Tcl makes it easy to eliminate this inefficiency because the **regsub** function returns the number of replacements that are done. If no replacements are done, the buffer doesn't need to be written:

```
if [ regsub -all "$old" "$inpBuffer" "$new" outBuffer ] {
  set f [open $file w];
  puts -nonewline $f $outBuffer;
  close $f;
}
```

This **if** statement is slightly condensed. If you like to spell things out, you might prefer:

```
if { [ regsub ... ] > 0 } {
  ... commands ...
}
```

The programming style you use is totally up to you. I prefer to rely on the fact that any non-zero value makes the conditional expression evaluate as true. Thus, when a replacement is done, the buffer is written.

Listing 12.18 shows the whole *replace.tcl* script in one piece.

Listing 12.18 *replace.tcl—Replace Text in More Than One File Using Tcl*

```
#!/usr/bin/tcl

# If fewer than two command-line parameters are used,
# display a usage message. Notice that the text with
# square brackets needs to be enclosed in curly-braces
# so that Tcl does not try to execute the text inside
# the square brackets as function calls.

if { $argc < 2 } {
  puts [ concat "Usage: $argv0 " \
        {[-d=directory] [-e=extension] oldtext newtext\n}
\
      ];
  exit 1;
}

# initialize variables to provide default values. If no
# option were specified on the command line, these defaults
# are used.
set dir      ".";
set ext      "";
set pattern "*";
```

```
# check the command-line parameter array (argv) to
# see which options were specified.
foreach iindex {0 1} {

  # each pass of the foreach loop stores a different
  # parameter into the parameter variable.
  set parameter [ lindex $argv $iindex ];

  # Use a pattern to extract the option letter and
  # value from the parameter.
  regexp {\-(.)=(.*)} $parameter temp letter value;

  # check to see if either of the two options we
  # need were specified.
  if { $letter == "d" } {
    set dir "$value";
  }
  if { $letter == "e" } {
    set pattern "*.$value";
  }
}

# Test for the specified directory's existence.
if { ! [ file isdirectory $dir ] } {
  puts "$argv0: $dir is not a directory!";
  exit 1;
}

# Extract the old text and the replacement text
# from the command line by reading the last and
# next-to-last elements in the argv array.
set iindex [ expr [ llength $argv ] - 1 ];
set new [ lindex $argv $iindex ];
set iindex [ expr $iindex - 1 ];
set old [ lindex $argv $iindex ];

# Find all of the relevant files. Create a list in
# the files array.
set files [ exec "find" "$dir" "-name" "$pattern" ];

# Iterate over the files array.
foreach file $files {

  # If the file is a directory or is not writeable, then
  # skip it and move onto the next.
  if [ file isdirectory $file ] continue;
  if {! [ file writeable $file ] } continue;
```

```
# open the file and store its contents into the
# inpBuffer variable.
set f [ open $file r ];
set inpBuffer [ read $f ];
close $f;

# Perform the text substitution. If any changes were
  # actually made, then write out the file to record
  # the changes.
  if [ regsub -all "$old" "$inpBuffer" "$new" outBuffer ] {
    set f [open $file w];
    puts -nonewline $f $outBuffer;
    close $f;
  }
}
```

Summary

At the beginning of this book, you might have had a wee bit of trepidation about learning the complexities of shell programming. Now you're conversant with three different languages. Did you think it was possible to learn so much in such a small book?

Let's quickly review the projects created in this chapter:

- A **find** command that asks for confirmation before allowing searches beginning at the root directory.

- A **write** command that asks questions of the user in order to avoid their having to remember the normal command's syntax.

- A **delete** command that hides files instead of deleting them.

- A login shell that only permits users to perform a limited number of commands.

- A script that locates a user's first name from the password file.

- A script that performs proper capitalization.

- A script that counts files.

- A script that replaces text in files.

These eight scripts provide a good diversity of experience. With these as a foundation, you are now conversant with most common scripting tasks.

Most of the scripts contain extensive comments. I hope you follow in my footsteps and add documentation to your scripts as you write them. Simple comments are rarely enough to decipher the action. Context, as well as simple mechanics, is needed. Try to indicate why a particular feature of the language is used. Alternately, you can indicate the goal of the code section.

Appendix A, "Internet Resources" points out where you can find additional information—and where you can find people willing to answer any question you can think up.

Internet Resources

This chapter introduces Internet Resources you can use to learn more about Bash, Perl, and Tcl. You can see which Usenet Newsgroups are available, where to find scripts you can modify for your own use, and other useful information.

Usenet Newsgroups

Usenet is an Internet service that distributes articles or messages between servers. Each message is targeted to one or more newsgroups. You need a news reader program in order to download messages from the news server to your local machine.

Before posting to any newsgroup, please read the FAQ, if any, associated with it. You can find the FAQ document at **http://www.faqs.org/faqs**. If you ask a question that is already answered in the FAQ document, you might be yelled at by other people reading the list. At all times, remember that you are asking other readers for their help. They are under no obligation to provide information or answers. If you are rude, insulting, unclear or lazy, you can expect the same treatment in return. Remember, "Be Polite!"

Bash

comp.os.linux.misc—Covers general Linux questions, including Bash.

Perl

comp.lang.perl.misc— Covers general Perl questions and issues.
comp.lang.perl.announce—Covers Perl-related announcements.
comp.lang.perl.modules—Covers new module announcements and questions.

Tcl

comp.lang.tcl—Covers general Tcl questions and issues. This newsgroup is quite active with postings about bugs and patches, new user questions, and general discussion.

comp.lang.tcl.announce—Covers announcements of new versions of Tcl and Tcl-related software packages.

Miscellaneous

comp.infosystems.www.authoring-cgi—Covers CGI issues for web authoring.

comp.infosystems.www.announce—Covers new developments on the web.

comp.infosystems.www.servers.misc—Covers general web
server questions and issues.

comp.internet.net-happenings—Covers new developments on
the web.

Web Sites

The web sites mentioned in this section are good places to visit to
build your knowledge base. Remember, the information you seek is
always found in the last place you look!

Bash

Since Bash is nearly synonymous with Linux, some of the links
below are to Linux web sites which have Bash sections.

http://metalab.unc.edu/LDP/— The *Linux Documentation
Project* or LDP web site. The LDP is a great source of Linux
knowledge. The overall goal of the LDP is to encourage collabora-
tion in taking care of Linux documentation, ranging from online
docs (man pages, texinfo docs and so on) to printed manuals covering such topics as installing, using, and running Linux. The LDP
is essentially a loose team of volunteers with no real central organi-
zation; anyone who is interested in helping is welcome to join the
effort.

http://www.linuxworld.com/—A free online magazine dedicated to the technical information needs of professional Linux
users. This is useful for system administrators, developers, web-
masters, IS managers and ISVs who need a basis for sound technical decision-making as they implement Linux and related open
source technologies in their computing environments.

http://www.landfield.com/faqs/unix-faq/—This web page lists
many FAQ lists related to Unix.

http://www.oase-shareware.org/shell/—This web site, created
by Heiner Steven, provides over 100 example shell scripts.

http://language.perl.com/versus/csh.whynot—This Usenet
message, written by Tom Christiansen, discusses why Bash is better
than Csh for script development.

http://alge.anart.no/linux/scripts/—This web site has example
Bash scripts. They are intended to be used as a tutorial.

http://clri6f.gsi.de/gnu/bash-2.01/examples/scripts.noah/—This web site has example Bash scripts. They are intended to be used as a tutorial.

http://www-usercgi.tu-chemnitz.de/~fachat/comp/mkhtml/mkhtml.html—This web page describes a tool that creates HTML pages. You probably won't use the tool, but perusing the source code might be useful.

http://www.cs.bgu.ac.il/~arik/usail/— The *Unix System Administration Independent Learning* web site. You might be interested in the *Understand Unix Concepts* link towards the bottom of the page.

http://linux.ucs.indiana.edu/edcert/session3/— This web site documents session three of the *Unix Workstation System Administration Education Certification Course*. You may be especially interested in reviewing the *Unix Shell Scripting* section.

http://www.informationfactory.com/ifc11.htm—This web site provides a video course introduction to shell programming using the Bourne Shell. This course, from *Training on Video,* is designed for experienced UNIX users and includes a 2-hour video presentation, course manual and a free book written by the course instructor.

Perl

http://www.perl.com/—The Perl home page.

http://www.perl.com/CPAN-local/— The *Comprehensive Perl Archive Network* or CPAN web site is one of the best places to go for Perl source code. Numerous Perl modules are archived here.

http://tpj.com/—The *Perl Journal* magazine calls itself the Voice of the Perl Community. It is a quarterly print magazine.

http://w3.stonehenge.com:80/merlyn/—The home page of Randal Schwartz—a person very knowledgeable about Perl. His home page has links to some of the columns that he wrote for the *Web Techniques* and *UNIX Review* magazines.

Tcl

http://www.scriptics.com/— Scriptics provides commercial Tcl development tools, extensions, and support and training services, as well as open source core technology for the Tcl community.

http://www.tkworld.org/ - tkWorld is an easy-to-use graphic user interface that replaces the command line for Linux and Unix. The product is free and open source.

http://www2.ssd.sscc.ru/misc/Tk-Tcl/Tcl.html—This web site is a compilation of links to Tcl resources.

http://www.links2go.com/more/starbase.neosoft.com/~claird/comp.lang.tcl/—This web page has many links to Tcl resources.

Miscellaneous

http://links2go.com/—An all-purpose links site. It purports to collect only URLs that are relevant to any given topic. I think they're worth a look.

http://www.gnu.org/— The GNU project seems like the birthplace of most open source software. You owe yourself a look at their site to see the wealth of free programs that are available.

http://whatis.com/—This incredible site provides cogent definitions for technical words, lists the meanings of every file extension, and much more. *whatis®* is a knowledge exploration tool about information technology — especially the Internet and computers. It contains over 1,500 individual encyclopedic definitions/topics and a number of quick-reference pages. The topics contain over 5,000 hyperlinked cross-references and over 3,000 links to others sites for further information.

http://www.leo.org/leo_home_e.html— The *Link Everything Online*, or LEO, web site provides a vast selection of software, "Information Service" with a large selection of links and documents on a wide range of topics, and information about the WWW, etc. For example, they have a page related to Bash at **http://www.leo.org/pub/comp/os/unix/gnu/bash/index.html** which archives Bash versions and related documentation.

http://www.linuxweb.com/frames/linux-quotes.html—This web page has hundreds of quotes, comments and other short funny items related to Linux.

http://www.dejanews.com/—This is the only Web site where you can read, search, participate in and subscribe to more than 80,000 discussion forums, including Usenet newsgroups.

http://www.faqs.org/faqs/—This web site is devoted to lists of
Frequently Asked Questions for many newsgroups. You can search
the archives by category and by author.

Internet Relay Chat (IRC)

The Internet Relay Chat service is a powerful tool. If you are lucky,
you can connect with very knowledgeable people who will answer
your questions. The advantage of IRC is that you can hold a real-
time conversation with other people. You ask a question, and they
respond. Then, you can ask for clarification or immediately try the
advice offered. If you still have a problem, you can ask for more
advice.

There are several networks that have arisen to support IRC. For
example: *EfNet*, *Undernet*, and *DALnet*. It seems to me that most
of the technical gurus hang out in *EfNet*—I use the **irc.phoenix.net**
server. If you first install one of the many IRC client programs, you
can type `/join #bash`, `/join #perl`, or `/join #tcl` and say hello to
everyone. You might even see me — my nickname is *WasWaldo*.

Until then...

Happy Programming!

The ASCII Table

Table B.1 lists all of the ASCII characters (the last column) and their numerical equivalents. Some ASCII characters were unprintable on my computer monitor. You might be using a different font and may get slightly different results.

Table B.1 *The ASCII Table*

Decimal	HexaDecimal	Binary	ASCII Character
X_{10}	X_{16}	X_2	& Description
000	0x00	0000 0000	
001	0x01	0000 0001	^A
002	0x02	0000 0010	^B
003	0x03	0000 0011	^C
004	0x04	0000 0100	^D end of file
005	0x05	0000 0101	^E
006	0x06	0000 0110	^F
007	0x07	0000 0111	^G bell
008	0x08	0000 1000	^H backspace
009	0x09	0000 1001	^I tab
010	0x0a	0000 1010	^J carriage return
011	0x0b	0000 1011	^K
012	0x0c	0000 1100	^L formfeed
013	0x0d	0000 1101	^M newline
014	0x0e	0000 1110	^N
015	0x0f	0000 1111	^O
016	0x10	0001 0000	^P
017	0x11	0001 0001	^Q
018	0x12	0001 0010	^R
019	0x13	0001 0011	^S
020	0x14	0001 0100	^T
021	0x15	0001 0101	^U
022	0x16	0001 0110	^V

Table B.1 *The ASCII Table (Cont'd)*

Decimal	HexaDecimal	Binary	ASCII Character
023	0x17	0001 0111	^W
024	0x18	0001 1000	^X
025	0x19	0001 1001	^Y
026	0x1a	0001 1010	^Z
027	0x1b	0001 1011	ESC
028	0x1c	0001 1100	^\
029	0x1d	0001 1101	^]
030	0x1e	0001 1110	^^
031	0x1f	0001 1111	^_
032	0x20	0010 0000	space
033	0x21	0010 0001	!
034	0x22	0010 0010	"
035	0x23	0010 0011	#
036	0x24	0010 0100	$
037	0x25	0010 0101	%
038	0x26	0010 0110	&
039	0x27	0010 0111	'
040	0x28	0010 1000	(
041	0x29	0010 1001	)
042	0x2a	0010 1010	*
043	0x2b	0010 1011	+
044	0x2c	0010 1100	,
045	0x2d	0010 1101	-
046	0x2e	0010 1110	.

Table B.1 *The ASCII Table (Cont'd)*

Decimal	HexaDecimal	Binary	ASCII Character
047	0x2f	0010 1111	/
048	0x30	0011 0000	0
049	0x31	0011 0001	1
050	0x32	0011 0010	2
051	0x33	0011 0011	3
052	0x34	0011 0100	4
053	0x35	0011 0101	5
054	0x36	0011 0110	6
055	0x37	0011 0111	7
056	0x38	0011 1000	8
057	0x39	0011 1001	9
058	0x3a	0011 1010	:
059	0x3b	0011 1011	;
060	0x3c	0011 1100	<
061	0x3d	0011 1101	=
062	0x3e	0011 1110	>
063	0x3f	0011 1111	?
064	0x40	0100 0000	@
065	0x41	0100 0001	A
066	0x42	0100 0010	B
067	0x43	0100 0011	C
068	0x44	0100 0100	D
069	0x45	0100 0101	E
070	0x46	0100 0110	F

Table B.1 *The ASCII Table (Cont'd)*

Decimal	HexaDecimal	Binary	ASCII Character
071	0x47	0100 0111	G
072	0x48	0100 1000	H
073	0x49	0100 1001	I
074	0x4a	0100 1010	J
075	0x4b	0100 1011	K
076	0x4c	0100 1100	L
077	0x4d	0100 1101	M
078	0x4e	0100 1110	N
079	0x4f	0100 1111	O
080	0x50	0101 0000	P
081	0x51	0101 0001	Q
082	0x52	0101 0010	R
083	0x53	0101 0011	S
084	0x54	0101 0100	T
085	0x55	0101 0101	U
086	0x56	0101 0110	V
087	0x57	0101 0111	W
088	0x58	0101 1000	X
089	0x59	0101 1001	Y
090	0x5a	0101 1010	Z
091	0x5b	0101 1011	[
092	0x5c	0101 1100	\
093	0x5d	0101 1101	]
094	0x5e	0101 1110	^

Table B.1 *The ASCII Table (Cont'd)*

Decimal	HexaDecimal	Binary	ASCII Character
095	0x5f	0101 1111	_
096	0x60	0110 0000	`
097	0x61	0110 0001	a
098	0x62	0110 0010	b
099	0x63	0110 0011	c
100	0x64	0110 0100	d
101	0x65	0110 0101	e
102	0x66	0110 0110	f
103	0x67	0110 0111	g
104	0x68	0110 1000	h
105	0x69	0110 1001	i
106	0x6a	0110 1010	j
107	0x6b	0110 1011	k
108	0x6c	0110 1100	l
109	0x6d	0110 1101	m
110	0x6e	0110 1110	n
111	0x6f	0110 1111	o
112	0x70	0111 0000	p
113	0x71	0111 0001	q
114	0x72	0111 0010	r
115	0x73	0111 0011	s
116	0x74	0111 0100	t
117	0x75	0111 0101	u
118	0x76	0111 0110	v

Table B.1 *The ASCII Table (Cont'd)*

Decimal	HexaDecimal	Binary	ASCII Character
119	0x77	0111 0111	w
120	0x78	0111 1000	x
121	0x79	0111 1001	y
122	0x7a	0111 1010	z
123	0x7b	0111 1011	{
124	0x7c	0111 1100	|
125	0x7d	0111 1101	}
126	0x7e	0111 1110	~
127	0x7f	0111 1111	Unprintable
128	0x80	1000 0000	Unprintable
129	0x81	1000 0001	Unprintable
130	0x82	1000 0010	Unprintable
131	0x83	1000 0011	Unprintable
132	0x84	1000 0100	Unprintable
133	0x85	1000 0101	Unprintable
134	0x86	1000 0110	Unprintable
135	0x87	1000 0111	Unprintable
136	0x88	1000 1000	Unprintable
137	0x89	1000 1001	Unprintable
138	0x8a	1000 1010	Unprintable
139	0x8b	1000 1011	Unprintable
140	0x8c	1000 1100	Unprintable
141	0x8d	1000 1101	Unprintable
142	0x8e	1000 1110	Unprintable

Table B.1 *The ASCII Table (Cont'd)*

Decimal	HexaDecimal	Binary	ASCII Character
143	0x8f	1000 1111	Unprintable
144	0x90	1001 0000	Unprintable
145	0x91	1001 0001	Unprintable
146	0x92	1001 0010	Unprintable
147	0x93	1001 0011	Unprintable
148	0x94	1001 0100	Unprintable
149	0x95	1001 0101	Unprintable
150	0x96	1001 0110	Unprintable
151	0x97	1001 0111	Unprintable
152	0x98	1001 1000	Unprintable
153	0x99	1001 1001	Unprintable
154	0x9a	1001 1010	Unprintable
155	0x9b	1001 1011	Unprintable
156	0x9c	1001 1100	Unprintable
157	0x9d	1001 1101	Unprintable
158	0x9e	1001 1110	Unprintable
159	0x9f	1001 1111	Unprintable
160	0xa0	1010 0000	Unprintable
161	0xa1	1010 0001	¡
162	0xa2	1010 0010	¢
163	0xa3	1010 0011	£
164	0xa4	1010 0100	Unprintable
165	0xa5	1010 0101	¥
166	0xa6	1010 0110	Unprintable

Table B.1 *The ASCII Table (Cont'd)*

Decimal	HexaDecimal	Binary	ASCII Character
167	0xa7	1010 0111	§
168	0xa8	1010 1000	¨
169	0xa9	1010 1001	©
170	0xaa	1010 1010	a
171	0xab	1010 1011	«
172	0xac	1010 1100	¬
173	0xad	1010 1101	–
174	0xae	1010 1110	®
175	0xaf	1010 1111	Unprintable
176	0xb0	1011 0000	°
177	0xb1	1011 0001	±
178	0xb2	1011 0010	2
179	0xb3	1011 0011	Unprintable
180	0xb4	1011 0100	Unprintable
181	0xb5	1011 0101	µ
182	0xb6	1011 0110	¶
183	0xb7	1011 0111	·
184	0xb8	1011 1000	,
185	0xb9	1011 1001	Unprintable
186	0xba	1011 1010	º
187	0xbb	1011 1011	»
188	0xbc	1011 1100	_
189	0xbd	1011 1101	_
190	0xbe	1011 1110	Unprintable

Table B.1 *The ASCII Table (Cont'd)*

Decimal	HexaDecimal	Binary	ASCII Character
191	0xbf	1011 1111	¿
192	0xc0	1100 0000	À
193	0xc1	1100 0001	Á
194	0xc2	1100 0010	Â
195	0xc3	1100 0011	Ã
196	0xc4	1100 0100	Ä
197	0xc5	1100 0101	Å
198	0xc6	1100 0110	Æ
199	0xc7	1100 0111	Ç
200	0xc8	1100 1000	È
201	0xc9	1100 1001	É
202	0xca	1100 1010	Ê
203	0xcb	1100 1011	Ë
204	0xcc	1100 1100	Ì
205	0xcd	1100 1101	Í
206	0xce	1100 1110	Î
207	0xcf	1100 1111	Ï
208	0xd0	1101 0000	Unprintable
209	0xd1	1101 0001	Ñ
210	0xd2	1101 0010	Ò
211	0xd3	1101 0011	Ó
212	0xd4	1101 0100	Ô
213	0xd5	1101 0101	Õ
214	0xd6	1101 0110	Ö

Table B.1 *The ASCII Table (Cont'd)*

Decimal	HexaDecimal	Binary	ASCII Character
215	0xd7	1101 0111	x
216	0xd8	1101 1000	Ø
217	0xd9	1101 1001	Ù
218	0xda	1101 1010	Ú
219	0xdb	1101 1011	Û
220	0xdc	1101 1100	Ü
221	0xdd	1101 1101	Ý
222	0xde	1101 1110	Unprintable
223	0xdf	1101 1111	ß
224	0xe0	1110 0000	à
225	0xe1	1110 0001	á
226	0xe2	1110 0010	â
227	0xe3	1110 0011	ã
228	0xe4	1110 0100	ä
229	0xe5	1110 0101	å
230	0xe6	1110 0110	æ
231	0xe7	1110 0111	ç
232	0xe8	1110 1000	è
233	0xe9	1110 1001	é
234	0xea	1110 1010	ê
235	0xeb	1110 1011	ë
236	0xec	1110 1100	ì
237	0xed	1110 1101	í
238	0xee	1110 1110	î

Table B.1 *The ASCII Table (Cont'd)*

Decimal	HexaDecimal	Binary	ASCII Character
239	0xef	1110 1111	ï
240	0xf0	1111 0000	_
241	0xf1	1111 0001	ñ
242	0xf2	1111 0010	ò
243	0xf3	1111 0011	ó
244	0xf4	1111 0100	ô
245	0xf5	1111 0101	õ
246	0xf6	1111 0110	ö
247	0xf7	1111 0111	÷
248	0xf8	1111 1000	ø
249	0xf9	1111 1001	ù
250	0xfa	1111 1010	ú
251	0xfb	1111 1011	û
252	0xfc	1111 1100	ü
253	0xfd	1111 1101	y
254	0xfe	1111 1110	Unprintable
255	0xff	1111 1111	ÿ

Index

The symbols in this index are sorted alphabetically by the symbol's name (ampersand, asterisk, at sign, etc.).

Symbols

Software and Information License

The software and information on this diskette (collectively referred to as the "Product") are the property of The McGraw-Hill Companies, Inc. ("McGraw-Hill") and are protected by both United States copyright law and international copyright treaty provision. You must treat this Product just like a book, expect that you may copy it into a computer to be used and you may make archival copies of the Products for the sole purpose of backing up your software and protecting your investment from loss.

By saying "just like a book," McGraw-Hill means, for example, that the Product may be used by any number of people and may be freely moved from one computer location to another, so long as there is no possibility of the Product (or any part of the Product) being used at one location or on one computer while it is being used at another. Just as a book cannot be read by two different people in two different places at the same time, neither can the Product be used in two different places at the same time (unless, of course, McGraw-Hill's rights are being violated).

McGraw-Hill reserves the right to alter or modify the contents of the Product at any time.

This agreement is effective until terminated. The Agreement will terminate automatically without notice if you fail to comply with any provisions of this Agreement. In the event of termination by reason of your breach, you will destroy or erase all copies of the Product installed on any computer system or made for backup purposes and shall expunge the Product from your data storage facilities.

Limited Warranty

McGraw-Hill warrants the physical diskette(s) enclosed herein to be free of defects in materials and workmanship for a period of sixty days from the purchase date. If McGraw-Hill receives written notification within the warranty period of defects in materials or workmanship, and such notification is determined by McGraw-Hill to be correct, McGraw-Hill will replace the defective diskette(s). Send request to:

Customer Service
McGraw-Hill
Gahanna Industrial Park
860 Taylor Station Road
Blacklick, Ohio 43004-9615

The entire and exclusive liability and remedy for breach of this Limited Warranty shall be limited to replacement of defective diskette(s) and shall not include or extend any claim for or right to cover any other damages, including but not limited to loss of profit, data, or use of the software, or special, incidental, or consequential damages or other similar claims, even if McGraw-Hill has been specifically advised as to the possibility of such damages. In no event will McGraw-Hill's liability for any damages to you or any other person ever exceed the lower of suggested list price or actual price paid for the license to use the Product, regardless of any form of the claim.

The McGraw-Hill Companies, Inc. specifically disclaims all other warranties, express or implied, including but not limited to, any implied warranty of merchantability or fitness for a particular purpose. Specifically, McGraw-Hill makes no representation or warranty that the Product is fit for any particular purpose and any implied warranty of merchantability is limited to the sixty day duration of the Limited Warranty covering the physical diskette(s) only (and not the software or information) and is otherwise expressly and specifically disclaimed.

This Limited Warranty gives you specific legal rights; you may have others which may vary from state to state. Some states do not allow the exclusion of incidental or consequential damages, or the limitation on how long an implied warranty lasts, so some of the above may not apply to you.

This agreement constitutes the entire agreement between the parties relating to use of the Product. The terms of any purchase order shall have no effect on the terms of this Agreement. Failure of McGraw-Hill to insist at any time on strict compliance with this Agreement shall not constitute a waiver of any rights under this Agreement. This Agreement shall be construed and governed in accordance with the laws of New York. If any provision of this Agreement is held to be contrary to law, that provision will be enforced to the maximum extent permissible and the remaining provisions will remain in force and effect.